British Writers, Popular Literature and New Media Innovation, 1820–45

Nineteenth-Century and Neo-Victorian Cultures
Series editors: Ruth Heholt and Joanne Ella Parsons

Recent books in the series

Domestic Architecture, Literature and the Sexual Imaginary in Europe, 1850–1930
Aina Martí-Balcells

Assessing Intelligence: The Bildungsroman and the Politics of Human Potential in England, 1860–1910
Sara Lyons

The Idler's Club: Humour and Mass Readership from Jerome K. Jerome to P. G. Wodehouse
Laura Fiss

Michael Field's Revisionary Poetics
Jill Ehnenn

Narrative, Affect and Victorian Sensation: Wilful Bodies
Tara MacDonald

The Provincial Fiction of Mitford, Gaskell and Eliot
Kevin A. Morrison

Women's Activism in the Transatlantic Consumers' Leagues, 1885–1920
Flore Janssen

Queer Books of Late-Victorian Print Culture
Frederick D. King

British Writers, Popular Literature and New Media Innovation, 1820–45
Alexis Easley

www.edinburghuniversitypress.com/series-nineteenth-century-and-neo-victorian-cultures

British Writers, Popular Literature and New Media Innovation, 1820–45

Edited by Alexis Easley

EDINBURGH
University Press

Edinburgh University Press is one of the leading university presses in the UK. We publish academic books and journals in our selected subject areas across the humanities and social sciences, combining cutting-edge scholarship with high editorial and production values to produce academic works of lasting importance. For more information visit our website: edinburghuniversitypress.com

Edinburgh University Press Ltd
13 Infirmary Street
Edinburgh EH1 1LT

Typeset in 11/13pt Sabon
by Cheshire Typesetting Ltd, Cuddington, Cheshire, and
printed and bound by CPI Group (UK) Ltd
Croydon, CR0 4YY

A CIP record for this book is available from the British Library

ISBN 978 1 3995 1400 2 (hardback)
ISBN 978 1 3995 1402 6 (webready PDF)
ISBN 978 1 3995 1403 3 (epub)

Contents

Illustrations

Figures

Table

Acknowledgements

First and foremost, I am grateful to the contributors to this volume, whose scholarship is a source of awe and inspiration to me and so many others in the Victorian studies community. I would like to thank Erik Wilkinson, Kari Aakre, Ellie Lange, Katherine Bruns, Cheniqua Morrison and the undergraduate students in my spring 2023 professional editing class for their assistance during the final stages of this project. This book would not have been possible without the encouragement of the brilliant editorial staff at Edinburgh University Press and the support of a University Scholars fellowship from the University of St. Thomas. My husband Brett Fried, as always, provides the domestic and emotional support that makes my scholarly life possible and my day-to-day life full of laughter and joy.

Series Preface

Nineteenth-Century and Neo-Victorian Cultures
Series Editors: Ruth Heholt and Joanne Ella Parsons

This interdisciplinary series provides space for full and detailed scholarly discussions on nineteenth-century and Neo-Victorian cultures. Drawing on radical and cutting-edge research, volumes explore and challenge existing discourses, as well as providing an engaging reassessment of the time period. The series encourages debates about decolonising nineteenth-century cultures, histories, and scholarship, as well as raising questions about diversities. Encompassing art, literature, history, performance, theatre studies, film and TV studies, medical and the wider humanities, *Nineteenth Century and Neo-Victorian Cultures* is dedicated to publishing pioneering research that focuses on the Victorian era in its broadest and most diverse sense.

Notes on Contributors

Françoise Baillet is Professor of British History and Culture and Head of the ERIBIA research team at Caen Normandie University, France. Her research addresses the role of the periodical press in the shaping of class, gender and national identities in nineteenth-century Britain. She is the author of *Visions et divisions: Discours culturels de Punch et ordre social victorien, 1850–1880* (2022), which examines *Punch* as a discursive and ideological construct. She has published several articles in areas related to Victorian cultural history and print culture, taking a particular interest in trade periodicals and in aestheticised renderings of working-class life in *The Illustrated London News* and *The Graphic*, and co-edited a forthcoming special issue of *Victorian Periodicals Review* on 'Revolution(s), Evolution(s), Circulation(s)'. Her current research activities include the design and implementation of *The Punch Pocket Book Archive*, an international digitisation project involving a group of researchers and curators from Manchester Metropolitan University and Caen Normandie.

Jennie Batchelor is Head and Professor of English and Related Literature at the University of York. She has published widely on periodicals, women's writing, book history and material culture in the long eighteenth century. Her most recent publications include *The Lady's Magazine (1770–1832) and the Making of Literary History* (Edinburgh University Press, 2022), which won the 2023 Colby Prize awarded by the Research Society for Victorian Periodicals. She also published *Jane Austen Embroidery: Regency Patterns Reimagined for Modern Stitchers* (2020) with Alison Larkin.

Alexis Easley is Professor of English at the University of St. Thomas in St. Paul, Minnesota. She is the author of *First-Person Anonymous: Women Writers and Victorian Print Media, 1830–70* (2004) and *Literary Celebrity, Gender, and Victorian Authorship, 1850–1914* (2011). She has also co-edited four books, including *Women, Periodicals and Print Culture in Britain, 1830s–1900s* with Clare Gill and Beth Rodgers (Edinburgh University Press, 2019). Her most recent book publication is *New Media and the Rise of the Popular Woman Writer, 1832–60* (Edinburgh University Press, 2021). This project was a 2019 recipient of the Linda H. Peterson Prize awarded by the Research Society for Victorian Periodicals. She is currently at work on a biography of Eliza Cook and a facsimile edition of a Victorian scrapbook.

Caley Ehnes teaches English literature and composition at the College of the Rockies in Cranbrook, British Columbia. She is the author of *Victorian Poetry and the Poetics of the Literary Periodical* (Edinburgh University Press, 2019). She has published articles on the poetess in *Women's Writing* and co-authored a forum article on the reception and poetics of Frances Browne for *Victorian Review* (2022). Her chapter on the nineteenth-century British literary magazine appeared in *The Routledge Companion to the British and North American Literary Magazine* in 2021.

Helena Goodwyn is Vice-Chancellor's Senior Research Fellow in the Department of the Humanities at Northumbria University. Her research interests include nineteenth-century periodicals, women's writing and transatlanticism. Her recent work has featured in *Women's Writing* and *Nineteenth-Century Gender Studies*. Her monograph, *The Americanization of W. T. Stead*, is forthcoming from Edinburgh University Press.

Chris Haffenden is a researcher at the Department of the History of Science and Ideas, Uppsala University, and research coordinator at KBLab at the National Library of Sweden. His research interests include memory studies, digital research infrastructure and the history of celebrity culture. His recent publications have explored the notion of erasure studies, the use of AI in research libraries and self-monumentalising in the Romantic period, including

Open Access articles in the journals *Memory, Mind & Media* and *College & Research Libraries*.

Elizabeth Howard is Assistant Professor of Literature at Bethlehem College in Minneapolis, Minnesota. She has published articles in *Victorian Poetry*, *Victorians Institute Journal*, *Religion and the Arts* and Palgrave's *Encyclopedia of Victorian Women's Writing*. Her most recent essay in *Victorian Periodicals Review* won the 2021 RSVP VanArsdel Prize.

Sofia Prado Huggins holds a PhD in English from Texas Christian University. Her research interests include late eighteenth- and early nineteenth-century global anglophone literatures, periodical studies and the geohumanities. Her dissertation, 'Blank Spaces: Global Geographies of Moral Capitalism in *The Anti-Slavery Reporter*, 1831–1833', historicises the geographic and conceptual centring of whiteness in liberal progressivism in late eighteenth- and early nineteenth-century antislavery archives. Sofia is the former editor-in-chief of the *Teaching Transatlanticism* website. Her work has been published in journals such as *Eighteenth-Century Fiction*, *Pedagogy* and *Symbiosis*. She is the project manager for The Uproot Project, a network of journalists of colour working in the climate, environment and science spaces.

Linda K. Hughes is Addie Levy Professor of Literature at Texas Christian University. She specialises in nineteenth-century literature and culture, gender and women's studies, and transnationality. Her recent monograph, *Victorian Women Writers and the Other Germany: Cross-Cultural Freedoms and Female Opportunity* (2022), includes a chapter on Mary Howitt's work across multiple genres. She is co-editor, with Sarah R. Robbins and Andrew Taylor, of *Transatlantic Anglophone Literatures, 1776–1920* (Edinburgh University Press, 2022) and editor of *The Cambridge Companion to Victorian Women's Poetry* (2019).

Brian Maidment is Emeritus Professor of the History of Print at Liverpool John Moores University and a former president of the Research Society for Victorian Periodicals. His two most recent books are *Comedy, Caricature and the Social Order, 1820–1850* (2013) and *Robert Seymour and Nineteenth-Century Print Culture* (2021).

Sara L. Maurer is Associate Professor of English at the University of Notre Dame. She is the author of *The Dispossessed State: Britain, Ireland, and Narratives of Ownership in the Nineteenth Century* (2012). Her current research is focused on the influence of Irish writers on British literature, as well as representations of charitable action, both in works of literature and in archival materials such as advice books for charitable workers, the annual reports of charities and the rules of newly established Anglican sisterhoods and brotherhoods.

Richard Salmon is Professor of Victorian Literature and Culture in the School of English, University of Leeds. He has published extensively on literary authorship and print culture in the nineteenth century, including a scholarly edition of *The Reverberator* for *The Cambridge Edition of the Complete Fiction of Henry James*, volume 10 (2018); an essay collection, *Thackeray in Time: History, Memory, and Modernity*, co-edited by Alice Crossley (2016); and a monograph, *The Formation of the Victorian Literary Profession* (2013). He is currently leading a four-year collaborative research project funded by the Leverhulme Trust on the formation and early history of the Incorporated Society of Authors (1884–1914).

Mark W. Turner is Professor of English at King's College London. His research interests include seriality, journalism, media history and nineteenth-century print culture. Among other publications, he is co-editor, with John Stokes, of Oscar Wilde's journalism for the Oxford English Texts *Collected Works* (2013) and author of *Trollope and the Magazines* (2000). He is a founding co-editor of the journal *Media History*.

To Brett Fried, *mudita*

Introduction: British Writers, Popular Literature and New Media Innovation, 1820–45

Alexis Easley

The period 1820–45 is often interpreted as a transitional phase between the Romantic and Victorian eras. As Richard Cronin notes, many scholars view this epoch as 'a shadowy stretch of time sandwiched between two far more colourful periods'.[1] Yet when viewed from a media history perspective, a different narrative emerges. The early nineteenth century was a period of new media innovation – an era that produced a wide variety of book, periodical and newspaper formats that were available to larger and more diversified reading publics than ever before. The efflorescence of print culture during this era was enabled by the rise of popular literature and education movements as well as the expansion of rail networks, advancements in printing and paper-making technology, and a reduction of the stamp duty from 4d to 1d in 1836.[2] During this period, publishers not only experimented with serial formats – from penny papers to the part-publication of novels such as Charles Dickens's *Pickwick Papers* (1836–7) – but also explored synergies between text and image, producing, for example, the elegant steel-cut engravings of literary annuals and the innovative woodcut illustrations incorporated into children's books and comic magazines.

This volume explores 1820–45 as a crucial era in the development of the modern press. While today we might associate 'new media' with digital technologies, new media innovation has a long history that precedes – and in many ways anticipates – the present moment. As Rachel Teukolsky reminds us, 'media invention itself is not new, and every epoch has had to confront the unruly and transformative effects of new communications technologies'.[3] During the early decades of the nineteenth century, innovation and 'unruliness' were produced not only through the competition for new readerships but also through practices of scissors-and-paste reprinting and the pirating of content enabled by ambiguities in international copyright law.[4] It was a media ecology, like our own, that was fueled by innovation and competition, as well as anxiety about the status of writers and readers in a time of accelerating social change. As Tom Mole notes, during the early nineteenth century, 'the future seemed to be open and uncertain, both promising and worrying'.[5] Then, as now, Mole asserts, 'media were the index of the new'.[6] At the same time that publishers developed new book and periodical formats designed to appeal to modern readers, they adapted older media forms to new publishing contexts. For example, as Clare Pettitt points out, 'twopenny and penny weeklies of the 1820s and 1830s owed as much to the format of the almanacs as to the newspaper press, or to the Enlightenment miscellany'.[7] By adapting old media and inventing the new, publishers, editors, artists and writers contributed to a print culture that was more robust and expansive than ever before. By mid-century, the habit of reading had become a part of everyday life for a wide range of readers, including women, children, activists, clerks and the lower classes.

As the press and book trades expanded, they produced a sense of 'unruly' plentitude. Magazines, newspapers and indexes took on the task of helping readers locate informative and entertaining content that suited their needs and desires. In 1832, *The Penny Magazine* compared itself to a 'small optic glass called "the finder", which is placed by the side of a large telescope to enable the observer to discover the star which is afterwards to be carefully examined by the more perfect instrument'.[8] This optical metaphor emphasises the increasing visuality of print culture as well as the need for curation and focus in a new media environment associated with overabundance. As Mark Algee-Hewitt et al. have noted, there were two main responses to this idea of 'print saturation' during the early nineteenth century:

> On the one side, cultural conservatives tended to view a world awash in new books and periodicals as one on the precipice of aesthetic, moral, and structural decline. [. . .] On the other side were those who hailed the profusion of writing as the leading edge of a march of intellect that would fulfill the greatest hopes of Enlightenment philosophers.[9]

This duality sparked various strategies of proliferation and control as editors and publishers navigated a print culture that was both old and new. The Chambers brothers' serially issued *Cyclopedia of English Literature* (1843–4), for example, included excerpts from both old and contemporary writers in a cheap, illustrated format, eventually achieving a circulation of 130,000.[10] At the same time, periodicals and newspapers, through processes of extraction, indexing and reviewing, attempted to help readers navigate their way through other realms of knowledge in an increasingly overwhelming world of print.

Key to the new 'popular' publications was price. As early as the 1820s, publishers were discovering ways to address broad readerships that included artisans and the lower middle classes. A vanguard publication in this regard was *The Mirror of Literature, Amusement and Instruction* (1822–47), which printed its first issue at the price of 2d. It aimed 'to afford the greatest quantity of "Amusement and Instruction" at the lowest possible expense, and to enable readers in the humblest circumstances to become acquainted with the current and expensive literature of the day'.[11] Editor John Limbird modeled his magazine after *Blackwood's Edinburgh Magazine* and other higher-priced monthlies in its miscellaneous content but aimed to reach a much broader audience.[12] Indeed, as Louis James notes, it achieved its aim, reaching a circulation of 150,000 with its first issue, eventually leveling out at 80,000 per week.[13] Key to the success of the *Mirror* was its repurposing of content cut and pasted from other periodicals, which enabled it to offer a broad range of appealing content. Thus, Jon Klancher concludes, 'The *Mirror* established the mass journal as a collage, a strangely constructed sequence of verbal and graphic images' that 'reflected' reality 'in discontinuous shards with no visible principle of continuity'.[14] Yet, at the same time that readers were invited to consume these scraps in nonlinear ways, they were also propelled 'speedily forwards in order to catch up with the culture of modern London', as Clare Pettitt asserts.[15] This idea of serial miscellaneity – and the interactive engagement with readers that it mobilised – would come to characterise many other forms of print in the decades to come.

The 1830s were a crucial era in the expansion of cheap publication. In 1838, Thackeray drew mocking attention to the 'vast mass of active, stirring life' in the cities that constituted the new market for cheap print.[16] Two years later, as Louis James notes, 'there were approximately eighty cheap periodicals circulating in London', ranging from magazines of popular progress to those offering down-market entertainment. In this decade, magazines of popular progress, such as *The Penny Magazine* (1832–45) and *Chambers's Edinburgh Journal* (1832–1956), achieved circulations over 80,000. Aimed at a broad family audience, these periodicals built upon earlier models of miscellaneous publication while emphasising healthful, improving content. For some of the new family periodicals, illustration was key to attracting a broad audience. *The Penny Magazine*, like the *Mirror*, included a woodcut illustration with each issue. As Pettitt notes, this 'newly available pictorial material was particularly important to forming new readerships and helping people to visualise themselves into a developing civic culture'.[17] This effect was amplified in the following decade with the founding of more expensive illustrated weeklies, including *Punch* (1841–1992) and *The Illustrated London News* (1842–1900).

Equally important to the formation of the idea of a mass reading public were weekly newspapers, including John Browne Bell's *News of the World*, launched in 1843, which claimed to offer 'news for the million'.[18] Although the paper did not achieve this circulation until the twentieth century, it was wildly successful in its first decade and achieved a circulation of 110,000 by 1855.[19] Like many other Sunday papers founded after the reduction of the newspaper duty in 1836, the *News of the World* was priced at three pence, was Radical in its political affiliations and was dedicated to addressing 'all classes of readers'.[20] As Richard Altick points out, the paper most likely appealed to 'artisans and small tradesmen' due to its combination of serious news and sensational crime reportage.[21] However, as a writer for the *London Journal* put it in 1845, the *News of the World* also had a 'tendency to *create* newspaper readers'.[22] These readers were in part defined by their weekly, rather than daily, access to news and information. Added to this was the lingering barrier of cost. As Clare Pettitt notes, there was a 'time lag of the news for most Londoners who were unable to afford expensive newspapers and instead relied on out-of-date information, or topical popular publication, and so were struggling to catch up'.[23]

Nonetheless, weekly newspapers of the 1840s were essential in imagining a mass-market readership that included artisans and the middle classes as well as family audiences that explicitly included women and children.[24] Sunday newspapers, along with other publications aimed at broad audience, were essential to the popularisation of literary genres such sentimental poetry, social-problem fiction and children's literature, as well as features such as reader correspondence, crime reports and 'facts and scraps' columns. Many writers during this era, such as Charles Dickens, Christian Johnstone, Louisa Sheridan and Charlotte Tonna, also worked as editors of periodicals, thus playing a crucial role in shaping the media formats in which popular literature would be accessed and consumed. Rather than simply harnessing existing audiences, the popular press constructed the mass and niche readerships that would consume print. As Jon Klancher puts it, the 'British periodical [was] a paradigm of audience-making'.[25]

Efforts to extend the reading habit resulted in the emergence of the first 'mass media' – a periodical and newspaper print culture aimed at a broad audience in the tens and hundreds of thousands.[26] While such circulation figures might not at first seem to qualify as sufficiently large to constitute a mass readership, it must be remembered that an individual copy of a book, newspaper or periodical would be consumed by multiple readers. As *The Westminster Review* noted in 1829, 'every newspaper is read by thirty persons, a very fair calculation, considering how great a proportion of the circulation of newspapers goes into reading-rooms and coffee-rooms, and other public places'.[27] Periodicals and newspapers were associated with leisure time, which, for most workers, was hard to come by. Thus, poetry, illustrations, scraps, excerpts and short articles became the predominate form of content in periodicals aimed at a mass readership. As *Chambers's Edinburgh Journal* noted in 1840, its aim was to reach 'that large department of society, who, being engaged in the duties of the counting-house, the shop, the work-room, or those of their private dwellings, have little leisure for the cultivation of their minds'.[28] *Chambers's* nonetheless acknowledged that there remained a 'vast substratum in society where the printing-press [had] not yet unfolded her treasures'.[29] To define the 'mass media' was both to imagine a broad audience for magazines, newspapers and books but also to realise the limits – both in terms of time and education – to the expansion of the reading habit.

The twelve chapters in this collection are intended to promote greater understanding of the period between 1820 and 1845 as an era of innovation in nineteenth-century print culture.

This included experimentation with new publication formats, the reinvention and remediation of older forms, and the definition of new kinds of contributors and audiences for print. The chapters in this collection are by no means intended to cover all genres, writers and themes during these decades or to provide a comprehensive overview of the period. Rather, each chapter is designed as a case study that models ways of entering into a vast field of study, drawing attention to the interactivity of readers, editors, publishers and print forms during a period of unprecedented change. These essays also draw attention to the ways in which our access to this history is enabled by twenty-first-century technologies – digitisation, keyword searches and distant reading – that provide access to the periodicals, newspapers and rare books that fuel and shape our research. Increased accessibility to rare books and periodicals in recent years has altered our understanding of early Victorian print culture. In her chapter for this volume, for example, Jennie Batchelor notes that scholars did not fully appreciate the complexity of *The Lady's Magazine* (1770–1847) until it became available for study in a digital archive. Her innovative reading of the magazine in relation to rival titles of the time period also demonstrates how digital accessibility enables us to see titles in relationship to each other within a broader media ecology. Of course, twenty-first-century scholars must always be cognisant of the fact that the remediation of selected nineteenth-century periodicals, books and newspapers in digital databases provides an incomplete picture of the wide range of publications produced during the period.[30] Archival research is still necessary for accessing rare books, periodicals and newspapers that have not been digitised. And the versions of texts that have been digitised in Google Books and other repositories are unique witnesses with specific histories of circulation and remediation.[31]

Digital accessibility has made it possible to discern broad patterns in the history of reprinting and excerption. In Chapter 1 of this volume, '"Collect and Simplify": Serial Miscellaneity and Extraction in the Early Nineteenth Century', Mark W. Turner explores forms of extraction in the early Victorian period – reprinted scraps, reviews, data and other mobile forms of print published in serial formats that were in part designed to help readers contend with an overabundance of information. While what Turner calls 'extractive miscellaneity' predates the nineteenth century, it became increasingly ubiquitous as periodicals and other serial formats expanded across the century, addressing new markets and experimenting with new rhythms of publication. This included Charles Knight's *Companion to the Newspaper* (1833–7) as well as entertaining parodies of scissors-and-paste journalism such as *The Thief* (1832–3). At the same time, consumers repurposed extracts from periodicals, cutting and pasting them into scrapbooks. Turner concludes by examining the *Australian Magazine*, launched in 1821, which printed extracts from correspondence and reprinted scraps from British periodicals in order to create a sense of connection to the mother country. At the same time, by printing extracts from other colonial papers, it constructed the idea of a global communications network. As Turner highlights, this sense of connectivity could be adapted to serve imperialist ends. For example, *Arden's Sydney Magazine*, founded in 1843, extracted data from other periodicals in order to make an argument for the oppression of aboriginal peoples. Turner's exploration of domestic and international forms of textual extraction demonstrates a broader tendency in Victorian scholarship toward exploring intersections within an expanding global economy of print. As Algee-Hewitt et al. remind us, 'print culture did not emerge only in the crucible of national fervor but also within an international context of translation, imitation, reprinting, and cultural cross-fertilization'.[32]

In addition to shedding fresh light on the history of book and periodical publication from 1820 to 1845, this volume draws attention to a wide range of writers, editors and publishers that have been neglected in current scholarship. While Byron may have died in 1824 and the canonical writers associated with high Victorianism were yet to produce their most memorable works, there were still a great many other authors working in the period whose innovations have yet to be fully appreciated or understood. This is especially true of so-called 'popular' writers and editors, such as Dinah Mulock, Mary Howitt and Charles Knight, who addressed broad readerships that included women, children and the lower classes. What made these writers significant was their engagement with the rise of new media – annuals, trade magazines, Sunday papers, cheap weekly periodicals, and illustrated books and magazines. An examination of writing produced between 1820 and 1845 also draws attention to the relationship of canonical writers such as Thomas Carlyle, Elizabeth Barrett Browning, Letitia Landon and William Hazlitt to developments in the publishing world – advertising, commemoration and celebrity culture.

During the early nineteenth century, forms of corporate, anonymous and pseudonymous publication disrupted the idea of the single, named author. *Blackwood's Edinburgh Magazine* (1817–1980) and *Fraser's Magazine* (1830–82), for example, printed most of their contributions without signature. While many magazines maintained a policy of anonymous publication or reprinted content from rival periodicals anonymously, some periodicals advertised author names – and drew attention to famous people in biographical profiles or celebrity portrait galleries. In periodicals and book collections, celebrity profiles and portraits were disseminated as never before, functioning not only to venerate canonical figures but also to construct living cultural heroes. As I have shown elsewhere, practices of transatlantic printing were crucial to the celebrity identities of writers such as Felicia Hemans and Eliza Cook.[33] In domestic and transatlantic contexts, author portraits were widely reprinted and were even remediated as collectable statuettes.[34]

In Chapter 2, 'William Hazlitt and Celebrity Culture: Periodical Portraits in an Age of Public Intimacy', Chris Haffenden situates Hazlitt's *The Spirit of the Age* (1825) within the proliferation of celebrity portraiture in print and visual culture. Just as the democratisation of print led William Thackeray to complain about the spread of cheap literature,[35] so too did William Hazlitt criticise the ephemeral fame produced by a proliferating popular print culture. Though Hazlitt critiqued celebrity culture and resisted including images with the profiles in *The Spirit of the Age*, he nonetheless participated in constructing the renown of famous Britons by providing the intimate details of their daily lives. Hazlitt contributed to a discourse on fame that simultaneously aimed to expand the definition of what kinds of subjectivities should be celebrated while also attempting to separate deserving from undeserving forms of celebrity.

While living authors were the focus of much celebrity media during the early decades of the nineteenth century, elegy and posthumous biography also proliferated in the periodical press. In Chapter 3, 'Periodical as Memorial: Remembering Felicia Hemans in *The New Monthly Magazine*, 1835', Elizabeth Howard explores the interlocking tributes to Hemans published after her death in May of 1835 that were created by Letitia Landon and Elizabeth Barrett Browning. Their elegies to Hemans, along with a portrait, a reprinted obituary and a retrospective review written by Landon, appeared serially in *The New Monthly Magazine* between June and October 1835. The serial publication of these commemorative pieces helped Landon and Barrett Browning bolster their authority as poets and enabled editor Samuel Carter Hall to spark fresh interest in his once-influential periodical. The idea of a serial, cross-referenced, multimodal tribute to a dead writer was made possible by a print culture dedicated to postmortem celebrity worship. This form of commemoration also played a crucial role in enabling the fame of living writers and editors who were eager to promote their own work while also honouring the dead.

'Multimodal' forms of publication were of course premised on techniques of illustration that encouraged reader participation. As Brian Maidment notes, the rise of wood engraving as an illustration technology 'vastly extended the possibility of integrating text and image into the same printed page' and thus promoted interactivity as readers navigated the 'intense relationship between an image and a written text'.[36] In Chapter 4 of this volume, '"Mirth" and "Fun": The Comic Annual and the New Graphic Humour of the 1830s', Maidment explores the redefinition of graphic humour as 'fun' rather than the more literary 'mirth' that characterised the Regency period. Like literary annuals, comic annuals were richly illustrated and were designed to appeal, in part, to a female readership; however, instead of incorporating steel-cut engravings, they employed woodcut illustration to achieve humorous effects – a method that would soon dominate Victorian comic illustration. Maidment highlights the self-consciousness of the comic annual genre through an analysis of a mock-heroic poem, *The Battle of the "Annuals"* (1835), and through analysis of frontispieces to *The Comic Offering*.

The invitation for readers to interact with images and text was perhaps nowhere more evident than in books and periodicals aimed at children. As Linda K. Hughes notes in Chapter 5, 'Fauna, Flora and Illustrated Verse in Mary Howitt's Environmental Children's Poetry', the combination of poetry and woodcut illustration produced a new kind of children's literature focused on cultivating joy rather than on inculcating religious dogma. Howitt contributed poetry to annuals early on in her career and brought her experience of writing illustrated poetry to her book series for children. Her *Sketches of Natural History* (1834) was innovative not only for its use of woodcut illustration but also for the ways in which it used text and image to promote ecological awareness of the relationships between all living creatures.

The proliferation of woodcut illustration in the early decades of the nineteenth century was part of a broader expansion of visual culture. Rachel Teukolsky reminds us that the word 'visuality' was 'coined by Thomas Carlyle in 1840 to describe a potent and revelatory form of seeing'.[37] Carlyle's timing was apt given the manifold expressions of visuality in the early decades of the nineteenth century. Just as the woodcut transformed popular print culture, so did advertisements, which assumed innovative forms during these decades. This included the horse-drawn advertising vehicles that Carlyle criticised in *Past and Present*, as well as the myriad print advertisements that proliferated after the advertising duty was reduced in 1833. T. R. Nevett notes that 'the first half of the nineteenth century was the period during which advertising evolved into something akin to its present form'.[38] This included the dissemination of visual spectacles, such as the poster hordes Dickens describes in 'Bill Sticking', an essay published in *Household Words* in 1851.[39] Posters were not subject to advertising duties, and consequently they covered the city, with hundreds of bill-stickers competing for the prime locations. In Chapter 6, 'Literature, Media and the "Advertising System"', Richard Salmon examines the ways in which advertising influenced broader political and cultural criticism, especially Thomas Carlyle's *Past and Present* (1840), which drew attention to advertising spectacles in the metropolis as well as the branding of products and individuals within a broader advertising system that included literary culture. Embedded in visually saturated urban environment, Carlyle could not help but participate in the advertising system he aimed to critique.

The increasing visual richness of print culture – both in terms of illustration and advertising – was part of a broader media ecology in which competition between publishers and titles produced innovation and change. The addition or subtraction of any new actant affects all other parts of the media system, as Neil Postman has observed.[40] Thus, Tom Mole notes, 'speaking in terms of media ecology makes visible the interplay of media, and draws attention to the porous boundaries between them'.[41] In Chapter 7, 'Keeping "pace with the growing spirit of the times": The Women's Magazine in Transition', Jennie Batchelor situates *The Lady's Magazine* within the media ecology of the early nineteenth century. While the magazine had a long history dating back to the 1770s, it was forced to adapt to rapidly shifting circumstances within periodical print culture as the decades unfolded. In response to the publication of annuals and new women's periodicals such as *The Lady's Monthly Museum* (1798–1832) and *La Belle Assemblée* (1806–37), it shifted its contents and strategies. This adaptability was key to its success – and made it a useful model for later women's periodicals as the decades unfolded. In recounting this history, Batchelor draws attention to the fluidity of periodical forms, which evolved in response to the editorial practices of rival magazines and to the shifting demands of the literary marketplace.

As Batchelor's chapter demonstrates, the period between 1820 and 1845 was crucial to the history of women's writing. Indeed, as Richard Cronin notes, it was a period 'in which it is possible neither to ignore the work of women writers nor to isolate their work from that of their male contemporaries'.[42] The expansion of the press during this period offered women many new opportunities to pursue careers as authors. While some writers, such as Felicia Hemans and Letitia Landon, became household names, many others worked anonymously, generating the content needed to address new family readerships. This was especially true of women's magazines such as *The Christian Lady's Magazine*, founded in 1834, and annuals such as *The Keepsake*, founded in 1828. At the same time, entertaining miscellanies such as *The London Journal* and *The Family Herald*, launched in 1842 and 1845, respectively, defined women as important consumers of cheap print. As Margaret Beetham notes, 'the "family" journal was the most significant development of the 1840s and it came to dominate Victorian popular publishing. These papers not only included "woman" in their readership, they assumed that her domestic management provided the scene of reading'.[43]

Just as important to the history of women's writing were magazines of popular progress, which explicitly addressed a family audience and employed a large number of women writers, most publishing their work anonymously. In Chapter 8, 'Beyond the Literary Annuals: Felicia Hemans, Letitia Elizabeth Landon and Periodical Poetry', Caley Ehnes explores the importance of one such magazine, *Chambers's Edinburgh Journal* (1832–1956), which published original poetry and reprinted verse from books and periodicals. While volume publications of poetry may have been in decline during this period,[44] periodicals and newspapers became major venues for poetry publication, making verse accessible to larger audiences than ever before. Given that the circulation of *Chambers's* was about 60,000 at the time of its founding, it was a crucial vehicle for the popularisation of poetry, especially women's verse, which reinforced the 'improving' domestic ethos of the magazine.[45] As Ehnes points out, Hemans's reprinted verse supported the editorial remit of *Chambers's*, and while Landon's verse was less adaptable to a popular audience, it could still be made to fit with carefully crafted editorial apparatus. Ehnes notes that the unintentional collaboration between the two poets and *Chambers's* laid the groundwork for the proliferation of family periodicals and popular poetry in the decades to come.

Studying women's engagement with new periodicals that arose between 1820 and 1845 enables us to gain a greater understanding of the kinds of barriers and opportunities they faced when choosing to pursue a literary career. In periods of new media change, when editorial policies are not yet solidified, writers from marginalised positions are often able to discover new opportunities for participation. In Chapter 9, 'A Familiar Transition: Dinah Mulock Craik's Early Career in Periodicals, 1841–45', Helena Goodwyn explores how one woman writer got her start in a rapidly changing literary marketplace. Craik made use of social networks and worked within popular genres – poetry set to popular tunes and translations of European fiction – to establish herself in a burgeoning field of letters. Later, she was able to leverage her work in popular genres to become a featured poet in *Chambers's Edinburgh Journal*. Goodwyn's chapter not only provides a framework for investigating women's routes to literary fame during the early nineteenth century but also serves as a model for how to use digital archives such as the Digital Victorian Periodical Poetry and Dinah Mulock Craik databases to shed fresh light on women's literary history.

As part of her study of Craik, Goodwyn draws attention to the role of *Chambers's Journal* in popularising abolitionist fiction. Indeed, Craik herself contributed to this discourse by publishing a translated story in the journal titled 'Eustace the Negro' in 1845. Of course, the period between 1820 and 1845 was one of the most prolific periods of abolitionist activism in Great Britain. The slave trade in the British Empire had been outlawed in 1807, but slavery continued in British colonies until it was prohibited, with some exceptions, in 1833. Meanwhile, in the United States, slavery continued on as before, fueling a transatlantic abolition movement. An awareness of the discourse on slavery in the early nineteenth century is crucial for understanding print culture of the time period. Rather than viewing Victorian studies as what Antoinette Burton calls an 'island of whiteness' in the academy, we can explore complexities and contradictions in the treatment of race in the transatlantic press.[46] While progressive journalism, both in Great Britain and the United States, was essential for promoting abolitionist thought, editors could not separate themselves from the discourse on white supremacy. The complex and often contradictory efforts of British abolitionists were bolstered by cheap family periodicals in Great Britain during the 1840s, which helped to disseminate arguments and generate financial support for the transatlantic antislavery movement. For example, Frederick Douglass's *North Star*, as Clare Pettitt has shown, was to some extent modeled on *Howitt's Journal* and regularly reprinted content from British magazines of popular progress.[47]

In Chapter 10, 'Paratextual Navigation: Positions of Witnessing in *The Anti-Slavery Reporter*', Sofia Prado Huggins focuses on a key periodical in the British antislavery movement. Through an analysis of selected issues of the *Reporter* published between 1831 and 1833, Huggins explores how footnotes and other paratextual elements established Great Britain as the centre of the international abolitionist movement and figured its readers as white witnesses to the horrors of chattel slavery. Although the *Reporter* made some inclusive references to colonial papers, particularly the *Christian Record*, it primarily focused on its own centrality in the transatlantic abolition movement. This had the effect of erasing Black narratives and other firsthand accounts, instead identifying a white British print culture as the primary site of antislavery activism. The *Reporter* thus assumed a complex role in transatlantic print culture – both as a site of progressive activism and a force of colonial erasure.

At the same time that activists were concerned with establishing Britain at the centre of abolitionist campaigns, the religious press imagined an active role for middle-class philanthropists in engaging with oppressed communities of workers on the domestic front. While the distribution of tracts and charitable visiting predated the early nineteenth century, editors and publishers viewed moral education as being increasingly urgent after the Peterloo Massacre (1819) and just as pressing later, with the expansion of industry, the rise of Chartism, and the proliferation of penny bloods and unstamped radical newspapers. Debates on 'The Condition of England' likewise produced countless tracts, novels, poems, essays and government reports. In Chapter 11, 'The Media System of Charitable Visiting', Sara L. Maurer focuses on the dissemination of tracts, books and forms associated with middle-class visits to the homes of the poor. This included Thomas Chalmers's *The Christian and Civic Economy of Large Towns* (1819–26), which envisioned charitable visiting as a method for collecting data and distributing church-based aid, along with promoting local and national circuits of communication. While such systems were designed to collect information, Maurer notes, they were also concerned with communicating an ethic of care. Middle-class visitors were encouraged to 'read' the homes and habits of the poor, while at the same time functioning as conduits of information and solace to those they served. Charitable visiting was a 'media system' in the sense that it involved the production of traveling books such as Jowett's *Christian Visitor* (1836), which contained biblical extracts and prayers, as well as a manual created by the Liverpool Visiting Provident Society (1838), which included blank forms visitors could use to document their charitable acts. Maurer's essay reminds us that the religious press in the Victorian era is a vast, understudied area of research – not only in terms of particular books and periodicals explicitly linked to religious organisations such as the Society for the Promotion of Christian Knowledge (1698–) and the Religious Tract Society (1799–1935), but also in terms of what Mark Knight identifies as 'the fluid interaction between theology and other discourses' such as 'literature, business, travel, and science'.[48]

As the press expanded in the early decades of the century, editors and publishers seized opportunities to reflect and construct the interests of niche audiences. The period covered by this volume corresponds with the development of trade journals, including *The Lancet*, *The Mining Journal* and *The Builder*, founded in 1823, 1835 and 1843, respectively. In Chapter 12, 'Invincible Brothers: The Pen and the Press in *The Compositors' Chronicle*, 1840–3', Françoise Baillet examines an overlooked periodical linked to another trade: compositing. Like other trade journals, it was concerned with self-advocacy and constructing a sense of creative community. It included a correspondence column that encouraged reader engagement, along with contents designed to provide instruction and entertainment for artisan workers and their families. In doing so, it reinforced the respectability of workers in the compositing trade, underscoring their domestic virtues, respectability and literary attainments. Nowhere was this more evident than in their poetry, which, as Baillet notes, created a sense of unity among printers and established their cultural capital as competent, and sometimes playful, masters of the written word.

As the reading habit became part of everyday life in Britain and its colonies, periodicals became increasingly differentiated, reaching out to niche markets of readers, including colonists, abolitionists, charitable visitors and compositors. At the same time, as the contents of this volume make clear, the period between 1820 and 1845 was an era in which the idea of a 'mass audience' for print first took shape, as shown in the efforts of publishers and editors to reflect and construct new readerships that included all members of the family and addressed large constituencies of artisan, lower-class and middle-class readers. These impulses toward expansion and differentiation produced competition and innovation that had lasting effects on print culture, shaping what would soon become the 'Victorian' publishing world – and anticipating what would eventually become our own twenty-first-century new media ecology.

This volume is not intended as an exhaustive introduction to innovations within print culture between 1820 and 1845 but as an invitation for further research. The topics and methods demonstrated in the pages that follow are meant to inspire scholarship in neglected areas of research, especially the writers, editors, illustrators and publishers who forged a sense of modernity through new media innovation, efforts that sparked both anxiety and excitement as the decades unfolded. These developments had wide-ranging implications both in Great Britain and in its current and former colonies. I hope that the publication of this volume will spark future research not only on individual actants but also on interactivity: the ways in which periodicals, books and newspapers sparked reader engagement – for example, through fan poetry, manuscript periodicals, correspondence and records of philanthropic activity. I also hope scholars will further investigate how readers engaged with multimodal textualities and repurposed print in scrapbooks and home decoration. Finally, I hope this volume will inspire scholars to explore intersections between periodicals, books and newspapers within the media system of the period, demonstrating how change affected not only individual titles but also a broader media ecology in which old media were adapted to new contexts.

Notes

1. Richard Cronin, *Romantic Victorians: English Literature, 1824–1840* (Houndmills: Palgrave, 2002), 1.
2. For background on changes in printing technology, see T. R. Nevett, *Advertising in Britain: A History* (London: Heinemann, 1982), 40–2.
3. Rachel Teukolsky, *Picture World: Image, Aesthetics, and Victorian New Media* (Oxford: Oxford University Press, 2020), 3.
4. For background on the unstamped press, see chapter 14 of Richard Altick, *The English Common Reader: A Social History of the Mass Reading Public, 1800–1900* (1957, reprint, Columbus: Ohio State University Press, 1998). For an overview of reprinting practices in transatlantic literary culture, see Meredith McGill, *American Literature and the Culture of Reprinting, 1834–1853* (Philadelphia: University of Pennsylvania Press, 2003).
5. Tom Mole, *What the Victorians Made of Romanticism: Material Artifacts, Cultural Practices, and Reception History* (Princeton: Princeton University Press, 2017), 13.
6. Ibid., 16.
7. Clare Pettitt, *Serial Forms: The Unfinished Project of Modernity, 1815–1848* (Oxford: Oxford University Press, 2020), 225.
8. 'Reading for All', *Penny Magazine* 1 (31 March 1832): 1.
9. Mark Algee-Hewitt, et al. (The Multigraph Collective), *Interacting with Print: Elements of Reading in the Era of Print Saturation* (Chicago: University of Chicago Press, 2018), 244.
10. Altick, *English Common Reader*, 389.
11. 'Preface', *Mirror of Literature, Amusement and Instruction* 1 (21 May 1823): n.p.
12. For background on Limbird's experiments in cheap periodical and book publication, see Altick, *English Common Reader*, 266–7.
13. Louis James, *Fiction for the Working Man, 1830–50* (1963, reprint, Brighton: Everett Root, 2017), 12–13.
14. Jon P. Klancher, *The Making of English Reading Audiences, 1790–1832* (Madison: University of Wisconsin Press, 1987), 79.
15. Pettitt, *Serial Forms*, 221.
16. [William M. Thackeray], 'Half-a-Crown's Worth of Cheap Knowledge', *Fraser's Magazine* 17 (March 1838): 280.

17. Pettitt, *Serial Forms*, 223.
18. Poster and handbill announcing the first issue of the *News of the World*, as reproduced in *A Catalog of Books and Newspapers Printed by John Bell and by John Browne Bell* (London: First Edition Club, 1931), 4.
19. Altick, *English Common Reader*, 394.
20. 'To the Public', *News of the World*, 1 October 1843, 4.
21. Altick, *English Common Reader*, 356.
22. 'The Newspaper Press in London', *London Journal* 1 (19 July 1845): 328. Emphasis in the original.
23. Pettitt, *Serial Forms*, 24.
24. Alexis Easley, 'Imagining the Mass-Market Woman Reader: *The News of the World*, 1843–77', in *The News of the World and the British Press, 1843–2011*, ed. Laurel Brake, Chandrika Kaul and Mark W. Turner (Houndmills: Palgrave Macmillan, 2016), 81–99.
25. Klancher, *The Making of English Reading Audiences*, 4.
26. Many other scholars have interpreted the period of this study as being instrumental to the development of the first 'mass market' press. David Kunzle identifies Pierce Egan's *Life in London and Sporting Guide*, founded in 1824, as the first mass-market newspaper due to its high circulation and broad appeal among the lower classes. David Kunzle, 'Between Broadsheet Caricature and "Punch": Cheap Newspaper Cuts for the Lower Classes in the 1830s', *Art Journal* 43, no. 4 (1983): 340. See also Klancher, who writes that the 'mass public as an idea must be continually tested, questioned and reimagined' and 'mapped on a disparate group of possible readers' in the periodical press (*Making of English Reading Audiences*, 77).
27. 'Weekly Newspapers', *Westminster Review* 10 (April 1829): 477.
28. 'Address of the Editors', *Chambers's Edinburgh Journal* 9 (25 January 1840): 8.
29. Ibid.
30. Patrick Leary, 'Googling the Victorians', *Victorian Literature and Culture* 10, no. 1 (2005): 72–86.
31. See James Mussell, 'Digitization', in *The Routledge Handbook to Nineteenth-Century British Periodicals and Newspapers*, ed. Andrew King, Alexis Easley and John Morton (London: Routledge, 2016), 17–28; Amaranth Borsuk, *The Book* (Cambridge: MIT Press, 2018), chapter 4.
32. Algee-Hewitt, et al. (The Multigraph Collective), *Interacting with Print*, 5.

33. Alexis Easley, *New Media and the Rise of the Popular Woman Writer, 1832–1860* (Edinburgh: Edinburgh University Press, 2021).
34. Ibid., chapters 1 and 2.
35. [Thackeray], 'Half-a-Crown's Worth of Cheap Knowledge', 290.
36. Brian Maidment, *Reading Popular Prints, 1790–1870* (Manchester: Manchester University Press, 1996), 15.
37. Teukolsky, *Picture World*, 4.
38. Nevett, *Advertising in Britain*, 25.
39. [Charles Dickens], 'Bill Sticking', *Household Words* 2 (22 March 1851): 601–6. See also Teukolsky, *Picture World*, 355–60.
40. Neil Postman, *Technopoly: The Surrender of Culture to Technology* (New York: Knopf, 1992), 18.
41. Mole, *What the Victorians Made of Romanticism*, 18.
42. Cronin, *Romantic Victorians*, 3.
43. Margaret Beetham, *A Magazine of Their Own?: Domesticity and Desire in the Woman's Magazine, 1800–1914* (London: Routledge, 1996), 46. See also Jennifer Phegley, 'Family Magazines', in *The Routledge Handbook to Nineteenth-Century British Periodicals and Newspapers*, ed. Andrew King, Alexis Easley and John Morton (London: Routledge, 2016), 276–92.
44. See Lee Erickson, *The Economy of Literary Form: English Literature and the Industrialization of Printing, 1800–1850* (Baltimore: Johns Hopkins University Press, 1996), chapter 1.
45. See Easley, *New Media*, chapter 4.
46. Antoinette Burton, *Empire in Question: Reading, Writing, and Teaching British Imperialism* (Durham: Duke University Press, 2011), 2.
47. Pettitt, *Serial Forms*, chapter 7.
48. Mark Knight, 'Periodicals and Religion', in *The Routledge Handbook to Nineteenth-Century British Periodicals and Newspapers*, ed. Andrew King, Alexis Easley and John Morton (London: Routledge, 2016), 364.

I

'Collect and Simplify': Serial Miscellaneity and Extraction in the Early Nineteenth Century

Mark W. Turner

One of the ways we can understand developments in serial print culture in the nineteenth century is through examining its innovations. Exploring how and why new titles emerged; attending to publishers' strategies in developing new readerships; analysing writers' and journalists' techniques as they developed and helped shape print forms – these are just some of the ways print and media historians have sought to capture the dynamism of print modernity. As I use it, 'print modernity' suggests an ongoing but geographically uneven set of developments within the print and media industry enabled through technologised, industrialised innovations across the nineteenth century. While it is a shorthand for new readerships and a complex set of processes and expansions in technologies of production and distribution, it is not intended to totalise how we think about industrial print. I am instead interested in tracking the broad tendencies and driving forces of how print works and develops over time. This chapter focuses on one significant and ever-present concept in print culture of the period – miscellaneity – and explores some of the ways it was established and consolidated in serials in the first decades of the nineteenth century. In particular, I consider one of the key techniques of miscellaneity – extraction – and explore how the common practice of what I call 'extractive miscellaneity' became embedded in serial culture early in the century. I conclude by gesturing toward the ways in which extractive methods in print suggestively align with extractive forces in colonialism by the end of the century. What is at stake here is an understanding not simply of how we conceptualise print but also how the techniques of print are deployed culturally and resonate politically as they develop across time.

Print modernity can partly be defined as a culture of seriality. As a number of scholars have shown, the serial provides shape and form to the proliferation of print across the nineteenth century, and the different forms and periodicities that were launched and tested in various markets attest to the extraordinary range of innovations by publishers and writers, drawing on new technologies and developing new processes and methods.[1] We need only think of the many terms in use for naming serial print (newspaper, review, magazine, miscellany, supplement, companion) with their different but overlapping periodicities (daily, weekly, fortnightly, monthly, annually) to appreciate the expansive nature of serial print in the period. While there were arguably dominant forms and formats emerging at particular moments – the penny magazine in the 1830s or the shilling monthly in the 1860s, for example – there was also an emphasis on innovation and differentiation. New serials frequently launched themselves, often hyperbolically, as being distinct, even if they were obviously following the lead of another successful title in the marketplace. They are 'new' but not always as new as they suggest, as they seek to become familiar and swiftly embedded in the rhythms of print. To that end, serial formats project regularity (even if they don't always manage to deliver on it), partly through forms of repetition. As James Mussell notes, serials 'announce their seriality through appearances', in other words through repeating aspects of format, including typeface, layout and departments, presenting the new instalment as recognisable and familiar, as something from the past and something of the present.[2] Each serial instalment is different but also the same, and each serial instalment is replaced by the next iteration in a temporal rhythm. But the serial is also imagined as long-term and projects a kind of endlessness: it continues to expand across time. We don't know when a newspaper or a magazine will end. All of the different forms and formats launched across the century are 'serials', reminding us that serial form was never singular or discrete any more than it was fixed. In what follows, I pay particular attention to the ways serials launch themselves in their prospectuses since it is often in these direct addresses to readers and the print industry that serials articulate their editorial practices and distinctive qualities as they bid to establish a readership in an always crowded print marketplace.

If the culture of seriality in print modernity developed forms for the proliferation and expansion of print and its many rhythms, then the culture of miscellaneity was all about brevity and selection within an abundant and expanding field.[3] In the face of the seemingly limitless amount of the 'new' arising out of the increasingly industrial cycles of print production across the century, selectivity was a necessary form of containment. Miscellaneity – as a mixture, a medley and a bringing together of separate things – works against the proliferation of seriality through such processes as reduction and compression. The use of extraction is one of the ways many miscellaneous publications achieved that reduction. Miscellaneity contains what otherwise would appear to be serially infinite, offering us a reassuring and apparently stable selection of all that we might read or know, whether in a daily newspaper, weekly magazine, monthly 'miscellany', quarterly review or other format.

Like seriality, miscellaneity was a long-established feature of print, at least since the seventeenth century and with the emergence of the newspaper format, although it has remained relatively under-studied. Recently, however, early modern scholars have begun to establish significant links between the 'miscellany' and early modern literary manuscripts, in Britain and abroad, suggesting the pervasiveness of miscellaneity as a conceptual practice in early modern literary culture. Joshua Eckhardt and Daniel Starza Smith, editors of a collection of essays on early modern miscellaneity, note that the practice of miscellaneity – of diverse gatherings of texts in various forms or what they call 'containers' – was, in the past, considered by scholars almost too commonplace to merit extensive discussion, but recently this has changed and early modern miscellanies are now receiving unprecedented attention.[4] They suggest that over the long seventeenth century, 'the English noun "miscellany" gradually came to refer not only to the miscellaneous parts or contents of a volume but also to the volume itself'.[5] The miscellany continued to develop thereafter 'as eighteenth-century stationers marketed hundreds of new books as miscellanies, as nineteenth-century editors reprinted early modern books under the name, and as twentieth-century scholars broadened their focus from the discrete contents to the entirety of these now-renamed early modern miscellanies'.[6] Miscellanies, then, have long been integral to manuscript and, later, print culture even if we haven't always noticed or known what to do with them. Eckhardt and Starza Smith argue that 'while early modernists have perfected methods for reading many of the individual texts and genres that one finds in miscellanies (poems and plays, sermons and speeches, letters and lyrics), only a few of them have begun to determine how to read a miscellany as a whole'.[7] In focusing on early nineteenth-century miscellaneity, therefore, I am not suggesting that miscellaneous practices in print culture were especially new; rather, I contend that as industrial print gathered force and as the birth of cheap press from the 1830s produced exponential growth in serial print, the dynamic between seriality and miscellaneity expanded in striking ways. From the 1830s to the 1840s, we see a proliferation not only in serial forms, ever testing out new markets and periodical rhythms, but also in miscellaneous practices. This chapter seeks to foreground the significance of miscellaneity in various ways as it embedded itself in the expanding field of cheap print in the first half of the nineteenth century.

A fortnightly serial launched in 1807 – *The Compiler; or, Literary Banquet. Consisting of Interesting Extracts from the Most Popular, Scarce, & Expensive Works* – helps us to see plainly the dual processes of seriality and miscellaneity at work early in the century. The *Compiler* was one of the many periodicals that announced its method in its title, and like other miscellanies at the time, it published excerpts from books organised under such generic topics as history; travel and biography; and fiction and poetry. The opening address to readers states that

> the enquiring curiosity of youth, the mature research of manhood, and the lighter taste of the female sex, may all find gratification in the pages of the 'Literary Banquet'; while the whole is made subservient to the noblest purposes of information, and the best ends of morality.[8]

The editor goes on to say, 'although this Work is published in Numbers, and various articles necessarily continued from one number to another, yet it has been, and shall continue to be, our care to render this and every succeeding Volume perfectly complete in itself'.[9] Two things stand out here. First, we see the link between miscellaneity and information, demonstrating that one of the functions of selection is to provide readers with necessary information and by implication a foundation for knowledge. This gets more pronounced throughout the century as, arguably, the nineteenth century heralds what we later call the 'information age', through developments in the documenting, indexing, cataloguing and storage of data and information. Miscellaneous information takes many forms, depending on the print context. In the *Compiler*, information is aligned with moral improvement, but in other publications, as we'll see, information is presented as entertainment. Second, the *Compiler* is a 'work published in numbers' but one that adheres closely to the cultural value and comparative permanence of the book, partly as a way of mitigating against the ephemerality of seriality. It relies on books for its miscellaneous content and presents excerpts in a single-column, book-like layout, assuring the reader that though the publication appears in instalments, there is an overriding vision of completeness at work.

The dynamics of seriality and miscellaneity and the methods of extracting and compressing that are inherent in serial print raise a number of significant questions: How are we meant to think about all the miscellaneous items that fill the pages of so many popular nineteenth-century serials? What is their status as text, representation or possibly as abstraction? Miscellaneous material has been understood in part as 'filler' that makes the pages of a serial number complete by filling in gaps in layout. Even if taking up space on the page is one function of some of this material, how might we start to process the miscellaneous information we see on the page? This chapter seeks to think closely about miscellaneity, partly as content but especially as process and method.

Extractive methods

Scissors-and-paste journalism was one of the defining characteristics of editorial and journalistic practice across the nineteenth century, beginning approximately from the 1820s and 1830s, which saw such striking growth and innovation in cheap print. Scissors-and-paste methods were also key to the culture of miscellaneity across the century. *The Dictionary of Nineteenth-Century Journalism* defines this widespread practice as 'excerpting from or recycling of articles from other publications'.[10] In particular, they point to news gathering in the provincial press, which relied on reprinting items from national papers, whether syndicated or pirated, but the metropolitan press was equally engaged in forms of excerpting. 'Excerpting' – or what some serial miscellanies called 'extracting' – included a variety of different practices, so 'scissors and paste', as we call it, really suggests a conceptual method rather than a singular editorial practice that produced a singular form.

One of the early examples of a scissors-and-paste serial in the century, *The Thief*, launched in 1832 and priced twopence, makes a cheeky virtue of their methods in their title. As the editor explains to a potential publisher (and bookseller) in the playful prospectus, imagined as a dialogue from a play:

> Editor: Sir, I have called upon you to know whether you will undertake the publishing of a new paper?
>
> Publisher: What, sir, *another* penny paper? Sir, my hands are so full of them, that I have already burnt my fingers. But what is the name of your intended paper?
>
> Ed: 'The Thief.'
>
> Pub: (*Starting from his seat*) Make my shop a receptacle for stolen goods! This is too bad – never, never!
>
> Ed: Gently, sir, gently, not so fast. – Is not 'published under the superintendence of the Forty Thieves' quite as good as 'published under the superintendence of the Society for Useful Knowledge'?
>
> Pub: No slander against the Society's Magazine, the most instructive –
>
> Ed: That is the very thing – they are all instructive, and none amusing.[11]

As with *The Compiler; or, Literary Banquet*, *The Thief* understands the link between miscellaneous contents and information or instruction, but part of what makes this title 'new' is that it seeks to buck the trend and focus on entertainment rather than instruction. The educative possibilities of print were being explored extensively beginning in the 1820s by Charles Knight and his cheap print innovations, which were partly associated with the Society for the Diffusion of Useful Knowledge (SDUK). It is Knight's and the SDUK's model of a popular, information-led, miscellaneous cheap press that *The Thief* defines itself against. The 'Magazine' noted in *The Thief*'s prospectus is Knight's enormously successful *Penny Magazine* (1832–46), the first cheap illustrated miscellaneous weekly that launched so many imitators in the burgeoning market for cheap periodicals.[12]

Many of Knight's innovative publications across his sprawling network of print relied on forms of excerpting and extracting for the purposes of recirculating information or retrospectively re-presenting 'news' after the fact. Seriality and miscellaneity work in tandem across his titles, and various modes of organising this expansive print were used to create order and organisation. In 1826–8, he developed an ambitious scheme for a 'National Library' of a hundred titles, the object of which was 'to condense the information which is scattered through voluminous and expensive works, into the form and substance of Original Treatises' on subjects like art, history, science and 'miscellaneous literature'.[13] It was to be both serial and miscellaneous, gathered under the framework of the unifying 'National Library' title. Knight is consistent across many of his publications in his mission to condense scattered information and materials for popular readers. Of his popular *Companion to the Almanac* launched in 1828, he writes that 'the knowledge conveyed shall be given in the most condensed and explicit manner', and this approach guided the publication for the next thirty-seven years.[14] Knight's *Companion to the Newspaper* (1833–7, initially priced 2d. monthly) sought to get round the stamp duty on news-oriented publications by publishing a monthly that would 'collect and simplify' materials gathered from other publications, including parliamentary reports and the foreign press, presenting them as 'political knowledge' for working people in a monthly cycle.[15] The publication is imagined as a 'storehouse of FACTS' which are otherwise 'scattered' across various forms of print and are therefore beyond the reach of the popular reader, who has neither the time nor the financial resources to explore such a range of publications.[16] The 'Advertisement' for *A Volume of Varieties*, a miscellaneous selection of Knight's contributions to periodicals from the 1820s to the 1840s, states that the author will 'collect a few scattered papers together', less for the education of readers in this instance than for their entertainment.[17] Collecting and gathering, simplifying and condensing – all of this editorial activity is conceived by Knight through a process in which serial expansion combines with some form of miscellaneous reduction, in which disparate and scattered materials are brought together, compressed and apparently contained and organised.

The Thief was less lofty in its ambitions than Knight's broad mission for cheap print from the 1820s to the 1840s, but the periodical shares similar methods for gathering scattered materials. As the editor and the publisher continue their dialogue in the prospectus to *The Thief*, the periodical's methods are revealed and its title justified:

Ed: No, no; it is to be edited by the *light-fingered* gentry, and will consequently contain no heavy articles. – The magazines, the various periodicals, will be our plunder; *they* will be, as it were, the shell and husk, *we* the kernel of literature; – *they* are the fatness, but *we* the marrow of fatness.

Pub: But the original matter, – the reviews, &c. The –

Ed: Nonsense[,] my good friend. Who writes any thing original now-a-days? We only steal from them what they have stolen from others. And as for reviews without extracts, what are they to a person who has never read the books? It is like telling a man that there is plenty of money in the Bank, when he asks you for a halfpenny. No, sir; we will leave original matter to more clever hands; and their name at the end of an article will act as an advertisement for them.[18]

Here the editor makes a virtue of his extractive methods of plundering entertaining content ('no heavy articles') from other publications, acknowledging that originality is not part of the plan. 'We only steal what they have stolen from others', he asserts, suggesting that the whole expanse of serial print is underpinned by the reconfiguration and repurposing of text from one form and format to another. The editor astutely notes the case of the highbrow, weighty quarterly 'reviews', which he says rely heavily on excerpting from the books being discussed. Part of the value of a review in the early nineteenth century (and thereafter) was precisely its extensive excerpts. The lengthy reviews in the quarterlies – and indeed, shorter reviews that appear more frequently across the century – reprint what the reviewer deems essential. The reviewer reads the actual book or books so that the reader doesn't have to. Finding the most important parts of a text, reducing a larger text to its essential bits – the kernel rather than the shell or the husk, as *The Thief* suggests – is one of the goals of miscellaneity. And the wry suggestion in the prospectus is that, already by 1832, this practice of excerpting is at work at all levels of the press, from the quarterly reviews to the cheap penny papers. Everyone cuts and pastes. Everyone steals from others. But for the emerging cheap press in the early decades of the century, extraction provided a relatively inexpensive way of gathering content through plunder.

The practice of scissors-and-paste journalism was integral to serial print culture across the nineteenth century, but it was not the only form of extraction in the culture of miscellaneity.

While various forms of serials were engaged in excerpting, readers, too, reused and repurposed the public world of print for more private, domestic aims through various modes of scrapbooking. As Brian Maidment has shown so persuasively, 'scraps' have an important place in the social history of visual culture. Indeed, he notes that they

> were an aspect of commercial print making in the 1820s, 1830s and 1840s and comprised images deliberately produced, either in sheets or as small separate images, in the expectation that they would be cut out and reassembled as decorative pages in albums or scrap-books.[19]

Maidment observes that 'scraps' have conventionally not been a subject of serious scholarly study, partly because it is difficult for literary and visual critics to know what to do with small bits of text that are apparently incomplete or are presented primarily as bits of circulating and recirculating information. A scrap seems unhelpfully incomplete in itself. Nineteenth-century readers, however, were less circumspect. The huge popularity of scrapbooking across the century attests not only to the centrality of the scrap in public culture but also to the ways individual readers used scraps to mediate public discourse in the private realm.

By the early decades of the nineteenth century, the word 'scrap' had made its way into the titles of miscellaneous books and periodicals, for example the book *Scrapiana; or, Elegant Extracts of Wit*, published in 1818, or the *Scrap Book of Literary Varieties*, launched in 1831. The idea of the scrap was popular and commonplace. Furthermore, as Alexis Easley notes, the term 'scrapbook' was coined in 1825. 'What was new', she notes,

> was its repurposing of the ephemera of popular print culture. In a scrapbook, an article on floral arrangement might be juxtaposed with a humorous poem or a paragraph about the vagaries of love – materials cut or copied from periodicals and arranged in a personally meaningful order. The selection and arrangement of scraps came to be associated with 'feminine' domestic culture, serving as both a leisure activity and a creative outlet. Miscellaneous columns were likewise designed to appeal to female readers and often served as a major source of content for scrapbooking. The cheap weekly periodical, the miscellaneous column, and the scrapbook thus co-evolved as interdependent genres.[20]

Easley discusses the way scrapbooking operates as a kind of gendered, domestic leisure activity enmeshed within networks of print. The coevolution and interdependence of genres and, by extension, the interlinkage of forms and formats is crucial in understanding the broader culture of miscellaneity of which scrapbooking was a part. What is important to recognise is the wider ecology of print at work here, in which forms, formats and genres borrow from each other, both in print and in the individual uses of that print in scrapbooking.

Ellen Gruber Garvey, who has written extensively about scrapbooking in the American context, suggests that this practice was in part a way of managing the abundance of print across interconnected genres and serial forms. 'Readers adapted to this proliferation of print', Garvey writes, 'by cutting it up and saving it, reorganising it, and sometimes recirculating it'.[21] She continues,

> Approaches for coping with the rising tide of print included library vertical files and cataloging systems like Melvil Dewey's, and commercial clipping bureaus that scanned a city's or nation's papers on behalf of clients. But at home, other readers [. . .] created scrapbooks to capture this value. [. . .] But each clipping scrapbook maker too created a private and idiosyncratic catalog, a reflection of personal identity made from mass-produced and distributed publication as much like Netscape Bookmarks or Microsoft Favourites as a library's vertical files. These Web management devices help users blaze a trail through a vast landscape of materials.[22]

Here, Garvey links individual scrapbooking to other forms and systems of nineteenth-century information and document management, as well as new forms of cataloguing that persist in various forms to this day. What both Gruber and Easley help us to see is how miscellaneity and extraction, whether thought about as domestic leisure and labour or as a broader cultural technique, lend themselves to systemisation. By the early Victorian era, miscellaneity as a form, practice and method was promiscuous across print culture in both private and public realms, and the systemisation of miscellaneity became ever more pronounced across the century.

Global systems of serial miscellaneity

Nowhere do we see the systemisation of early nineteenth-century print as strikingly as in the development of newspaper press directories, first launched in the 1840s. As Laurel Brake has noted in her study of the pioneering *Newspaper Press Directory*, launched in 1846 by the advertising agent Charles Mitchell, the genre emerged in the context of a broader interest in forms of print that organised and disseminated information.[23] Across the century, new serial forms of directory, index, guide and companion focused on gathering, organising and shaping information for specific industries and general public use. We see that clearly in Charles Knight's constellation of SDUK print titles and other serials including, for example, the *Companion to the Newspaper*. The newspaper press directory genre was a product of the press industry, an annual trade publication focused on encouraging advertising in the newspapers and exploiting the commercial possibilities of an ever-expanding serial press. To that end, Mitchell's (as the *Newspaper Press Directory* was more commonly known) and other directories sought to capture information about all the newspapers published in Britain and to organise that information according to categories such as location and frequency. One effect of such organisation was to provide an abstracted overview of the industry through information. Thus, the way we get a glimpse of the entirety (or supposed entirety) of the newspaper press is through its representation as information. A genre that began with a focus on newspapers expanded to include many other forms of serial literature, not only in Britain but across the globe. And other countries, of course, developed their own national and international press directories. A title like Mitchell's offers a seemingly stable vantage point for readers to 'see' the ever-expanding and diversifying serial press industry. It is the management of press industry information, presented as a system of serial print, that enabled its vastness to appear organised and coherent.

As an article in the first volume of Mitchell's makes clear, an alignment of new and innovative technologies of communication helped to drive the spread of serial print. An anonymous author writes,

> Within an incredibly brief space of time from the application of steam to machinery, not only the stream press turns out its countless thousands of double sheets by the hour, but locomotive conveyance has

> attained to so vast an extent and importance as to demand an entire and numerous class of newspapers for the recording of its events, and the advocacy of the multitudinous questions to which its interests continually give birth.[24]

As we see here, the expansion of the press due to steam and locomotion created the need for more print; seriality produces yet more seriality. Railway timetables and railway industry papers and periodicals recording the railway's events are now needed as the industry expands. Furthermore, this expansion of the press traversed ever greater distances which, in turn, also created the context for more serial print circulating ever more widely. The article notes 'the immense impulse given to commerce and the arts of life, by the enlarged means of communication with distant parts' and suggests that the monthly *Railway Magazine*, launched by the radical publisher Effingham Wilson in 1835, constituted a 'new medium of public information' with a goal of gathering and presenting the specific commercial concerns of the new railway industry.[25]

The expansion of serial print due to increased means of technical production (steam press) and dissemination (railways) became even more pronounced with the development of the telegraph. In his autobiography, Charles Knight notes that at the time of the pioneering cheap serial *Penny Cyclopaedia*, completed in 1844, 'we were only in the infancy of that vast change in the intercourse of the world which has been effected by the railways.'[26] And just as the impact of the railways was being felt, the arrival of the telegraph further developed the possibilities for communication across great distances. 'The "Penny Cyclopaedia" could scarcely contemplate the wonderful ramifications of this marvellous invention,' Knight writes.[27] He goes on to note how 'the whole business of journalism in this country' had 'utterly changed' at the introduction of the telegraph.[28] The 'greatest marvel of all', he notes, is

> that, through the application of the Submarine Telegraph, whilst the battle of the dawn is still raging on the shores of the Baltic, the types which are to tell us of the progress of an undecided event are being set up in the evening in a dozen print offices in London.[29]

The global implications of this integrated new system of production and dissemination made itself felt over the coming decades, and by the 1880s, the international press became an important feature of press directories as well – for example, *Sell's Dictionary of the World's Press*, launched in 1883–4, which makes the international reach of the volume a feature in the title.

However, the dynamics of seriality and miscellaneity were embedded in global print long before the railways, steam press and telegraph would rapidly expand the industry and its global reach. The 1821 launch of the first magazine to be published in Australia, the monthly *Australian Magazine; or, Compendium of Religious, Literary, and Miscellaneous Intelligence*, shows how seriality and miscellaneity worked in tandem to enable a concept of transnational and specifically colonial connectedness early in the century. The 'Preface' to volume 1 reminds readers of the principles of the miscellany, noting that the magazine's aim is 'to disseminate useful knowledge, religious principles, and moral habits' and avoid politics.[30] From the beginning, the editors 'endeavoured to select the most interesting' material related to '*Colonial* occurrences', while also publishing one original article each month.[31] As Elizabeth Webby discusses in her overview of the nineteenth-century Australian periodical press, the *Australian Magazine* focused on 'providing information on important topics from the Mother Country, defending the vital principles of Christianity, and providing an outlet for local writers'.[32] The index to volume 1 organises the contents in ways that would have been familiar to readers of other miscellaneous books and periodicals, with topics and genres such as biography, theology and natural philosophy, along with the two longest sections – religious intelligence and miscellanies. 'European incidents' are indexed as a separate category, indicating the ways the magazine integrated the settler colonial context with the wider 'home' culture. As a serial 'compendium' of miscellaneous 'intelligence', the *Australian Magazine*'s extractive methods are perhaps unsurprising, but miscellaneity in this colonial context may provide a function different from that seen in the contemporaneous titles discussed above. Here, extractive miscellaneity – the assembling of scattered intelligence and information in a serial pattern – not only links the magazine and the settler colony back to the 'Mother Country', as Webby suggests, but also to other colonial sites in a network of global print and communications.

By way of an introduction to the magazine, the first issue leads with what is almost entirely a single, brief letter, an '*Extract of a Letter from His Excellency* General Macquarie, *Governor and Commander in Chief*' of Australia, which offers his sanction and support.[33] The extraction of letters as miscellaneous intelligence – sometimes from personal correspondence sent to the editor, sometimes from print sources – features across the periodical in ways that bind the letter with global print circuits of communication. The first article of the inaugural issue is the beginning of a biographical serial on the 'Life of the Eminent Missionary [Christian Frederick] Swartz', a German missionary based in India. The article is 'chiefly taken' from another periodical, the *Missionary Register*, and is largely comprised of reprinted letters that Swartz wrote from Tanjore where he was stationed. Later in the same issue, an article entitled 'Allegory on Impudence and Modesty' is a transcription of a mid-eighteenth century discussion of allegory published in Edinburgh but here framed as a letter to the editor of the *Australian*.[34] A few pages later, another letter to the editor appears – this time from Samuel Marsden, the Church of England's leading cleric in New South Wales and an important missionary. Marsden's letter encloses yet another letter, from Rev. John Campbell of Cape Town, South Africa, which states, 'you have my permission to insert, in your Monthly Publications, any part you may approve.'[35] The letter by Rev. Campbell is then published as an 'Extract of a Letter from the Rev. J. Campbell in Africa, to the Rev. S. Marsden', providing an account of Campbell's journey to missionary stations in South Africa between 1818 and 1820. In the 'Miscellanies' section of the second issue of the *Australian Magazine*, still more letters to the editor embed yet more letters, for example on the subject of spade husbandry:

> I send you, here with, Copies of Correspondence on this subject, for which I am indebted to the kindness of a friend; and which, as it contains the observations and experiments of a practical man, will fully prove the benefits resulting from this practice. Should you think fit to indulge it with a place in your Miscellany, you will confer a favor on,
>
> Sir,
>
> your obedient servant,
>
> A Farmer.[36]

The reprinted letter from a farmer in Newcastle, sent to a farmer in New South Wales, provides an account of his experience of cultivating the soil using a spade, along with what he calls the 'data' connected to his agricultural experiments. In issue three of the magazine, a transcription from another periodical appears in a letter to the editor, along with an extract from the journal of 'Captain Raine's Narrative of a Visit to Pitcairn's Island in the Ship Surry, 1821'. The editor notes, 'We shall proceed to select extracts from that gentleman's journal, to whom we beg to make our public acknowledgments for the obliging manner in which he furnished our Miscellany with so valuable an article.'[37]

Letters to editors were nothing new in the serial press in the 1820s: there is a long history of periodicals relying on readers' correspondence (whether they are 'real' letters or not) to frame the discourses of a periodical and to provide a seemingly unified world for the reader. What I would emphasise here, however, in my study of the early run of the *Australian Magazine*, is the way the particular method of miscellaneous extraction of letters connects the settler colonialists in Australia in a wider network of communications with other colonial contexts – for example, South Africa and India. On the one hand, there is the global circulation of communications through letters (travelling by ship rather than railway at this time); on the other hand, there is the emergence of colonial serial print which relies partly on those global communications to create a unified vision of the colonial world. Seriality and miscellaneity – the ongoing promise of continuity and the bringing together of scattered information – combine in an attempt to articulate a unified understanding of 'the Australian' in the *Australian Magazine*.

Another early monthly periodical in settler Australia, *Arden's Sydney Magazine*, launched in 1843, demonstrates a similar use of extractive methods but with a more pointed political effect. Like the *Australian Magazine*, *Arden's* uses miscellaneous methods to collect and simplify key information. The 'Monthly Colonial Chronicle' uses short paragraphs to report on legislative news, council and other committee meetings, as well as shipping arrivals and departures, while the 'Colonial Statistics' section gives informational tables on agriculture as well as the import and export of wool, oil and livestock, along with lists of land sales, population data and yet more shipping information. None of this monthly material is discursively framed; rather, it takes the form of lists and tables of data turned into information. The statistics and chronicle sections resemble any number of SDUK publications or other information and knowledge-led publications of the early nineteenth century. However, an article on the 'Civilization of the Aborigines' asserts a racist argument in favour of what is called the 'Coercive System' of 'managing' the native aboriginal peoples of Australia based on extensive quotation from various reports, correspondence between government officials and excerpts from the press, including the *Melbourne Gazette*. The author of the article quotes 'an extract from a Port Phillip paper' that states, 'We (Port Phillip Patriot) have been favoured with the following extract of a letter from a settler at the Grange, giving an account of a *rencontre* between a small part of Captain Dana's native police and a horde of predatory savages.'[38] Here, *Arden's* publishes an extract of an extract previously printed in another newspaper as part of its gathering of scattered bits of information and its construction of a broader narrative supporting an oppressive and violent system for controlling aboriginal peoples. Miscellaneous extraction, as a process and method, was never neutral; thus, its uses need to be examined more particularly and specifically in relation to print contexts.

Conclusion: A print politics of colonial extraction?

As the century progressed, cheap serial print covered the globe. Publishing nodes in media, communications and transport networks – Melbourne, London, Boston, Kolkata and Cape Town, among others – suggest overlapping networks of connectedness, an apparently seamlessly mediated world. Seriality and miscellaneity, their forms and methods, helped produce that apparent unity. Extraction continued to be an important way that miscellaneous methods were imagined, and the metaphors attached to extractive miscellaneity became ever more prominent. If early in the century *The Thief* uses the image of the kernel being extracted from the shell to describe its miscellaneous practice, later in the century, in innovative miscellanies such as the enormously popular *Tit-Bits* and the *Review of Reviews*, the processes of selective extraction and reduction at work in serial miscellaneity are represented through the language of ploughing, digging up and winnowing away. These images and methods provide a way of holding forth against the abundance of print modernity, offering reassurances that readers won't get lost in the maze of print by printing only the essentials.

By the end of the century, extractive miscellaneity was deployed in a more systematised way than in earlier decades – with information being mined from other sources and then reimagined, recirculated and repurposed. The nineteenth century, as Elizabeth Carolyn Miller has discussed in her study *Extraction Ecologies* (2021), was 'a period when Britain came to understand itself as an empire thoroughly dependent on extraction: an extraction-based industrial society irretrievably bound up with the mining of underground material, with no viable alternative capable of preserving social relations'.[39] As she persuasively demonstrates in her account of literary genre and form, 'literature is not merely a passive register of industrial extraction's impacts[;] [. . .] it was the discursive site where this transformation was mediated'.[40] She helps us see how an extraction ecology is aligned with aesthetic forms. The dynamic created between seriality and miscellaneity similarly produces its own kinds of compressive aesthetics, of gathering and simplifying. Miller's understanding of extraction ecologies relies on the notion of de-plenishing resources and the idea of finitude, which provides value within the system. What gets de-plenished in extractive miscellaneity is time – the reader's ability to spend time understanding the ever-accumulating abundance of global material. Print modernity, as we have seen in the examples of cheap print in the early nineteenth century, assumes that time is running out for readers to get a grip on the constantly increasingly amount of material that might be known. Time is a precious commodity in modernity as the growth, expansion and spread of global print across integrated networks and systems make connectivity more necessary than ever.

Extractive miscellaneity is not the same thing as extractive colonialism with its particular forms of violence against the human and natural worlds. Yet it is striking that some of the conceptual methods, processes and techniques of print modernity – driven by those twin engines of seriality and miscellaneity, with its movement of expansion and compression – are connected to extractive colonialism through forms of mediation and communication, representation and abstraction. We see this early in the century in the way scattered texts get brought together and reduced and used in colonial contexts like Australia; by the end of the century, there is an even greater alignment of serial print with a broader project involved in shaping how we think about the colonial world and the liberal subject's enmeshed place within that world. Part of what is at stake in identifying extractive miscellaneity as it develops across the century is a gathering of readers in a global world of print.

That is where the extractive logic of serial miscellaneity heads. But as early as the 1820s, the *Australian Magazine*, the first magazine published in that settler colony, arguably did exactly that in its threading together of letters and miscellaneous data from scattered sources. That unity is, of course, partly illusory, enabled by processes of excerption and extraction, underpinned by the fantasy of the too-easy global spread of print and communication, itself underpinned by the fantasy of empire as the century unfolds.

In the systemisation and abstraction of material, then, we see a process at work – not only a way of delimiting and managing abundance but also a way of making the individual a part of a cohesive but much larger whole. The individual scattered text is made part of another whole; the individual reader is made to connect to a larger collective. Already, in the birth of cheap print in the early decades of the century, we can begin to ask: how do we conceptualise serial and miscellaneous print in relation to forms of colonialism? In what ways do the methods, processes and techniques of print enable, circulate, represent and/or abstract the political and cultural forces being mediated? The metaphors of plundering that we see early in the century later align with the larger forces of extractive colonialism at work across other kinds of imperial systems, a more violent version of extracting the kernel and leaving the rest behind.

Notes

1. There is a long list of excellent scholarship on the forms of the nineteenth-century serial dating back to the pioneering work by Linda K. Hughes and Michael Lund, *The Victorian Serial* (Charlottesville: University of Virginia Press, 1991), and Graham Law, *Serializing Fiction in the Victorian Press* (Basingstoke: Palgrave, 2000). For recent work on the proliferation of serial print specifically, see Laurel Brake, 'The Serial and the Book in Nineteenth-Century Britain: Intersections, Extensions, Transformations', *Memoirs du Livre Studies in Book Culture* 8, no. 2 (2017): 1–16; James Mussell, 'Elemental Forms: The Newspaper as Popular Genre in the Nineteenth Century', *Media History* 20 (2014): 4–20; Mark W. Turner, 'Serial Culture in the Nineteenth Century: G. W. M. Reynolds, the Many *Mysteries of London*, and the Spread of Print', in *Nineteenth-Century Serial Narrative in Transnational Perspective, 1830s–1860s, Popular Culture – Serial Culture*, ed. Daniel Stein and Lisanna Wiele (Basingstoke: Palgrave, 2019), 193–211.

2. James Mussell, '"Of the making of magazines there is no end": W. T. Stead, Newness, and the Archival Imagination', *English Studies in Canada* 41, no. 1 (2015): 72.
3. See Mark W. Turner, 'Seriality, Miscellaneity and Compression in Nineteenth-Century Print', *Victorian Studies* 62, no. 2 (2020): 283–94. For other recent work on miscellaneity, see Daniela Gretz, Marcus Krause and Nicolas Pethes, eds, *Miszellanes Lesen Reading Miscellanies/Miscellaneous Reading* (Hannover: Wehrhahn Verlag, 2022).
4. Joshua Eckhardt and Daniel Starza Smith, *Manuscript Miscellanies in Early Modern England* (London: Routledge, 2019), 2. For another recent discussion of early modern miscellaneity, see Megan Heffernan, *Making the Miscellany: Poetry, Print, and the History of the Book in Early Modern England* (Philadelphia: University of Pennsylvania Press, 2021).
5. Eckhardt and Starza Smith, *Manuscript Miscellanies*, 2.
6. Ibid.
7. Ibid.
8. 'Address', *Compiler; or, Literary Banquet* 1 (London: A. Neil, 1807): iii.
9. Ibid.
10. Catherine Feely, '"Scissors-and-Paste" Journalism', in *The Dictionary of Nineteenth-Century Journalism* (online edition), ed. Laurel Brake and Marysa Demoor (Ghent and London: Academia Press and the British Library, 2009).
11. 'Our Leader', *Thief* 1 (21 April 1832): 1.
12. Thomas Arnold, uncertain about the proliferation of cheap miscellaneous print, characterised the *Penny Magazine* as 'all ramble-scramble'. See Charles Knight, *Passages of a Working Life During Half a Century; with A Prelude of Early Reminiscences* (London: Bradbury and Evans, 1864), 2:182.
13. Knight, *Passages of a Working Life*, 2:47.
14. Ibid., 2:64. On Knight's *Companion to the Almanac* and other almanacs, see Brian Maidment, 'Beyond Usefulness and Ephemerality: The Discursive Almanac, 1828–60', in *British Literature and Print Culture*, ed. Sandro Jung (Woodbridge: Boydell and Brewer, 2013), 158–94.
15. 'Prospectus', *Companion to the Newspaper* 1 (1 March 1833): 1. On Charles Knight and his publishing ventures, see Valerie Gray, *Charles Knight: Educator, Publisher, Writer* (Aldershot: Ashgate, 2006), especially chapter 3. On the *Companion to the Newspaper*, see Mark

W. Turner, 'Companions, Supplements, and the Proliferation of Print in the 1830s', *Victorian Periodicals Review* 43, no. 2 (Summer 2010): 119–32.

16. 'Prospectus', *Companion to the Newspaper*, 1.
17. Charles Knight, 'Advertisement', in *A Volume of Varieties* (London: Knight, 1844), v.
18. 'Our Leader', *Thief*, 1.
19. Brian Maidment, 'Scraps and Sketches: Miscellaneity, Commodity Culture and Comic Prints, 1820–40', *19: Interdisciplinary Studies in the Long Nineteenth Century* 5 (2007), http://www.19.bbk.ac.uk.
20. Alexis Easley, 'Scrapbooks and Women's Leisure Reading Practices, 1825–60', *Nineteenth-Century Gender Studies* 15, no. 2 (2019), http://w.ncgsjournal.com/issue152/easley.html.
21. Ellen Gruber Garvey, 'Scissorizing and Scrapbooks: Nineteenth-Century Reading, Remaking, and Recirculating', in Lisa Gittelman and Geoffrey B. Pingree, eds, *New Media, 1740–1915* (Cambridge: MIT Press, 2003), 209. See also Garvey's more recent *Writing with Scissors: American Scrapbooks from the Civil War to the Harlem Renaissance* (Oxford: Oxford University Press, 2013).
22. Gruber Garvey, 'Scissorizing and Scrapbooks', 209.
23. Laurel Brake, 'Nineteenth-Century Newspaper Press Directories: The National Gallery of the British Press', *Victorian Periodicals Review* 48, no. 4 (2015): 569.
24. 'Railway Press', *Newspaper Press Directory* 1 (London: C. Mitchell, 1846): 27.
25. Ibid., 31.
26. Knight, *Passages of a Working Life*, 2:218.
27. Ibid., 2:220.
28. Ibid., 2:221.
29. Ibid.
30. 'Preface', *Australian Magazine* 1 (1821): iii. The preface appears in the volume edition rather than in a monthly issue.
31. Ibid., iv.
32. Elizabeth Webby, 'Australia', in *Periodicals of Queen Victoria's Empire: An Exploration*, ed. J. Don Vann and Rosemary T. VanArsdel (Toronto: University of Toronto Press, 1996), 24.
33. 'Prospectus', *Australian Magazine* 1, no. 1 (1 May 1821): 3.
34. 'Allegory on Impudence and Modesty', *Australian Magazine* 1, no. 1 (1 May 1821): 21–2.
35. 'To the Editor of the Australian Magazine', *Australian Magazine* 1, no. 1 (1 May 1821): 27.

36. 'To the Editor of the Australian Magazine', *Australian Magazine* 2, no. 2 (1 June 1821): 49.
37. 'Captain Raine's Narrative of a Visit to Pitcairn's Island, in the Ship Surry, 1821', *Australian Magazine* 1, no. 3 (1 July 1821): 80.
38. 'Civilization of the Aborigines', *Arden's Sydney Magazine* 1, no. 2 (October 1843): 65–82, 78.
39. Elizabeth Carolyn Miller, *Extraction Ecologies and the Literature of the Long Exhaustion* (Princeton: Princeton University Press, 2021), 2–3.
40. Ibid., 14.

2

William Hazlitt and Celebrity Culture: Periodical Portraits in an Age of Public Intimacy

Chris Haffenden

In 'On Sitting for One's Picture' (1810), William Hazlitt connected the intimate practices of portraiture with wider questions of public recognition. While opening the essay with a particular discussion about the 'conscious vanity' involved in becoming the subject of a portrait, he concluded with broader reflections on the limitations of such pictures for 'perpetuating our names in the wide page of history'.[1] By dwelling upon the relation between media form and cultural value, Hazlitt embodied the early nineteenth-century preoccupation with the effects of wide-ranging media change on the production of renown. With the growth of the reading public and the expansion of print culture enabled by technological developments, a new type of public visibility emerged, one that produced novel emotive relations between readers and celebrities, what Joseph Roach has called 'public intimacy'.[2] Through enhanced techniques for circulating images and texts, the private lives of celebrities became a source of fascination, familiarity and identification among readers. Insofar as he sought to understand the workings of these new conditions, Hazlitt has been described as 'the first great fame theorist of the modern age'.[3]

This chapter uses innovations of print portraiture as a lens to examine Hazlitt's complex relationship with modern celebrity. While considerable attention has been focused on his role as a theorist of fame – with scholars such as Andrew Bennett and Lucy Newlyn on the one hand, and Claire Brock on the other, presenting contrasting views – a lot less has been written about him as a producer of celebrity culture.[4] By situating the portraits in *The Spirit of the Age* (1825) within the media and material context of celebrity, I highlight how Hazlitt generated intimacy effects that were central to literary culture in the 1820s. The first part of the chapter explores the new conditions of publicity produced by media proliferation in the Romantic period as a frame for understanding Hazlitt's response to celebrity culture, while the second part turns to a closer examination of the representational strategies of his print portrait gallery. In showing how an apparent critic of celebrity could still engage in its practices, this chapter suggests just how pervasive celebrity culture had become by the 1820s.

Media proliferation and personality overload

'We are become public creatures.'[5] So declared Hazlitt in an 1820 essay that attempted to account for what he saw as the 'poverty [. . .] of our present dramatic genius'.[6] His use of the phrase was relatively particular in this instance, forming part of an argument about how, in directing attention towards more general abstractions following the French Revolution, 'the press had been the ruin of the stage'.[7] Yet this sense of becoming 'public creatures' also constitutes a broader statement about the impact of media change on shifting conditions of publicity from the closing decades of the eighteenth century to the 1820s. In the opening sections of this chapter, I outline some of these changes and show how media and technological developments were contributing to new forms of – and pressures on – public personality. Doing so establishes a vital context for making sense of Hazlitt's varied interactions with celebrity culture, highlighting the ways in which he could both resist and reproduce the norms of this culture.

A salient way of characterising the media change of the early nineteenth century is in terms of proliferation.[8] The first and most significant form – one that had helped transform the public culture that Hazlitt was writing and commenting upon – was that of print. The course of Hazlitt's life saw not only a rapid expansion of print media but also a steady flow of commentary from contemporary critics who sought to make sense of what this new and protean world of print might mean. When the emergence of industrialised print production combined with broader infrastructural changes from the closing decades of the eighteenth century, the result, as Tom Mole has shown, was an exponential increase in the volume of printed material available.[9] By the 1820s, this increase was both enabled and driven by the rise of new media forms, such as serial publication and weekly periodicals and the growth of new groups of readers, including women and children. From the perspective of a critic such as Hazlitt, who aspired to at least something of an overview, this generated a palpable feeling of overload: 'Who is there', he wondered, 'that can boast of having read all the books that have been written, and that are worth reading? Who is there that can read all those with which the modern press teems, and which, did they not daily disappear and turn to dust, the world would not be able to contain them?'[10] With an increasing abundance of texts now being produced by print capitalism, the challenge became one of prioritising scarce attention: of establishing what should be read and why.

Beyond the sensation of an unmanageable volume of printed material, this period also witnessed a dramatic expansion of the visual field. The second form of proliferation I wish to point towards is that of Romantic visual culture; not only was there too much to read but also the risk of there being too much to see. Late eighteenth-century London had offered a growing range and extent of visual entertainment that would only intensify into the nineteenth century: from art exhibitions and theatrical performances to freak shows and funeral effigies on show at Westminster Abbey, as well as the spectacular displays of the real provided by panoramas.[11] The experience of this space of increasingly popular visual attractions could be enticing yet also overwhelming. Such ambivalence was captured by William Wordsworth who, in detailing his encounters with the 'spectacles' of the metropolis, had spoken both of the 'allurement' of the diverse performers at Sadler's Wells and the 'perpetual whirl of trivial objects' he saw at St Bartholomew's Fair.[12] This sense of disorientation was heightened by the increase of printed images that circulated during this period and the new constellations of image and text premiered at commercial exhibitions such as Boyd's Shakespeare Gallery.[13] When readers morphed into spectators and vice versa and when the dizzying effects of this multimedia culture of exhibition were experienced as a 'perpetual whirl', it was evident that this had become, in Edward Bulwer Lytton's formulation, a 'Staring Nation' preoccupied with the visual.[14]

In particular, this entailed a fixation with viewing – and commenting upon – images of the famous. The third and final proliferation I highlight is that of portraiture, since, as part of what Antoine Lilti has described as 'the first media revolution', this proved a notable marker of the emerging conditions of publicity during this period.[15] While previously an exclusive representational form connected to the court and nobility, one rarely seen in public, the portrait was significantly democratised from the mid-eighteenth century onwards.[16] This can be connected, in part, to the new vogue for public exhibitions, such as the Royal Academy's annual exhibition, which offered novel opportunities for self-display amidst the growing trade in portrait painting. But more significantly, it was about establishing a new market for portrait images made possible by innovations in print technology and commercial design. With new techniques for reproducing images like steel-plate engraving and the development of improved distribution infrastructures, there was a spectacular increase in the circulation of the heads and bodies of the renowned during this period: from the growing trend of grangerising via the extra-illustration of books to the widely popular portrait prints, busts, medallions and ceramics that became available in print shops and country fairs.[17] The effect of this proliferation was to produce a visual culture suffused with images of the well known, where an overwhelming volume of bodies was effectively competing for public attention.

Contemporary observers recognised the unmanageable proliferation of claims to public recognition. Commentators of a more conservative bent were especially worried that this amounted to an overproduction akin to opening the floodgates – a saturation of the forms involved in producing value that could only lead to a debasement of the currency of renown. Writing in 1796, for instance, the Earl of Fife suggested that 'when every body almost who can afford twenty pounds, has the portraits of himself, wife, and children painted', a cheapening of the genre was inevitable.[18] Future collectors, he explained, 'even with the aid of the annual Exhibition, will hardly be able to find out the numerous bad painters, and the uninteresting obscure persons so represented'.[19] Isaac D'Israeli made much the same point, though in more satirical terms, highlighting the dangers attached to the emerging genre of autobiography: 'If the populace of writers become thus querulous after fame (to which they have no pretensions) we shall expect to see an epidemical rage for auto-biography break out.'[20] The 'pernicious' effects of such an outbreak, D'Israeli sardonically surmised, would be a London 'peopled solely by "men of genius"'.[21]

The rapid increase in texts, sights and images produced by media change was thus generating concern about overload by the turn of the nineteenth century. With the proliferation of the means for creating visibility, a wider range and extent of public personalities had been made possible and brought into circulation. Contemporary figures such as Wordsworth observed countless such 'candidates for regard' in London, those who 'in hall, Court, theatre, conventicle, or shop, in public room or private, park or street, each fondly reared on his own pedestal, looked out for admiration'.[22] Once the number of candidates competing for attention became difficult to manage, critics needed to devise new strategies of appraisal, which I will consider in the next part of this essay.

Managing excess: Techniques of priority

This overflow of public personalities necessitated concerted efforts to address the problem of priority. When critics such as D'Israeli and Hazlitt worried about surveying an insurmountable volume of print and when Wordsworth and other observers like Mary Robinson pointed towards the expanding range of aspirants for public recognition, what type of appraisive infrastructure might be relied upon to ascertain value and direct focus? One response to this challenge of overload was the numerous canonisation projects that appeared during the early decades of the nineteenth century. While these projects could span a range of cultural production and assume a variety of material forms, including anthologies of national poetry, biographical encylopaedias and sculptural pantheons, they were united by the shared ambition of sorting the wheat from the chaff and presenting a manageable selection of the worthy. In this sense, the assertion of a canon of lasting value became a way of imposing order on the crowded arena of public names during the early nineteenth century.

Another pertinent means of determining value was through the branded identities of popular celebrities. Responding to forms of celebrity that had been established as a new and more open form of recognition during the eighteenth century, publics were exposed to an expanding range of images of the renowned yet were increasingly aware of their remoteness from these idols.[23] To reduce this sense of alienation, the emerging celebrity system invested in various strategies for creating public intimacy and offering the sensation of close proximity to the new icons of public life.[24] By the turn of the nineteenth century, a constellation of practices was being used to circulate the private lives of celebrities and transform them into brand names: from puffs and promotions to biography, illustrations and scandalous gossip. The effect of this was to foreground particular celebrities, such as Lord Byron, whose profiles were so visible that they overshadowed competitors and completely dominated the marketplace. Celebrity could thus function as a pointed mechanism to focus attention upon a select few.

As a commentator reflecting upon these partly overlapping and partly competing techniques of priority, Hazlitt sought to elevate the canon and protect it from what he judged to be the degraded character of popular celebrity.[25] Addressing the problem of value in an age of mechanical reproduction, he effected a temporal and qualitative divide between the two forms of recognition that left little doubt as to where his sympathies lay. The proper 'fame' of the canon, Hazlitt insisted, 'is not popularity, the shout of the multitude, the idle buzz of fashion, the venal puff, the soothing flattery of favour or friendship; but it is the spirit of a man surviving himself in the minds and thoughts of other men, undying and imperishable'.[26] While canonicity was a posthumous award that was built to last, celebrity was discounted as a fickle and ephemeral form of renown: one encapsulated by the fleeting worth of a 'newspaper puff'.[27] Indeed, in expanding upon the appraisive process of establishing lasting fame, Hazlitt explained that the material practices of celebrity and the creation of public intimacy were irrelevant:

> Death is the great assayer of the sterling ore of talent. At his touch the drossy particles fall off, the irritable, the personal, the gross, and mingle with the dust – the finer and the more ethereal part mounts with the winged spirits to watch over our latest memory.[28]

In other words, a precondition for entering the canon was a gradual stripping away of the paraphernalia of contemporary recognition.

Such scepticism about the worth of celebrity was part of Hazlitt's broader ambivalence towards the popularisation of cultural production and judgement. This was evident, for instance, in his comparison of viewing print images in a shop with the experience of seeing a painting in a gallery. If visiting a printshop such as 'Molteno's or Colnaghi's' might offer some 'relief and satisfaction in the motley confusion, the littleness, the vulgarity of common life', he judged that it still proved but 'a mean, cold, petty' substitute for 'a fine Collection of Pictures'.[29] The imitations of fine art engravings provided tantalising hints of greatness, yet they could hardly compete with the aura-making force of the 'bright originals'.[30] This privileging of the fine art original over the mechanically produced copy dovetailed with his conviction that 'the multitude' could not be trusted to recognise and appreciate 'the highest excellence'.[31] Indeed, he insisted that taste was not subject to the 'principle of universal suffrage' but was instead limited to 'those few persons whom nature intended for judges', who were in possession of 'the most refined understandings'.[32] Rather than having been produced by 'popular consent or the common sense of the world', the reputations of lasting works had been the result of the appraisal of a select 'few persons in every successive period'.[33] For Hazlitt, then, criticism was a necessarily elite project that operated at a considerable remove from 'the generality of mankind'.[34]

Although he was suspicious of popular judgement, Hazlitt did not reject the reading public entirely. While dismissive of mass taste as 'the caprice of fashion, the prejudice of the moment', he was far from committed to the reactionary politics of Wordsworth and Coleridge and instead articulated a progressive, broadly democratic politics of knowledge.[35] Drawing upon his optimistic conception of print culture as 'the great organ of intellectual improvement and civilization', he highlighted the importance of continued popularisation efforts to further the process of dissemination.[36] In the context of information overload and the 'superabundance of raw materials' produced by advances in print technology, he argued that 'the grand desideratum now, is to fashion and render them portable. Knowledge is no longer confined to the few: the object therefore is, to make it accessible and attractive to the many'.[37] Hazlitt could still make nostalgic gestures towards earlier periods prior to this broadening of the reading public, when 'literature was not then cheap and vulgar', but in general he asserted that expanded print circulation had produced a new, irreversible reality that 'we must conform to'.[38] It might not be possible to improve popular taste, but given that 'the cells of learning' had been 'thrown open', he certainly thought that the public now needed to be reckoned with.[39]

This sense that the emergence of modern conditions of publicity had constituted 'a change in the world' prompted Hazlitt to develop a more complex relationship with forms of contemporary recognition than simply a blanket dismissal. Despite his many objections to celebrity culture, he did on occasion seem to embrace it. Whereas previously the neglect of authors by their contemporaries necessitated a '*forlorn hope* in the prospect of immortality', modern authors could now enjoy the 'prompt payment' of immediate recognition since the 'effort and the applause go together'.[40] Such formulations have led Claire Brock to argue that, far from promoting the canon as a defence against popular renown, Hazlitt was actually a keen proponent of 'contemporary celebrity'.[41] And certainly, the effusive praise he bestowed upon Sarah Siddons, as 'the stateliest ornament of the public mind' and 'the idol of the people', might seem to support this line of argument.[42] Yet on the other hand, he also clearly emphasised that Siddons proved an 'exception' to the clearly defined distinctions that he consistently sought to maintain between mere celebrity and posthumous fame. As he explained in his clarification of the different orders of recognition that he identified in the public sphere of the early nineteenth century, 'popularity is neither fame nor greatness', just as any feats or attainments that 'are confined to the momentary, individual effort, and construct no permanent image or trophy of themselves without them' are necessarily of lesser worth.[43] While he could concede that there was a place for the popular recognition of celebrity in the bustling marketplace of the age of the periodical press, he remained convinced that the canon was a superior arbiter of value.

Periodical portraits as critique

Having grasped how Hazlitt responded to media proliferation by committing, at least for the most part, to canonicity as opposed to celebrity, we can now use this insight as a lens through which to consider his engagement with the practices and norms of early nineteenth-century celebrity culture. This discussion will focus on the 'contemporary portraits' he offered to the public in *The Spirit of the Age*. In her study on the emergence of what she describes as the 'portraitive mode' in Romantic Britain, Elizabeth A. Fay has argued that Hazlitt's volume constituted a principal challenge to this culture: a site of 'resistance' against the tendency to turn 'subjects into consumer commodities' amidst a 'hovering fear of thingification'.[44] While certainly suggestive as an extension of the argument that Hazlitt was a staunch critic of mass celebrity, Fay's interpretation risks overlooking the ways in which he could actually reproduce the norms of this culture. In the following sections, I consider Fay's argument about the disruptive character of *The Spirit of the Age* before analysing how far Hazlitt was imbricated in the representational protocols of the celebrity culture he variously sought to critique. As a foundation for this argument, we need first to turn our attention to the particular form of the portrait gallery that he deployed in this text.

The wide-ranging changes in print culture that had enabled the formation of Romantic reading publics also dramatically transformed the portrait gallery as a media form. As with the expansion of portraits mentioned above, the portrait gallery was democratised in significant ways over the course of the long eighteenth century, principally as a result of the proliferation of print. Having previously been an exclusively aristocratic form of self-fashioning designed to display and reinforce social authority, the emergence of print galleries made portraiture considerably more open by the time Hazlitt came to publish *The Spirit of the Age*.[45] This was due in part to the increased access that came with the metamorphosis of the 'gallery' from a place to a reproducible object: rather than being tied to a physical site like the ancestral gallery of painted portraits, the paper portrait gallery could circulate and be consumed in a range of social settings, including the home. In becoming what Fay described as 'a coffee table book', such galleries in book form provided a way of popularising the images and lives of the great and the famous and bringing them from the great house into the drawing room.[46] Beyond broadening availability, the printification of the portrait gallery also served to widen access to who could be represented in such a form for public display and veneration. By the early nineteenth century, as Christopher Rovee has demonstrated, there was a 'dizzying array' of such volumes available on the market, with 'every profession, every class, every type' seeming to have 'its gallery'.[47] As this diversification suggests, the print gallery had rapidly become a means of representation and identity production for a far wider range of social groups than simply the elite.

A key instance of this promotion of group identity was the galleries of authors that started to appear in the periodical press from the 1810s and quickly became a standard feature in literary magazines.[48] What these periodical portrait galleries sought to do, as Richard Salmon has explained, was to 'represent contemporary or recent authors as a visible collective body'.[49] In doing so, the galleries aligned with the representational protocols of an emergent celebrity culture in notable ways. First, by focusing exclusively upon the portraits of *living* authors rather than historical figures, they adhered to the temporal regime of contemporaneity that is foundational to the workings of modern celebrity.[50] Whereas the function of an aristocratic portrait gallery was to stage the permanence of genealogy by connecting the present to a long line of images from the past, the periodical portrait gallery instead produced a synchronic frame of reference that suggested what mattered was the here and now of the present moment. Second, by conflating the life and the work of celebrities, periodical galleries produced significant intimacy effects. Interweaving portrait images and biographical sketches, such magazines offered their readers the prospect of revealing details of the personal lives of these public figures. Like the 'hermeneutic of intimacy' exploited by Romantic poets, literary portrait galleries formed part of a wider repertoire of techniques that responded to the alienating effects of an anonymous mass public and an overflow of mass-produced texts and images by offering the promise of close contact with celebrity authors.[51] In sanctifying authors' status as idols to be venerated, periodical portrait galleries simultaneously contributed to this period's 'domestication of genius', both in terms of allowing prominent public lives to enter the home and in making domestic dimensions of these personal lives available for consumption within such homes.[52]

Hazlitt worked within this genre of the periodical gallery, with various of his portrait essays having first appeared in *The New Monthly Magazine* (1824) before later being subsumed into a single volume. However, he sought to subvert some of its principal characteristics. Tom Mole has suggested that *The Spirit of the Age* constituted a discursive pantheon forming part of a broader nineteenth-century concern with establishing and displaying a national pantheon of 'notable individuals'.[53] Yet if that were the case, it was a decidedly deflationary pantheon. Rather than providing any straightforward celebration of the twenty-four figures he selected to represent the zeitgeist, Hazlitt used these portraits to highlight what he regarded as the shortcomings of the cultural moment. Indeed, in adopting the perspective of posterity to cast judgement upon the expected future reputations of these contemporary figures, he offered a scathing verdict as to their chances for lasting value. As he wryly asserted in his essay on Jeremy Bentham, 'his name will hardly live so long' despite the philosopher's recurrent fantasies of the utilitarian impact of his writings over 'the next six to eight centuries'.[54] In marked contrast to encouraging veneration, then, this was a project centred on criticism. By putting forth a pantheon of public personalities only to undercut their claims to worth, Hazlitt made his print gallery a potent site of critique.

The most striking way in which he challenged the formal workings of the periodical portrait gallery was through the concerted absence of images: his book provided a series of 'portraits' that abstained from the use of visual portraiture. This is significant because it suggested an attempt to sidestep the economy of visual representation that had become such an important feature in the conditions of publicity of the early nineteenth century, as outlined in the opening section of this chapter. By omitting portrait busts or profiles that otherwise proliferated among the frontispieces of published books and print galleries of the period, Hazlitt seemed to be asserting a sense of distance from the predominant regime for producing unique and instantly recognisable individuals, which celebrity culture both presumed and reproduced. In doing so, as Fay suggested, he appeared to resist the 'reproductive technologies that naturalize visual portraits', thereby refusing to make public lives into consumable items.[55] Insofar as he declined to visualise the public profiles he used to critique the spirit of the age, the blank frontispiece of Hazlitt's volume can be aligned with the veiled portrait used to depict the 'author of Waverley' before Walter Scott revealed himself as the creator of the series in 1827 (Fig. 2.1).

In both instances, there was a refusal to conform to the imperative to make the profiles of public personalities visible through consumable images. In Hazlitt's case, this was entirely in keeping with his rejection of the role of 'the personal' dimensions of celebrity culture in appraising cultural value that we noted previously. Viewed in this way, *The Spirit of the Age* appears as something closer to an anti-portrait gallery.

Hazlitt's production of intimacy effects

Hazlitt's seeming rejection of the visual in his critique of celebrity tells only one side of the story. Just as Scott's veiled portrait effectively constituted a marketing ploy – a commercial game in which the personal and visual features of the author were withheld

Fig. 2.1 Frontispiece engraved by A. Wilson for Robert Chambers, *Illustrations of the Author of Waverley, Being Notices and Anecdotes of Real Characters, Scenes and Incidents Supposed to Be Described in His Works* [1822], 3rd ed. (London: W. & R. Chambers, 1884).

chiefly as a means of fuelling further interest in the question of his authorial identity – so did Hazlitt deploy various techniques for creating public visibility that had become an established feature of celebrity culture in this period. He engaged with the star system and hero worship that both preceded, and later became enmeshed with, a modern publicity regime. This was evident, for instance, in his particular obsession with Napoleon, as symbolised by the bust of the emperor in *Liber Amoris* (1823), and in his celebrity worship of Bentham, from whom he rented a cottage and who he was, therefore, able to observe up close. Indeed, his friend and fellow literary pilgrim Benjamin Haydon emphasised that it was 'with a longing eye' they had gazed at Bentham.[56] Such a concern with coming into close contact with the great also shaped aspects of *The Spirit of the Age*, which we now turn to consider.

Hazlitt might not have used visual portraiture in *The Spirit of the Age*, but he nonetheless devoted particular attention to the physical appearance of his subjects in many of the essays. Consider how he introduced Bentham via comparison with Milton's portraits – 'the same silvery tone, a few dishevelled hairs, a peevish, yet puritanical expression' – before offering the following sketch:

> In modern times, he is something between Franklin and Charles Fox, with the comfortable double-chin and sleek thriving look of the one, and the quivering lip, the restless eye, and animated acuteness of the other. [. . .] Add to this physiognomical sketch the minor points of costume, the open shirt-collar, the single-breasted coat, the old fashioned half-boots and ribbed stockings; and you will find in Mr. Bentham's general appearance a singular mixture of boyish simplicity and of the venerableness of age.[57]

Similar instances are to be found throughout the book, with, for instance, Godwin's face 'not unlike the common portraits of Locke', Wordsworth looking like 'some of Holbein's heads' and Lord Eldon possessing 'one of the best-natured faces in the world'.[58] In positing a firm distinction between the visual portrait and the biographical essay, Fay discarded such descriptions as 'a superabundance of caricature-like visual metaphors'.[59] Yet this is to brush over their effect: for just like other forms of popular visual culture such as the satire or the street sign, caricature could provide an effective means of enhancing celebrity visibility.[60] Indeed, beyond overlooking Hazlitt's use of famous portraits from the past as a visual index to render present figures legible, such an argument also disregards how words were used to invoke images in the 'lively tradition of verbal portraiture' that Julian North has identified in biographical works from the 1820s.[61] In directing focus upon the visual profiles of celebrities in text form, Hazlitt offered his readers the intimate promise of – to borrow North's apt phrase – 'pictured presence'.[62]

Hazlitt's focus on presence was intensified by his emphasis on the particularity of the celebrities in his volume. By depicting his characters in social settings and highlighting the idiosyncratic characteristics of their personalities, he participated in the domestication of genius that simultaneously created the prospect of intimacy, as outlined above.[63] Such illusions of closeness were produced by the character sketches Hazlitt deployed in many of the essays. For example, he describes Wordsworth as having 'a peculiar sweetness in his smile, and great depth and manliness and a rugged harmony in the tones of his voice'.[64] He then suggests:

> In company, even in a *tête-à-tête*, Mr. Wordsworth is often silent, indolent, and reserved. If he is become verbose or oracular of late years, he was not so in his better days. He threw out a bold or an indifferent remark without either effort or pretension, and relapsed into musing again.[65]

Through dwelling on what he characterised as 'domestic habits' and 'little peculiarities of temper', Hazlitt therefore participated in the economy of celebrity biography that he had variously critiqued and elsewhere sought to theorise.[66] As he explained, such biographies 'reveal to us the private history of eminent individuals' and were capable of throwing a 'spell' over the 'reader's mind', principally due to the connection created by the 'individuality of the details'.[67] Given that *The Spirit of the Age* also utilised such 'details' and thereby offered what he termed as the 'gratification of our curiosity', it formed part of a wider response to an increasing public demand for intimacy with celebrity figures.[68]

The desire for revealing insights into the private world of celebrated figures was also evident in the domestic details Hazlitt dwelt upon. As with his earlier essay capitalising on his first acquaintance with Coleridge and other poets, he deployed his personal experience of such encounters to produce intimacy effects in his textual portraits.[69] Once again, this was evident in his depiction of Bentham, where he could draw upon firsthand material of his previous landlord. Hazlitt thus placed the philosopher in the idiosyncratic setting of his 'house in Westminster, overlooking the Park', outlining his distinctive walking habits and noting the particular features of his domestic environment: from the 'playing on a fine old organ, and [. . .] a relish for Hogarth's prints' to the exercise set-up of 'wooden utensils in a lathe' and the house being 'warmed and lighted by steam'.[70] At one level, as Fay suggests, these details highlight Hazlitt's critique of the overemphasis upon abstraction at the expense of the particular.[71] Yet viewed from the perspective of celebrity biography, such characterisations can be understood as part of a broader preoccupation with the specific places and objects associated with revered writers. Indeed, a significant cultural development of this period was the emergence of increasingly organised forms of literary pilgrimage, which saw readers travelling to visit the houses of both dead and living authors.[72] As Hazlitt noted, there was a 'romantic interest' in such tourism, as well as in the attention devoted to 'relics' like 'a poet's lock of hair, a *fac-simile* of his handwriting, an ink-stand, or a fragment of an old chair belonging to him', since they enabled 'a sort of personal contact with such characters'.[73] By gesturing towards similar details, *The Spirit of the Age* anticipated the virtual literary tourism that would later become an established feature of Victorian print culture.[74]

Despite his critique of 'popularity', then, Hazlitt's portrait gallery did not involve a complete rejection of the representational protocols of celebrity culture. While not employing printed images, his volume made use of facial description, character sketches and domestic detail to offer at least something of the 'personal contact' and intimacy effects that were a central component of this culture. However critically inclined these descriptions might have been, they still had the effect of making the personal lives of his 'spirits' more readily available to his readers in print form. That an apparent critic of celebrity came to reproduce some of its principal preoccupations – emphasising the appearance and lifestyles of seemingly unique individuals – suggests how pervasive these concerns had become by the early nineteenth century. In a culture increasingly characterised by an overflow of industrially produced texts and images, Hazlitt could also contribute to the making of intimate public creatures.

Portraiting public intimacy in longer perspective

In his classic study on the history of fame, Leo Braudy suggested a significant shift had occurred between Samuel Johnson's *Lives of the Poets* (1779–81) and Hazlitt's *The Spirit of the Age* (1825): while Johnson could discuss poets without mentioning how 'they presented themselves to their immediate audiences', Hazlitt could hardly mention their works without also discussing the question of public attention to their 'personal nature'.[75] If the neatly schematic character of this contrast has been complicated by the rich and varied research on eighteenth-century celebrity culture, Braudy's point about the inescapable force of celebrity in the public space of the 1820s is reinforced by my arguments in this chapter.[76] Hazlitt may have responded to the prospect of overload by proposing an ethereal form of posthumous canonicity, but he could still engage in the practices of celebrity worship he occasionally disparaged. And though his deflationary portrait gallery appeared to abstain from the demands of an industrialised visual culture, the textual devices of his print portraits nonetheless offered some of the personal details necessary for his audience to imagine an intimate relationship with celebrity figures.

The conventions and strategies for producing such intimacy effects would become important components in the formation of celebrity culture throughout the nineteenth century. In this emerging media ecology, the widening range of genres employed to create the unique yet accessible star – from the gossip columns and portrait galleries of the illustrated press to the 'homes and haunts' guidebook and the 'at home with' celebrity interview and profile – made it possible for a growing body of readers to imagine affective relationships with public figures. This expansion was precisely due to the affordances of print portraiture (visual, textual or a combination of both), which enabled the bodies, domestic details and personal lives of celebrities to become objects of both mass-market attention and of intimate affection for individual readers. While sceptical as to the critical acumen of such a popular readership, Hazlitt's volume formed part of a shift towards innovative forms of media that would bring celebrities into a wider range of homes over the course of the century. *The Spirit of the Age* therefore substantiated the compelling appeal of 'the personal' that Hazlitt otherwise railed against: the works and the lives of celebrities had become inseparable.

Notes

1. Hazlitt, 'On Sitting for One's Picture', in *The Plain Speaker* (1826), *The Complete Works of William Hazlitt*, ed. P. Howe (London: J. J. Dent, 1930–4), 12:108.
2. Joseph Roach, 'Public Intimacy: The Prior History of "It"', in *Theatre and Celebrity in Britain, 1660–2000*, ed. Mary Luckhurst and Jane Moody (Basingstoke: Palgrave Macmillan, 2005), 15–30. For the emergence of modern celebrity in the eighteenth century, see Antoine Lilti, *The Invention of Celebrity: 1750–1850*, trans. Lynn Jeffress (Cambridge: Polity Press, 2017).
3. Leo Braudy, *The Frenzy of Renown: Fame and Its History* (New York: Oxford University Press, 1986), 434.
4. Andrew Bennett, *Romantic Poets and the Culture of Posterity* (Cambridge: Cambridge University Press, 1999); Lucy Newlyn, *Reading, Writing, and Romanticism: The Anxiety of Reception* (Oxford: Oxford University Press, 2000); Claire Brock, *The Feminization of Fame, 1750–1830* (Basingstoke: Palgrave Macmillan, 2006).
5. Hazlitt, 'The Drama: No. IV', *London Magazine* (April 1820), *The Complete Works of William Hazlitt*, 18:304.
6. Ibid.
7. Ibid., 18:305.
8. See the insightful discussion of this theme in Mark Algee-Hewitt, et al. (The Multigraph Collective), *Interacting with Print: Elements of Reading in the Era of Print Saturation* (Chicago: University of Chicago Press, 2018), 243–59.
9. Tom Mole, *Byron's Romantic Celebrity: Industrial Culture and the Hermeneutic of Intimacy* (Basingstoke: Palgrave Macmillan, 2007), 9–11.
10. Hazlitt, 'The Periodical Press', *Edinburgh Review* 38 (May 1823); *The Complete Works of William Hazlitt*, 16:213–14.
11. Richard D. Altick, *The Shows of London: A Panoramic History of Exhibitions, 1600–1862* (Cambridge: Belknap Press, 1978); Gillen D'Arcy Wood, *The Shock of the Real: Romanticism and Visual Culture* (Basingstoke: Palgrave, 2001). Hazlitt had gestured towards this growing space of public exhibition when comparing reading fiction to 'a peep at the raréé-show of the world [. . .] gazing at mankind as we do at wild beasts in a menagerie, through the bars of their cages, – or at curiosities in a museum'. Hazlitt, 'On Reading Old Books', in *The Plain Speaker* (1826), *The Complete Works of William Hazlitt*, 12:222.

12. William Wordsworth, *The Prelude; Or, Growth of a Poet's Mind. An Autobiographical Poem* (New York: D. Appleton, 1850), 7.182.
13. Luisa Cale, *Fuseli's Milton Gallery: Turning Readers into Spectators* (Oxford: Clarendon Press, 2006).
14. Edward Bulwer Lytton, *The Siamese Twins: A Tale of the Times*, 2nd ed. (London: H. Colburn and R. Bentley, 1831), 50; Sophie Thomas, *Romanticism and Visuality: Fragments, History, Spectacle* (New York: Routledge, 2007), 1–6.
15. Lilti, *Invention of Celebrity*.
16. Lilti, *Invention of Celebrity*, 53; Marcia Pointon, *Hanging the Head: Portraiture and Social Formation in Eighteenth-Century England* (New Haven: Yale University Press, 1993).
17. Lucy Peltz, *Facing the Text: Extra-Illustration, Print Culture, and Society in Britain, 1769–1840* (San Marino: Huntington Library, 2017); Eric Eisner, *Nineteenth-Century Poetry and Literary Celebrity* (Basingstoke: Palgrave Macmillan, 2009), 1, 154.
18. *Catalogue of the Portraits and Pictures in the Different Houses Belonging to the Earl of Fife* (1798), cited in Pointon, *Hanging the Head*, 2.
19. Ibid.
20. Isaac D'Israeli, 'Review of "Memoirs of Percival Stockdale"', *Quarterly Review* 1 (May 1809): 339.
21. Ibid.
22. Wordsworth, *The Prelude*, 7.195.
23. Roach, 'Public Intimacy', 16.
24. Mole, *Byron's Romantic Celebrity*, 16–22.
25. For influential readings that take this view of Hazlitt, see Bennett, *Romantic Poets*, and Newlyn, *Reading, Writing*.
26. Hazlitt, 'On the Living Poets', in *Lectures on the English Poets* (1819), *The Complete Works of William Hazlitt*, 4:144.
27. Ibid.
28. Hazlitt, 'Lord Byron', in *The Spirit of the Age; Or, Contemporary Portraits* (1825), *The Complete Works of William Hazlitt*, 11:78.
29. Hazlitt, *Sketches of the Principal Picture-Galleries in England* (1824), *The Complete Works of William Hazlitt*, 10:8.
30. Ibid. Compare Walter Benjamin, 'The Work of Art in the Age of Mechanical Reproduction', in *Illuminations*, ed. Hannah Arendt, trans. Harry Zorn (London: Pimlico, 1999).
31. Hazlitt, 'On Different Sorts of Fame', *The Round Table* (1817), *The Complete Works of William Hazlitt*, 4:94.

32. Hazlitt, 'Why the Arts Are Not Progressive?' *The Round Table* (1817), *The Complete Works of William Hazlitt*, 4:164.
33. Ibid.
34. Ibid.
35. Hazlitt, 'On Different Sorts of Fame', *The Round Table* (1817), *The Complete Works of William Hazlitt*, 4:94.
36. Hazlitt, *The Life of Napoleon Buonaparte, Vol. 1* (1828), *The Complete Works of William Hazlitt*, 13:37–60.
37. Hazlitt, 'Periodical Press', *Edinburgh Review* (May 1823), *The Complete Works of William Hazlitt*, 16:219–20.
38. Hazlitt, *Sketches of the Principal Picture-Galleries in England* (1824), *The Complete Works of William Hazlitt,* 10:8; Hazlitt, 'Periodical Press', *Edinburgh Review* (May 1823), *The Complete Works of William Hazlitt*, 16:218.
39. Hazlitt, 'Periodical Press', *Edinburgh Review* (May 1823), *The Complete Works of William Hazlitt*, 16:220.
40. Hazlitt, 'On Different Sorts of Fame', *The Round Table* (1817), *The Complete Works of William Hazlitt*, 4:95; see also similar arguments in Hazlitt, 'Periodical Press', *Edinburgh Review* (May 1823), *The Complete Works of William Hazlitt*, 16:219.
41. Brock, *Feminization of Fame*, 171.
42. Hazlitt, 'Mrs Siddons', *Examiner* (16 June 1816), *The Complete Works of William Hazlitt*, 5:312. See also Hazlitt, 'On Actors and Acting', *The Round Table* (1817), *The Complete Works of William Hazlitt*, 4:158.
43. He also writes, 'No man is truly great who is great only in his life-time.' Hazlitt, 'The Indian Jugglers', *Table-Talk* (1821), *The Complete Works of William Hazlitt*, 8:84.
44. Elizabeth A. Fay, *Fashioning Faces: The Portraitive Mode in British Romanticism* (Durham: University of New Hampshire Press, 2010), 75.
45. Christopher Rovee, *Imagining the Gallery: The Social Body of British Romanticism* (Stanford: Stanford University Press, 2006).
46. Fay, *Fashioning Faces*, 69–70.
47. Rovee, *Imagining the Gallery*, 8.
48. For more on this genre, see David Higgins, *Romantic Genius and the Literary Magazine: Biography, Celebrity, Politics* (London: Routledge, 2005), 60–1, 163.
49. Richard Salmon, *The Formation of the Victorian Literary Profession* (Cambridge: Cambridge University Press, 2013), 3.
50. James K. Chandler, *England in 1819: The Politics of Literary Culture and the Case of Romantic Historicism* (Chicago: University of Chicago Press, 1998).

51. Mole, *Byron's Romantic Celebrity.*
52. Julian North, *The Domestication of Genius: Biography and the Romantic Poet* (Oxford: Oxford University Press, 2009).
53. Tom Mole, *What the Victorians Made of Romanticism: Material Artifacts, Cultural Practices, and Reception History* (Princeton: Princeton University Press, 2017), 134.
54. Hazlitt, *The Spirit of the Age; Or, Contemporary Portraits* (1825), *The Complete Works of William Hazlitt*, 11:7.
55. Fay, *Fashioning Faces*, 75.
56. Haydon, *Life of Benjamin Robert Haydon*, ed. Tom Taylor (New York: Harper & Brothers, 1853) 1:216–17.
57. Hazlitt, 'Jeremy Bentham', in *The Spirit of the Age; Or, Contemporary Portraits* (1825), *The Complete Works of William Hazlitt*, 11:6–7.
58. Hazlitt, 'William Godwin', 'Mr. Wordsworth' and 'Lord Eldon—Mr. Wilberforce', in *The Spirit of the Age; Or, Contemporary Portraits* (1825), *The Complete Works of William Hazlitt*, 11:28, 91 and 145. (For similar instances of facial or physical description, see 11:27, 38–40, 44, 78, 134, 140.)
59. Fay, *Fashioning Faces*, 72–3.
60. Clara Tuite, *Lord Byron and Scandalous Celebrity* (Cambridge: Cambridge University Press, 2015), 203–9.
61. Julian North, 'Portraying Presence: Thomas Carlyle, Portraiture, and Biography', *Victorian Literature and Culture* 43, no. 3 (2015): 466.
62. Ibid.
63. He also writes, 'We draw down genius from its air-built citadel in books and libraries, and make it our playmate and companion.' Hazlitt, 'Spence's *Anecdotes of Pope*', *Edinburgh Review* (May 1820), *The Complete Works of William Hazlitt*, 16:153.
64. Hazlitt, 'Mr. Wordsworth', in *The Spirit of the Age; Or, Contemporary Portraits* (1825), *The Complete Works of William Hazlitt*, 11:91.
65. Ibid., 91–2.
66. Hazlitt, 'Spence's *Anecdotes of Pope*', *Edinburgh Review* (May 1820), *The Complete Works of William Hazlitt*, 16:153.
67. Hazlitt, 'Lady Morgan's *Life of Salvator*', *Edinburgh Review* (July 1824), *The Complete Works of William Hazlitt*, 16:284–85.
68. Hazlitt, 'Spence's *Anecdotes of Pope*', *Edinburgh Review* (May 1820), *The Complete Works of William Hazlitt*, 16:153; North, 'Portraying Presence', 473.
69. Hazlitt, 'My First Acquaintance With Poets', *Liberal* (1823), *The Complete Works of William Hazlitt*, 17:106–22.

70. Hazlitt, 'Jeremy Bentham', in *The Spirit of the Age; Or, Contemporary Portraits* (1825), *The Complete Works of William Hazlitt*, 11:16.
71. Fay, *Fashioning Faces*, 73.
72. Paul Westover, *Necromanticism: Traveling to Meet the Dead, 1750–1860* (Basingstoke: Palgrave Macmillan, 2012).
73. Hazlitt, 'Spence's *Anecdotes of Pope*', *Edinburgh Review* (May 1820), *The Complete Works of William Hazlitt*, 16:153
74. Charlotte Boyce, 'At Home with Tennyson: Virtual Literary Tourism and the Commodification of Celebrity in the Periodical Press', in *Victorian Celebrity Culture and Tennyson's Circle*, ed. Charlotte Boyce, Páraic Finnerty and Anne-Marie Millim (Basingstoke: Palgrave Macmillan, 2013), 18–52.
75. Braudy, *Frenzy of Renown*, 392.
76. For a recent example exploring eighteenth-century celebrity, see Heather McPherson, *Art & Celebrity in the Age of Reynolds and Siddons* (University Park: Pennsylvania State University Press, 2017).

3

Periodical as Memorial: Remembering Felicia Hemans in *The New Monthly Magazine*, 1835

Elizabeth Howard

During the 1820s and 1830s, biographies and postmortem commemorations[1] – as well as adjacent genres of elegies, engravings and 'character of writing' essays – helped to shape popular conceptions of professional authorship and authorial fame in a time of literary transition. Published across a range of periodicals, these genres individually and collectively offered a writer's life and work as an object of assessment, asking not only who an author was but also what an author's enduring contribution might be.[2] The cultural authority of poets, including female poets, depended on the judgements conferred by critics as well as the content and arrangement of periodicals, which were changing in response to the literary markets of the 1820s and 1830s.

When Felicia Hemans died in May of 1835, the amount of periodical space devoted to her death offers one metric for measuring her perceived authority as a female poet and the developing expectations for authorship in the 1830s. Reviewing the constellation of writing about Hemans at her death also allows us to identify who else sought to gain from her poetic authority and what role commemorative poetry, specifically the elegy, played in this effort. In their elegies to Hemans in *The New Monthly Magazine*, Letitia Elizabeth Landon and Elizabeth Barrett Browning both laid claim to Hemans's poetic status by means of their responses to her and to each other. This chapter, therefore, considers Landon and Barrett Browning's choice of *The New Monthly Magazine* as a strategic site for engaging with Hemans. Landon and Barrett Browning submitted their elegies for critical evaluation even as they assessed Hemans's literary legacy, publishing their verse alongside other memorials to Hemans's life and career.[3] At the same time,

Landon and Barrett Browning established their own poetic fame and authority in the periodical's contingent and contiguous serial context.

In July of 1835, David Macbeth Moir informed the readers of *Blackwood's Edinburgh Magazine* that Hemans had died of an illness two months earlier, inserting the announcement in a passing 'critical comment' appended to Felicia Hemans's 'Sabbath Sonnet'.[4] 'Without disparagement of the living', Moir eulogises, 'we scarcely hesitate to say that in Mrs. Hemans our female literature has lost perhaps its brightest ornament'.[5] Moir compares Hemans to her female peers, Joanna Baillie, Anna Brownell Jameson, Letitia Elizabeth Landon, Caroline Bowles and Mary Mitford, but he concludes that none is quite her equal. Despite high praise from Moir, *Blackwood's* published no other notice of Hemans's death even though it had published the majority of her periodical poetry in the last years of her life.[6] *The New Monthly Magazine* made a decidedly different choice following Hemans's death. Editor Samuel Hall published commemorative content across four genres in six consecutive issues, including three elegies: two by Landon and one by Barrett Browning. Between June and October of 1835, these elegies were published alongside a reprinted 'biographical sketch' of Hemans, an essay by Landon on the 'character' of Hemans's writing and an engraved image of the late poet. Their tributes to Hemans provide insight into the status of the female poet in the 1830s, a relatively flexible category that Landon and Barrett Browning both sought to shape. The *New Monthly*'s attention to Hemans's death also demonstrates the perceived economic value of her popularity to a once-influential periodical.

Within London's periodical scene of the 1820s and 1830s, *The New Monthly Magazine* at first experienced significant popularity and then a steady decline. Together, editors Thomas Campbell, Henry Colburn and Cyrus Redding reorganised the magazine in 1821, recruited popular writers and expanded their readership. Throughout the 1820s, the *New Monthly* competed with *Blackwood's* and *The London Magazine* for top popularity in England and ultimately rose to prominence during the mid-1820s as the 'leading magazine' in London.[7] Beyond a complicated and carefully curated political image among its editors, a significant part of the *New Monthly*'s success is attributable to Colburn and Campbell's ability to attract new poetry and prose from popular authors, including Hemans and Lady Morgan. Nonetheless, when

Campbell left the magazine in 1830 under new and changing editorship, the *New Monthly* lost its reputation of balanced political diversification among its readers, initiating a slow but sure decline.

When they reorganised the *New Monthly* in 1821, Campbell, Colburn and Redding titled the first hundred pages of the magazine as 'Original Papers' to distinguish the literary content from the 'Historical Register' of agricultural reports, news, patents and death notices in its second half.[8] In addition to highlighting political essays, the revised format of the *New Monthly* gave increased attention to literary works from new contributors like Charles Lamb, William Hazlitt and Leigh Hunt. Within the 'Original Papers', poetry shared an equivalent status to essays and fiction in its position on the page and in its indexing.[9]

Stuart Curran argues that late Romantic poets saw themselves as peripheral cultural influences, yet Landon's and Barrett Browning's elegies on Hemans do not occupy a marginal position in *The New Monthly Magazine*.[10] Instead, the location of their elegies suggests the centrality of poetry in popular discourse, even during a period that was 'doubtful' of the poetic genre.[11] Landon and Barrett Browning respond to Hemans's death in a way that directly contributes to their own literary authority. Whilst commemorating the life of Felicia Hemans, the *New Monthly* creates a public space for Barrett Browning and Landon in which they can simultaneously mould and critique the status of the poetess in popular print culture.

Today, Landon's and Barrett Browning's elegies on Hemans are best remembered for their association in a longer 'elegiac chain' stretching from Hemans's elegy on Mary Tighe (1827) to Christina Rossetti's memorial to Landon (1863). Yet analysis of this tradition has paid little attention to the periodical contexts in which the elegies appeared. Assessments of this 'elegiac chain' tend to focus on the emotive, experimental and argumentative quality of the poems rather than their contribution to the development of periodical poetry or to the evolution of the elegiac form in print.[12] In this chapter, I situate Landon's and Barrett Browning's elegies to Hemans within the context of *The New Monthly Magazine*'s six months of commemorative contributions on Felicia Hemans in 1835.

In June 1835, the *New Monthly* began its memorialisation of Hemans by publishing 'Biographical Particulars of Celebrated Persons, Lately Deceased: Mrs. Hemans'.[13] A month later, Samuel Hall published Landon's 'Stanzas on the Death of Mrs. Hemans',[14] and in August he printed Landon's 'On the Character of Mrs. Hemans's Writings',[15] along with James Thomson's engraving of the late poet.[16] Barrett Browning's 'Stanzas Addressed to Miss Landon, and Suggested by Her "Stanzas on the Death of Mrs. Hemans"' followed in September.[17] The sequence of memorials to Hemans ends in October 1835 with the publication of Landon's 'The Parting Word'.[18] All six commemorations in the *New Monthly* work in tandem as a serial tribute, marking the death and legacy of Felicia Hemans in a range of genres – postmortem biography, elegy, essay and engraving. In this chapter, I interrogate the critical and aesthetic gains made possible by the publication of this extended memorial to Hemans, demonstrating how elegies by Landon and Barrett Browning function in tandem with other genres of death writing in the shifting literary market of the 1830s. Landon and Barrett Browning experiment with ways to reinforce Hemans's – and their own – fame within *The New Monthly Magazine*'s specific periodical context.

Hemans, poetry and periodicals in the 1820s and 1830s

Twenty-first-century scholars and nineteenth-century critics have characterised the 1820s and 1830s – Hemans's most prolific years – as an extended literary lull. Judith Fisher, for example, borrows a description from *Fraser's Magazine* to characterise these decades as a literary 'famine'.[19] David Stewart notes that poetry was still widely written and read over these decades, yet he also discerns an anxiety in the 1820s and 1830s over poetry's future status and cultural value. Stewart characterises poetic experimentation during these decades as a response to this anxiety.[20] Rather than reading this anxiety negatively, however, Stewart recasts the 1820s and 1830s as a historical moment in which poetic anxiety translated into an interest in 'Living Poets' in post-Waterloo anthologies and essays 'because the very constitution of the category was "living", unsettled, contingent [. . .] guessing what the future would think of the present'.[21] This interest in living authors renders visible the efforts of critics, editors and readers to claim the present moment as one in which significant literary achievement was possible, if uncertain. Jock Macleod likewise traces a sustained interest in 'living poets' until the 1840s when, he argues, aesthetic interests pivoted towards postmortem biographical sketches. Macleod reads this pivot as a shift from an interest in living authors to dead ones and, further, as a working out of the 'multiple and variable debates [. . .] since at least the 1820s about the nature of authorship and the differences between kinds of writing'.[22] Hazlitt's 'Contemporary Portraits' in *The New Monthly Magazine* beginning in 1824 and William Maginn's eighty-one portraits of living authors in *Fraser's Magazine* between June of 1830 and July of 1838 affirm Stewart's and Macleod's characterisations of the professional author as a living figure during this period.[23]

Print cycles of periodicals also shaped the literary market's interest in what was 'living'. As weeklies and monthlies published poems that first appeared in the daily press, periodical seriality also contributed to the impression of a living and lively literary market. Seriality not only connected a past print moment to a present one but also framed the present as an open, incomplete timeline.[24] The periodical was building contingency into habits of reading such that the *New Monthly* in 1833 could coyly describe periodical intervals as echoing and even replacing ecological rhythms:

> This is the true millennium of the printers. [. . .] The earth is at once an Annual, laden with all the accumulated treasures of the year; a Quarterly Review, delighting us with the varieties of each succeeding season; and a daily Newspaper, teeming with new events which keep us, its readers, in a state of constant excitement. The moon, what is it but a perpetual *New Monthly Magazine*?[25]

Even overlooking the rather too prominent place the article ascribes to the *New Monthly* in the 'periodicity [. . .] of the heavens', Samuel Hall underscores periodicals' capacity to shape their readers' perception of time passing – to change the ways in which they marked time.[26] The serial openness of periodicals served a literary climate that was 'unsettled'.[27] Periodicals as sites of critique further confirmed perceptions of their 'living' authority.

In addition to circulating critical assessments of specific works, literary monthlies like *Fraser's* or the *New Monthly* also judged the broader state of literature, including acerbic indictments of other monthlies as curators of literary content. When *Fraser's* and the *New Monthly* repeatedly dismissed the 1820s and 1830s as decades of secondary status in literary history, they attacked competitors as the parties responsible for the decline.[28] Yet *Fraser's* and the *New Monthly* were simultaneously quick to note any remaining fragments of literary vitality in their own journals. William Maginn opened the new year in 1833 by attacking the *New Monthly* as an obsolete monthly precisely because *Fraser's* had poached its best contributing authors. In his pseudonymous editorial persona as Oliver Yorke, Maginn proclaims, 'Have we not sucked the blood from the very bones of the "*New Monthly*"?'[29] A year later, Hall offered his own assessment that an 'effusion now and then finds its way into the periodical journals as if to show that the fire of genius is not as yet wholly extinguished amongst us'.[30] Periodical editors laboured to persuade their readers that whatever literary spark of genius might remain, it would be found in their own publications. Maginn in *Fraser's Magazine* and Samuel Hall in the *New Monthly* both suggested that to read outside of the periodical was to miss the best current examples of literary achievement. This claim to literary exclusivity reflects the 'growing power' of periodical publishers in what Fisher calls 'an emerging marketplace system'.[31]

The New Monthly Magazine's prominence in the English literary scene during the 1820s corresponded with the publication of Hemans's poetry in the journal. In the late 1820s, Hemans was publishing in every issue of the *New Monthly*, often more than once per issue. Between July of 1825 and February of 1828, Hemans's poetry appeared in thirty-one consecutive issues of the *New Monthly*. Between 1827 and 1829, Hemans shifted her preference from the *New Monthly* to *Blackwood's* after William Blackwood published her *Records of Woman* in 1827, but she continued to send poems to the *New Monthly*, doubling the rate of pay she received from Hall as late as 1834.[32] In the years between 1829 and 1834, Hemans still contributed new poems to every other issue or every third issue of the *New Monthly*. In 1835, Samuel Hall reclaimed Hemans as a house poet by publishing a serial cluster of commemorative pieces. Like Campbell's initial decision to publish Hemans's poetry liberally to boost periodical sales in the early 1820s,[33] Hall's attention to Hemans's death likewise appears to have been a calculated economic decision based on the idea that commemorating the late poet would be good for business.

The New Monthly Magazine and genres of commemorative claiming

After Hemans's death on 16 May 1835, the first of the *New Monthly*'s commemorative publications appeared in the June issue in a section titled 'Biographical Sketches of Celebrated Persons, Lately Deceased'. Hall cut and pasted Hemans's obituary from the May 23 issue of the *Athenaeum*,[34] publishing it alongside sketches of Sir George Tuthill,[35] Richard Sharp, ESQ,[36] and Mr. Douglas, the botanist.[37] While the 'Biographical Sketches' of these three men range in length from half a page to a page and a half, Hemans's sketch is three and a half pages, uncharacteristically long for the column in the 1830s. Beyond the length of Hemans's biographical sketch, Hall gives particular attention to Hemans as a poet particularly associated with the *New Monthly* by adding a new introduction. He begins by apologising for the monthly print cycle that inevitably delayed the publication of the obituary. He also promises further content on Hemans: in July, he will provide 'our own thoughts of her character and writings',[38] along with an engraving of the late author.[39] Hall's introduction to the biographical sketch reprinted from the *Athenaeum* also claims a particular familiarity with Hemans, including his knowledge of her illness.[40] Hall references the 'melancholy intelligence' of her 'impending death' that he received in a 'note from her sister'.[41]

Hall also adds two footnotes to his obituary – an unusual practice in the *New Monthly* – to directly address Hemans's relationship with the magazine. In the first note, Hall corrects a passage in the *Athenaeum* article suggesting that Hemans's articles on 'Foreign Literature' in *Constable's Edinburgh Magazine* were 'the only specimens of that style of writing [i.e., the essay genre] ever attempted by her'.[42] His footnotes explain that she also published prose works in the *New Monthly*: 'She had, as our readers are aware, commenced a series of German prose studies in "New Monthly Magazine"', the continuation of which her ill-health compelled her to postpone'.[43] Likewise, when the *Athenaeum* article cites *Blackwood's Magazine* as the location of 'her last lyric', Hall writes in a footnote, 'We have reason to believe that the writer is in error; and that the last productions of her pen were the series of Sonnets which so recently appeared in the "New Monthly Magazine".[44] Hall is referring to Hemans's 'Thoughts During Sickness' from the March issue, unaware or perhaps overlooking the fact that her 'Despondency and Aspiration' had appeared in the May issue of *Blackwood's Magazine*. Nonetheless, in both notes, Hall communicates his desire to position *The New Monthly Magazine* as the true 'home' for Hemans's verse. In doing so, he alludes to the rivalry among editors to harness Hemans's popularity. Hemans's death offered Hall an opportunity to harken back to the *New Monthly*'s former glory when Hemans had published prolifically in its pages. The editors of *Blackwood's* did not dispute Hall's claims since by 1835 Hemans's popularity provided less marginal value to them than it did for *The New Monthly Magazine*.

The New Monthly Magazine's attention to the legacy and literary contributions of Hemans enhances her status as a poet, not only through its use of postmortem biography as a genre with which to confirm literary merit and cultural authority but also through its use of a multi-genre, serial form of commemoration. If in the Victorian 'culture of mourning' individuals carried about 'accouterments' of grief,[45] Hall provides an early example of how a periodical could extend and amplify this process. The commemorative materials on Hemans are linked by more than the appearance of consecutive monthly issues; they also cross-reference other memorials in the series. Hall, for example, previews the publication of Landon's memorial essay and Thomson's engraved portrait. Likewise, Barrett Browning makes a titular reference to Landon's elegy in her 'Stanzas Addressed to Miss Landon, and Suggested by Her "Stanzas on the Death of Mrs. Hemans"'. Other parts of the serial commemoration link together internally. Landon's essay 'On the Character of Mrs. Hemans's Writings', for example, opens with a French epigram – '*Oh! mes amis, rappellez-vous quelquefois mes vers; mon ame y est empreinte*' – initially from Germaine de Staël's *Corinne* (1807) but also the epigraph for Hemans's 'A Parting Song'. The biographical sketch on Hemans reprinted from the *Athenaeum*, in turn, quotes the last stanza of Hemans's 'A Parting Song'. Thus, the biographical sketch and Landon's 'Character' essay touch, end to beginning, through Hemans's 'A Parting Song' just as the two pieces were supposed to follow one another sequentially in the June and July issues of the *New Monthly*. In the October issue, Landon invokes Hemans's 'A Parting Song' yet again by publishing 'The Parting Word', which meditates on loss. The commemorative pieces published in *The New Monthly Magazine* are held together by allusions to Hemans's work, which serve as a barely visible connecting thread.

Though distinct from written commemorations, Hemans's engraved portrait in *The New Monthly Magazine* also helps to hold together the serial material memorialising her death. Using Angus Fletcher's 1829 marble busts as a model,[46] James Thomson's engraving provided a likeness of Hemans printed just before Landon's review of her writing. The *New Monthly* was not an illustrated magazine, so the inclusion of the engraving of Hemans catches the reader's eye. The engraving was designed as a memorial, yet in the publication process, it was printed apart from the rest of the pages and inserted into the magazine on a page of its own before the binding. The absence of type on the verso page makes the image easy to remove from the magazine and repurpose in scrapbooks and other contexts. The page's independence weakens its relationship to any particular print issue. The engraving page is also unnumbered and is absent from the monthly table of contents and annual index. The engraving did not participate in any of the periodical's primary structures for identifying a print object's location. Its placement in the periodical, particularly when monthly issues were bound into a volume, was contingent on the binder's discretion. Not unlike a ghost, Hemans's bust is present on the page, but it is simultaneously, and even disquietingly, absent from the periodical's organising apparatus.

Due perhaps to its lack of placement markers, Thomson's engraving of Hemans changes locations in various bound volumes of *The New Monthly Magazine*. Before the publication of the annual edition of the magazine, the June issue anticipated the placement of Thomson's engraving alongside Landon's remembrance of Hemans. The image most likely appeared two months later in volume 44, issue 176, between pages 424 and 425.[47] In some annual volumes, however, the engraving is used as a frontispiece, appearing before the lead article of volume 45, just prior to the beginning of issue 177.[48] Conversely, in the bound copy in the Wisconsin Historical Society's collection, the engraving appears at the front of volume 44, before issue 173. While it is striking to find Hemans's bust on the page facing Landon's essay, it is striking in a different way to find her portrait as a frontispiece to the volume edition of the *New Monthly*, either introducing or concluding the commemorative materials. Without a page number to discipline our expectations, Fletcher's engraving of Hemans seems to fit everywhere: in the front of volume 44, at the front of volume 45, and in a specific issue housed between pages 424 and 425. Her portrait fits in any of these issues – but, most appropriately, it hovers over the six consecutive issues that comprise *The New Monthly Magazine*'s memorial to Hemans.

Two ballad 'stanzas' as competitive elegies

In the same way that Samuel Hall lays claim to Hemans as a contributor to *The New Monthly Magazine* by commemorating her death in consecutive, coordinating issues, Letitia Landon and Elizabeth Barrett Browning use the occasion of Hemans's death to assert their own poetic authority. They memorialise Hemans not in the pages of *Fraser's Magazine*, where Landon was better known, or in *Blackwood's Magazine*, where Hemans preferred to publish after 1827, but in *The New Monthly Magazine*, where they can participate in and extend its serial memorial. Landon knew as early as June, when Hall announced forthcoming additional materials on Hemans, that the magazine's memorial to the late poet would extend across multiple issues. Before Landon published her essay on Hemans's character and writing, she published an elegy to her in the July issue of the *New Monthly*. Barrett Browning's elegy, published in the September issue, includes the title of Landon's poem within her own title, thereby appending her poem to the content Landon had already provided. Just as Hall takes the opportunity to capitalise on Hemans's death to increase the circulation of the *New Monthly*, Landon and Barrett Browning align themselves with her legacy. These memorials not only underscore Hemans's cultural capital during the 1830s but also shed light on who might seek to leverage that authority.

While Landon and Barrett Browning link their poetic careers to Hemans through their elegies, they demonstrate some ambivalence about her status as a popular poetess.[49] Over the course of the century, the term 'poetess' became increasingly unstable. Early in the century, it was used to describe not only female poets writing in a tradition of affect and sentiment but also writers who wished to distinguish their craft from these gendered conventions.[50] The generic ambiguities associated with the poetess figure echoed the instability of the literary marketplace in the 1820s and 1830s, as theorised by David Stewart. That the 'poetess' was under formation during this period means that

Landon and Barrett Browning could only define their authority – and Hemans's legacy – in complex terms.

Since the content of Landon's elegy and essay overlaps significantly, we can read them in tandem. What begins as Hall's promise to print a piece on Mrs. Hemans's 'character *and writings*' appears as Landon's essay titled 'On the Character *of* Mrs. Hemans's Writings'.[51] The original topic proposed by Hall suggests two subjects: the author's character and the character of her writings. Landon's essay elides the two: the author is known and assessed by the character of her work. Landon's elegy on Hemans does the same by considering Hemans's character in her poetry. In elaborating on the life and writing of Hemans, both in prose and poetry, Landon blends her voice with Hemans's. For example 'Stanzas on the Death of Mrs. Hemans' opens with an epigram from Hemans's 'The Nightingale's Death Song', suggesting that the bird mourns the late writer's passing.[52] Just past the inscription, the initial stanzas of Landon's poem repackage Hemans's 'Bring Flowers'.[53] The first two mourning voices in Landon's poem belong to Hemans, not Landon. Landon compresses Hemans's thirty-six-line poem into four and a half lines, each of which opens with 'Bring flowers'. She ascribes this chorus to Hemans's 'lovely song'; at the same time, the command to 'bring flowers' defines Landon's elegy. By appropriating the line 'Bring flowers to strew the bier! / Bring flowers!', Landon reimagines Hemans as calling for flowers to adorn her own grave, while at the same time providing metaphorical lyric flowers for Hemans's bier. Although Landon borrows Hemans's language, retaining the dominant image of each stanza (feast, bride, captive and grave), she makes strategic alterations. She reiterates Hemans's penultimate stanza, 'Bring flowers pale flowers, o'er the bier to shed'.[54] However, in Hemans's poem there is one more verse – 'Bring flowers to the shrine where we kneel in prayer'.[55] Landon cuts off Hemans's song to serve her own elegiac purposes.

Although Landon mimics the alternating long and short lines from Hemans's 'Bring Flowers', she deviates from her heroic meter – couplets of alternating hexameter and pentameter – to create a metrical scheme that alternates tetrameter and trimeter with a rhyme scheme reminiscent of two ballad quatrains spliced together: ABCBDEFE. It was an unconventional metrical choice given the popularity of Thomas Gray's 'Elegy Written in a Country Churchyard', with its pentameter meter and alternating rhyming scheme: ABAB. By transforming Hemans's heroic stanzas from 'Bring Flowers' into ballad meter at the opening of her elegy, Landon makes Hemans familiar and old at the same time. Landon joins those who 'loved and honoured thee [Hemans] / [but] Who only knew thy name', announcing, 'I cannot choose but think thou wert / An old familiar friend'.[56] On the one hand, Hemans's familiarity to those who 'knew' her in name only suggests that she was a 'living' author for her readers. Yet by referring to Hemans as 'old familiar friend', Landon alludes to the late poet's timelessness. Despite Hemans's proximity to her readers, Landon describes her as though her aesthetic authority has been long confirmed:

The meteor wreath the poet wears
Must make a lonely lot;
It dazzles, only to divide
From those who wear it not.[57]

Landon underscores the fact that Hemans has indeed obtained the 'prize' of fame even if she notes that it has given her a 'lonely lot'.

In her elegy, Landon not only claims timeless fame for Hemans but also for herself. After referencing lines from Hemans's poetry, Landon's speaker takes over halfway through the fifth line as a mourner ('thus said the lovely song'), then as an interrogator ('And shall they not be brought[?]'), then as the echo who takes up Hemans's cry ('Bring flowers'), and finally as the new singing voice addressing Hemans in second person ('I feel as thou hadst been').[58] In the penultimate stanza, Landon identifies Hemans as her animating force – 'The charm that dwelt in songs of thing / My inmost spirit moved' – suggesting that Landon's poetic commemoration can surpass all others.[59] Landon links her own poetic potential to Hemans's achievement: 'Thy heart [. . .] left within our hearts'.[60]

Elizabeth Barrett Browning's 'Stanzas Addressed to Miss Landon, and Suggested by Her "Stanzas on the Death of Mrs. Hemans"' adopts Landon's ballad stanzas and second-person address, but she addresses herself to Landon, not Hemans. Barrett Browning reinforces Hemans's poetic authority by reminding Landon that she belongs among the living poets. Barrett Browning rebukes Landon as 'Thou bay-crown'd living one' whom she instructs to 'Go! Take thy music from the dead' rather than to 'bring' it.[61] At the end of the poem, Barrett Browning claims the privilege of writing

Hemans's elegy. Indeed, she gives herself the opportunity to write for all of 'England': 'Albeit softly in our ears / Her silver song was ringing, / The footsteps of her parting soul / Were softer than her singing'.[62] Hemans's 'soft' song is still louder than her departing soul because Barrett Browning takes it up and carries it on. As a funerary genre, the elegy arrests readers' attention, encouraging them to slow down. The net result is to make readers linger longer over Hemans's memory while admiring Barrett Browning's poetic skill. At the same time, Barrett Browning calls out to Landon, as a mourner, to instruct her how to engage with Hemans as a literary foremother.

While Barrett Browning scolds Landon, she nonetheless recognises her as a poet who is capable of taking Hemans's place. Barrett Browning identifies Landon as the 'bay-crown'd living one' bending over the 'bay-crown'd dead', recognising that Landon now casts her shadow over Hemans. If Barrett Browning names Landon as the ascendant poet in Hemans's wake, the editors of *The New Monthly Magazine* likewise confer on Landon the status of poet-critic. The editors announced in their June obituary that a forthcoming review of Hemans's writings would provide '*our* own thoughts of her character and writing'.[63] Landon, as author of 'On the Character of Mrs. Hemans's Writings', is endorsed by the editors as the voice of the periodical itself.

Landon's long-form essay on Hemans's work, published one month after her elegy, likewise mingles her voice with Hemans's, often in the same sentence, sometimes with a dash and sometimes merely with a line break. In her liberal quotations of Hemans, Landon sometimes sutures two poems together, back-to-back, without interruption.[64] What makes the transition from Landon's voice to Hemans's and back again so seamless is, in part, Landon's lyric prose. For example, Landon's sentence 'We have quarrelled in some embittered moment with an early friend, and when too late lamented the estrangement' transitions gently to Hemans's '[They] laid their youth as in a burial urn, / Where sunshine may not find it'.[65] An exchange between poets may be a contest, but that contest is intermingled with respect – one of both sorority and seniority. Landon never met Hemans, yet in her poem she syntactically converses with her through quotation. Landon finishes Hemans's sentences and Hemans finishes hers. Landon's inclusion of Hemans's lines demonstrates respect even as she relies upon the late poet's imagery to enhance the lyric quality of her prose.

What did it mean to the readers of *The New Monthly Magazine* to find so much writing about Hemans after she had died? If, as Landon contends, there was a 'relief of expression' when a poet conveyed deep feelings, there seemed to be a reciprocal 'relief of encounter' with a familiar dead poet when her name and work were evoked in the pages of a periodical that was known for printing her verse. Consolation comes first from a literary encounter with the absent dead and then from the words of those who grieve her passing. Landon quotes from Hemans's own elegy on Mary Tighe, 'At the Grave of the Poetess', to mark Hemans's death in the *New Monthly*, thus modeling the activity of borrowing grief. Landon describes this act of consolation as poetry's 'haunted words', which become 'to us even as our own [words]'.[66] Landon offers the *New Monthly*'s readers Hemans's words to grieve the late poet's own passing.

By choosing to memorialise Felicia Hemans in *The New Monthly Magazine*, Letitia Landon and Elizabeth Barrett Browning capitalised on trends in periodical publication, which included the interaction between elegies and other commemorative genres as well as instabilities in the 'poetess' persona. Although the 1830s still marked an uncertain present and future for the status of poetry in England, this very uncertainty appears to have offered Landon and Barrett Browning opportunities for experimentation. While Eric Eisner characterises the 1820s and 1830s as 'decades when the professional woman writer lacks a secure model through which to occupy the public stage as a professional',[67] Susan Wolfson explains that feminising poetry offered one possible way to save it – to 'rehabilitate' the genre if male cultures of poetry were failing.[68] Part of this rehabilitation of poetry for Landon and Barrett Browning includes setting the elegy in dialogue with other commemorative genres in the periodical that helped to reaffirm poetry's contribution to assessing and defining the status of authorship and the living author. By participating in *The New Monthly Magazine*'s serial commemoration of Hemans, Letitia Landon and Elizabeth Barrett Browning find ways to affirm their own poetic achievements while confirming Hemans's significance as an important female poet.

Notes

1. Susan Wolfson identifies the death of Byron in 1824 as launching a '*post-mortem* industry'. See Susan J. Wolfson, *Romantic Interactions:*

Social Being and the Turns of Literary Action (Baltimore: Johns Hopkins University Press, 2010), 257. David Stewart, by contrast, describes the 1820s and 1830s as a period notable for its biographical interest in living authors. See David Stewart, *The Form of Poetry in the 1820s and 1830s: A Period of Doubt* (London: Palgrave Macmillan, 2018), 2.

2. David Higgins draws a direct connection between the 'cultural fascination with genius' and the magazine as 'the predominant literary form'. See David Higgins, *Romantic Genius and the Literary Magazine: Biography, Celebrity, Politics* (London: Routledge, 2005), 6.
3. See Stewart, *Form of Poetry*, 36, and Jock Macleod, 'Noticing the Dead: The Biographical Sketch in Victorian Periodicals', *Victorian Periodicals Review* 50, no. 3 (2017): 534. Although Stewart and Macleod underscore the importance of the living author for definitions of professional authorship across the 1820s and 1830s, the chronological divide between pre-mortem and postmortem biographies is not as clear as Macleod suggests. For example, as early as 1833 *The New Monthly Magazine* published its postmortem 'Biographical Particulars of Celebrated Persons Lately Deceased' series, which recognised literary figures alongside political ones.
4. David Moir, '[Critical Comment on] Sabbath Sonnet', *Blackwood's Magazine* 38 (July 1835): 96–7.
5. Ibid., 96.
6. Linda Jones asserts that Hemans sent more original poetry to *Blackwood's* than to the *New Monthly* as early as 1827. Linda Jones, 'The *New Monthly Magazine*, 1821 to 1830', PhD diss., University of Colorado at Boulder, 1970 (ProQuest Dissertations Publishing, 7121596). Paula Feldman's income analysis, however, suggests that Hemans published more substantially in the *New Monthly* as late as 1829. See Paula Feldman, 'The Poet and the Profits: Felicia Hemans and the Literary Marketplace', *Keats-Shelley Journal* 46 (1997): 150.
7. See Jones, 'The *New Monthly Magazine*', 19; Nanora Sweet, 'The *New Monthly Magazine* and the Liberalism of the 1820s', *Prose Studies* 25, no. 1 (1 April 2002): 147; Richard Cronin, *Paper Pellets: British Literary Culture after Waterloo* (Oxford: Oxford University Press, 2010), 187; and David Higgins, *Romantic Genius*, 7.
8. This dual format for *The New Monthly Magazine* lasted from 1821 to 1836. See Jones, 'The *New Monthly Magazine*', 15.
9. While the shortest poems in the *New Monthly* are used as 'filler' (placed in the last few inches of space remaining on a page after a

long-form essay), more often than not poems receive their own full-page prints. In some cases, an essay fills up the remaining space on a page that begins with poetry. See, for example, the transition between 'The Ladies and the Parliament' and 'Monthly Commentary' in *The New Monthly Magazine* 44 (August 1835): 502.

10. Stuart Curran, 'Romantic Elegiac Hybridity', in *The Oxford Handbook of the Elegy*, ed. Karen Weisman (Oxford: Oxford University Press, 2010), 238–50.
11. Stewart, *The Form of Poetry*, 8.
12. See Derek Furr, 'Sentimental Confrontations: Hemans, Landon, and Elizabeth Barrett', *English Language Notes* 40, no. 2 (2002): 29–47; Brandy Ryan, '"Echo and Reply": The Elegies of Felicia Hemans, Letitia Landon, and Elizabeth Barrett', *Victorian Poetry* 46, no. 3 (2008): 249–77; and Monika Irene Cassel, 'Poetesses at the Grave: Transnational Circulation of Women's Memorial Verse in Nineteenth-Century England, Germany and America', PhD diss., University of Michigan, 2002 (ProQuest Dissertations Publishing, 3042050), 90.
13. 'Biographical Particulars of Celebrated Persons, Lately Deceased: Mrs. Hemans', *New Monthly Magazine* 44 (June 1835): 265–8.
14. Letitia Elizabeth Landon, 'Stanzas on the Death of Mrs. Hemans', *New Monthly Magazine* 44 (July 1835): 286–8.
15. Letitia Elizabeth Landon, 'On the Character of Mrs. Hemans's Writings', *New Monthly Magazine* 44 (August 1835): 425–33.
16. 'F. Hemans, Engraved by Thomson, from a Bust by Fletcher', *New Monthly Magazine* 44 (August 1835): inserted between pages 424 and 425.
17. Elizabeth Barrett Browning, 'Stanzas Addressed to Miss Landon, and Suggested by Her "Stanzas on the Death of Mrs. Hemans"', *New Monthly Magazine* 45 (September 1835): 82.
18. Letitia Elizabeth Landon, 'The Parting Word', *New Monthly Magazine* 45 (October 1835): 155.
19. Judith L. Fisher, '"In the Present Famine of Anything Substantial": *Fraser's* "Portraits" and the Construction of Literary Celebrity; Or, "Personality, Personality Is the Appetite of the Age"', *Victorian Periodicals Review* 39, no. 2 (2006): 108.
20. Stewart, *The Form of Poetry*, 23.
21. Ibid., 36.
22. Macleod, 'Noticing the Dead', 548.
23. Ibid., 538.
24. See Margaret Beetham, 'Open and Closed: The Periodical as a Publishing Genre', *Victorian Periodicals Review* 22, no. 3 (1989):

96–100; and James Mussell, 'Repetition: Or, "In Our Last"', *Victorian Periodicals Review* 48, no. 3 (2015): 345–6.

25. Samuel Carter Hall, 'Notes on Periodicals', *New Monthly Magazine* 39, no. 156 (December 1833): 424.
26. Ibid.
27. Stewart, *The Form of Poetry*, 36.
28. See, for example, the *New Monthly*'s claim that 'the most saleable species of literature [is], at present, that which is stitched up from old materials by the literary cobblers'. Samuel Carter Hall, 'Literature in 1834', *New Monthly Magazine* 40 (April 1834): 503.
29. [William Maginn], 'Address to Contributors and Readers', *Fraser's Magazine* 7 (January 1833): 7.
30. Samuel Carter Hall, 'Literature in 1834', 498.
31. Fisher, 'In the Present Famine', 109.
32. Feldman, 'The Poet and the Profits', 150.
33. See Sweet, 'The *New Monthly Magazine*', 148.
34. The *Athenaeum*'s obituary on Hemans is an impersonal review of her life and literary accomplishments as opposed to the intimate 'first-hand account of having known Mrs. Hemans' that Henry Chorley wrote for the *Athenaeum*. Henry Chorley, 'Personal Recollections of the Late Mrs. Hemans, No. I', *Athenaeum* 398 (13 June 1835): 452. The *Athenaeum* recognised Felicia Hemans every other week for four weeks, transitioning from the genre of the obituary (23 May) to Chorley's memorial essays (13 June, 27 June and 11 July) as time passed. Its 'Biographical Sketches' are dramatically longer and more detailed than the one-sentence notices listed in its 'Marriage and Death' section.
35. 'Biographical Particulars of Celebrated Persons, Lately Deceased: Sir George Tuthill', *New Monthly Magazine* 44 (June 1835): 268.
36. 'Biographical Particulars of Celebrated Persons, Lately Deceased: Richard Sharp, ESQ', *New Monthly Magazine* 44 (June 1835): 268–9.
37. 'Biographical Particulars of Celebrated Persons, Lately Deceased: Mr. Douglas, the Botanist', *New Monthly Magazine* 44 (June 1835): 269–70.
38. 'Biographical Particulars of Celebrated Persons, Lately Deceased: Mrs. Hemans', *New Monthly Magazine* 44 (June 1835): 265.
39. It was, however, not until August of that year that the engraving and Letitia Landon's article on the 'Character of Mrs. Hemans's Writing' finally appeared.
40. Felicia Hemans, 'Thoughts During Sickness', *New Monthly Magazine* 43 (March 1835): 328–30.

41. 'Biographical Particulars of Celebrated Persons, Lately Deceased: Mrs. Hemans', 265.
42. Ibid.
43. Ibid., 266. The *Athenaeum* had only attributed 'her scattered lyrics' and her more popular 'Welsh Melodies' and 'Siege of Valencia', not her prose works. See 'Original Papers: Mrs. Hemans', *Athenaeum* 395 (23 May 1835): 391–2.
44. 'Biographical Particulars of Celebrated Persons, Lately Deceased: Mrs. Hemans', 267.
45. Erik Gray, 'Victoria Dressed in Black', in *The Oxford Handbook of the Elegy*, ed. Karen Weisman (Oxford: Oxford University Press, 2010), 273.
46. For the original bust, see Angus Fletcher, *Felicia Hemans*, c. 1829, marble, 26 × 17 ¾ inches, National Portrait Gallery, London, npg.org.uk.
47. 'F. Hemans, Engraved by Thomson, from a Bust by Fletcher', *New Monthly Magazine* 44, no. 176 (August 1835).
48. 'F. Hemans, Engraved by Thomson, from a Bust by Fletcher', *New Monthly Magazine* 45, no. 177 (September 1835): i. In the bound copy in the Wisconsin Historical Society's collection, the engraving appears at the front of volume 44, before issue 173. 'F. Hemans, Engraved by Thomson, from a Bust by Fletcher', *New Monthly Magazine* 44, no. 173 (May 1835): i.
49. See, for example, William Maginn, 'Female Fraserians', *New Monthly Magazine* 13 (January 1836): 78–9.
50. We might contrast, for example, Maria Jewsbury's depiction of Hemans as a 'female poetess' in 1831 to the later Victorian reception of Hemans as an 'essentially feminine poet'. See Eva Hope, 'Felicia Hemans: The Poet of Womanhood', in *Queens of Literature of the Victorian Era* (London: Walter Scott, 1886), 261–301.
51. My emphasis.
52. Landon, 'Stanzas', 286.
53. Ibid.
54. Felicia Hemans, *The Poetical Works of Mrs. Felicia Hemans* (London: Evert Duyckinck, 1828), 69
55. Ibid., 70.
56. Landon, 'Stanzas', 288.
57. Ibid., 287.
58. Ibid., 286, 288.
59. Ibid., 288.
60. Ibid.

61. Barrett Browning, 'Stanzas', 82.
62. Ibid.
63. 'Biographical Particulars of Celebrated Persons, Lately Deceased: Mrs. Hemans', 265. Emphasis added.
64. Landon, 'On the Character of Mrs. Hemans's Writings', 428.
65. Ibid., 426.
66. Ibid.
67. Eric Eisner, *Nineteenth-Century Poetry and Literary Celebrity* (Basingstoke: Palgrave Macmillan, 2009), 118.
68. Susan J. Wolfson, *Borderlines: The Shiftings of Gender in British Romanticism* (Stanford: Stanford University Press, 2006), 43.

4

'Mirth' and 'Fun': The Comic Annual and the New Graphic Humour of the 1830s

Brian Maidment

The outpouring of annuals and gift books in the 1820s and 1830s, 'though treated with disdain by many contemporary writers and artists',[1] has long been recognised as a significant feature of late Regency print culture. Part of the interest in the early history of annuals has been bibliographical[2] – locating and defining the annual as a print form among the many similar literary innovations that characterised the experimental and entrepreneurial publishing ventures of the 1820s and 1830s.[3] Annuals and gift books were significantly innovative in the history of print. They introduced elaborate embossed bindings for the mass market that employed the new technology of the fly-embossing press, giving the small volumes what Eleanore Jamieson has rather dismissively called 'a semi luxury' look.[4] With their decorative covers and gilded fore edges, annuals sought to attract new if not especially ambitious readers, 'particularly those of the ladies who for the first time [were] considered worthy of commercial attention', as Jamieson wryly notes.[5] Annuals also exploited the glossy sheen and tonal complexity of their illustrations, becoming 'the first type of book to benefit from steel engraving'.[6] At a time in the 1820s and 1830s when the cheapness of wood engraving was beginning to be widely exploited, steel engraving had become largely associated with topographical illustration, in which 'the wide range of tones it could produce and the maximum contrast between black and white' were of considerable value.[7]

Beyond the acknowledgement of such commercially innovative elements, recent interest in the annual has centred on its importance as a print form that was both for and, to a significant extent, by women. Books by Linda Peterson, Barbara Onslow, Alexis Easley and Kathryn Ledbetter have emphasised the presence and significance of women as editors and contributors, especially of poetry, to a wide range of print forms, including annuals, in the 1820s and 1830s.[8] In *Poetry, Pictures and Popular Publishing: The Illustrated Gift Book and Victorian Visual Culture, 1855–1875*, Lorraine Janzen Kooistra has addressed many of the issues involved in reading texts, especially poetry, together with their related illustrations.[9] Two more recent studies have concentrated more precisely on the importance of annuals to the history of women's writing. Katherine Harris's *Forget Me Not: The Rise of the British Literary Annual, 1823–1835*, provides the most comprehensive account of the annual form, including a lengthy discussion of Hood's *Comic Annual* and Louisa Sheridan's *Comic Offering* as opposing models of gendered comedy. Barbara Onslow's recent essay, 'Gendered Production: Annuals and Gift Books', highlights the difficulty of untangling the precise generic properties of annuals from the many gift-book formats produced during this period and emphasises the commercial and aesthetic importance of these publications to the professionalisation of women authors and editors.[10]

The central concern of this paper is a consideration of the variety of ways in which comic annuals – a small, interconnected and highly visible group of publications from the 1830s – began self-consciously to debate, develop and enact the modes of graphic humour available within late Regency print culture. A further interest is the extent to which such reconceptualisations of humour were gendered in order to accommodate women within the marketplace for graphic humour. New interest in the genres and modes of 'comicality' and 'fun', in which the pleasures of humour were unalloyed by any form of social purposiveness, began in the 1830s to overlay longstanding belief in the social value of wit and satire as mechanisms of social accountability. The formulation of comic modes as pleasurable or even diversionary, when considered in relation to earlier forms of humour that carried a minatory socio-political weight, marks a major refocusing of comic energy in the 1830s. The following discussion centres on the comic annual as one of the sites in which changing modes of graphic comedy, especially the shift from 'mirth' to 'fun', were being developed. These changes evolved not only because comic annuals were deliberately addressing women readers and wood engraving was becoming a widely acceptable form of visual humour but more widely because conceptualisations of comedy were undergoing change. These modal changes in graphic humour were to some extent discussed and theorised within the comic annuals themselves. Evidence of such generic self-consciousness is provided by the complex frontispieces and title pages drawn for each of the volumes, which often use a much more sophisticated graphic vocabulary than that used for the smaller textual illustrations. This self-consciousness is also demonstrated in *The Battle of the "Annuals"*, a mock-heroic poem issued anonymously in 1835 that both celebrated and satirised the annual as a literary form. After a discussion of the comic annual as a print form and a more detailed consideration of the widespread celebration of 'fun' rather than 'mirth' as the central project of literary and graphic humour, this chapter centres on the ways in which comic annuals exhibited their commitment to, and awareness of, a new kind of humour in which woodcuts were not so much cutting as amusing or diverting.

The comic annual as a print form

Comic annuals were ostensibly and ostentatiously a humorous reinvention of the literary annual, but they nevertheless comprised a distinct group of publications, nearly all of them originating between 1830 and 1832.[11] With the exception of *Hood's Comic Annual* (published by Hurst, Chance, R. Baily and then Charles Tilt, 1830–42), none survived past 1836. *Hood's Comic Annual* was, and remains, the best known, but there were at least five other titles – *The Comic Offering* (Smith, Elder, 1831–5); *The New Comic Annual* (Hurst, Chance, 1832); *The Humourist* (Rudolph Ackermann, 1832); *Seymour's Comic Album* (W. Kidd, n.d.) and *The Squib Annual* (Chapman and Hall, 1836). Only *Hood's Comic Annual* and *The Comic Offering* made the transition from a single issue into serial publication. These few but relatively widely known and commercially successful comic annuals were neither enormously condescending nor outspokenly satirical in providing commentary on the literary annuals from which they derived their origin. On the chart of generic or modal forms of humorous remaking that runs from servile imitation through mock-heroic pastiche to parody (admiring and mocking at the same time) and on into the outrage of travesty or the contempt of satire, comic annuals were rather gentle ripostes to the form from which they originated and which they sought to reimagine.

Their main significance, perhaps, was not to provide satirical commentary on the literary preciousness and self-conscious gentility found in the annuals but to offer an important mechanism in the democratisation of humour as it shifted modally from late Georgian wit and the transformative literary and graphic experimentation of the Regency period to early Victorian concepts of 'comic' and 'fun'.

One key aspect of this democratisation of comic texts and, especially, graphic humour was the recognition of women readers as a potential audience. In her recent study of the annual, Katherine Harris highlights conflicting views of the appropriateness of graphic humour for ladies that Thomas Hood and Louisa Sheridan debated in their jousting prefaces to *Hood's Comic Annual* and *The Comic Offering* in 1831.[12] According to Harris, Hood freely admitted to 'entering not only the publicly private drawing room but also the very private dressing room' and notes that while Sheridan considered Hood's annual 'too coarse for a lady's viewing', her own publication offered 'a remedy to include women in the jocularity'.[13] While Tamara Hunt's substantial study of *The Comic Offering* has little to say about graphic content, it nonetheless stresses the ways in which the annual specifically aimed to avoid any hint of 'coarseness' that might offend women readers.[14]

The comic annuals all had a similar material format that included small page sizes, plentiful wood-engraved vignettes or full-page illustrations, and gimcrack but flashy bindings – characteristics that they shared with gift books and annuals more broadly. Their difference from the 'serious' annuals was largely expressed through their graphic content – simple linear wood engravings, rather than highly finished and tonally complex full-page metal engravings – and by their focus on comedy rather than on the literature of feeling and sentiment that filled out *Friendship's Offering*, *The Literary Souvenir* and *The Keepsake*. *The Comic Offering*, however, did make use of elaborate engraved frontispieces and title pages that included complex vignette illustrations, and all of the comic albums sought to introduce themselves with more sophisticated prefatory images. Harris views the use of the wood engraving as a deliberate practical response to the cost of commissioning illustrations.[15] It was a move 'backward in technology', she argues, that utilised 'a simplified woodcut engraving (taken from a crude line drawing)'.[16] 'The engravings appear to be of no higher quality than a line drawing', she concludes, nonetheless noting that in Hood's case (as with all the comic annuals) the engravings, together with their brief, often punning captions, formed a central textual element in *The Comic Annual* rather than serving as illustrations that responded to typeset content.[17] Harris's account perhaps underestimates the centrality of the graphic content of *The Comic Annual*. As this essay will go on to suggest, the use of illustration in the comic annuals in the early 1830s established the wood engraving, with all of its linear simplicity, as a form that would come to dominate early Victorian cartoons and comic art.

Given their deliberately downmarket mode of illustration and focus on the traditionally 'coarse' male discourse of humour, comic annuals might seem to belong more appropriately to the lists of publishers such as Robins, Duncombe, Strange, Horace Mayhew or Steill,[18] which specialised in cheap illustrated publications and had extensive experience with the demands of serial publication. However, despite their incorporation of vulgar wood engravings as the chosen mode of illustration, comic annuals were published by precisely those firms that were also producing genteel and entirely unironic annuals. With the possible exception of *The Squib Annual*, all the comic annuals were published by ambitious publishers whose books were aimed at sophisticated literary readers. Hurst, Chance issued *The Keepsake* between 1828 and 1831, but they also launched *Hood's Comic Annual*. After the first volume, ownership passed to Charles Tilt, but this did not stop Hurst, Chance from founding a rival title, *The New Comic Annual*, in 1832 that mimicked *Hood's Comic Annual* in almost every respect, including its title. From a publisher's point of view, it seems that comic annuals were seen as complementary to literary annuals rather than as a rival form of publication, which in turn suggests that comic annuals for a few years offered amusing commentary on, rather than ridicule of, their immediate peers. Put more simply, despite their content, comic annuals were aimed at exactly the same kinds of readers as their more traditional and more obviously genteel counterparts.

A further mark of the relatively high status accorded to comic annuals was the decision to name the artists who produced their illustrations. It was uncommon for wood engravings to be signed in periodicals published in the 1820s and 1830s and rarer still for the artists to be given title-page credit. Yet most of the comic annuals named their illustrators, with *The New Comic Annual* going so far as to publish a list of illustrations that credited not just the draughtsman, William Brown, but also the engravers, most of them extremely obscure figures now lost to record. The plates in *The Comic Offering*, while not specifically crediting their makers, nonetheless frequently included signatures on their plates, and the *Annual*'s editor, Louisa Sheridan, went out of her way in editorial comments to highlight her own contributions as a draughtswoman. As already suggested by Harris, the use of the term 'illustrator' is perhaps somewhat confusing because the central attraction of comic annuals was not particularly their illustrations but rather their extensive use of autonomous free-standing graphic jokes, jokes that did not need any form of textual explication (Fig. 4.1).

AN OFFER IN BLACK AND WHITE.

Fig. 4.1 A characteristic wood-engraved joke from the first volume of *The Comic Offering* (London: Smith, Elder, 1831), 115. The engraving illustrated a poem describing how a Miss Green was being wooed by a baker's boy and a sweep's apprentice, the 'white' and 'black' of the title.

Comic annuals were not always interested in promoting an interactive relationship between text and image, and, as is shown in Figure 4.1, the image was well able to stand on its own as a discrete humorous element. The graphic elements formed an immediate visual attraction in these volumes, with their accessible humour standing in evident contrast to the finished sheen of the steel engravings found in the literary annuals and gift books.

The two best-known and longest-running comic annuals – *The Comic Offering* (1831–5) (Fig. 4.2) and *Hood's Comic Annual* (1830–42) (Fig. 4.3) – were close contemporaries and show distinct similarities in form and content. Both shared 'The Comic' in their title as a declared field of activity, a term that became widely used in the humorous literature of the early Victorian period. They made extensive use of wood engravings, both full-page images and vignettes. Similar in size, they offered distinctive bindings – red leather with impressed decoration in the case of *The Comic Offering* and quarter leather with glazed paper boards for *The Comic Annual*.[19] Both used gold edging on their pages as

Fig. 4.2 Frontispiece and title page to the first volume of *The Comic Offering* (London: Smith, Elder, 1831).

Fig. 4.3 Cover of the first volume of Thomas Hood's *Comic Annual* (London: Hurst, Chance, 1830) in quarter-leather and glazed boards. 'Anniversary of Literary Fun' was the publication's subtitle.

a decorative feature intended to catch the eye. The content of both combined comic verse, tales and illustrations that were suitable for the Christmas market. It was only the declared focus on the comic that differentiated these two annuals from their many competitors for seasonal consumers. Both titles have been included in many studies of late Regency gift books. One crucial element of difference, however, has been widely acknowledged – that *The Comic Offering* was edited by a woman, Louisa Henrietta Sheridan, and that it sought, as the preface to the first volume emphasises, 'the patronage of BRITISH LADIES'.[20] The volume also firmly asserted in its subtitle that it formed the '*Ladies*' Melange of Literary Mirth' and prominently included the name of its female editor on the same page. While Thomas Hood announced himself as the editor and primary contributor to *The Comic Annual*, he noted in the preface to the first volume that he 'was indebted [. . .] in particular to one highly talented young Lady' for drawings that were subsequently turned into illustrations.[21] The gendering of printed humour is one of the concerns that informs the following discussion.

There has been a considerable amount of scholarly attention devoted particularly to the literary, bibliographical and print-historical aspects of the annual in the 1820s and 1830s, with both Faxon's and Harris's books providing comprehensive listings of publications. This essay focuses rather on the comic annual as a distinctive and to some extent progressive presence in the history of comedy, and, particularly, graphic humour. The chosen illustrative medium for comic annuals, the wood engraving, was in the 1820s and 1830s slowly accommodating itself to comic purposes, and the success of Sheridan and Hood's publications, as well as the presence of a number of less prominent but nonetheless significant comic annuals, marks a moment when the stark linearity and simply drawn outlines of their illustrations, despite their evident artistic crudity, became an acceptable humorous medium even for women readers. As Hood declared in the preface to the first volume of *The Comic Annual*, inevitably throwing out puns on the way, 'Preferring Wood to Copper or Steel, I have taken to *Box* as the medium for making hits'.[22] The nature and force of those comic 'hits' form the subject of this essay.

Despite a shared avowal of the 'comic' as their field of operation, the subtitles of the first volumes of *The Comic Annual* and *The Comic Offering* suggest that the two publications operate in two quite distinct humorous universes. *The Comic Offering*, after its rather deferential self-definition as an 'offering', declares itself to be a 'melange of mirth', while *The Comic Annual* announces itself as 'an anniversary of literary fun'. The distance opening up between mirth and fun is, in the history of comic modality in the early nineteenth century, a substantial one. The following discussion considers mirth and fun separately as distinctive humorous categories.

Mirth

'Mirth' was a category that looked back to eighteenth-century literary humour. It manifested itself through such literary subgenres as drollery, facetiae and whimsicality, as well as the jest, bon mot and anecdote. Often mirth was personified as the antidote to melancholy and evoked under the presence of the guiding divinity of Momus. Figure 4.4, the frontispiece to the 1837 volume of *The Comic Annual*, makes this attack on melancholy explicit.

Fig. 4.4 Frontispiece to *The Comic Annual* (London: A. H. Baily, 1837).

With its suggestion of pleasant and harmless sociability, mirth was constructed in opposition to the sharper and more purposive forms of late eighteenth-century humour such as the lampoon, the parody and the caricature – satirical forms that offered a critique of contemporary society and, more widely, human folly. Wit, inventiveness and cleverness remained widely admired qualities in humorous writing, but they were, by the 1830s, becoming less central to graphic comedy.

The humorous modes that comprised the concept of 'mirth' for late Regency readers can be immediately identified in many of the titles and contents of comic publications dating from the 1820s and 1830s. During this earlier period, 'wit' and 'humour' presided over comic literature. A provincial publication from 1826 called *The Cream of the Jest* offered 'a fund of Chaste Wit and Humour' and was organised in three parts: 'the punnery', 'a feast of facetiae' and 'Momus in measure'.[23] Punning was a widely mobilised form of humour in the 1820s and 1830s that was theorised in such slightly self-mocking treatises as Bernard Blackmantle's *The Punster's Pocket-Book*, illustrated with Robert Cruikshank's wood engravings.[24] Punning, of course, was central to *Hood's Comic Annual* in both verbal and graphic forms, but it was also widely used and acknowledged in other comic annuals. *The New Comic Annual*, itself full of punning humour, nonetheless warned that 'A good Pun like good *pun*-ch must possess plenty of spirit, but care must be taken that it does not call forth a *pun*-ch on the head, as is generally the case with *pun*-chinello'.[25] One author in the 1832 volume of *The Comic Offering* likewise acknowledged, 'I steal the pith / Of many a punster good / She says I'm robbing Hook and Smith / She swears in robbing Hood.'[26] 'Facetiae', widely used as a term for a brief comic anecdote in the 1820s, became a distinct commercial subgenre in 1830, with several publishers issuing pamphlet-length, paper-bound publications of humorous poems with wood-engraved illustrations.[27] The invocation of Momus as the presiding genius of comedy was widespread, reaching its most famous iteration in George Cruikshank's graphic characterisation of *Hood's Comic Annual* as 'Broad Grins' (Fig. 4.5).[28] Momus, the god of mockery, blame, scorn, complaint and harsh criticism, was expelled by Zeus from heaven for ridiculing the gods and was therefore a somewhat discomforting figure to choose as a comic muse.

Fig. 4.5 George Cruikshank, 'Hood's Comic Annual – Broad Grins from Year to Year', plate 19 of *My Sketch Book* (London: George Cruikshank, 1834).

Beyond 'wit' and 'humour', 'mirth' was frequently opposed to melancholy and became a widespread overarching definition of humour in the 1820s and 1830s. An undated provincial publication titled *The Book to Keep the Spirits Up in Dull and Gloomy Hours* made it clear that the battle between mirth and melancholy undergirded contemporary ideas of humour. In this instance, the book offered 'manifestations of fun, mirth, humour, drollery, repartee, wit with funny anecdotes, laughable incidents, poetry & c.', a more or less comprehensive listing of available comic subgenres at the time, and introduced 'fun' as a category alongside more traditional humorous subgenres.[29] A similarly extended list appeared on the title page of *Mirth in Miniature* (1825), which offered 'a collection of the very best bon mots, witticisms, smart repartees, bulls and laughable anecdotes'.[30] The 1825 7th edition of George Colman's *The Circle of Anecdote and Wit* boasted of an additional 'choice selection of comic and humorous tales, epigrams and facetious morceaux, in verse'.[31] The subtitle of an 1822 publication by Dean and Mundy – 'a diverting selection of droll stories, queer adventures, wise sayings, Irish bulls, strange whims and original jests' – seems entirely in the continuing tradition of late Regency literary humour.[32] However, the periodical's main title, *The New Fun-Box Broke Open*, suggests the ways in which the grandiloquently presented modes of low humour that belonged to the Regency were being transformed during the 1820s to the simpler pleasures of 'fun'. The fun-box had indeed been broken open.

One of the most suggestive uses of 'mirth' as a category comes from the subtitle to the extensive *Universal Songster* published in three volumes between 1825 and 1828.[33] These volumes brought the lyrics of both traditional songs and lyrics drawn from the supper rooms, concert halls and stages of contemporary London together in an elaborate form that made even the most ephemeral ditty something acceptable in the genteel drawing room. The subtitle of these volumes was 'The Museum of Mirth', which suggests that the volumes were not just a contemporary anthology but also a memorial to forms of comic verse that were in danger of being lost. *The Universal Songster* was illustrated with small-scale humorous wood engravings by George and Robert Cruikshank, whose status and popularity validated the use of the wood engravings in these volumes as an ambitious and aesthetically sophisticated medium. While wood engravings had been widely used on ballad sheets, songsters and garlands, along with the emerging genre of the serialised song book, *The Universal Songster* brought them into respectability and offered them as an expression of a more refined taste. It thereby established an important precedent for combining humorous wood engravings with textual manifestations of mirth in forms that could be adapted by comic annuals.

By the 1830s, 'mirth' was thus in widespread use as a catch-all term for the potential kinds of comic literary expression that might be drawn on to fill out a volume of humorous text. The subgenres of literary humour rehearsed in the titles of the late Regency anthologies cited above included jests, witticisms, repartee, drollery, facetiae, puns, bon mots and laughable anecdotes. The elements in this rather literary list of comic possibilities are largely characterised by their brevity, with only anecdotes and drolleries suggesting more extended forms of narrative humour. Despite inheriting the generic potential of all these forms of popular humour, the comic annuals draw very little on this inheritance. Instead, they seek to draw on the elements that had made the literary annual such a commercial success. The relationship between the comic annuals and the literary annuals is not so much parodic as commercial. Hood and Sheridan saw the comic annual as a mechanism for translating the traditional bookish codes of mirth into something less oppressively literary and more fitting for a wider, less genteel readership. The use of the comic wood engraving, which was at the same time being deployed widely in other forms of humorous publications, was central to this project.

It was a quite deliberate act to use 'The Ladies' Melange of Mirth' as the subtitle for *The Comic Offering*. A 'melange of mirth' evoked the kind of accumulated anthology of brief jokes, anecdotes and puns that had served previous generations as down-market but respectable humorous literature. But in practice *The Comic Offering* was much less deferential to the traditions of humorous print culture than its subtitle suggested. Instead, it along with other contemporary comic annuals, established an important new form of graphic humour: fun.

Fun

To this day, 'fun' remains a term frequently used to describe a slightly debased mode of humour that is linked to the idea of frolic. Negative inversions of the term like 'make fun of', 'not much fun' and the often ironic 'fun and games' are frequently to be heard, along with the trivialised potential of doing things 'for fun' or 'in fun'. 'What fun' is usually used to imply the opposite. But 'fun' became a slightly more substantial humorous possibility in the 1820s and 1830s. In these decades, 'fun' enters the literary vocabulary as a term used to describe a kind of humour to be enjoyed sociably at leisure, free from the literariness of mirth and with less stress on wit and social purposiveness. One anthology from the 1820s, *Odds and Ends*, boasted of 'a Groat's worth of fun for a Penny' in its subtitle.[34] By the 1830s, the well-known publishers Sherwood, Gilbert and Piper were happy to produce *Fun for the Million*, a traditional-enough assembly of 'the best jokes, witticisms, puns, epigrams, humorous stories, and witty compositions' marketed under the less ponderous banner of 'fun'.[35] The volume was extensively reprinted. Some of the immensely popular editions of the play text of *Tom and Jerry, or Life in London* branded the drama 'a burletta of fun, frolic, and flash', thus linking fun to the raffish social adventures widely shown on the London stage.[36] A similar link between fun and frolic was made in a provincial collection of 'all the most popular and new puns, jests and witty sayings' gathered together as *The Comical Budget of Fun and Frolic*.[37]

Fun was certainly a category of humour that began to identify itself closely with illustrated comic publications in the 1830s. By 1835, Robert Cruikshank, doubtless under the guidance of his publisher William Kidd, designated the third volume of his *Cruikshank at Home* series as *Cruikshank's Offering of Mirth, or, Evergreen of Fun*. Even before Cruikshank sought to merge mirth and fun in a single volume, Seymour had used the subtitle 'A Perennial of Fun', over-optimistically as it turned out, on the sole volume of *Seymour's Comic Album* (Fig. 4.6).

Hood, too, was rethinking mirth as fun. Although the opening statement of the first volume of *The Comic Annual* asserts that 'In the Christmas holidays [. . .] we naturally look for mirth', 'fun' soon became its central guiding spirit.[38] The printed paper cover to the first volume carries the subtitle 'The Anniversary of Literary Fun'[39] (see Fig. 4.3), and the book's 'Preface' described the ways in which Hood's two previous volumes of *Whims and Oddities* had morphed into a new form. The preface averred that this new form, in contrast to previous practice, would not involve 'equivocating between Mirth and Melancholy' but would rather be 'exclusively devoted to the Humorous'.[40] Despite the apparently conventional evocation of 'mirth' and 'the humorous' here, a new vocabulary of comic potentialities was being evoked largely through verbal equivocations on the meanings of 'annual' and 'anniversary'. 'Annual' for Hood meant both a literary form and good-humoured domestic celebration linked to a festive calendar. 'Christmas is strictly a Comic Annual', he declares resonantly, thus eliding the traditional and evolving celebratory year and the publication of annuals into a single event.[41] He returned to this elision between the festive calendar and shared sociability in 'Five Comic Annuals', one of the best-known images in *The Comic Annual* (Fig. 4.7).[42] In this image, Hood humorously represents the comic annual as a series of public celebrations on the streets as annually recurring moments of frolic.

SEYMOUR'S

COMIC ALBUM;

OR,

MUSEUM OF ENTERTAINMENT:

A PERENNIAL OF FUN.

THE ILLUSTRATIONS

DESIGNED BY ROBERT SEYMOUR,

AND

ENGRAVED ON WOOD BY SAMUEL SLADER.

"MONUMENTUM EXEGI, ÆRE PERENNIUS."

EXTREME PENALTY OF THE LAW.

LONDON:
W. KIDD, 14, CHANDOS-STREET, WEST-STRAND;
SIMPKIN AND MARSHALL, STATIONERS'-HALL-COURT;
ADAM AND CHARLES BLACK, EDINBURGH;
AND W. F. WAKEMAN, DUBLIN.

Fig. 4.6 Title page for *Seymour's Comic Album* (London: William Kidd, n.d.). The volume formed an element of 'Kidd's Entertaining Library'.

Fig. 4.7 Thomas Hood, 'Five Comic Annuals' frontispiece to *The Comic Annual* (London: Charles Tilt, 1834).

The Comic Annual and *The Comic Offering* join battle

An interesting contemporary commentary on the relative qualities of *The Comic Annual* and *The Comic Offering* as the two most significant comic annuals is offered by an extended mock-heroic poem, *The Battle of the "Annuals"* (Fig. 4.8).

Published anonymously in 1835 using the format of one of the comic literary fads of the 1830s – the *jeu d'esprit* – the poem is the work of Charles Robert Forrester, who, with his brother Alfred, formed one half of the comic writing and illustrating team of 'Crowquill'. While maintaining his career as a lawyer, Charles nonetheless was a fluent and prolific writer working in a humorous mode who was more interested in absurdity than satire. In his early career, Alfred provided illustrations to Charles's texts. Charles Forrester had himself contributed to *The Comic Offering* from 1832 on, but despite any notions of self-interest, *The Battle*

Fig. 4.8 Frontispiece and title page to *The Battle of the "Annuals"*, written and drawn by 'Crowquill' and published by A. H. Baily, c. 1833.

of the "Annuals" is an extremely helpful guide to the perceived differences between, and distinct qualities of, contemporary comic annuals. Combining a wood engraving with a pamphlet-length text, it also provides an interesting example of the kind of facetious humour that fell short of outright satire yet had become widespread by the 1830s.

As might be expected from a writer who had published something called *Absurdities*, Charles Forrester largely saw annuals as little more than a short-term commercial fad. In *The Battle of the "Annuals"*, he asserts that 'They seek for fame, but History / Will blink them by the mass!'[43] However, they also provided Forrester with an excellent opportunity for a comic exegesis that mocked the pretentiousness and refinement of the genre by using the tropes of heroic conflict. *The Comic Offering* and *The Comic Annual* were central protagonists in this battle.

Forrester began his poem by noting the specific physical manifestations of 'annualness': 'In leather trappings some appear, / While others silk reveal; / And most, like knights of other days, / Are armed with plates of steel.'[44] The punning use 'plates of steel' here expresses delight in the satirical and humorous potential of new reprographic media at the time. Here, for example, is an advertisement from *Figaro in London* for the launch of *The Comic Magazine* in 1832:

> In order to render the work [*The Comic Magazine*] *lighter* the proprietors propose availing themselves considerably of the assistance of the *graver*, confident that the best way of *making hits* is by giving *good outs*, and from the artist possessing the double advantage of being a good *cutter* and being *funny* at the same time, we look forward to a rapid *sale*.[45]

The playing off 'lighter' against 'graver' and the multiple meanings of 'cutter' invoke the newly discovered potential of the wood engraving in the 1830s as a comic medium. It thus makes sense that Forrester right at the beginning of his poem characterises the physical appearance of the annuals through their 'plates of steel'.

Nonetheless, the poem is at considerable pains to differentiate between the genteel sheen and tonal brightness of the steel engravings characteristic of the literary annuals and the wood engravings that characterised *The Comic Offering* and *The Comic Annual*. The voice of *The Comic Annual* speaks in defence of its chosen mode of picture making: 'For all their grave and serious looks / I do not care a pin; / For though I wield a wooden sword, / My *cuts* shall make them *grin*!'[46] This comes after Forrester's earlier characterisation of *The Comic Annual* as a jester 'with lath in hand, and cap and bells, / And coat of motley hue'.[47] Despite Forrester's assertions of the ability of wood engravings to create 'grins', there remains something of a discrepancy between wielding 'laths' and being truly 'cutting'. This is important because Forrester's account of the two comic annuals turns on how 'pointed' and 'cutting' they are. In this respect, *The Comic Offering* comes across as a lightweight:

> The 'Comic Offering' unfolds
> Her banner to the breeze –
> Just like a satin pincushion
> All full of points – that please –
>
> But never wound! – the leader is
> Far too polite, that's poz!

So *honest* too – some wish that she
 A '*little sharper*' was![48]

Forrester suggests that perhaps this damaging and 'pointless' politeness has something to do with the annual's material presence:

The 'Comic Offering' appears
 In white muslin array'd;
Quite *recherchee* and *a-la-mode*,
 And well used to – parade!

In look a hero! – and her wit
 So delicate and fine;
Its *point* is quite invisible –
 Tis *jest* in a decline![49]

Given that Forrester had been a contributor to *The Comic Offering*, these are pointedly unkind remarks, with even the clever pun on 'jest' and 'just' sounding rather sneering. It is not difficult to read the comments about 'delicacy' and 'fineness' as allusions to the gender of the annual's editor, especially given the characterisation of *Friendship's Offering* as 'her'. Forrester assumes that comic annuals should perform a role quite distinct from the lane occupied by literary annuals. He argues that the humour in a comic annual, especially the graphic humour, should be pointed and cutting rather than diverting and anodyne. Forrester acknowledged that *The Comic Offering*, despite being open to criticism for using coarse wood engravings rather than more ambitious steel-engraved plates, did strain towards the edginess that comic illustration provided: 'Yes! They may laugh at my "designs", / While they design in vain; / I'll ne'er retreat – or if I cut, / I'll cut and come again.'[50] Whether wood engraving – the use of 'laths' rather than pointed 'gravers' to produce the image – could maintain a 'pointed' tradition of graphic comedy was a matter of some doubt, especially given Forrester's wider critique in *The Battle of the "Annuals"* of the fashionable gestures and lack of seriousness that characterised annuals more widely. He saw them engaged in a self-obsessed battle to win over readers to their charms.

The Battle of the "Annuals" was primarily concerned with describing the circulation wars between the annuals published during the early 1830s; on the slightest evidence, Forrester mocks their attempts to differentiate themselves from their rivals. His account of the competition for readers and pursuit of cultural status exemplified by the annuals was deliberately structured within the mock-heroic mode in order to bring a soothing joviality to what in practice was a quite acerbic account of the pretentiousness and preening vanity displayed by the annuals. But his poem also alludes to other conflicts and 'battles' beyond the circulation wars and issues of identity. Forrester included two comic annuals among his discussion of annuals without any apparent sense that they might breach the distinctive characteristics of the genre. Yet his poem makes two clear distinctions between comic and 'literary' annuals. The first concerns illustration – the steel plates that characterise literary annuals and the wood engravings that define comic annuals. The second concerns the wider aspirations of the annual form – the 'point' and 'cut' of humorous and satiric content against the refinement and cultural aspirations of the gift-book annuals aimed at genteel readers, presumably women. A further conflict emerges from the ways in which the comic annuals themselves formulated their purpose as a battle between the forces of comicality and melancholy. Underlying this conflict is a sense of the difficulty of formulating a conceptual model of humour, especially visual comedy, that was appropriate at a moment when the minatory and reproving powers of wit and satire, as well as the coarse pleasures of male sociability, were giving way.

Robert Seymour and the comic wood engraving

Robert Seymour, the artist who produced many of the illustrations for *The Comic Offering*, was an important and prolific figure in the short-lived heyday of the comic annual. Thomas Hood had largely relied on his own drawings for *The Comic Annual* but had used well-known commercial engravers like Branston and Bonner to reproduce his work, meticulously crediting them in the prefatory lists of illustrations in each volume. The single volume of *The New Comic Annual* relied exclusively on an obscure artist, William Brown, for its graphic content. Neither Hood nor Brown was widely visible elsewhere in furthering the development of small-scale humorous wood engraving, although of course Hood's illustrations for his own publications were well known. Seymour, on the other hand, was by the early 1830s working in many forms of comic illustration – etched and lithographed single-plate caricatures, elaborate frontispieces for books, and wood engravings for play texts – and was beginning to be well enough known to publish serial works under his own name, with the lithographed *New Readings of Old Authors* launched in 1832. That same year, he also contributed to a pioneering periodical, *The Comic Magazine*, which was largely dependent on his wood engravings. Seymour, along with George Cruikshank, was a versatile artist who was attuned to the developing marketplace for humorous images in the early 1830s. His dedication to the potential of the comic annual as a mechanism for displaying the new wood-engraved manifestations of fun led him to launch two of his own annuals, neither of which seems to have been particularly successful.[51] He was nonetheless a pivotal figure in negotiating the transition in humorous image-making, from caricature to the new small-scale visual jokes that characterised downmarket print culture. Seymour had a unique understanding of both traditional modes of graphic comedy and the potential of small comic wood engravings wrapped into the pages of various new print forms, including songbooks, play texts, almanacs, magazines and comic annuals.

It is unsurprising that Louisa Sheridan, in pursuit of respectability and quality, would engage Seymour to work on *The Comic Offering* alongside the up-and-coming illustrator Kenny Meadows and highly skilled commercial engravers such as Gorway, Slader, Jackson and G. D. (presumably George Dorrington). It is important to note that none of these artists and engravers is acknowledged in the 'list of embellishments' included in the printed text of *The Comic Offering*; they are visible only through the monograms on those plates which are signed. Seymour drew the frontispieces for volumes 1 and 4 as well as the title page used for all five volumes.[52] Signed work by Seymour is visible elsewhere in volumes 1 (three images), 2 (nine images), 3 (sixteen images) and 4 (one image). Seymour seems to have been the main illustrator for the first three volumes, though much of his work seems to have been unsigned. Volume 5 (1835), which carries no signed contributions from Seymour, nonetheless has the frontispiece he drew from a design by Sheridan and engraved by Samuel Slader (Fig. 4.9).

It depicts 'The Wag-on' of fun, shown leaving the 'General Wag Office' laden with parcels of 'puns', 'jests' and 'stories', and leaving behind 'the blues', 'low spirits' and 'fogs', thus reiterating the traditional trope of mirth conquering despair. The image

"The Wag-on of Fun."

Fig. 4.9 Frontispiece to the 1835 volume of *The Comic Offering*, designed by Louisa Sheridan, drawn by Robert Seymour and engraved by Samuel Slader.

is much less sophisticated than Seymour's previous frontispiece designs; it thus reflects the broader shift in *The Comic Offering* to a simple linear mode and lithography.

Satire versus fun: The frontispieces to *The Comic Offering*

Seymour, along with Robert Cruikshank and Bonner, was the most prolific and experienced practitioner of the new small-scale humorous wood engravings that gave commercial impetus to a whole new range of comic print forms in the early 1830s. His name, even when visible only as initials on plates, gave *The Comic Offering* a respectability and cachet appropriate to the tastes of its targeted readers. His engraved frontispieces and title pages were even more crucial in formulating the comic identity of *The Comic Offering* and provide a sophisticated gloss on the changing ways in which comedy might be manifested and named at a moment of fluidity and experimentation within print culture.

In the 1831 frontispiece, the 'march of comicality' manifested itself in smoke and dust, raised spears and banners, and even a bomb-like smoking Christmas pudding brandished at the top left-hand corner of the image (Fig. 4.10). 'Comicality', it seems, is something of a cultural onslaught that uses revolutionary practices to overthrow the forces of melancholy, as evidenced in the two black devils being scattered underfoot[53] and the snake-haired mask of melancholy banished to the image's nether regions. Seymour here offered a highly theorised iconographic and verbal account of comedy rendered through the tumbling figures and fluttering banners of a street procession. The riotous accumulation of detail is anchored by two strap lines: 'away with melancholy' is spread across the base of the image in a ribbon, while 'the march of comicality' is displayed at the centre of the image by three substantial young female circus figures cartwheeling across the scene, apparently free of the laws of gravity. 'Away with melancholy' draws on the tropes through which comedy was frequently represented in the 1830s as a battle between 'melancholy' and 'comicality', with comicality used as a generalised term to embrace the wide range of modes available to both graphic and literary humourists.

'The march of comicality' was a politicised phrase that inevitably evoked 'the march of intellect', a complex and continuing

Fig. 4.10 Frontispiece for *The Comic Offering* for 1831, drawn by Robert Seymour.

development in the social, economic and technological fabric of British society that brought with it fear and anxiety about the rate and effects of radical social change. Seymour had caricatured the march of intellect more extensively than any of his contemporaries, frequently in detailed satires that depicted technological and educational 'progress' as a threat to the traditional social order that could potentially lead to civil unrest. Here he invented a 'march' that represented the powers of the satirical artist/observer to offset socio-cultural fears with 'comicality'.[54]

The ways in which Seymour represented 'the march of comicality' ran the risk of rendering comedy as a disruptive rather than a meliorating social force. In the aftermath of Peterloo, all street marches and demonstrations, especially those that featured such disorderly features as drums, banners and fairground zaniness, were widely regarded with suspicion and even fear. The density of Seymour's crush of participants, many of whom wave banners and stare confrontationally out of the image at the imagined spectators, created a claustrophobic graphic space that positioned the viewer as a bystander at a passing circus show of zanies and grotesques. This sense of enclosure and pressure on space is reinforced by the 'away with melancholy' banner pressing down on the snake-haired head at the bottom of the image and by the ovoid shape and sharply defined edges of the image as it appears on the white sheet of the page. Many participants, most obviously the central figure bearing a flag for 'puns' on a pole, defiantly fix their gaze on the artist/spectator, asserting their right to participate in representing their cause in the theatre of the London streets. The high-stepping fustian figure, seemingly stepping out from his study, loftily bears a placard for 'tales' and stares into the future with a look of wonder on his face. Other marchers, such as the figure on the far right bearing the colours of 'ton' (presumably with the rest of 'bon ton' hidden), glances over his shoulder at some distraction at the side of the road. The entire image gathers together the allusive plenitude of the caricature tradition into the miniaturised new form of the wood engraving held within the small page of a printed text.

Despite its satirical and politicised allusiveness, Seymour's frontispiece was clearly intended to both celebrate the feast of comedy and to encourage the reader to fight off melancholy by reading *The Comic Offering*. The banners firmly announce the range of the annual's contents. 'Tales' in the form of short fiction and whimsical poetic narratives were certainly part of the book's 'offering'. 'Puns' were also ever-present, though mainly in the illustrations, which exploited the widespread fashion for visual/verbal linguistic and graphic interplay, where the visual image would be frequently undercut or reinterpreted by its caption. Literary punning was also a frequent feature of the poetic contributions. 'Bon Mots', a distinctive genre of short and incisive verbal wit expressed in a sentence or two, had become a characteristic feature of general-interest magazines of the 1820s and 1830s, but such contributions were not to be found in *The Comic Offering*. Nor was 'Satire', cut back to 'tire' on the half-hidden banner at the back right of the frontispiece. A lack of satirical content was an obvious feature of the annual because the humour tended to be more whimsical and frivolous. What Seymour had assembled here on his banners was a generalised definition of the comic mode rather than a precise description of the contents of Sheridan's editorial choices. His frontispiece is to some extent an elegy for the vanishing world of caricature.

Conclusion: Comic annuals and the history of graphic humour

Comic annuals have been thoroughly discussed in recent scholarship as representing an important element within the mass of literary annuals produced in the 1820s and 1830s. These decades offered new forms of bookmaking linked to seasonal occasions and opened up new literary opportunities for writers, especially women. The innovative use of wood- engraved illustration in comic annuals, in contrast to the steel plates found in literary annuals, has been widely acknowledged. That women formed the dominant implied readership for annuals has also been established. Louisa Sheridan's important role as a woman editor of a comic annual has been recognised, along with her innovative efforts to address women readers. But little has been said about the role of the visual content of the comic annuals as a manifestation of a significant transitional moment in the history of British graphic comedy. Such a transition was signalled by a shift from etched and engraved satire to punning jokes rendered in crudely linear wood-engraved forms. Underlying this transition – and propelled by the commercial opportunities offered by the development of new, cheaper and more accessible print forms – was a fundamental reconceptualisation of comedy that sought to democratise visual humour. In the comic annuals of the 1830s, the complex allusiveness and imagistic density of satire and the literariness of 'mirth' began to give way to a more genial, less introverted kind of visual humour that was evolving towards 'fun'.

Notes

1. Barbara Onslow, 'Gendered Production: Annuals and Gift Books', in *Journalism and the Periodical Press in Nineteenth-Century Britain*, ed. Joanne Shattock (Cambridge: Cambridge University Press, 2017), 66.
2. Frederick W. Faxon, *Literary Annuals and Gift Books: A Bibliography 1823–1903* (London: Private Libraries Association, 1973). This revised edition of Faxon's *Bibliography*, originally published in 1912, is prefaced by two essays on the physical characteristics of the genres by Eleanore Jamieson and Iain Bain. Katherine D. Harris's *Forget Me Not: The Rise of the British Literary Annual, 1823–1835* (Athens: Ohio University Press, 2015) combines a detailed study of annuals with appendices listing published annuals in both America and Britain and their major contributors, editors and publishers.
3. Katherine D. Harris, 'Borrowing, Altering and Perfecting the Literary Annual Form – Or What It Is Not: Emblems, Almanacs, Pocket-Books, Albums, Scrapbooks and Gift Books', Poetess Archive 1 (2007): https://paj-ojs-tamu.tdl.org/paj/article/view/23; Brian Maidment, *Comedy, Caricature and the Social Order, 1820–1850* (Manchester: Manchester University Press 2013), 72–5.
4. Faxon, *Literary Annuals and Gift Books*, 15.
5. Ibid., 17.
6. Basil Hunnisett, *Engraved on Steel: The History of Picture Production Using Steel Plates* (Aldershot: Ashgate, 1998), 121.
7. Ibid., 131.
8. Linda H. Peterson, *Becoming a Woman of Letters: Myths of Authorship and Facts of the Victorian Market* (Princeton: Princeton University Press, 2009); Barbara Onslow, *Women of the Press in Nineteenth-Century Britain* (Basingstoke: Macmillan, 2000); Alexis Easley, *First-Person Anonymous: Women Writers and Victorian Print Media, 1830–70* (Aldershot: Ashgate, 2004); Kathryn Ledbetter, *British Victorian Women's Periodicals: Beauty, Civilization, and Poetry* (New York: Palgrave Macmillan, 2009).
9. Lorraine Janzen Kooistra, *Poetry, Pictures and Popular Publishing: The Illustrated Gift Book and Victorian Visual Culture, 1855–1875*

(Athens: Ohio University Press, 2011).
10. Onslow, 'Gendered Production', 66–83.
11. Harris, *Forget Me Not*, 154–66.
12. Ibid., 160–6.
13. Ibid., 166.
14. Tamara L. Hunt, 'Louisa Sheridan's *Comic Offering* and the Critics: Gender and Humour in the Early Victorian Period', *Victorian Periodicals Review* 29, no. 2 (1996), 95–115.
15. Harris, *Forget Me Not*, 157.
16. Ibid., 156.
17. Ibid.
18. For background on Robins, see Robert Patten, *George Cruikshank's Life, Times, and Art* (Cambridge: Lutterworth Press, 1992), 1:269–70, 361–2. For Duncombe, Strange and Steill, see Robert J. Kirkpatrick, *Pennies, Profits and Poverty: A Biographical Dictionary of Wealth and Want in Bohemian Fleet Street* (London: Kirkpatrick, 2016). For Mayhew, see Christopher G. Anderson, *London Vagabond: The Life of Henry Mayhew* (London: Anderson, 2018).
19. Alternative bindings in publisher's cloth were also available.
20. Preface to *The Comic Offering* (London: Smith, Elder 1831), viii.
21. Preface to *The Comic Annual* (London: Hurst, Chance 1830), viii.
22. Ibid.
23. *The Cream of the Jest: A Fund of Chaste Wit and Humour* (Derby: Henry Mozley, 1826).
24. Bernard Blackmantle, *The Punster's Pocket-Book, or The Art of Punning* (London: Sherwood, Gilbert, and Piper, 1826).
25. 'Puns on Punning; or, Hints to a Punster', *New Comic Annual* (London: Hurst, Chance, 1831), 69.
26. Isabel Hill, 'A Stage Driver', *Comic Offering* (London: Hurst, Chance, 1832), 90.
27. Maidment, *Comedy, Caricature and the Social Order*, 154–7; Brian Maidment, '"Thief of the name of Kidd": Unscrupulous Opportunism and Cheap Print in Late Regency London', *Victorian Popular Fictions* 3, no. 2 (2021): 21–44.
28. George Cruikshank, *My Sketch Book* (London: George Cruikshank, 1834), plate 19.
29. John Duncan [John Brighte], *The Book to Keep the Spirits Up* (Wakefield: William Nicholson, n.d.).
30. *Mirth in Miniature, or Bursts of Merriment* (Derby: Henry Mozley, 1825).
31. George Colman, *The Circle of Anecdote and Wit*, 7th ed. (London:

John Bumpus, 1825).

32. *The New Fun-Box Broke Open* (London: Dean and Munday, 1822).
33. *The Universal Songster or Museum of Mirth*, 3 vols. (London: John Fairburn, 1825–8).
34. *Odds and Ends, Being a Collection of the Best Jokes, Comic Stories, Anecdotes, Bon mots, Etc.* (Glasgow: n.p., c. 1830).
35. *Fun for the Million* (London: Sherwood, Gilbert and Piper, n.d.).
36. *Tom and Jerry, or Life in London: A Burletta of Fun, Frolic and Flash* (London: J. Robinson, 1825).
37. 'Godfrey Gimcrackiana', in *The Comical Budget of Fun and Frolic* (Derby: Thomas Richardson, c. 1830).
38. Preface to *The Comic Annual*, v.
39. The printed title on the glazed paper cover of the first volume of *The Comic Annual* actually reads, 'The Anniversary of the Literary Fund'. This remained unaltered in subsequent volumes up to 1838. The 1842 volume was printed in a different format.
40. Preface to *The Comic Annual*, viii.
41. Ibid., v.
42. *The Comic Annual* (London: Charles Tilt, 1834). 'Five Comic Annuals' formed the frontispiece to the volume.
43. Alfred Forrester and Charles Forrester, *The Battle of the "Annuals": A Fragment* (London: A. H. Baily, 1835), 27.
44. Ibid., 3.
45. 'Advertisement', *Figaro in London* 1 (17 March 1832): 60.
46. Forrester, *Battle of the "Annuals"*, 28.
47. Ibid., 26.
48. Ibid., 6.
49. Ibid., 16.
50. Ibid., 28.
51. The first chapter of my monograph *Robert Seymour and Nineteenth-Century Print Culture* (Abingdon: Routledge, 2021) provides an overview of Seymour's varied career.
52. The frontispiece for volume 2 was drawn by Kenny Meadows.
53. Post-Peterloo trampling was a widespread caricature trope for social disorder.
54. Maidment, *Robert Seymour*, 44–70.

5

Fauna, Flora and Illustrated Verse in Mary Howitt's Environmental Children's Poetry

Linda K. Hughes

If in *The Second Common Reader* Virginia Woolf consigned Elizabeth Barrett Browning to the 'downstairs [. . .] servants' quarters' in 'the mansion of literature' (a judgement now radically reversed), Mary Howitt, whose ballads Browning praised in 'Lady Geraldine's Courtship', has seemingly been locked in an unvisited basement storage room by most scholars of the twentieth and twenty-first centuries, even those who study popular nineteenth-century literature and print forms.[1] Despite Howitt's numerous contributions to that landmark new media innovation of the early nineteenth century, the literary annual, she is not listed among the 'authors' in Laura Mandell's 'Poetess Archive' (though several of her poems' titles are cited), and Katherine D. Harris's *Forget Me Not: The Rise of the British Literary Annual, 1823–1835*, omits mention of Howitt altogether – though Howitt contributed to the *Forget Me Not* in 1834, among other annuals, and later edited *Fisher's Drawing Room Scrap-book* from 1840 to 1842 after L. E. L.'s premature death in Africa. Howitt was a prominent figure from the 1830s through the 1850s, whose literary and social networks included Felicia Hemans, Elizabeth Gaskell, Alfred Tennyson, Charles Dickens and members of the Langham Place Group. More than a once-prominent writer now fallen into relative obscurity, Howitt demands inclusion in this volume because she was an important new media innovator from the 1820s to the 1840s, both in her material forms and in her content, especially, as I argue, with respect to her eco-poetry in *Sketches of Natural History*, a multimodal volume for children published in 1834.

Rudolph Ackermann inaugurated the fashion of multimodal literary annuals with his *Forget Me Not* in 1823. As Katherine

Harris remarks, 'Annuals were something new, different, and substantial. [. . .] The literary annual made its British debut at a moment in print culture when innovative technological advances, literacy rates, demand for reading materials, and publishing and book-selling practices increased the production of printed materials.'[2] Packaged in a genteel pocket-sized volume inspired by German *Taschenbücher* (pocket-sized books), annuals featured illustrations as well as tales and poems written by a range of celebrity, up-and-coming and anonymous authors to illustrate images rather than the reverse.[3] By 1829, Mary Howitt was contributing signed poems to several annuals, including *Friendship's Offering*, *The Winter's Wreath*, *The Gem* and *The New Year's Gift and Juvenile Souvenir*, which featured Howitt's most famous poem, 'The Spider and the Fly'.[4] Howitt, then, was on the front lines almost from the beginnings of the literary annual. In the process of working with a range of annuals, Howitt was gaining first-hand experience in how images might be intriguingly, productively and profitably integrated with her verses. For example, one of her four poems included in the 1829 *Winter's Wreath*, a lyric entitled 'Mountain Children' (later reprinted in Howitt's 1847 *Ballads and Other Poems*), was directly paired with an illustration, *View from Ambleside – Children Returning from School*, based on a John Renton painting engraved by Edward Goodall (Fig. 5.1).[5]

Even when her own poems were not immediately linked to illustrations, Howitt was immersing herself in the multimodal aesthetic that defined the literary annual. In other ways, too, Howitt generated or participated in important media innovations. From the time of her marriage to fellow Quaker William Howitt at age twenty-two, the couple began to write and publish collaboratively.[6] They were unusual in collaboratively writing poetry. Though their co-authored poems were likely assemblages more than interactive compositions (as were Mary Howitt's collaborative childhood poems with her sister), the married couple insisted on their corporate authorship, as the title page of their second collaborative volume, *The Desolation of Eyam and Other Poems* (1827), indicated (Fig. 5.2).[7]

Today the collaborative poetry of Michael Field, the publishing signature of two women poet-lovers, compels wide interest in nineteenth-century gender and poetry studies. The Howitts were gender-conforming (rather than queer) antecedents in the 1820s of

Fig. 5.1 'View near Ambleside – Children Returning from School', by Edward Goodall, from a Picture by J. Renton, in *Winter's Wreath* (London: George B. Whittaker, 1829), 397. Courtesy of the Lilly Library, Indiana University.

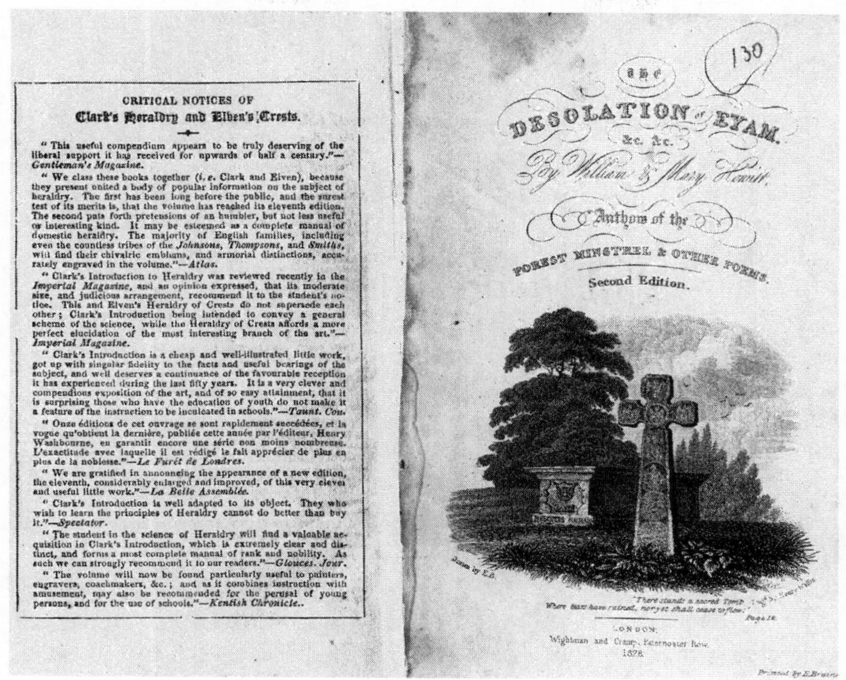

CRITICAL NOTICES OF

Clark's Heraldry and Elven's Crests.

"This useful compendium appears to be truly deserving of the liberal support it has received for upwards of half a century."—*Gentleman's Magazine.*

"We class these books together (*i. e.* Clark and Elven), because they present united a body of popular information on the subject of heraldry. The first has been long before the public, and the surest test of its merits is, that the volume has reached its eleventh edition. The second puts forth pretensions of an humbler, but not less useful or interesting kind. It may be esteemed as a complete manual of domestic heraldry. The majority of English families, including even the countless tribes of the *Johnsons*, *Thompsons*, and *Smiths*, will find their chivalric emblems, and armorial distinctions, accurately engraved in the volume."—*Atlas.*

"Clark's Introduction to Heraldry was reviewed recently in the *Imperial Magazine*, and an opinion expressed, that its moderate size, and judicious arrangement, recommend it to the student's notice. This and Elven's Heraldry of Crests do not supersede each other; Clark's Introduction being intended to convey a general scheme of the science, while the Heraldry of Crests affords a more perfect elucidation of the most interesting branch of the art."—*Imperial Magazine.*

"Clark's Introduction is a cheap and well-illustrated little work, got up with singular fidelity to the facts and useful bearings of the subject, and well deserves a continuance of the favourable reception it has experienced during the last fifty years. It is a very clever and compendious exposition of the art, and of so easy attainment, that it is surprising those who have the education of youth do not make it a feature of the instruction to be inculcated in schools."—*Taunt. Cou.*

"Onze éditions de cet ouvrage se sont rapidement succédées, et la vogue qu'obtient la dernière, publiée cette année par l'éditeur, Henry Washbourne, en garantit encore une série non moins nombreuse. L'exactitude avec laquelle il est rédigé le fait apprécier de plus en plus de la noblesse."—*Le Furét de Londres.*

"We are gratified in announcing the appearance of a new edition, the eleventh, considerably enlarged and improved, of this very clever and useful little work."—*La Belle Assemblée.*

"Clark's Introduction is well adapted to its object. They who wish to learn the principles of Heraldry cannot do better than buy it."—*Spectator.*

"The student in the science of Heraldry will find a valuable acquisition in Clark's Introduction, which is extremely clear and distinct, and forms a most complete manual of rank and nobility. As such we can strongly recommend it to our readers."—*Glouces. Jour.*

"The volume will now be found particularly useful to painters, engravers, coachmakers, &c.; and as it combines instruction with amusement, may also be recommended for the perusal of young persons, and for the use of schools."—*Kentish Chronicle.*

130

THE DESOLATION OF EYAM, &c. &c.

By William & Mary Howitt,

Authors of the FOREST MINSTREL & OTHER POEMS.

Second Edition.

"There stands a sacred Tomb
Where tears have rained, nor yet shall cease to flow;"

Page 18.

LONDON:
Wightman and Cramp, Paternoster Row.
1828.

Fig. 5.2 Title Page, *The Desolation of Eyam*, by William and Mary Howitt, 2nd ed. (London: Wightman and Cramp, 1827; rpt. 1828). Courtesy of the Perry Casteñeda Library, University of Texas.

what still strikes scholars as a radical collaborative model of poetic composition.

The Howitts' poetry volumes also chime with another important media innovation of the nineteenth century: transatlantic publication and authorship. Even as William Howitt was publishing his rural sketches in the same *Kaleidoscope* issues that circulated the now-canonical transatlantic writer Washington Irving, their collaborative poems, influenced by Felicia Hemans's North American poetic subjects, were hailing American readers with poems such as 'The Emigrant – A Tale of the American Woods' and 'Penn and the Indians' in their 1827 volume, the latter poem representing Quaker William Penn as a model of keeping faith with the indigenous and, in turn, Native Americans peacefully keeping faith with him and his Quaker community. Felicia Hemans expanded their reach toward America by forwarding a copy of *The Desolation of Eyam* to friends in America.[8] The Howitts would continue to be mindful of their American readers. As Karen Karbiener notes, 'Howitt's role in the development of an independent American culture is even more noteworthy than her contributions to British literary history,' and after Hemans's death in 1835, Mary Howitt went on to become the single most popular British woman poet in the United States.[9]

Above all, though, Mary's principal new media innovations from the 1820s to the 1840s were in her writings for children.[10] According to Woodring, 'The greater of the Howitts' two most important contributions to the stream of European letters, in fact, was their cultivation of the fanciful in juvenile literature, which had already begun to put forth a few timid shoots out of the previously unirrigated didacticism.'[11] I have mentioned her contribution of 'The Spider and the Fly' to a juvenile annual in 1829, which featured a visual tailpiece in the form of children flying a kite (Fig. 5.3), and as noted earlier, her *Sketches of Natural History* was generously illustrated.

From 1836 to 1839, she published three more illustrated verse collections for children, *Tales in Verse for the Young* (1836); *Birds and Flowers and Other Country Things* (1838), clearly a sequel of sorts to *Sketches of Natural History*; and *Hymns and Fireside Verse* (1839), which went into a second edition. Her successes with these titles clarify her unusual position and form the backstory of her innovative role as a series children's author with an advance contract. The success of her *Tales in Verse* enabled her to publish *Tales in Prose: For the Young* (1836), which opened with 'A Night-Scene in a Poor Man's House', a fantasy tale in which the dreary penury of David Maclean and his wife and eight children is vividly shown, then suddenly erased when he finds himself heir to a nobleman and his estate. At some point, a London publisher, Thomas Tegg, read that first story and decided to approach her.[12]

Tegg was best known for buying up remaindered or out-of-copyright books and reselling them as cheap literature. However, as James J. and Patience P. Barnes observe, despite his 'publish[ing] relatively little original fiction [. . .] occasionally he made an exception, as in the case of Mary Botham Howitt'.[13] Based on reading 'A Night-Scene', Tegg offered Howitt £1,000 in 1839 for a series of thirteen children's books 'to illustrate as he said "household virtues"', and, as biographer Amice Lee comments, though the series was 'never advertised, the books went through many editions', most

THE SPIDER AND THE FLY. 53

—And now, dear little children, who may this story read,
To idle, silly, flattering words, I pray you ne'er give heed :
Unto an evil counsellor, close heart, and ear, and eye,
And take a lesson from this tale, of the Spider and the Fly.

F 3

Fig. 5.3 Tailpiece, 'The Spider and the Fly', by Mary Howitt, *The New Year's Gift and Juvenile Souvenir*, 1829. Courtesy of the Baldwin Library of Historical Children's Literature, Special and Area Studies Collections, George A. Smathers Libraries, University of Florida.

of them reprinted (or pirated) in the United States.[14] In this respect, Howitt pioneered the idea of creating a book series for children. Her titles included *Strive and Thrive* (1839), *Hope On, Hope Ever* (1840) and *Work and Wages* (1842), though the second of these titles and one other may have been written by William Howitt since, as Howitt explained in the preface to her last series book, 'two were written by my husband at a time when I was otherwise unavoidably occupied' – presumably during the time of her last pregnancy and the birth of her daughter Margaret in 1839.[15]

Howitt's final book in the series, *My Own Story* (1844), was another important innovation: an autobiography of childhood written not from the perspective of life's end but from its middle (Howitt was then forty-five and the mother of both grown and young children). Wordsworth's landmark autobiography of childhood, *The Prelude*, would not become public until six years later, and the subject was then relatively uncommon. Howitt's midlife autobiography ended with Mary and her sister Anne Botham's departure from home to attend school. This choice, when the end point of Howitt's life had not been reached, meant that hers could not be a teleological account in service to spiritual ends or claims to prominence. However, Rebecca Styler sees a strategic rhetorical purpose insofar as Howitt's 'entirely secular' autobiography capped her series books' presentation of family virtues with a loving, idealised model of family life and early childhood.[16] In the childhood autobiography, Howitt also shares her notions of what children's literature should and should not do as she recalls the early books she and her sister were given:

> The books which we had then were very different to those which children have now-a-days. They were externally mostly square, and bound, many of them, in beautiful paper. [. . .] Beautiful books they were to look at on the outside; but alas! – I grieve to say it – they were very dry within. At that time the Taylor's charming Original Poems, and more charming Nursery Rhymes, were not written – nor had any of Maria Edgeworth's earlier ones penetrated into our out-of-the-world region. Our books bore such titles as The Castle of Instruction, The Hill of Learning, The Rational Dame, and so on; and seemed written on purpose to deter children from reading.[17]

Later she details how she and her sister turned from reading children's literature, in part inspired by John Aikin and his sister

Anna Barbauld's *Evenings at Home*, to composing their own, thus becoming child writers as well as readers.[18]

Howitt's comments, published a decade after *Sketches of Natural History* appeared, help shed light on the earlier volume's aesthetic and ethical approach. Clearly, like many other pioneering early nineteenth-century children's writers, Howitt affirmed that books written for children should inspire delight and curiosity rather than offering rigid moral lessons, and like her non-teleological narrative in *My Own Story*, the most notable 1834 poems did not aim to teach or wrench her subject matter into overt lessons or worship of God's creation. 'The Spider and the Fly' will always remain the volume's best-known poem, but other notable poems in the volume anticipate elements of contemporary environmental writing, particularly their commitment to viewing flora and fauna as co-inhabitants of earth that exist as intrinsically valued life forms apart from any human use – except children's delight in reading about them.

Mary Howitt's love of nature and natural observation is evident in *Forest Minstrelsy* and in *My Own Story*, which abound in natural description and delight in gardens.[19] In contrast to contemporary eco-poets, she harboured no anxieties about the Anthropocene or awareness of the dangers it would increasingly pose. But she represented the fundamental interconnection of all living things – animals, plants and humans – in *Sketches of Natural History*, a position that resembles the 'ethical commitment to the lives of nonhuman creatures' as ends in themselves that today underlies animal studies, environmental writing and eco-poetry.[20] Domination of nature is never her point (though one poem has imperialist and racist overtones).[21] She mentions flora and fauna in passing as creations of God several times, but she also sidesteps explicit religious teaching or assertions that the created earth exists for the use of humankind. And in the final poem I discuss, on the unlikely topic of 'The Water-Rat', she goes further: she celebrates the animal she praises and memorably brings it before her readers as a living being of intrinsic worth like the humans whom she encourages to appreciate the water rat and all other living things in the animal's 'tangled bank' of residence. This is a peaceable, vegetarian creature whose only fear of harm comes from human beings – members of the reading audience, in short.[22] Rather than insisting on anthropocentric utilitarian relations of flora and fauna to humans, *Sketches* as a whole encourages children's joy, merriment, wonder and delight in animals' and plants' existence as companionable life-forms on earth.

As an illustrated children's book designed for the interactive consumption of word and image, *Sketches of Natural History* participated in the new media innovations of its time. Illustrated children's books dated back to the eighteenth century, but most of these were steel-engraved. Thomas Bewick's great innovation in *History of British Birds* (1797, 1804) was to create woodcut illustrations that enabled text and image to appear on the same page in an interactive relationship visually and ideationally.[23] Significantly, Howitt's volume was inspired by her husband's and children's huddling around Bewick's volumes and reacting to their illustrations, particularly the tailpiece vignettes at the end of each entry:

> My husband used to amuse our children with off-hand explanations of Bewick's vignettes. It is impossible to describe the fascination of those evening hours, when the father, with the children clustered round him or on his knee, told the imaginary story of the wonderful picture. [. . .] My little poetical sketches had reference to Bewick's woodcuts of birds and animals, and were written down because the children liked them.[24]

Sketches was published by Effingham Wilson, the publisher of Alfred Tennyson's first volume, *Poems, Chiefly Lyrical* (1830) and Robert Browning's *Paracelsus* (1835). Eric Nye classes Wilson as a radical publisher, though by the 1830s, according to Nye, his radicalism was modulating into a kind of advanced liberalism. The telling connection to the press for Howitt, however, was that the year before *Sketches* appeared, Wilson published her husband's *Popular History of Priestcraft*, which went into five editions.[25] Both the Howitts, then, had become allied to an advance guard of innovative publishers. Mary's 1834 volume was generously illustrated, with twenty-four woodcuts in all, counting the kingfisher frontispiece and swallows on the title page. These were engraved by Ebenezer Landells, who himself has a place in new media history as an apprentice to Thomas Bewick at fourteen and later as a principal motivator and initial proprietor of *Punch Magazine*.[26] Mary expressed dissatisfaction with the illustrations in her 1889 *Autobiography*: 'I [. . .] made my appearance from [Effingham Wilson] in a very humble guise, a small square volume, with poor woodcuts, entitled "Sketches of Natural History"; in a very unattractive form, I thought, in comparison with Mrs. Austin's "The Story without an End," which Wilson has just before published.'[27] But the reviewers did not agree, and Christian Johnstone, who devoted generous space to the new volume in *Tait's Edinburgh Magazine*, averred, 'The publisher and artist have executed their respective departments as if desirous of doing due honour to these sweet inspirations of maternal love. The engraver almost deserved to have had his name on the title page, in company with that of Mary Howitt' – testimony to the integral multimodality of *Sketches*.[28]

The poems anticipating modern eco-poetry stand out from the volume's more traditional fare, with which I begin. The opening two poems, 'The Coot' and 'The Camel', emphasise God's beneficence, and the second salutes an animal marked by utilitarian use for humans. Both lyrics model behaviours obliquely encouraged in children. The coot models bravery and trust in God when its nest is picked up by a sudden 'mountain flood' and carried over a waterfall to the sea as it travels safely in its 'little ark';[29] the camel is characterised by its generous kindness to the humans it safely carries across deserts, so gentle it 'Might'st be guided by a child'.[30] Both are illustrated in their natural environments, the coot amidst sedges and bulrushes by running water over which a visiting kingfisher flies, the camels in arid open spaces led by children of colour. Self-evidently, the perspective in the latter poem is human-centred.

Anthropocentrism by way of anthropomorphism also characterises several poems focused on promoting childish delight and imagination. Clearly the flattering spider-host and timid fly are stand-ins for humans in 'The Spider and the Fly'. And 'The Monkey' celebrates 'nature's punchinello', who resembles a merry, energetic and rather naughty ('roguish') child who frisks about, pretends to sleep yet 'takes a peep' at a proffered nut.[31] Perhaps the absence of an illustration in this case is a deliberate decision not to fix the creature's species so that it blurs the line between animal and human (which is fitting since the two are linked scientifically). 'The Nettle-King' is one of the poems representing flora rather than fauna and is an allegory of the cost of overweening human pride. As the nettle grows, so does its lust for power, and it exults, 'I am as great as a plant can be!' as its expanding height and breadth strangle nearby plants.[32] It even has the power to frighten any child who wanders nearby. But its exultation is literally cut short when a 'Woodman stout' passes by and smartly cuts it at the root with a single swipe of his scythe.

Yet the last two lines turn the poem in a different direction. The first stanza mentions that within the nettle's canopy 'there was a toad that sate below, / Chewing his venom sedate and slow', that is, turning poison into nourishment in one of nature's symbiotic relationships.[33] After the woodman tramples the nettle into the ground, 'he saw where the Toad in its shadow lay, / But he said not a word, and went his way'.[34] Under no threat from the toad, the woodman respects its independent life and walks away. The nettle's lesson about aggressive power and domination is overturned and replaced in the final two lines by the alternative lesson of coexistence with nonhuman forms of life. Landells's accompanying engraving positions the human woodman at the centre as his scythe strikes the nettle's root, but the toad is nowhere to be seen – reinforcing the fitness of the lowly toad's secret, ongoing life in the woods, which the child reader is invited to imagine but cannot directly see.

'The True Story of Web-Spinner' uses anthropomorphism in unexpected ways as well, in this case as one of the volume's poems offering scientific information in a delightful guise. The poem is a gothic horror tale of an evil spider that lives in a corner of his seven-storey house and lures in guests that he then pounces upon and kills with grisly gusto before eating them. When faced with a large, elegant bluebottle, he has to improvise and cleverly ties up the large visitor with thread spun from its own body and hoists it up to await feasting bit by bit. When a 'Magistrate' bursts in, the murderer escapes through a trapdoor, and its body is never found. To this ballad horror story Howitt attached a prose gloss, dissipating children's potential fears by explaining that the details came from a human observer's natural history account of a spider in his house whose behaviour supplied every detail in the poem, down to the spider's spinning its thread around a bluebottle and hoisting it up to the highest elevation in its excavated multilevel living space. Together, poem and gloss give child readers both the thrill of a horror story and a model of what patient scientific observation of living forms in the environment can reveal about fascinating behaviours in the animal world. Notably, in terms of the attitudes toward all living things that the volume encourages, the spider, too, escapes at the end, like the toad; the point is not to squash the loathsome creature but to learn about the natural world from it.

The wonder that can accompany scientific learning about nature marks 'The Long-Tailed Titmouse Nest'. The title references an English bird whose wondrous nest, Howitt claims, outdoes the famous Asian tailorbird. This is a xenophobic note to be sure. But then the child reader can actually go visit the nearby titmouse nest, which Howitt describes in minute detail:

all knit together [are]
Moss, willow-down, and many a feather;
So soft, so light, so wrought with grace,
So suited to this green-wood place,
And spangled o'er, as with the intent
Of giving fitting ornament,
With silvery flakes of lichen bright,
That shine like opals, dazzling white!
Think only of the creature small,
That wrought this soft and silvery ball,
Without a tool to aid her skill;
Nought but her little feet and bill –
Without a pattern whence to trace
This little roofed-in dwelling-place.[35]

Inside, astonishingly, are '*sixteen* merry things alive – / Sixteen young chirping things, all set / Where you, your little hand could not get!'[36] Admiration is the keynote here, encouraging children to cultivate an enlarged sense of the wonder of animal life nearby and the curiosity to observe it with no harm done to observer or observed.

Perhaps the most fascinating of the scientifically oriented poems is one that may register the new findings of Georges Cuvier and Charles Lyell but seems more directly inspired by William Buckland's pamphlet on a fossilised elephant and other 'antediluvian' bones found in a Yorkshire cave in 1821.[37] This poem is 'The Fossil Elephant', which cuts between old and new geology by emphasising a time before humans existed, when huge animals were 'kings of all the world'[38] and there were no ships, no buildings, 'no silver and no gold' (Fig. 5.4).[39] This can be read as a corrective to human pride in domination and 'progress'. For the poem closes with the foretelling of the world's end in a fiery apocalypse, which suggests that all attempts to dominate nature fail and that humanity, like these large creatures of old, are ephemera fated to disappear from the face of the earth.

A more distinctly ecological orientation emerges in 'The Beaver' and its preceding illustration, which provides a vivid image of

Fig. 5.4 Ebenezer Landells, illus., 'The Fossil Elephant', in *Sketches of Natural History*, by Mary Howitt (London: Effingham Wilson, 1834), preceding p. 19. Courtesy of Special Collections, Mary Coutts Burnett Library, Texas Christian University.

what a child's eye would rarely see. This poem provides an even more direct corrective to human pride and human impulses to dominate creation than 'The Fossil Elephant', for the beaver, as presented by Howitt, exists on an equal plane with humans in skill and knowledge, as evidenced by its remarkable building skills. To approach the beaver's home, she explains, is to see 'a mighty work [. . .] / That would do no shame to human hands', a 'well-built dam' that can 'stem the tide' of a strong, wide 'northern river', with 'fairest masonry' that 'The waters cannot o'erpass'.[40] Not only is the beaver as 'wise' as an 'old learned [human] sage', but in some ways the beaver's possession of knowledge is the more impressive. It can carry out sophisticated building projects without books. And, thanks to the beaver's creator, the beaver knew 'as much' five thousand years ago 'as now ye know'.[41] Juxtaposed to the beaver's accomplishments, 'man's' achievements are rather puny:

But man! How hath he pondered on,
Through the long term of ages gone;
And many a cunning book hath writ,
Of learning deep, and subtle wit;
Hath compassed sea, hath compassed land,
Hath built up towers and temples grand,
Hath travelled far for hidden lore,
And known what was not known of yore,
Yet after all, though wise he be,
He hath no better skill than ye![42]

The poem additionally denies superior virtue to humankind, first because the beaver, 'As gentle and mild as a Lamb at play', models a distinctive ethic of care, securing life to its families: 'Happy they live 'mong kith and kin – / As happy as living things can be, / Each in the midst of his family!'[43] Second, and more important, beavers are 'peaceable creatures'[44] that model coexistence with others who are not like themselves, and thus they are fit moral instructors of humankind:

Ay, there they live and the hunter wild
Seeing their social natures mild,
Seeing how they were kind and good,
Hath felt his stubborn soul subdued;
And the very sight of their young at play
Hath put his hunter's heart away;
And a mood of pity hath o'er him crept,
As he thought of his own dear babes and wept.*[45]

Here, notably, it is a human, not an animal, that is 'wild' and in need of being 'subdued'. And the beaver, according to Howitt's asterisked footnote ('*A Fact') achieved this softening of the human heart in actuality. Like 'The Nettle-King', 'The Beaver' actively promotes the preservation of animal life in English woods and an ethic of coexistence while also gently endorsing family virtues and avoidance of human pride in knowledge or morality.

I conclude this look at *Sketches of Natural History* with the poem that is closest to modern eco-poetry, 'The Water-Rat'. That the title is so unpromising, given the negative associations summoned by the very word 'rat', makes its overt embrace of the animal world all the more emphatic. On the one hand, the poem offers pure joy in another being for its own sake. On the other, the poem obliquely insists that humans see themselves in relation to all living things, not above them, and value their intrinsic worth. And more overtly than in some poems, 'The Water-Rat' actively critiques human depredations on the environment.

The image engraved by Landells shows the water rat environed by water, flora and fauna (note the birds and ducks in the sky) (Fig. 5.5). With this visual prelude immediately above, the poem, too, represents not a solitary animal but an ecosystem complete with a scientific floral term:

I'll shew you a sight you love better than these,
A little field-stream overshadowed with trees,
Where the water is clear as a free mountain-rill,
And now it runs rippling, and now it is still;

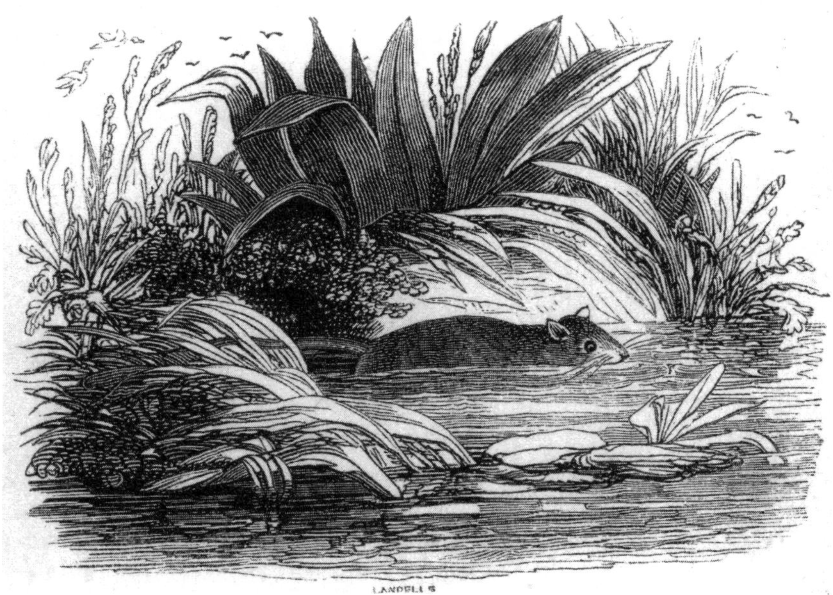

Fig. 5.5 Ebenezer Landells, illus., 'The Water-Rat', in *Sketches of Natural History*, by Mary Howitt (London: Effingham Wilson, 1834), preceding p. 47. Courtesy of Special Collections, Mary Coutts Burnett Library, Texas Christian University.

Where the crowned Butomus is gracefully growing,
Where the long purple spikes of the Loose-strife are blowing,
And the rich, plumy crests of the Meadow-sweet seem
Like foam which the current has left on the stream;
There I'll shew you the brown Water-Rat at his play –
You will see nothing blither this blithe summer day;
A glad, innocent creature, for whom was ordained
The quiet of brooks, and the plants they contained.[46]

The poem's opening eight lines, which reference humans involved in merry haymaking at a distance and invite the reading audience to come into a meadow, are patterned in four lines per sentence in the poem's tripping measure of anapestic tetrameter verse. With the poem's 'arrival' at the meadow and the new scene it unfolds, Howitt deliberately shifts to an alternate pattern: a single twelve-line sentence in which every element is connected to everything else. The performative syntax of interconnectedness alone conveys the sentence's complete thought. And in the meantime, the speed of the anapests reinforces the speed of the flowing water and its rippling sounds, together preparing for the rat's own quick, merry movements.

This same ecosystem also supplies all the water rat's wants so that it can live in peacable harmony with his surroundings, taking only what will grow back:

He has not a want which he cannot supply
In a water like this, with these water-plants nigh;
And he asketh no bounty from man; he can find
A plentiful table spread out to his mind;
For this little field-stream hath all good that he needs,
In the budding tree-roots and the clustering reeds,
And the snowy-flowered arrow-head thick growing here.[47]

The creature's self-sufficing coexistence with its surroundings is counterpointed throughout by the water rat's principal threat: humankind. Howitt here directly conveys judgement of human violence against other living things by deliberately juxtaposing the threats humans pose to fellow creatures with the gentle water rat's merry playfulness – when no human, not even the poet and child-reader, are present:

A glad, innnocent creature, for whom was ordained
The quiet of brooks, and the plants they contained.
But hush! Step as lightly as leaves in their fall;
Man has wronged him, and he is in fear of us all.
See! there he is sitting, the tree-roots among,
And the Reed-sparrow by him is singing his song.
See how gravely he sits; how demure and how still,
Like an anchorite old at his mossy door-sill!
Ah, no, now his mood of sedateness is gone,
And his harlequin motions he'll shew us anon.
Look! Look now! How quickly the water he cleaves,
And again he is up 'mong those arrow-head leaves;
See his little black head, and his eyes sparkling shine.[48]

Of course, the human element is virtually present if safely hidden. Still, the human observer elicits a second judgement of the danger humanity poses to the water rat – 'Ah, pity it is man has taught him to fear!'[49] – before the poem resumes celebrating the water rat's playful merriment. It concludes with the gentle creature's symbiotic relationship with his environment as he creeps into his burrow to sleep the winter away. The sustained joyousness of the poem, aided by its chiming rhymes, is best appreciated when the whole (too long for reproducing here) is read straight through, as Howitt's gossamer light verse imparts complementary delight without diverging into sentimentality or prosiness. In many ways, the pure, disinterested joy and gladsome recognition of a fellow earthly creature is the poem's strongest ecological message that checks the human urge to place themselves at the centre of nature and all creation.

Sketches did not lead to an immediate sequel in the same vein. Though the title of Howitt's 1838 volume for children, *Birds and Flowers and Other Country Things*, is promising, its longer poems point to a slightly older child-reader, and the sure, light touch and simplicity of her verse when she wrote for her own children in *Sketches* is diminished when she writes a frankly commercial book for other people's children, though it, too, was warmly received. Howitt's preface to *Birds and Flowers* reveals its origins in the book market: 'It being the intention of the Publishers of this little work, to bring out, at the close of each year, a volume for the young, to be entitled THE CHRISTMAS LIBRARY, I have been engaged by them to furnish the material for the volumes.'[50] As a whole, these poems are more human-centred, more willing to show the use of flora and fauna for humans, though 'Summer' also evokes a woodland ecosystem of plant and animal life-forms (with the water rat making a cameo appearance). 'The House-Sparrow' and gloss, one of the lengthiest selections, treats 'Jack Sparrow' as a kind of country rough who is mischievous and calculating and lacks charm ('The bully of his tribe – to all beyond / The gipsey, beggar, knave, and vagabond!' according to the final couplet).[51] Shockingly, as a sequel to the 1834 poetic *Sketches*, the appended prose gloss to 'The House-Sparrow' reveals that the poet and her family had the sparrows shot at, and at least one was killed after the sparrows harrassed and prevented the peaceable martins from nesting. Here humans are free to dominate other creatures after all. Even the title page of *Birds and Blooms* disappoints compared to *Sketches*: rather than presenting animals in their environments, disparate species are arranged symmetrically on tree branches and reed-like plants as if posed for a daguerreotype. Perhaps the most memorable poem of *Birds and Flowers* is its grimmest, 'The Carrion-Crow', which stints nothing in detailing the bird's grim sustenance from death but does so without judgement or an extraneous lesson.[52]

The contrast between Howitt's 1834 and 1838 volumes is less a judgement on Howitt's poetic skill than an indication of just why her 1834 *Sketches of Natural History* is indeed a new media innovation. Its illustrations and Howitt's verse built upon the prior innovations of literary annuals, Bewick's woodcuts, Romantic descriptive poetry and the turn toward delight and imagination in children's literature. But from an environmental standpoint, its most notable poems and illustrations invited children to comprehend the interconnectedness of all living things, to envision themselves in relation to the natural world, not above it, and to reject longstanding assumptions of human entitlement and human domination of the earth.

Notes

My thanks to Mason Patterson, Addie Levy Research Associate (2022–23), as well as to Julie Christenson, Rare Book Librarian, and Kerri Menchaca, Library Specialist, in Special Collections, Mary Couts Burnett Library, Texas Christian University, for assistance with images.

1. Virginia Woolf, 'Aurora Leigh', *The Second Common Reader* (1932), reprinted in *Aurora Leigh*, by Elizabeth Barrett Browning, edited by Margaret Reynolds (New York: Norton, 1996), 439. Exceptions to the erasure of Howitt include scholars Carl Woodring, Brian Maidment, Paula Feldman, Linda Peterson, Karen Karbiener and Joanne Shattock. In *Serial Forms: The Unfinished Project of Modernity, 1815–1848*, (Oxford: Oxford University Press, 2020), Clare Pettitt devotes a chapter to the biopolitics of *Howitt's Journal*, co-edited by Mary and William Howitt.
2. Katherine D. Harris, *Forget Me Not: The Rise of the British Literary Annual, 1823–1835* (Athens: Ohio University Press, 2015), 38, 114–20.
3. For a brief discussion of Howitt's poem 'The Morning Walk', published next to John Clare's 'Sonnet' in *Friendship's Offering* (1831), see my article 'Women Poets and the Poetess Tradition', in *Victorian Literature: Criticism and Debates*, ed. Lee Behlman and Anne Longmuir (London: Routledge, 2015), 82.
4. No exhaustive bibliography of Mary Howitt's publications is available. Her complete works may never be fully known since she published prolifically under signature and anonymously in multinational books and periodicals. My assertion about the initial date of her participation in annuals is based on a partial search of the HathiTrust database.
5. Mary Howitt, 'Mountain Children', *Winter's Wreath* (London: George C. Whittaker and George Smith, 1829), 397–8. Howitt's first stanza was admirably suited to a view of Ambleside in the Lake District:

   Dwellers by lake and hill!
   Merry companions of the bird and bee,
   Go gladly forth, and drink of joy your fill,
   With unconstrained step, and spirit free!

6. The couple married on 16 April 1821 and went on a tour of Derbyshire; before this date, William had been contributing poems and a series of rural sketches under the pseudonym 'Wilfred Wender' entitled 'A Pedestrian Pilgrimage of Five Days' to the *Kaleidoscope*, a Liverpool periodical in which Washington Irving's *Geoffrey Crayon* sketches were published. Mary may have collaboratively written 'A Pedestrian Pilgrimage' with William almost from the start, since his 3 July 1821 continuing instalment included a poem by 'Wilfreda Wender'. In 1822, after the couple hiked across Scotland,

they published, as Linda Peterson notes, 'A Scottish Ramble' in the *Mercury* in 1824, signing themselves as 'Wilfred and Wilfreda Wender'. See Linda H. Peterson, *Becoming a Woman of Letters: Myths of Authorship and Facts of the Victorian Market* (Princeton: Princeton University Press, 2009), 99. For details of the wedding of the Howitts, see Carl Woodring, *Victorian Samplers: William and Mary Howitt* (Lawrence: University of Kansas Press, 1952), 9–10.

7. William and Mary Howitt, *The Desolation of Eyam* (London: Wightman and Cramp, 1827), title page; Mary Howitt, *An Autobiography*, ed. Margaret Howitt, 2 vols. (London: William Isbister, 1889), 1:176.
8. See Woodring, *Victorian Samplers*, 23. Woodring speculates that the volume travelled to the family of Professor Andrews Norton, the father of Charles Eliot Norton, in Boston.
9. Karen Karbiener, 'Scribbling Woman into History: Reconsidering a Forgotten British Poetess from an American Perspective', *Wordsworth Circle* 32, no. 1 (2001): 49.
10. See my *Victorian Women Writers and the Other Germany: Cross-Cultural Freedoms and Female Opportunity* (Cambridge University Press, 2022), 59–65, for discussion of Howitt's print multimedia innovations in children's literature in the *Child's Picture and Verse Book: Commonly Called Otto Speckter's Fables* (1844) and cross-cultural young adult novel, *Which is the Wiser?* (1842).
11. Woodring, *Victorian Samplers*, 33.
12. Amice Lee, *Laurels and Rosemary: The Life of William and Mary Howitt* (London: Oxford University Press, 1955), 114.
13. James J. Barnes and Patience P. Barnes, 'Reassessing the Reputation of Thomas Tegg, London Publisher, 1776–1846', *Book History* 3 (2000): 56.
14. Lee, *Laurels and Rosemary*, 114.
15. Mary Howitt, *My Own Story; or, the Autobiography of a Child* (London: Thomas Tegg, 1844), vii.
16. Rebecca Styler, 'Revelations of Romantic Childhood: Anna Jameson, Mary Howitt, and Victorian Women's Spiritual Autobiography', *Life Writing* 11, no. 3 (2014): 317. As Styler astutely remarks, Howitt's 1845 venture, unlike a spiritual biography, gives 'a model of ideal family life to complete her popular series for the common reader'.
17. Howitt, *My Own Story*, 29. Howitt refers to the children's verse volumes *Original Poems for Infant Minds* by Ann Taylor Gilbert (1782–1866) and her sister Jane (1783–1824), published from 1804 to 1805.

18. Howitt, *My Own Story*, 98.
19. See, for example, Howitt, *My Own Story*, 112–14.
20. See, for example, John Miller, 'The Evolving Forms of Animal Studies', *Victorian Studies* 62, no. 2 (2020): 308.
21. 'The Swallow', the volume's penultimate poem, traffics in imperialist and racist rhetoric yet simultaneously questions automatic assumptions of British superiority. The poem opens with the poet asking where the swallow has been in its six months' migration and imagining its flight across the Middle East and Africa, as well as its encounters with foreign peoples. Some inscriptions of racial difference seem neutral, for example, depictions of the Arab storyteller. But Howitt swerves into racist diction in referencing the 'Caffres'. And the poem ends thus:

    Tell but this, we'll leave the rest,
    Which is wisest, which is best;
    Tell, which happiest, if thou can,
    Hottentot or Englishman? –
    Nought for answer can we get,
    Save twitter, twitter, twitter, twet!

    While her likely audience would expect the implied answer to her last question to be the white Englishman, the bird is perfectly indifferent to the question and speaks an alternative, distinctive language. Hence, the question remains intriguingly unresolved. See Mary Howitt, *Sketches of Natural History* (London: Effingham Wilson, 1834), 159–62.
22. The British 'water rat' is actually the European water vole; unlike the carnivorous rat, the water vole feeds on vegetation alone.
23. Ina Ferris, 'A Bookish Intervention: Thomas Bewick's *British Birds* and the Reconfiguration of Illustrated Natural History', *Romanticism* 28, no. 1 (2022): 74–6.
24. Howitt, *An Autobiography*, 1: 241. Howitt dedicated *Sketches of Natural History* to her children Anna Mary and Alfred William. Both Ferris and Hilary Thompson note that Bewick himself termed his tailpieces 'tale-pieces'. His small vignettes, often depicting humans, followed the larger-sized illustrations of birds and explanatory text and encouraged readers to imagine scenarios for what the tailpieces pictured. See Ferris, 'A Bookish Intervention', 82, and especially Hilary Thompson, 'Enclosure and Childhood in the Wood Engravings of Thomas and John Bewick', *Children's Literature* 24 (1996): 13.
25. Eric W. Nye, 'Effingham Wilson, Radical Publisher of the Royal Exchange', *Publishing History* 36 (1994): 87–96.

26. Patrick Leary, *The Punch Brotherhood: Table-Talk and Print Culture in Mid-Victorian London* (London: British Library, 2010), 13, 140–4. For Landells's brief apprenticeship with Bewick, see Amanda-Jane Doran, 'Landells, Ebenezer (1808–1860)', *Oxford Dictionary of National Biography* (online edition), 2004.
27. Howitt, *Autobiography*, 1:241.
28. [Christian Johnstone], 'Mary Howitt's Sketches of Natural History. Dr. Bowring's Minor Morals for Young People', *Tait's Edinburgh Magazine* 1 (August 1834): 446. Note the first billing given to Howitt, though Johnstone began with Bowring.
29. Howitt, *Sketches of Natural History*, 2, 4.
30. Ibid., 5, 8.
31. Ibid., 13, 18.
32. Ibid., 39.
33. Ibid., 38.
34. Ibid., 41.
35. Ibid., 131.
36. Ibid., 132.
37. See 'Buckland – on Antediluvian Fossil Bones', *Quarterly Review* 27 (July 1822): 459–76. Carl Woodring observes that Howitt stays prudently within the biblical limit of Ussher's 6,000 years, as did Buckland in calling the fossils 'antediluvian' (Woodring, *Victorian Samplers*, 33).
38. Howitt, *Sketches of Natural History*, 21.
39. Ibid., 20.
40. Ibid., 67–8.
41. Ibid., 69.
42. Ibid., 70.
43. Ibid., 67, 68. I borrow 'ethic of care' from Talia Schaffer, *Communities of Care: The Social Ethics of Victorian Fiction* (Princeton: Princeton University Press, 2021).
44. Howitt, *Sketches of Natural History*, 68.
45. Ibid., 68–9.
46. Ibid., 48.
47. Ibid., 50–1.
48. Ibid., 49–50.
49. Ibid., 51.
50. Mary Howitt, *Birds and Flowers and Other Country Things* (London: Darton and Clark, 1838), v.
51. Ibid., 178.
52. Ibid., 125–8.

6

Literature, Media and the 'Advertising System'

Richard Salmon

During the first wave of historical studies of advertising, the first half of the nineteenth century was often dismissed as a relatively insignificant period. Writing in his seminal essay 'Advertising: The Magic System', Raymond Williams argued that the 'Industrial Revolution, and the associated revolution in communications, fundamentally changed the nature of advertising' but that this transformation did not immediately give rise to distinctively modern advertising forms.[1] By the 1850s, advertising practices and media, he claimed, were still largely unchanged from the previous century, and it was not until the late nineteenth century that 'the formation of modern advertising' was clearly established in tandem with the development of a new 'corporate' phase of capitalism.[2] In *The Commodity Culture of Victorian England: Advertising and Spectacle, 1851–1914*, Thomas Richards identified an earlier turning point in the development of organised forms of commodity spectacle in the Great Exhibition of 1851, but he took a largely similar view to Williams of earlier nineteenth-century advertising and likewise argued for a time lag of some thirty years after this epochal event for its effects to be fully realised in advertising practices. Prior to the Great Exhibition, according to Richards, 'the year 1851 had found advertising in a primitive state', and even after the event, mid-century advertising commonly had 'modest objectives and paltry means'.[3]

Both Williams and Richards, however, were convinced of the importance of the cultural and ideological shifts embodied by the development of modern advertising. Advertising should be understood not merely as a genre of print or textual production but as a new 'medium' and a 'major form of modern social communication' to be analysed in relation to its 'economic, social, and cultural' impacts.[4] More recent studies, though, have called into question the historical accuracy of these accounts, drawing attention to advertising culture in the early to mid-nineteenth century, prior to the widespread application of new technologies of visual reproduction. In particular, literary scholars of the Romantic period, such as John Strachan and Nicholas Mason, have demonstrated that the 'common genealogy' of literature and advertising from the late eighteenth century produced a rich field of intertwined commercial practices and mutual parody or satire.[5] Early nineteenth-century advertisements for products such as shoe blacking and cosmetics, for example, often drew on the form of poetry to devise advertising 'jingles', leading in turn to W. F. Deacon's literary parody *Warreniana* (1824), which imagined celebrated Romantic poets such as Wordsworth and Byron 'being paid to provide advertising copy' for Robert Warren, a manufacturer of branded shoe blacking and one of the most prominent advertisers of the period.[6]

Advertising also impinged on popular fiction genres of the 1820s and 1830s, blurring the boundaries between literary and commercial discourse. The 'fashionable' ('silver fork') novels of this period were sometimes suspected of informally advertising the branded commodities consumed by their wealthy protagonists – an early form of 'product placement'.[7] Similarly, with monthly serialised fiction in the format pioneered by Dickens's *Pickwick Papers* (1836), the novel was printed with an advertising supplement, sometimes yielding a surprisingly sustained dialogue between the literary text and its advertising paratext.[8] Mason accordingly dismisses as 'myth' the notion that 'advertising did not begin to assume its modern forms until the late nineteenth century', contending that 'by the dawn of the nineteenth century [. . .] advertising [had] emerged as a system'.[9] This revisionist account draws on the earlier work of the advertising historian T. R. Nevett, who, contrary to Williams, argued that 'the first half of the nineteenth century was the period during which advertising evolved into something akin to its present form'.[10]

Support for this claim draws primarily on the recognition that the 'growth of advertising' was 'linked inextricably with the development of newspapers'.[11] During the period covered by this volume, advertisements were generally published in two primary media: the periodical press and what can loosely be termed 'street advertising'. Nevett records that the annual total number of newspaper advertisements rose from 801,083 in 1820 to 1,933,476 in 1845, and that expenditure on newspaper advertising in Britain doubled from £252,340 to £507,540 over the same period.[12] At the same time, Nevett suggests that the long-standing taxation duties levied on individual newspaper advertisements (the source of the above figures) 'may actually have helped to stimulate the growth of alternative advertising media'.[13] Notwithstanding these impressive figures, the tax on advertisements (not abolished until 1853) constrained the growth and potential of newspaper advertising during this period. The tax contributed to what many contemporary observers saw as an anarchic proliferation of advertising in the public spaces of London and other British cities: a medium characterised by James Dawson Burn in 1855 as the 'language of the walls'.[14] Both of these media were prominently featured in critical commentaries and satires on advertising during the period, often within the same text.

In this chapter, I discuss a significant cluster of critical writings published in the early 1840s that demonstrate some of the ways in which contemporary literary authors responded to these new forms of advertising, alongside some of the advertising texts with which they engaged. Thomas Carlyle's *Past and Present* (1843) – his influential account of the 'Condition of England' – is often cited in histories of Victorian advertising, but the extent of this book's engagement with advertising culture and the significance of advertising to Carlyle's broader cultural critique has not been fully acknowledged. Known for a passage deriding a 'seven feet' tall effigy of a hat paraded through the streets of London as an embodiment of 'English Puffery', *Past and Present* also links newspaper advertisements for patent medicines to the discourse of social reform. Carlyle's critical text conveys a sense of the cultural pervasiveness of advertising at this historical moment, which is similar to Abraham Hayward's account of the 'Advertising System' in a lengthy review essay for the *Edinburgh Review*, also published in 1843. Long before Williams's characterisation of advertising as 'the magic system' and preceding the organised commodity spectacles of the later nineteenth century, early Victorian critics such as these were conscious of advertising as an increasingly unavoidable cultural practice.

Advertising and periodical criticism

Numerous essays on advertising were published in the periodical press from the 1820s to the mid-1840s that discussed its distinctive features and wider cultural implications from a variety of perspectives. While most of these commentaries voiced concerns, sometimes in humorous or satirical form, not all of them were straightforwardly dismissive or condemnatory. For some, advertising was a distinct 'art' that rivalled or was equivalent to more established literary forms. While this view was ironically expressed in Thomas Hood's 'The Art of Advertizing Made Easy' [*sic*], published in the *London Magazine* in February 1825, it was presented more seriously in 'On Advertisements; and Advertising, Considered as One of the Fine Arts', published in *Tait's Edinburgh Magazine* in September 1835, and in 'Advertising Considered as an Art', from *Chambers's Edinburgh Journal*, December 1844. For the writer in *Tait's,* advertising has an aesthetic dimension because it appeals to the 'imagination of the Public, by the exercise of your own imagination, combined with factual experience'.[15] As 'the imagination is boundless', so the scope for artistic invention within advertising is 'illimitable'; elevating 'desire' and 'temptation' above material need, successful advertisers are not restrained by an obligation to truth or even plausibility.[16] Somewhat cynically, the writer advises prospective advertisers to 'always remember to suggest largely to the imagination, and insist upon your power of realizing its desires', even if the result amounts to a 'lie'.[17] The artfulness of advertising is also emphasised by the writer for *Chambers's*, who considers the more informal, less explicit types of advertisement commonly described as 'puffs', for example, when a brand name is casually inserted into a newspaper paragraph ostensibly on a different topic. 'In this department of advertising, literary resources of a high character are necessary', the writer contends, since 'the great aim is to weave the various advertisements into the text without allowing the non-experienced reader to detect them'.[18] Here, advertising composition is seen as an exercise of literary craft capable of blending seamlessly with other forms of fictional writing.

Abraham Hayward's 1843 essay 'The Advertising System' stands out from other periodical commentaries of the time as a broader account of the sheer presence of advertising and commercial spectacle in British society prior to the Great

Exhibition. Mason describes it as 'the most important essay on British advertising from the first half of the nineteenth century', although he does not discuss it in any detail.[19] The essay is nominally a review of two recent French novels concerned with advertising, Honoré de Balzac's *César Birotteau* (1841) and *Histoire de M. Jobard* (1842) by Cham, neither of which is examined beyond the title particulars and initial framing of the discussion. Instead, Hayward offers a sweeping characterisation of contemporary advertising culture supported by a miscellaneous catalogue of examples. While 'The Advertising System' does not provide a particularly cohesive analysis of the ways in which different manifestations of advertising embody an overarching economic and ideological structure, as its title might suggest to readers versed in modern cultural or media theory, it nevertheless contains some striking generalised observations. For example, 'there is no disguising it, the grand principle of modern existence is notoriety; we live and move and have our being in print. [. . .] The universal inference is, that, if a man be not known, he cannot be worth knowing'.[20] Mediation through print as the condition of 'modern existence' is rendered synonymous with advertising in its broadest sense. Moreover, Hayward aims to show 'that no trade, profession, walk, or condition in life is entirely free' from 'modern puffery'; social life is already saturated with advertising culture.[21]

Writing in the early 1840s, Hayward observed a shift in the relationship between advertising and higher forms of literature from the earlier decades of the nineteenth century while maintaining a sense that these forms were not categorically different. It was no longer common for advertisements to feature adapted extracts from canonical poets or specially composed verse jingles as it was in the 1810s and 1820s when Lord Byron was reputedly employed as an advertising copywriter for Warren's Blacking. Prose was now the preferred literary genre for adaptation to print advertising, according to Hayward, yet 'there is no denying that Advertisements constitute a class of composition intimately connected with the arts and sciences'.[22] The essay offers a considered view of the place of advertising within a broader spectrum of modern cultural forms, rather than outright condemnation of its questionable moral basis. Like most commentators of the period, Hayward acknowledges that advertisers practice deception through the illusions they create. At the same time, he is far from certain of the instrumentality of advertising, of whether it stimulates desire or indifference in the reader-viewer. It is unclear 'what is likely to be the effect of living in an atmosphere of falsehood [. . .] where nobody says what he means, or means what he says – where every thing is seen through the smoked glass of interest, or the Claude Lorraine glass of flattery – where copper gilt passes current for gold'.[23] The deceptive practice does not necessarily lead to its intended result. Despite the article's imposing title, then, Hayward presents advertising more as a miscellaneous collection of unpredictable acts of persuasion than as a totalising 'system' heralding the seamless integration of production and consumption within an advanced commodity culture. Nevertheless, as a marker of the development of advertising during the first half of the nineteenth century, the terminology is significant. Nearly a decade later, in the final instalment of a series of articles for *Fraser's Magazine* published under the title 'The Age of Veneer', George Henry Francis argued in similar but more emphatic terms that 'puffery' had become 'regularly reduced to a system':

> The practical adoption of the science [of advertising] in any extended and systematic form has grown up almost under our own eyes. It is barely older than the Stephenson locomotives. The non-risen generation will, indeed, reckon it among the great world-changing inventions whose development it has been their privilege to witness. Catholic Emancipation, Reform Bills, and a few trifles of that sort, will be thrust back into the second rank; but steam locomotion and the puff-advertisement system will stand forth as the grandest of world-phenomena – as the symbols of the strides which society has made during the past quarter of a century.[24]

For Francis, the 'science of puffing' is one concrete manifestation of a broader cultural propensity to be swayed by a 'superficial' and illusory spectacle: the 'art of veneering the public mind'.[25] Situating the growth of print advertising in an even wider cultural and historical scope, 'The Age of Veneer' offers a more comprehensive interpretation of its significance than Hayward's accretive approach to describing the effects of the 'system'. The more portentous tone of the later critique shows the influence of Carlyle's intermediate commentary on advertising 'phenomena'.

Carlyle and advertising spectacle

This study is not the first to cite *Past and Present* as a significant reference point in nineteenth-century responses to advertising culture. Generally, though, Carlyle is seen as an unsophisticated critic of advertising, whose moralistic judgements are mentioned only in passing. Mason, for example, dismisses Carlyle's 'rants against the evils of modern advertising', although his focus is on earlier Romantic-period writing.[26] More substantively, Richards uses *Past and Present* as evidence of the 'very small scale' of advertising in Britain in the decades preceding the Great Exhibition.[27] In this book, he suggests that 'practically all advertising takes place in the streets. Far from being carefully arranged in a clean, well-lighted space, Carlyle's advertisements are part of the unplanned and unregulated contagion of London street life'.[28] This indicates that the forms of advertising observed by Carlyle are not 'modern' but rather are remnants of a traditional culture of urban spectacle rendered 'obsolete' after 1851.[29] Richards's argument is based primarily on book 3, chapter 1 of *Past and Present*, titled 'Phenomena', in which Carlyle discusses a series of grotesque, phantasmagorical urban spectacles, culminating in the 'great Hat seven-feet high, which now perambulates London streets', considered by Carlyle's fictitious persona Sauerteig to be the 'culminating and returning point, to which English Puffery has been observed to reach'.[30] Carlyle refers here to a type of street advertising popularised in the late 1820s and 1830s by a hatmaker named Perring who decided to promote his wares by mounting a giant effigy of a hat emblazoned with his brand name and address on the Strand on a horse-drawn carriage (Fig. 6.1).

In their illustrated history of Victorian advertising, Diana and Geoffrey Hindley note that Perring justified this innovation in his advertising handbills, which describe a 'HAT ON WHEELS [. . .] perambulating the town daily, reminding the observer where good cheap hats may be bought'.[31] More grandiosely, Perring promoted his specialty brand of 'Light Hats' with the promise that 'A LIGHT HAT is of the greatest importance to the studious; it allows our ideas to expand and prevents depression of the spirits'.[32] For Carlyle, the 'seven-feet' hat became a visual emblem of 'this all-deafening blast of Puffery' that encapsulates the nightmarish condition of England.[33] The inflated size of the effigy in relation to the modest item of clothing which it represents graphically reveals

Fig. 6.1 W. Weir, 'Advertisements', in *London*, ed. Charles Knight (London: Knight, 1843), 5:38.

the disconnection between 'sham' and reality, providing a visual embodiment of 'puffery' in action (the etymology of the word suggesting an enlargement of size beyond the natural dimensions of an object). Carlyle views the 'self-trumpeting Hatmaker' as 'the emblem of almost all makers, and workers, and men, that make anything' in the modern world.[34] The spectacle of Perring's mobile advertisement overshadows the labour required to produce useful objects.

> [I]nstead of making better felt-hats than another, [the hatter in the Strand] mounts a huge lath-and-plaster Hat, seven-feet high, upon wheels: sends a man to drive it through the streets; hoping to be saved *thereby*. He has not attempted to *make* better hats, as he was appointed by the Universe to do [. . .] but his whole industry is turned to *persuade* us that he has made such.[35]

Characteristically, Carlyle does not see a 'comic' side to the grotesquerie of this mode of representing commodities. It is, rather, a 'tragic' spectacle that such phenomena are an increasingly familiar urban presence: 'that we view him as a thing of course, is the very burden of the misery'.[36]

While Richards views such innovations in street advertising as premodern elements of commodity culture, he notes that by the 1840s 'the streets of London were clogged with the effigies of things'.[37] As indicated above, restrictions on newspaper advertising during this period led advertisers to devise what Strachan terms 'multi-media strategies' for promoting their products.[38] In addition to the use of sandwich boards and advertising vans, other forms of mobile advertising included the placing of ads on the exterior of horse-drawn omnibuses (from 1829) and, later on, inside buses (from the 1840s). Static street advertising largely took the form of posters ('bill-sticking') or, less frequently, the writing of advertising messages directly onto walls. Altogether, Strachan concludes, London was 'saturated with the language and imagery of advertising'.[39] Carlyle was not the only contemporary observer to protest the incursions of advertising into public space. In 'The Age of Veneer', Francis described the difficulty of avoiding advertising messages in different media whilst traversing the city streets:

> If one takes a cab, they come flying in sheaves in at the windows. If one enters an omnibus, the roof is lined and the seats covered with them. [. . .] Upon the kerbstone, traced in black, is the outlined coffin, with the puff of the dealer inscribed therein. Is the street blocked when one wishes to cross? We will lay you ten to one that five out of the ten vehicles are lumbering parallelopipeds [*sic*], covered with typography, gilt tea-cannisters on wheels, japanned and colossal boot-legs, rival Brobdignagian [*sic*] tea-kettles, and supernatural coffee-pots, or some other of the multifarious tribe of what, in theatrical parlance, would be termed 'property' advertisements.[40]

Francis vehemently denounced the 'demoralization' caused by the 'modern system of puffing', which afflicted manufacturers and consumers alike.[41] He endorsed Carlyle's 'bitter' commentary on the 'poor hatter', recognising the urgency of Carlyle's 'mission [. . .] to demolish "shams"', though Francis was more sympathetic to the economic rationale behind Perring's advertising campaign: 'even if our friend the hatter had made articles of unrivalled quality, his skill would be wholly wasted, unless he used some glaring, eye-attracting means of letting the world know of it'.[42]

In 1846, a correspondent to the *Times* similarly complained of the 'nuisance' of mobile street advertising, lamenting 'the entire destruction of the retail trade which is taking place through the walking placards and advertising vans being allowed to perambulate through the great thoroughfares' and urging that 'something ought to be done to remedy so crying an evil'.[43] By the 1850s, street advertising had reached a level of saturation that provoked legislative countermeasures. Advertising vehicles of the kind that promoted Perring's Light Hats were prohibited by the London Hackney Carriage Act of 1855, ostensibly on the grounds of obstructing traffic rather than for any moral objection to their promotion of 'shams'. Looking back over recent decades in *A History of Advertising from the Earliest Times*, published in 1874, Henry Sampson thought there had been a decisive shift and improvement in public advertising practice from the first half of the century resulting from this and other reforms: 'The huge vans, plastered all over with bills, which used to traverse London, to the terror of the horses and wonder of the yokels, were improved off the face of the earth a quarter of a century ago; and now the only perambulating advertisement we have is the melancholy sandwich-man and the dispenser of handbills'.[44] Likewise, according to Sampson, the practice of 'bill-sticking', which Dickens had memorably described in a *Household Words* article of 1851, was no longer a 'disfigurative' trade in which rival operatives deliberately pasted over competing advertisements, resulting in an illegible palimpsest of advertising messages: 'habits have changed very much for the better', he declared.[45]

Advertising and the 'maladies of Society'

Advertising plays a more extensive role in Carlyle's diagnosis of the 'Condition of England' than his discussion of the 'seven-feet Hat' alone suggests. While the references to street advertising in *Past and Present* have received some critical attention, albeit cursory and dismissive, his use of one of the most famous branded commodities of the nineteenth century – Morison's Universal Pills – within the same text has attracted surprisingly little notice. Book 1, chapter 4 of *Past and Present*, titled 'Morrison's Pill' [*sic*], and book 3, chapter 15, 'Morrison Again' [*sic*], directly allude to the exorbitant claims made by contemporary advertisements for patent medicines. Moreover, Morison's Pills were extensively advertised in the newspaper press and other periodical forms, broadening the scope of Carlyle's critique beyond urban spectacle. The references to Morison's Pills in *Past and Present* are abstract and detached from any material space or concrete visual form. In 'The Advertising System', Hayward specifies that 'the boldest appeals to credulity are made by those who profess to cure diseases or improve personal appearance', in other words, by manufacturers and vendors of patent medicines, clothing and cosmetic products.[46] Both patent medicine and clothing/cosmetic advertisers appealed to the consumer through promises of personal transformation, bodily health and cure. As historians of advertising have shown, the manufacturers of these two types of commodities pioneered advertising strategies in the eighteenth and nineteenth centuries; significantly, both feature in Carlyle's examination of advertising culture. As Richards observes, 'the essence of every patent medicine's claim was that it, and it alone, possessed the one true remedy, the magic potion, the healing draught, the elixir of life'.[47] Advertising campaigns for patent medicines thus sought to promote a 'therapeutic system by and through which English consumers might construe their bodies as a field for advertised commodities'.[48] Richards does acknowledge that Carlyle 'perceived this conjuncture of cure-alls' in *Past and Present* and 'transformed a quack's pill into an emblem of all easy solutions to persistent social problems'.[49] In the following discussion, I develop this insight in greater textual detail and set it in a wider context of the use of advertising in political discourse of the 1840s.

Early on in *Past and Present*, Carlyle implicitly compares his authorial stance as a prophetic social critic to the role of an advertiser, only to disavow this connection by issuing a firm disclaimer. In response to the imagined reader's question, 'what is to be done, what would you have us do?', he dismisses the notion that there is 'some "thing," or handful of "things," which could be done' to cure this 'social malady':

> Brothers, I am sorry I have got no Morrison's Pill for curing the maladies of Society. It were infinitely handier if we had a Morrison's Pill, Act of Parliament, or remedial measure, which men could swallow, one good time, and then go on in their old courses, cleared from all miseries and mischiefs! [. . .] There will no 'thing' be done that will cure you. There will a radical universal alteration of your regimen and way of life take place; there will a most agonising divorce between you and your chimeras, luxuries and falsities take place; a most toilsome, all but 'impossible' return to Nature, and her veracities, and her integrities take place: that so the inner fountains of life may again begin, like

> eternal Light-fountains, to irradiate and purify your bloated, swollen, foul existence, drawing night, as at present, to nameless death! Either death or else all this will take place. Judge if, with such diagnosis, any Morrison's Pill is like to be discoverable.[50]

Carlyle understands that by venturing to characterise the condition of England through metaphors of disease and malady, he casts himself in an authoritative professional role as diagnostic interpreter of the health of the nation. But to suggest a 'remedial measure' for the diseased social body places him in a position uncomfortably close to that of the medical 'quack', whose branded products – usually in the form of pills or ointments – promised to cure all manner of illnesses and were vociferously promoted in print media. The more radical the writer's social critique or suggestions for reform, the more he runs the risk of appearing to offer a 'universal' solution for social problems of the kind familiar, in the realm of individual bodily health, to readers of classified ads. Carlyle is thus at pains to announce that he has no 'cure' for the manifold social problems of poverty and injustice described in *Past and Present*; readers of the book should not approach it as an advertising text. Of course, Carlyle's attempt to distance his work of cultural criticism from the discourse of advertising could be said to produce its own version of a familiar sales pitch. His desired 'return to Nature' and to the 'inner fountains of life' are themselves redolent of the generic language of contemporary advertisements for medical and cosmetic products. In so vehemently denouncing the 'quack', Carlyle associates his message with that of 'true Heroes and Healers', echoing a standard rhetorical gesture of brand advertising: accept no imitations, only the original and true remedy. Later in the text, it becomes clear that Carlyle's rejection of the 'Morrison's Pill hypothesis' also implies a mistrust of religious doctrines that offer a panacea to believers (who 'have only to swallow once, and all will be well').[51] However compromised, though, this appeal to an 'inner' truth and source of authority points to a desire to evade the heavily mediated language of advertising: 'The clearer my Inner Light may shine, through the *less* turbid media; the *fewer* Phantasms it may produce, – the gladder surely shall I be, and not the sorrier!'[52] While no act of self-reflection can produce entirely unmediated, spontaneous insight, advertising represents a particularly opaque example of 'turbid media', through which any source of light is heavily filtered.

Roy Porter notes that 'the advent of newspaper advertising constituted an epoch in quack medicine promotion by vastly multiplying the number of potential buyers accessible to a vendor'.[53] In the 1830s, James Morison began extensive advertising in the press for his 'Vegetable Universal Pill', a laxative that was claimed to purify the blood. Containing only 'natural' ingredients (including rhubarb and aloe), Morison's Pills were recommended for consumption in large doses of up to thirty pills per day. The numerous testimonials that accompanied advertisements often advised purchasers whose ailments were not immediately cured to go on consuming more pills until they were. Morison established an institute, the 'British College of Health', to promote his products, presenting himself as a 'Hygeist' rather than an ordinary vendor of medicines, and was thereby able 'to turn the selling of health into a cause and crusade'.[54] Morison's Pills were marketed as a type of what would now be called 'alternative medicine', a more natural remedy than the treatments provided by the medical establishment. In response, Porter notes, medical professionals such as Thomas Wakley, editor of the *Lancet*, sought to expose Morison as a quack and campaigned against the unregulated sale of patent medicines.[55] There were also many humorous satirical responses to Morison's Pills in visual and literary form that emphasised the dangers of overconsumption.[56] By the 1840s, Morison's Universal Pills were both a hugely successful commercial brand and a notorious example of the deceptive illusions of advertising. For Hayward, James Morison – who died in 1840 – was literally a victim of his own publicity, 'a martyr to his own fame':

> When the cases, necessarily rare, in which his pills had failed, were mentioned, he invariably said that the patients wanted faith, and should have gone on taking them till they got well. In his last illness his practice corresponded with his theory; he rejected all other medicine, took more pills as he grew worse, and was in the very act of calling for a fresh box when he expired.[57]

Four years earlier, in 1836, a London apothecary and associate of Morison, Robert Salmon, was convicted of the manslaughter of John McKenzie as a result of his excessive prescription of Morison's Pills. Salmon was fined £200 and cautioned not to repeat the offence, a warning which he seems to have ignored.[58]

The role of nineteenth-century print advertising in the dubious success of Morison's Pills and other patent medicines has been examined by several cultural historians. The notion of advertising as a medium widely invested with magical properties – Williams's 'magic system' – lends itself to, and perhaps reflects, the desired efficacy of medicinal commodities. Writing about the development of advertising in an American context, Jackson Lears observes that patent medicines 'held out the promise of new life and dramatic self-transformation', corresponding to advertising's 'modern version of a magical worldview'.[59] Similarly, Sara Thornton points out the congruence between print advertising as a medium and the medicinal 'pill' as a product: 'In the advertisement, the law of the knife, of surgery, is avoided in favour of the pill, which is a magical remedy even though its effects are quite as violent as the illnesses themselves.'[60] Whereas other forms of medical intervention promised, at best, a painful means of restoring the body to health, pills appeared to offer an easy cure, no more demanding than reading the advertisement in which its magical effects were described. The author of 'Advertising Considered as an Art' in *Chambers's Edinburgh Journal* made precisely this analogy between the print medium and the advertised commodity when they remarked that readers of advertisements 'seem condemned to be taking ocular doses of Potts' pills, till you are as familiar with the name of Potts as you are with that of Newton or of Shakespeare'.[61] The advertisement itself performs the ascribed function of the pill; though only appealing to the visual ('ocular') sense of the consumer, it has the sedative or therapeutic effect of a 'dose'.

More broadly, Carlyle's application of advertising discourse to the 'maladies of Society' in *Past and Present* broaches the relationship between advertising, social class and radical politics within the early Victorian period. One aim or implication of Carlyle's message to readers of the book ('I advise thee to renounce Morrison; once for all, quit hope of the Universal Pill') may have been to discredit more radical solutions to the 'Condition-of-England Question' by associating them with the quackery of patent medicine advertisers.[62] Carlyle's well-known view of Chartism as an authentic but chimerical and destructive expression of working-class suffering seems congruent with his use of Morison's Pill as a metaphor for social remedy. This more radical response to social injustice may hold out the promise of more comprehensive reform akin to the search for a 'universal' cure, but through Carlyle's analogy with the language of advertising, such panaceas appear superficial and glib. As such, his advice to 'renounce Morrison' could plausibly be read as a warning of the dangers of involvement in the Chartist movement. Whether advertising itself, as a cultural form often portrayed as vulgar and disreputable, held wider associations with political radicalism or even with working-class culture is more difficult to establish. According to Richards, Victorian print advertising was largely associated with 'middle-class periodicals': 'Until the very end of the nineteenth century advertising consisted almost entirely of the bourgeoisie talking to itself'.[63] Strachan, however, convincingly demonstrates that advertising played a significant role within early nineteenth-century periodicals aimed at a working-class readership. While some radical journalists refused to publish advertisements on principle, others embraced the practice, whether through economic necessity or because they saw nothing wrong with doing so. Henry Hunt – most famous for his role in the reform movement which led to the Peterloo Massacre in 1819 – was also a manufacturer of shoe blacking (amongst other products), who unashamedly used his political credentials to support the targeted advertising of his business to supporters. This was only one example of 'brand proprietors or shopkeepers overtly pitching their advertisements at the ideological sympathies of radical readers'.[64] Even the leading Chartist weekly newspaper, *The Northern Star* (1837–52), incorporated an advertising page aimed at its largely working-class readership featuring copious advertisements for patent medicines.[65]

Indeed, advertisements for Morison's Pills were regularly inserted in the early issues of *The Northern Star*. On 20 January 1838, for example, Robert Salmon (mentioned above) published a 'Manifesto' that claimed to expose the sale of 'spurious imitations' of Morison's Pills and declared his own company (Salmon and Hall) to be the 'sole proprietors' of the 'Original' product.[66] In a second 'address' published the following month, Salmon explained that he had left his former position as an associate of Messrs. Morison, claiming that since 1835 pills sold under their name had not been made to the original recipe and that only Morison's Pills accompanied by his own signature on the packet were the authentic product. Joshua Hobson, editor of the *Star* at the time, is listed on these advertisements as an authorised retailer of Salmon's Morison's Pills, which could be purchased from the offices of the newspaper in Leeds. Over the ensuing months, the

Star printed several advertisements for 'THE ORIGINAL MORISON'S PILLS, OR UNIVERSAL MEDICINE', as 'prepared only by Salmon and Hall'.[67] But then, in October 1838, it published a riposte from James Morison describing Salmon's product (alongside those of other rival manufacturers) as itself a 'spurious imitation': 'None can be genuine without the words "MORISON'S UNIVERSAL MEDICINES" [. . .] engraved on the Government Stamp, in white letters upon a red ground' (Fig. 6.2).[68]

Henceforth, the *Star* appears to have endorsed the version of Morison's Pills supplied by Morison and the British College of Health within its advertising pages. In March 1841, after the death of James Morison, it published the notice of a legal judgement won by the family firm against 'certain Impostors for counterfeiting their medicines', seemingly issued as an advertisement-cum-threat of legal action.[69] Hobson, though, does not appear to have been an authorised retailer of the brand of Morison's Pills stamped by the British College of Health. It is perhaps not coincidental, then, that from around 1840 other proprietary medicines were far more frequently advertised in *The Northern Star* than Morison's Pills. In addition to brands such as Frampton's Pill of Health, Holloway's Pills and Ointment (a cure for 'all diseases'), Kerman's Celebrated Golden Packets of Specific Medicines (pills for gout and rheumatism as well as a 'Universal Ointment'), and various treatments for venereal disease, the product most persistently advertised by and associated with the *Star* was Parr's Life Pills.

The first advertisement for Parr's Life Pills appeared in *The Northern Star* in September 1840. It took what was to become the customary form of a testimonial from Thomas Parr, 'Old Parr's Last Will and Testament', a fictitious document purporting to date from 1630. Reputedly 'the oldest man, with one exception, which England ever produced', Parr – according to the legend – lived to the age of 152 years, married his first wife at age 88 and remarried at 120. The secret to Parr's longevity was an herbal remedy, which, much like Morison's Pills, was claimed to effect 'perfectly miraculous' cures to all manner of diseases whose origins lay in the impurity of the blood: 'Cases of every description have all been cured simply by the use of PARR'S LIFE PILLS, thus showing that what has been considered different disorders, and requiring different treatment, all originated in the same cause, and can be cured by one uniform treatment'.[70] Like Morison's Pills, then, Parr's Life Pills were marketed on the grounds of their universality, rather than

MORISON'S PILLS,

OF THE BRITISH COLLEGE OF HEALTH, LONDON.

CAUTION.

WHEREAS spurious imitations of my Medicines are now in circulation, I, JAMES MORISON, the Hygeist, hereby give notice, that I am in *no wise* connected with the following Medicines purporting to be mine, and sold under the various names of "*Dr. Morrison's Pills*," "*The Hygeian Pills*," "*The Improved Vegetable Universal Pills*," "*The Original Morison's Pills, as compounded by the late Mr. Moat*," "*The Original Hygeian Vegetable Pills*," "*The Original Morison's Pills*," &c. &c.

That my Medicines are prepared only at the British College of Health, Hamilton Place, King's Cross, and sold by the General Agents to the British College of Health and their Sub-Agents, and that no chemist or druggist is authorised by me to dispose of the same.

None can be genuine without the words "MORISON'S UNIVERSAL MEDICINES" are engraved on the Government Stamp, in white letters upon a red ground.—In witness whereof I have hereunto set my hand.

JAMES MORISON,
The Hygeist.

British College of Health, Hamilton Place, New Road, May, 1838.

Sold by W. STUBBS, General Agent for Yorkshire, at 56, Cross-Church-Street, Woodhouse, Leeds, to whom applications for Agencies must be made, and the following regular appointed Agents.

Leeds, Mr. W. H. Walker, stationer, 27, Briggate, and Mrs. Senior, No. 1, South Market.
Sheffield, Mr. Badger, 47, West-street.
Bradford, Mr. Stead, grocer, Market-street.
Doncaster, Mr. Clayton, perfumer, &c.
Wakefield, Mr. Nichols and Son, printers.
Halifax, Mr. Hartley, stationer.
Huddersfield, Mr. Thornton, tailor.
Dewsbury, Mr. Brown, furniture warehouse.
Bawtry, Mr. Grosby, Stamp-office.
Aberford, Mr. Wilkinson, draper.
East Witton, Mr. Mc Collah.
Knaresbro' and Harrogate, Mr. Langdale stationer.
Pontefract, Mr. Standish, artist.
Richmond, Mr. Norman, grocer.
Ripon, Mr. Vant, tailor.
Rotherham, Miss Wilson, post-office.
Selby, Mr. Richardson, draper.
Barnsley, Mr. Harrison, stationer.
Skipton, Mr. Tasker, printer.
Tadcaster, Mr. Bee, perfumer, &c.
Wetherby, Mr. Sinclair, bookseller
Paddock, Mr. Allison, grocer.
Hightown, Mr. Lister, bookseller.
Middleham, Mr. Close.
Sherborne, Miss Johnson, draper.
Otley, Mrs. Fox, grocer.
Beeth, Mr. Close.

Fig. 6.2 Advertisement for Morison's Pills, *Northern Star* 1 (6 October 1838): 1.

as treatments for specific complaints. Joshua Hobson was listed in advertisements as an approved wholesale supplier of Parr's Life Pills from the offices of *The Northern Star*, and, as in the case of Morison's Pills, advertisements often warned consumers against inefficacious counterfeit products.[71] An interesting example of the extent to which advertising for Parr's Life Pills was targeted specifically at the working-class, Chartist readership of the newspaper can be seen in an advertisement from 2 July 1842 headed 'LOVE OF COUNTRY'. Beginning with an appeal to the reader's 'patriotism', the advertisement points out that the 'strength and bulwark of any nation lies in the happy frames of her Sons and Daughters' whereas 'in the pale and languid invalid, there is seldom the spirit to maintain an independent position when assailed by the insidious or threatening attacks of the Oppressor'.[72] Healthy bodies are required to support the stance of liberty and resistance espoused by Chartism, and for this purpose consuming Parr's Life Pills can be beneficial:

> In Politics, every one seems to be well-acquainted with the various evils that afflict society, and yet, but few are found sufficiently enlightened or bold enough to prescribe a remedy. It is just so with the diseases incident to the human frame; all can talk of and lament their existence, and yet few indeed can be found to point out the means, sufficiently within the reach of all men, for obtaining their removal. The extensive use of Parr's Life Pills has, however, dispelled the mist of ignorance, and tens of thousands who have been cured of the most inveterate maladies are now gratefully employed in recommending their more general adoption. If every family in the kingdom would keep a supply of this incomparable Medicine by them, premature old age would never happen, and seldom indeed should we behold in our streets the pale and haggard look, the consumptive cheek, or tottering debility; we should rise as a people and improve as a nation.[73]

Here, the analogy between individual bodily disease and the 'maladies of Society' invoked by Carlyle in *Past and Present* is more fully developed but in a direction that runs counter to Carlyle's critique of the illusory promises of advertising. The argument presented in the advertisement suggests that just as finding a 'remedy' for social ills falls to those 'sufficiently enlightened or bold', so curing the ills of the body requires sound advice. Once the 'means' for achieving the latter are recognised, however, it becomes easier to address the former as well: with healthier bodies, 'we should rise as a people and improve the nation'. The advertisement thus makes a direct claim for the efficacy of Parr's Life Pills in fostering the conditions for social reform or even revolution. Given the careful alignment of this text with both the ideological stance and commercial interests of the newspaper in which it appeared, it seems plausible that it may have been written by a member of the *Star's* editorial staff. The paragraph quoted above was followed by a testimonial letter attributed to William Hick, also a staff member at the *Star's* office, documenting 'very many cases of extraordinary cures [that] have occurred among the aged workpeople, both male and female', including one in which 'an aged couple, enfeebled by disease and debilitated by premature old age [. . .] were persuaded to try a few boxes of Parr's Life Pills, and in a week were restored and strengthened that they could pursue their employment with pleasure and profit'.[74] The persistent promotion of Parr's Life Pills as a miracle cure – 'the wonder of the age' – in the advertising pages of *The Northern Star* cannot simply be dismissed, then, as an extraneous commercial feature of the paper's production, at odds with, or irrelevant to, its editorial and campaigning functions (Fig. 6.3).[75]

It is not my aim in this chapter to consider whether the advertising of patent medicines played a useful role in supporting Chartist periodicals through commercial revenue and by helping their readers to imagine radical cures to social problems, or whether – as Carlyle thought – it merely promoted a delusive panacea, inadequate to the disease in need of remedy. Rather, both Carlyle's *Past and Present* and *The Northern Star* have served to illustrate some of the ways in which advertising practices of the 1830s and 1840s informed wider literary discourse: here, that of political reform and the Condition of England debate. It is evident that the prominent role of patent medicines within the early development of modern advertising gave a unique inflection to the coalescence of individual and collective narratives around what Richards terms the 'therapeutic commodity'.[76] As Strachan puts it, 'Advertising offers the possibility of personal reinvention and renewal', a discourse that was readily available for wider societal applications.[77]

Similarly, during this period, advertising addressed both individual reader-consumers, through specifically targeted newspapers and other periodical forms, and the wider public realm, through the medium of urban spectacle. While newspapers themselves

PARR'S LIFE PILLS.

THE amazing Cures performed by this Medicine are truly astonishing. Instances are occurring daily of persons who were almost at death's door being restored to sound and vigorous health. The following are selected from hundreds of a similar nature. Forwarded by Mr. Mottershead, Chemist, Market-place, Manchester.

"To the Proprietors of Parr's Life Pills.

"Gentlemen,—I feel it my duty, for the good of suffering mankind, to send you this true statement of the astonishing effects which Parr's Life Pills have produced upon me, and also upon my wife and daughter. Myself and wife have both been strangers to good health for nearly twenty years, until we accidentally heard tell of your Pills, which we have taken for several weeks, and their effects upon us have been almost miraculous, both now feeling young, strong, and in health; my daughter, also, has found them equally beneficial.

"You may refer any one to me who at all doubts the truths of this, and you may make any use you think proper of this testimonial.—I remain, in health,

"Your obliged, grateful servant,

"JAMES LESCHERIN,

"Grove-place, Ardwick,

"near Manchester."

"Witness—JOHN WHITWORTH."

"May 13, 1841."

Sir,—I am happy to add my evidence as to the efficacy of Parr's celebrated Pills, having been long ailing with a complication of disorders in the Head, Stomach, and Liver, and now, since taking two of your boxes of Pills, I am quite restored to a perfect state of health. You may make whatever use of this you please, only I think the good effects ought to be made public.

"I am, Sir, yours, obliged,

"CHAS. EDWD. HARDERN."

"Oldham, April 30, 1841."

Sir,—Mrs. Sarah Stansfield, of Dale-street, Salford, says, after taking two 2s. 9d. boxes of Parr's Life Pills, she has received more benefit from their use than from any medical advice or medicine she has been able to procure. She has been afflicted with Sick Head-ache and Bilious Complaints for a period of seven years, and has scarcely passed a day during that time without pain, until taking the above Pills, and now, is happy to say, she is quite recovering.

(Signed)

"SARAH STANSFIELD.

"April 17, 1841."

"Stalybridge, April 13th, 1841.

"Sir,—My brother, William Carnson, No. 8, John-street, Butcher-gate, Carlisle, was cured of Gravel by taking two boxes of Parr's Life Pills; Betty Marey, of Stalybridge, has been cured of a Head-ache of many years' standing, by taking three boxes of Parr's Life Pills, after spending many pounds with doctors; John Taylor, a man who fell into the canal, and afterwards broke out in blotches all over his body, the doctors could do nothing for him; a person that had tried the Pills advised him to get some; he did, and is now perfectly restored, and many others I do not remember. I am much better myself for taking Parr's Pills. I will inform you more fully in a short time of more cases.

"I remain, dear Sir,

"Your obedient servant,

"J. CARNSON.

"To Mr. Mottershead, Manchester."

Fig. 6.3 Advertisement for Parr's Life Pills, *Northern Star* 5 (2 July 1842): 2.

were often shared amongst readers, collective experiences of public space were increasingly infiltrated by street advertising of the kind observed by Carlyle in the form of the 'seven-feet' hat. Advertising spectacle was characteristically anarchic and unregulated during the early Victorian period, in contrast to the more orchestrated mid- to late nineteenth-century world of trade fairs and expositions, but no less pervasive. Indeed, for many contemporary observers, advertising already appeared to have reached saturation levels within print culture and public space well before the middle of the century. Advertising amounted to a 'system': a unitary method of representing objects as branded commodities – and, by extension, people as commodified brands – which encompassed seemingly disparate fields of cultural life. Both formal paid advertisements for named products and informal techniques of 'puffery', which sought to manipulate the publicity of individual brands within print media while concealing their commercial interests, were components of this overarching 'advertising system'. The 'system' also extended to 'literature' – to the very writers whose critical reflections this chapter has discussed. The arguments made by Carlyle against advertising spectacle were presented with the knowledge that he, too, could be suspected of belonging to the system.

Notes

1. Raymond Williams, 'Advertising: The Magic System', in *Problems in Materialism and Culture* (London: Verso, 1980), 173.
2. Ibid., 177–9.
3. Thomas Richards, *The Commodity Culture of Victorian England: Advertising and Spectacle, 1851–1914* (Stanford: Stanford University Press, 1990), 6.
4. Williams, 'Advertising: The Magic System', 185. In a similar vein, see Jennifer Wicke, *Advertising Fictions: Literature, Advertisement, and Social Reading* (New York: Columbia University Press, 1988).
5. Nicholas Mason, *Literary Advertising and the Shaping of British Romanticism* (Baltimore: Johns Hopkins University Press, 2013), 5.
6. John Strachan, *Advertising and Satirical Culture in the Romantic Period* (Cambridge: Cambridge University Press, 2007), 2.
7. William Hazlitt, for example, wrote in the *Examiner* in 1827, 'You dip into an Essay or a Novel, and may fancy yourself reading a collection of quack or fashionable advertisements'. Quoted in Edward

Copeland, *The Silver Fork Novel: Fashionable Fiction in the Age of Reform* (Cambridge: Cambridge University Press, 2012), 18.

8. See Andy Williams, 'Advertising and Fiction in *The Pickwick Papers*', *Victorian Literature and Culture* 38, no. 2 (2010): 319–35; and Emily Steinlight, '"Anti-Bleak House": Advertising and the Victorian Novel', *Narrative* 14, no. 2 (2006): 132–62.
9. Mason, *Literary Advertising*, 6, 13.
10. T. R. Nevett, *Advertising in Britain: A History* (London: Heinemann, 1982), 25.
11. Ibid., 16.
12. Ibid., 26–8.
13. Ibid., 28.
14. For a critical discussion of Burn's text, see Sara Thornton, *Advertising, Subjectivity and the Nineteenth-Century Novel: The Language of the Walls* (Houndmills: Palgrave Macmillan, 2009), 48–53.
15. 'On Advertisements; and Advertising, Considered as One of the Fine Arts; in Which the Theory and the Practice Are Combined', *Tait's Edinburgh Magazine* 2 (September 1835): 575.
16. Ibid., 576.
17. Ibid.
18. 'Advertising Considered as an Art', *Chambers's Edinburgh Journal* 52, n.s. (28 December 1844): 402.
19. Mason, *Literary Advertising*, 123.
20. [Abraham Hayward], 'The Advertising System' [review of *César Birotteau* by Honoré de Balzac and *Histoire de M. Jobard* by Cham], *Edinburgh Review* 77 (February 1843): 2.
21. Ibid., 4.
22. Ibid.
23. Ibid., 43.
24. [George Henry Francis], 'The Age of Veneer', *Fraser's Magazine* 45 (January 1852): 90.
25. [George Henry Francis], 'The Age of Veneer', *Fraser's Magazine* 42 (October 1850): 441.
26. Mason, *Literary Advertising*, 138.
27. Richards, *Commodity Culture*, 20.
28. Ibid.
29. Ibid., 21.
30. Thomas Carlyle, *Past and Present* (London: Chapman and Hall, 1843), 191.
31. Diana Hindley and Geoffrey Hindley, *Advertising in Victorian England, 1837–1901* (London: Wayland, 1972), 87.

32. Ibid.
33. Carlyle, *Past and Present*, 190–1.
34. Ibid., 195.
35. Ibid., 192.
36. Ibid. This passage echoes Wordsworth's famous phrase, the 'burden of the mystery', in 'Tintern Abbey' (from *Lyrical Ballads*, 1798).
37. Richards, *Commodity Culture*, 48.
38. Strachan, *Advertising and Satirical Culture*, 16.
39. Ibid., 22; see also Nevett, *Advertising in Britain*, 56–9.
40. Francis, 'The Age of Veneer', *Fraser's Magazine* 45 (January 1852): 91.
41. Ibid., 93.
42. Ibid.
43. Quoted in Nevett, *Advertising in Britain*, 58–9.
44. Henry Sampson, *A History of Advertising from the Earliest Times* (London: Chatto and Windus, 1874), 31.
45. Ibid., 26–7. See also Charles Dickens, 'Bill-Sticking', *Household Words* 2 (22 March 1851): 601–6.
46. Hayward, 'The Advertising System', 4.
47. Richards, *Commodity Culture*, 178.
48. Ibid., 183.
49. Ibid., 188.
50. Carlyle, *Past and Present*, 30–1.
51. Ibid., 282.
52. Ibid., 33–4, 305–6.
53. Roy Porter, *Health for Sale: Quackery in England, 1660–1850* (Manchester: Manchester University Press, 1989), 117.
54. Ibid., 231.
55. Ibid., 225–9.
56. See Strachan, *Advertising and Satirical Culture*, 76–80.
57. Hayward, 'The Advertising System', 8.
58. See Strachan, *Advertising and Satirical Culture*, 78.
59. Jackson Lears, *Fables of Abundance: A Cultural History of Advertising in America* (New York: Basic Books, 1994), 42–3.
60. Thornton, *Advertising, Subjectivity and the Nineteenth-Century Novel*, 117.
61. 'Advertising Considered as an Art', 401.
62. Carlyle, *Past and Present*, 305.
63. Richards, *Commodity Culture*, 7.
64. Strachan, *Advertising and Satirical Culture*, 146–7, 66–9.

65. I am grateful to Victoria Clarke for drawing my attention to this point during discussions of her research on *The Northern Star*. See Clarke, 'Reading and Writing *The Northern Star*, 1837–1847' (PhD thesis, University of Leeds, 2020).
66. *Northern Star* 10 (20 January 1838): 1.
67. *Northern Star* 12 (3 February 1838): 1; 19 (24 March 1838): 1; 39 (11 August 1838): 1; 40 (18 August 1838): 1; 45 (22 September 1838): 1; 46 (29 September 1838): 1.
68. *Northern Star* 47 (6 October 1838): 1. The notice was reprinted on 13 October, 10 November and 8 December 1838; 4 May, 7 September, 2 November and 28 December 1839.
69. *Northern Star* 173 (6 March 1841): 2.
70. *Northern Star* 163 (26 December 1840): 6.
71. *Northern Star* 173 (6 March 1841): 2; 181 (1 May 1841): 2; 208 (6 November 1841): 2; 212 (4 December 1841): 2.
72. *Northern Star* 5 (2 July 1842): 2.
73. Ibid.
74. *Northern Star* 242 (2 July 1842): 2. Hick also provided testimonials for Parr's Life Pills on 1 October 1842, 31 December 1842 and 14 January 1843.
75. *Northern Star* 384 (22 March 1845): 2.
76. Richards, *Commodity Culture*, 196.
77. Strachan, *Advertising and Satirical Culture*, 123.

7

Keeping 'pace with the growing spirit of the times': The Women's Magazine in Transition

Jennie Batchelor

In 1820, *The Lady's Magazine; or Entertaining Companion for the Fair Sex* (1770–1832) marked its fiftieth anniversary with the launch of a new series. The move was unavoidable. As Samuel Hamilton (1778–c. 1850), the periodical's sometime printer, proprietor and editor, elaborated in a prospectus, times and 'the taste of the day' had changed since the publication of the magazine's first issue in August 1770.[1] In response to these shifts, the periodical vowed to 'discard a few of the subjects which have hitherto entered into the regular list of our resources'; to 'extend' its range of contents; and to raise its production standards via the use of 'finer paper, a more elegant type, and engravings of exquisite beauty'.[2] These final two objectives would be met by the magazine's headline reviews section – introduced a few years earlier – which featured extended, serialised extracts of 'the best poems, novels, or historical narratives' by the likes of Lord Byron, Thomas Moore and Sir Walter Scott, illustrated with original designs by 'SMIRKE, WESTALL, STOTHARD, AND H. CORBOULD' and engraved by 'JAMES AND CHARLES HEATH, W. FINDEN, ENGLEHEART AND ROBINSON'.[3]

Other 'improvements' included an intensified commitment to 'natural history', 'botany', 'mineralogy' and 'social philosophy', which had become increasingly popular in the magazine since 1800, and to 'OEconomics' and 'religion and morality', which had always been prominent subjects.[4] To avoid alarming loyal subscribers, the prospectus was coy about what was to be discarded. The dedicated news section and items on current affairs that the magazine had carried would be dropped – owing to the 'increased circulation of newspapers'.[5] The annual supplement would also be cut in a bid to defray the production costs associated with its superior engravings.[6] Finally, the magazine's hugely popular serial fiction would be replaced with stories running to 'two or three numbers' at most.[7] Hamilton neglected to admit that the magazine would also cease issuing its monthly needlework patterns for embellishing clothes and household objects – one of the periodical's major innovations at its launch. More significantly, he would all but drop its longstanding commitment to reader-submitted content in favour of excerpts from previously published works and submissions by paid contributors.

The prospectus attributed the changing 'taste of the day' to 'momentous' developments in 'the education of females', developments it claimed to have pioneered, at least in part.[8] The truth was more prosaic, however. The newly precarious position of 'one of the oldest' and most widely read 'periodical miscellanies of this metropolis' in a diversified and professionalised periodical marketplace undoubtedly preoccupied Hamilton when devising the new series.[9] *The Lady's Magazine* was not the first periodical to court or address female readers, nor was it the first miscellany to target women subscribers or to call itself a lady's magazine.[10] Yet this *Lady's Magazine* was a truly innovative publication that cultivated a large audience of readers.[11] It offered an eclectic blend of essays on household management and on moral, educational and philosophical subjects, as well as news, biographies, poetry, short stories, serial fiction, fashion content, travel writing and advice columns. It was unique when it was founded by veteran periodical proprietor John Coote in 1770 and warrants recognition as the first recognisably modern, mass-market women's magazine.[12] Its monthly print run was an estimated 10,000 to 15,000 monthly copies at its height, but it had a considerably larger readership since a single copy of the magazine might be shared by multiple readers via family or library circulation. By contrast, the average print run of a novel at the time was just 750 copies. Several attempts were made to capitalise on the journal's popularity over the next five decades. While the prospectus confidently dismissed its 'ephemeral rivals', *The Lady's Magazine* was forced to compete for women readers after the mid-1780s, when its first direct rival, the piratical *New Lady's Magazine* (1786–96), was founded.[13] These pressures increased considerably at the end of the century, with the founding of *The Lady's Monthly Museum* (1798–1828) and *La Belle Assemblée* (1806–32), not to mention indirect competition from other periodical formats, including the magazine's '*cater-cousins*': reviews, specialist fashion magazines and, from the mid-1820s, annuals.[14] In 1823, just three years after the new series was launched, *The Lady's Magazine* was reported to have a circulation of just 250 copies a month due to increased competition, a difficulty that was compounded by a series of financial and editorial crises.[15] This downward trajectory was successfully reversed in the next few years through the introduction of various formal and technological 'improvements' that restored something of the magazine's former glory.

The Lady's Magazine has long been marginalised in literary history and periodicals scholarship. In part, its marginalisation can be accounted for by its inconvenient periodisation, which pushes at the limits of a generously defined Romantic period even without consideration of its mergers with the *Ladies' Museum* (1832) and *Court Magazine and Belle Assemblée* (1838), which gave it an extended afterlife to 1847. Until recently, *The Lady's Magazine* was usually featured in the small body of scholarship that acknowledged it as a coda to studies of eighteenth-century periodicals, or as a precursor to the Victorian women's magazine. Kathryn Shevelow has argued that *The Lady's Magazine* marked the beginning of the end for pedagogically ambitious women's periodicals, with its emphasis upon instructing readers in the arts of becoming the ideal domestic woman.[16] Margaret Beetham's pioneering work on the Victorian women's magazine, by contrast, presents *The Lady's Magazine* as an elite, amateurishly produced and naïve periodical that only realised the potential of its 'radical heterogeneity' in later decades.[17] Both characterisations, which predate digitisation of *The Lady's Magazine*, present partial accounts of the magazine derived from brief chronological snapshots and a primary focus on the magazine's fashion reports, plates and conduct essays at the expense of the vast majority of its eclectic and more intellectually ambitious and politically savvy content.

I have argued elsewhere that *The Lady's Magazine* was a key publication of the Romantic era that was widely and lastingly influential in championing women's education, reading and writing.[18] In this essay, I shift focus to explore the publication's legacies for the women's magazine. Hamilton's claim in the 1820 prospectus that *The Lady's Magazine* was entering a pivotal and necessarily self-reflective moment in its history was prescient. What he fails to acknowledge explicitly is that for the next two decades the women's magazine, as we would come to know it, was entering a significant transitional phase that shaped the genre's forms and mission into and beyond the Victorian period. Using *The Lady's Magazine* as a principal case study, this chapter elucidates how rivalries and intimacies between different 1820s periodicals and periodical formats, especially literary magazines, fashion periodicals and annuals, drove the development of the women's magazine. It also sheds light on the roles that male editors, such as Samuel Hamilton and Charles Heath, and women writers, such as Mary Russell Mitford, played in these innovations.

Developments in the format, content and tone of the women's magazine from the 1820s and 1830s were far from linear. As Hamilton intuited, the future of the women's magazine from the mid-nineteenth century would depend as much on returning to past formulae as on trialling new innovations. Taking account of this overlooked yet dynamic period illuminates an important missing link in the history of the women's magazine. Constructing such an account also challenges longstanding misconceptions about the generic, ideological and class inflection of Romantic women's periodicals and forces a reassessment of the so-called innovations associated with women's magazines of the 1840s and beyond. More than simply providing a default template – or 'basic pattern' – for its Victorian successors, *The Lady's Magazine* engaged in a prolonged deliberation about what and who makes a women's magazine.[19] In doing so, it demonstrates that the Victorian women's magazine was more indebted to its Romantic predecessors than we have hitherto recognised.

Subjects 'appropriated to the Fair': Defining the women's magazine before 1800

In an inaugural 'Address' to readers, the editor of *The Lady's Magazine* expressed how 'surprizing [*sic*]' it was that 'no periodical publication should at present exist calculated' for the 'particular amusement' of women.[20] The claim was misleading. Editors had wrestled with the question of how to make a women's periodical from the genre's inception in the 1690s when the short-lived question-and-answer sheet, the *Ladies Mercury* (1693), was launched as a spin-off to John Dunton's *Athenian Mercury* (1690–7). It took another forty years and the founding of Edward Cave's *Gentleman's Magazine* (1731–1922) before the commercial rewards of gender specialisation in periodical publishing became fully visible and another thirty before any magazine explicitly marketed to female subscribers approximated the popularity of its masculine counterparts.[21] With varying degrees of explicitness, each of the early miscellanies for women that sought to capitalise on Cave's venture meditated on how to differentiate a lady's from a gentleman's magazine. Usually, these accommodations centred on the topics covered, the nature or volume of news coverage and the inclusion of fiction or other imaginative content, the latter of which had been largely absent from the *Gentleman's Magazine*. Some periodicals introduced new forms of content. *The Lady's Magazine; or Polite Companion for the Fair Sex* (1759–63), for instance, included occasional fashion plates. It presented itself as a 'by women, for women' publication even though its pseudonymous female editor was almost certainly a man – and aspired to address upper-middle-class and aristocratic readerships. While eighteenth-century women's magazines are often described in Victorian periodicals scholarship as elite in their orientation, most in fact used the adjectives 'lady's' or 'ladies'' more neutrally to connote all literate women.[22] This was especially true for the later and more famous *Lady's Magazine*, which replaced the word 'polite' in its subtitle with 'entertaining' to differentiate itself from its namesake and to signal the inclusiveness of its anticipated readership. It addressed women in the 'country' as well as the metropolis and promised 'something suitable' to women in 'different walk[s] of life', from the 'house-wife' to the 'peeress', along with the shopgirls and dressmakers whose lives featured prominently in the periodical's fiction and agony aunt columns.[23]

The Lady's Magazine promised this wide readership an extensive 'bill of fare' carefully adapted for 'the patronage of the fair sex'.[24] It adopted the two-column, densely printed and lightly illustrated magazine format of contemporary titles such as the *Gentleman's Magazine*. It also included many of the same types of content as the *Gentleman's Magazine*, including poetry, news columns and essays on diverse subjects, as well as birth, marriage and death notices. To 'meet with the patronage of the fair sex', however, it promised to pay equal attention to women's 'persons' and 'minds' in the form of 'new' initiatives, including monthly 'patterns for the Tambour, Embroidery, or every kind of Needlework' and 'engravings [to] inform our distant readers with every innovation that is made in female dress'.[25] While the magazine vowed to ransack 'every branch of literature' in the service of educating its women readers in disciplines as varied as science, history, geography and philosophy, it sought to distinguish itself from other magazines and promised to better serve its 'Fair' readers by giving new weight to narrative nonfiction, especially travel writing, and 'Interesting Stories, Novels, Tales, Romances' designed to promote 'chastity' and 'virtue'.[26]

As a manifesto for a new type of mass-market publication, a genre that would later become the women's magazine, *The Lady's Magazine*'s 'Address to the Public' (1770) is bold. It is also partly misleading. While needlework patterns were a mainstay of the magazine until the new series launched in 1820, dress was not a regular feature for at least another three decades. Moreover, the plots of the periodical's hugely popular short and serial fiction – which shine a searing light on the universality of the economic, cultural and sexual oppression of women – often resist their moralising narrative frames.[27] The 'Address' also fails to account for the breadth of the magazine's content, which prominently included medical columns by the likes of Drs Cooke, Leake and Turnbull tailored to the complaints of women readers and their children; series on household management from child-rearing to cookery; and agony aunt columns, the most successful of which, 'The Matron', ran from 1774 until 1791 (relaunched as 'The Matron Revived' in 1817). These columns relied upon the participation of readers, who actively sought the wisdom of Mrs Grey (the titular 'Matron') on how to endure an abusive marriage, the expertise of Dr Cook on how to relieve mastitis or treat cradle cap, or the advice of a fellow reader on how to cure warts, headaches or freckles. Such reliance on unpaid reader copy has sometimes been cast as a source of 'embarrassment' or marker of amateurism.[28] Yet reader participation via the publication of subscriber letters and reader contributions was at the heart of *The Lady's Magazine*'s popularity in its first five decades. Reader participation bound women readers in villages, towns and cities within a virtual community united by fellow feeling and mutual interest.[29] It was an ethos that for many years served the women who read, wrote for or conversed with fellow contributors in the pages of *The Lady's Magazine*. Not coincidentally, it was an ethos that served the commercial interests of the periodical's publishers, George Robinson and his associates, by cultivating a sense of brand loyalty and communal ownership built upon the shared investment of its subscribers – any of whom could, in theory, become one of its unpaid authors.

Fashionable rivalries: The women's magazine in transition, 1800–20

There were relatively few changes in *The Lady's Magazine*'s content, format or business model until the new series in 1820. The threat of rival publications such as Alexander Hogg's *New Lady's Magazine*, which shamelessly declared Robinson's publication obsolete while pirating a significant percentage of its content, caused the editors of *The Lady's Magazine* few sleepless nights. The launch of Vernor and Hood's *The Lady's Monthly Museum* (in 1798) and John Bell's *La Belle Assemblée* (in 1806), however, sparked intense competition, evolution and innovation in the women's magazine genre, establishing the parameters for a new century.

The Lady's Monthly Museum did not present itself as a direct rival to *The Lady's Magazine*, instead claiming erroneously that it was the first periodical to cater specifically to women readers. Its 'Prospectus' (1798) nonetheless contains a series of thinly veiled attacks on its competitor. The first of these lies in the periodical's full title, which designates the *Museum* a 'Polite Repository of Amusement and Instruction [. . .] By A SOCIETY OF LADIES'.[30] Here, the term 'LADIES' (coupled with 'Polite') carries an element of class-inflection absent in the title of *The Lady's Magazine*, as well an air of female editorial and writerly professionalism that was important to its identity. Given the professionalism of its contributing authors, the 'Prospectus' continued, *Museum* subscribers should be reassured that they will not be 'taxed by the necessity of pursuing unending narratives', a thinly veiled dig at the several *Lady's Magazine* serials produced by reader-contributors who occasionally left them unfinished, much to the irritation of readers who had devoured them for months or years.[31] The *Museum* looked different both inside and out. It adopted a single-column page layout, its wrappers were 'done up in coloured paper' and it was smaller: 'a convenient size for the pocket'.[32] While there was considerable overlap in the *Museum*'s and *Lady's Magazine*'s contents – 'Novels, Tales, and Romances', 'Poetry original and selected', short pieces in French, and 'Charades and Enigmas' – the *Museum* promised novelties, including monthly headline biographies and an extensive reviews section offering advice on the most suitable female reading materials.[33] The *Museum*'s most significant innovation was to capitalise on the recent growth in the market for fashion magazines, especially titles published in France, including *Les Cabinet des Modes* (1785–93), Niklaus Wilhelm von Heideloff's *Gallery of Fashion* (1794–1803) and *Le Journal des Dames et des Modes* (1797–1837). The *Museum* similarly offered readers a monthly 'Cabinet of Fashion' section featuring verbal descriptions of the latest styles and hand-coloured plates depicting fashionably adorned figures.[34] The costs involved in producing the plates levied a higher cover price of a shilling compared to the sixpence still being commanded by *The Lady's Magazine* three decades after its founding.

La Belle Assemblée – a lavish royal octavo publication launched by experienced periodical editor and publisher John Bell – raised the stakes further. While it did not claim to be the first publication to target women, it promised to lay 'the foundation of a Work, which, in the comprehensiveness of its instruction, the variety of its amusements, and the elegance of its embellishment, has had no parallel in the history of periodical publications'.[35] The boast was justified. *La Belle Assemblée*'s contents were of a piece with those of *The Lady's Magazine* – a succession of 'Original Communications' and a variety of reprinted excerpts, as well as poetry, news, announcements, song sheets, theatrical intelligence, needlework patterns and elegant 'embellishments'. Yet *La Belle Assemblée*'s production values and fashion coverage were more impressive than those of its predecessor. The first issue in February 1806 set the bar high with an essay entitled 'General Observations on Fashions and the Fashionables', eight full-length 'Portraits' of London and Paris fashions, another plate featuring new styles in London headdresses and no less than four needlework patterns. Bell's magazine was also the first to cite named authorities in its fashion coverage. Its first issues featured plates by Mr Devis designed by his wife and former editor of the short-lived fashion journal *Le Miroir de la Mode* (1803–4), Madame (Margaret) Lanchester. Three years later, Lanchester gave way to Mrs (Mary Anne) Bell, John Bell's daughter-in-law, who would later serve as co-editor of the *World of Fashion and Continental Feuilletons* (1824–51), the famous 'inventress' of millinery-, dress- and corset-making designs and the proprietor of shops in Bloomsbury and, later, St James's Park.

The Lady's Magazine might have publicly prided itself on 'standing like a rock amidst the dangers of rivalry and the fluctuations of caprice', but its confidence was shaken by the extent and quality of fashion coverage in its two key competitors.[36] Despite its claims in its inaugural issue that dress would be prominent among its contents, the editors found fashion intelligence hard to gather and prohibitively expensive given its 6d cover price. Only four fashion plates appeared in the magazine between 1770 and 1798; consequently, readers who sought such content were forced to turn to the growing number of dedicated fashion journals. Within eighteen months after the launch of *The Lady's Monthly Museum*, hand-coloured plates and detailed accompanying descriptions appeared monthly in *The Lady's Magazine*, and in the 1810s it also began to promote styles invented by London dressmakers such as Mrs Smith of Old Burlington Street, Miss Macdonald of Bond Street and Miss Pierpoint of Portman Square, the latter two of whom also published designs in *The Lady's Monthly Museum*. *The Lady's Magazine*'s fashion coverage nevertheless differed from that of its rivals. As Hilary Davidson has documented, all fashion plates from this period were to a large extent 'aspirational' rather than representing an accurate reflection of what people were wearing at the time.[37] This was especially the case for the middling sort of readers *The Lady's Magazine* aimed to attract. The implied contradiction between the magazine's consumer-focused fashion content and its dedication to socioeconomic, moral and educational values has long been taken as symptomatic of the impossibly contradictory demands it placed upon its readers. Yet there is considerable evidence that before the 1830s at least, the magazine saw its fashion 'intelligence' as just another 'branch of information'[38] – not unlike its miscellaneous essays on news, history, geography, natural history and travel writing – designed to help women readers navigate the world in which they lived.[39] The place of fashion coverage within the magazine, like so much else of its contents and format, would change in the new 'age of periodical publications' to become even more aspirational.[40]

Surviving the 'age of periodical publications': Defining and negotiating the competition, 1820–32

In 1820, *The Lady's Magazine*, *La Belle Assemblée* and *The Lady's Monthly Museum* (now published by Dean and Murray) seemed, on the surface at least, to coexist relatively peaceably, although they all used editorial addresses and newspaper advertisements to claim their superiority to their competitors in elegance, taste and variety. Moreover, in a newly professionalised era of magazine production, payment for contributor copy was becoming routine, and despite their belief in the loyalty of different reader demographics, women's magazines shared several contributors, including the extraordinarily prolific poet James Murray Lacey, the Scots writer Beatrice Grant and the poet and novelist Mary Leman Rede (later Grimstone). Yet for commercial reasons, the rapid ascendancy of periodicals in the early nineteenth century had produced inevitable shifts in reader expectations, taste and 'mental vigor'.[41] As such, *The Lady's Magazine*, once the leader in its field, recognised that it needed to track changes in the competition carefully.[42] It responded swiftly and enthusiastically to reader demand for more extensive fashion coverage, while quietly introducing other changes, including the adoption in 1817 of the same section heads and content organisation used in *La Belle Assemblée*.[43] *The Lady's Magazine* nevertheless avoided introducing change for change's sake and stayed true to the magazine's 'Plan', what we might call its brand identity.

The editors of *The Lady's Magazine* not only realised the necessity of moving with the times in order to respond to consumer demand and increased competition but also understood the importance of retaining the magazine's identity in order to please loyal subscribers. Striking this balance was a feat that was more difficult to achieve after *The Lady's Magazine* and its rivals made the case for the commercial viability of the women's magazine. The question of whether gender specialisation had a future in periodical print culture became particularly pressing when other non-gender-specific periodicals such as *The New Monthly Magazine* and *Blackwood's Edinburgh Magazine* were attracting ever more women readers and regularly reviewing and publishing the work of women writers such as Anne Grant, Felicia Hemans and Letitia Landon. More than any other women's periodical of the time, *The Lady's Magazine* ruminated upon this question, investing in a series of 'improvements' in content and relationships with other periodical types as it sought to reimagine itself for a new generation of readers and writers.

'[E]nlarging the plan'

As Hamilton signalled in his 1820 'Prospectus', the reviews section was one of the key 'improvements' introduced by *The Lady's Magazine* in the 1820s. Notices of recently published or forthcoming titles had been commonplace in magazines from the middle of the eighteenth century. *The Lady's Magazine* was anomalous in not publishing reviews earlier, an anomaly made more visible when *The Lady's Monthly Museum* launched with its own evaluative reviews section in 1798. Yet when *The Lady's Magazine* belatedly changed its position regarding critical notices, it did so in the spirit of innovation rather than imitation. Eschewing the capsule reviews characteristic of other magazines and styling itself instead after the prominent literary review journals, notices in *The Lady's Magazine* commonly ran several pages, with many extending over several issues and featuring evaluative commentary and extensive extracts from works by the likes of Lord Byron, Thomas Moore, Jane Porter and Sir Walter Scott. Many were also beautifully accompanied by specially commissioned engravings, including contributions from James Heath and Thomas Stothard that accompanied the magazine's extensive review extracts from Sir Walter Scott's *Tales of My Landlord* (1816–32). These illustrations later found their way into the first illustrated edition of Scott's *Tales*.

The reviews section was one of several signs that *The Lady's Magazine* in the 1820s was attempting to style itself as a competitor to prominent literary journals and magazines such as the *Literary Gazette* and that 'snarling cur' *Blackwood's Magazine*, both of which had been dismissive of *The Lady's Magazine* and vocal about the fact that it '[had] no business, and should not interfere with its masculine contemporaries'.[44] Yet interfere it did. In 1819, *The Lady's Magazine* began reprinting content from *Blackwood's*, including essays by John Wilson and an extract from Coleridge's *Biographia Literaria* (1817). This led to a bitter and very public war of words in which the editor of *The Lady's Magazine* responded to *Blackwood's* accusations of plagiarism by claiming imitation was the best form of flattery. He then satirically reassured Blackwood that his 'literary journal' was 'safe from our plunder in general, as its articles are often too erudite, and sometimes of too local a description, to suit our miscellany'.[45]

From 1820, *The Lady's Magazine* also committed to following broader trends in literary journals and magazines by significantly reducing volunteer contributions. Gone was the lively dialogue between correspondents and nominated (or self-appointed) advice-givers. Also missing were the prose and poetry contributions of readers, as well as serial fiction – a genre *The Lady's Monthly Museum* and *La Belle Assemblée* continued to publish. According to James Grant, it was 'the first among the Lady's Magazines to pay for contributions', typically offering 'four guineas per sheet for poetry, and three guineas and a-half for prose' in the 1820s, although some contributors earned five times as much.[46] Some of the first contributors to benefit from this arrangement, while still retaining their anonymity, included prolific novelist and short story writer Barbara Hofland; her husband, artist Thomas Christopher Hofland (author of *The Lady's Magazine*'s recently introduced 'Fine Arts' column); poet, playwright and prose fiction writer Mary Russell Mitford; and journalist, critic and playwright Thomas Noon Talfourd, who authored several biographies, critical essays and reviews for *The Lady's Magazine* and negotiated the publication of Mitford's 'Our Village' with the periodical's editor, Samuel Hamilton.

Mitford's relationship with *The Lady's Magazine* is better documented than that of any other contributor in the periodical's history. Her correspondence with the periodical's editor, printer and fellow correspondents Talfourd and Hofland help to illuminate the transformations the periodical underwent in the first half of the 1820s. Mitford was already a familiar name to *Lady's Magazine* readers when her series of sketches first appeared in the December 1822 issue. Several of her published poems had been reprinted in the periodical under her signature in the 1810s, although most readers were unable to connect these verses to 'Our Village' and Mitford's other prose contributions to the magazine over the next two years, all of which were unsigned or appeared under the signature 'M'. Mitford did not write the series specifically for *The Lady's Magazine*. She placed the sketches there only after they were first rejected by *The London Review* and *The New Monthly Magazine*. Yet, from the outset, 'Our Village' aligned neatly with the new direction that Hamilton was imagining for *The Lady's Magazine*, newly subtitled, *or, Mirror of the Belles-Lettres, Fashions, Fine Arts, Music, Drama &c.* Indeed, Mitford's famous opening for 'Our Village' might be read as a quiet manifesto, not only for a new kind of prose fiction but also for the periodical in which the sketches appeared. Gone were the days of the magazine's commitment to fantastic oriental tales, overtly didactic moral tales or sprawling gothic serials that spanned months or even years, during which readers would be 'whirled half over Europe at the chariot-wheels of a hero'.[47] Inspired by the intimacy of 'Miss Austen's delicious novels' and eschewing the melodrama of *Blackwood's* 'Tales of Terror' or the more sensational short fiction and serials that continued to run in *The Lady's Monthly Museum*, Mitford's series hones in on the rural, the local and the particular.[48] It marks a decisive shift in the periodical's sensibility, which William Hazlitt described as being 'all at home'.[49] Written at a time of rapid change in which industry was transforming rural lives and the periodical marketplace was changing apace, 'Our Village' preserved a largely comforting – though far from politically complacent – sense of place suspended in time. Nor was there a danger that this serial would or could be left unfinished. Mitford's sketches, like pieces in a mosaic or the individual fields, woods, meadows and residences described in 'Our Village', formed a pleasing whole, with each constituent piece having its own integrity and shining in isolation. In terms of subject matter, structure and tone, 'Our Village' chimed with Hamilton's objective to bring a modicum of cohesion, stability and literary professionalism to a miscellany that had once been unapologetically eclectic and somewhat uneven. According to Mitford, the new professionalism helped to raise subscriptions of the periodical tenfold.[50]

This stability was shaken, however, when Hamilton declared bankruptcy and absconded to France in April 1823. He still owed money to several contributors, including more than £40 to Mitford.[51] In order to avoid the magazine's collapse, Hamilton's brother-in-law Charles Heath took the helm. He was an engraver and entrepreneur whose family had a long connection with the magazine and several generations of the Robinson family who published it. Heath did not – probably could not – pay Hamilton's debts but continued to publish Mitford's work for a lower fee and requested that she concede the copyright for future sketches so that he could publish them as a standalone volume.[52] Mitford refused these terms. Her sketches continued to appear in *The Lady's Magazine* until August 1824, when 'Lucy Revisited' appeared, but she declined to relinquish her copyright and published them in volume form as *Our Village* (1824). Her publisher was George Whittaker, the new editor of *The Lady's Magazine*'s old rival, *La Belle Assemblée.*

While Charles Heath's role as engraver of many of the periodical's plates in the 1820s is known, his editorship of *The Lady's Magazine*, revealed by Mitford's correspondence, is unacknowledged in accounts of his career. Yet his involvement in reimagining the magazine in the 1820s was at least as important as Mitford's. Heath played an instrumental role in introducing steel-plate engravings to the periodical – the first of which was published in April 1823, the same month that he assumed the editorship. As editor, he was more consistent in crediting artists and engravers of the growing number of engravings the magazine was publishing each month. Heath also seems to have been responsible for one of the most striking developments in the magazine in the 1820s and 1830s: its increasing alignment with the annuals, a new periodical publishing phenomenon aimed primarily at young, well-to-do readers.

The changes that *The Lady's Magazine* instituted in response to competition from the annuals in the mid-1820s were much more decisive than those changes it introduced when it styled itself as a worthy competitor to literary magazines and fashion journals. *The Lady's Magazine* first formally noticed the annuals in an October 1824 review of Ackermann's *Forget Me Not* for 1825. In the months and years that followed, an ever-increasing amount of space within *The Lady's Magazine* was dedicated to reprinted prose fiction and poetry from the annuals, including works by Letitia Landon, Percy Shelley and Susannah Strickland, as well as work from *The Lady's Magazine*'s regular contributors, including Hofland and Mitford. By 1831, *The Lady's Magazine*'s increasingly close relationship with the annuals was official. As the *Morning Advertiser* noted on 3 November 1831, the magazine had 'committed matrimony' with the *Companion to the Annuals*, a short-lived monthly periodical.[53] The incorporation of the *Companion* into *The Lady's Magazine* was widely viewed as a canny and successful move. In showcasing the 'merits of these beautiful periodicals, so highly honourable as they are in every respect to the progress of literature, and to our excellence in the fine arts', alongside its own 'pretty stories and some good poetry', *The Lady's Magazine* tapped into the huge market for the annuals, forty of which were now in print. It extended that audience by reprinting content from the annuals, making it available to those who could not afford their considerably higher cover price. Not coincidentally, it was also a move that the correspondent noted could not 'fail to ensure a continuance of the distinguished success which *The Lady's Magazine* has long enjoyed'.[54]

Following its marriage to *The Companion to the Annuals*, *The Lady's Magazine* became more enthusiastically bigamous. A second union followed in the winter of 1831 when the editors made a deal with Theophile Lafuile and Adolphe Goubaud, proprietors of the weekly Parisian fashion magazine *Le Follet, Courrier des Salons* (1829–92). The arrangement was brokered by the little-known James Page, who launched an 'Improved Series' of *The Lady's Magazine* when he became proprietor in 1830 after the periodical finally fell out of the Robinsons' hands. Marianne Van Remoortel has recently argued that Samuel Beeton's contract to import plates and patterns from Goubard's *Le Moniteur de la Mode* for the *Englishwoman's Domestic Magazine* (1852–79) marked a 'pivotal moment in the history of the British fashion press', but the precedent was established by Page some three decades earlier.[55] During the 1810s and 1820s, British women's magazines looked primarily to London styles and dressmakers for their fashion plates and copy, but by the 1830s Paris was reinstated as the style capital of Europe. *La Belle Assemblée* and *The Ladies Museum* (formerly *The Lady's Monthly Museum*) provided regular updates from Parisian-based correspondents, but both were outmaneuvered by Page's deal with *Le Follet*. The arrangement gave *The Lady's Magazine* the exclusive 'right of publishing certain Engravings' published simultaneously in *Le Follet* in Paris and granted 'the use of our names in all proceeding which the said parties may find it necessary to institute, for the prevention of the counterfeit publication', a right Page was forced to exercise on several occasions in the coming years.[56] The subsequent changes to the magazine were material. Initially, *The Lady's Magazine* simply inserted individual *Le Follet* plates where its London fashion plates had previously appeared. But within three months, an eight-page *Le Follet* supplement, written in French and printed on rose-coloured paper, was sandwiched in the middle of each issue. While the finer details of the deal with Lafuile and Goubaud remain obscure, the magazine hinted on more than one occasion that it was financially risky, a risk that Page sought to mitigate by a strikingly modern innovation: giving subscribers the opportunity, for a fee, to have portraits of their faces drawn into the plates.[57] The deal paid off. The 'originality' of Page's collaboration with his Parisian colleagues was widely celebrated in the press. While *The Lady's Magazine*'s circulation during this period remains a matter of speculation, it was widely referred to as both the largest and most successful of the various 'Ladies' Magazines' in production at the time.

Within eighteen months of *The Lady's Magazine*'s union with *Le Follet* and *The Companion to the Annuals*, its market position was strong enough that it was able to enter into a new business arrangement – the absorption of one of its most tenacious competitors, *The Ladies Museum*. The events that led to this most unlikely of marriages are similarly murky, though it is perhaps no coincidence that it occurred in the same year that Caroline Norton threatened the future of both publications by taking on the editorship of the still-popular *La Belle Assemblée*. The union would most likely have surprised regular readers of both titles because of the palpable animosity between them. Just one year earlier, *The Ladies Museum* issued a bitter invective against the 'intellectual sterility' of the 'poor old dame' it sought to succeed.[58] But the 'old dame' had life in her yet. The 'Address' that opened the July 1832 issue celebrated the new title's entrance with a promise that, by securing the *Museum*'s 'distinguished writers', which included Isabella Hill, Mary Howitt and Mary Jane Jewsbury, *The Lady's Magazine and Museum* would be the foremost 'periodical for the ladies of England' and the best 'suited to the advanced state of their intellectual acquirements'.[59]

It is tempting to see the succession of changes to the tone, form and content of *The Lady's Magazine* in the 1820s and early 1830s as a prolonged period of floundering for a magazine that in 1831 could not even remember when its first issue was published.[60] While some of the changes made to the magazine were likely unanticipated – such as those instituted by Heath after Hamilton absconded – many more were carefully planned as the magazine carefully tracked and responded to new periodical titles and genres and attempted to outmaneuver some of its closest competitors. In 1847, *The Lady's Magazine* finally ceased publication after an 1838 merger with the *Court and Lady's Magazine and Monthly Critic* (formerly *La Belle Assemblée*). In the late 1840s, it became a much less dynamic publication with a static format containing short fiction, fashion news, short memoirs with illustrations and essays on current affairs.[61] It was also beset by 'vexatious interruptions' and 'hindrances' with securing and publishing content.[62] *The Lady's Magazine* ceased with little fanfare or lament. Yet in many ways its work was done. It had successfully made the case for the viability of the women's magazine and, in the process, had entered into an extended and experimental interrogation of what a women's magazine was, who its audience was and what its priorities should be.

As periodical publication entered a new epoch in the 1840s and 1850s, editors of magazines that specifically targeted women readers responded to the lessons learned from the evolution of *The Lady's Magazine*. Like Hamilton in the 1820 prospectus, they took a 'look into the past' and adopted a similar structure to *The Lady's Magazine* (essays, fashions, literature and culture) as it settled in the 1830s. But they also took a longer view, with many reintroducing innovations that Hamilton and his successors dropped: popular serial fiction, reader dialogue, advice columns, dress patterns and essays on domestic management. In doing so, *The Lady's Magazine* negotiated its place amongst the literary magazines, reviews, annuals and high-end fashion journals that flourished in the first third of the nineteenth century. Taking a longer view of the history of women's magazines to include the vibrant decades of the 1820s and 1830s helps nuance our understanding of the Victorian women's magazine. While new technologies and various socioeconomic factors undoubtedly account for the form's greater reach and market share, the women's magazine – formally, materially, stylistically and culturally – was a periodical genre whose parameters and commercial viability were wrestled into existence by the innovative contributors, editors, artists and publishers of the early nineteenth-century periodical marketplace.

Notes

1. Samuel Hamilton, 'Prospectus for a New Series of the *Lady's Magazine*' (1820), John Johnson Collection, Prospectuses of Journals 32 (36), 1, Bodleian Library, University of Oxford.
2. Ibid.
3. Ibid.
4. Ibid., 3–4.
5. Ibid.
6. Ibid.
7. Ibid.

8. Ibid., 2.
9. Ibid., 1.
10. Jennie Batchelor and Manushag N. Powell, 'Introduction', in *Women's Periodicals and Print Culture in Britain, 1690s–1820s*, ed. Jennie Batchelor and Manushag N. Powell (Edinburgh: Edinburgh University Press, 2018), 1–19.
11. On periodicals and audience building in this period, see Jon P. Klancher, *The Making of English Reading Audiences, 1790–1832* (Madison: University of Wisconsin Press, 1987).
12. A growth in population and literacy rates as well as technological advancements in print production and distribution meant that 'the possibility of a mass market existed even before 1790' even though the 'mass production of printed material did not take hold until after 1830', H. J. Jackson, *Romantic Readers: The Evidence of Marginalia* (New Haven: Yale University Press, 2008), 8.
13. Hamilton, 'Prospectus', 1.
14. William Hazlitt, 'The Periodical Press', *Edinburgh Review* 38 (May 1823): 359.
15. Mary Russell Mitford to Benjamin Robert Haydon [May 1823], qB/TU/MIT, vol. 4, f. 472. Reading Central Library.
16. Kathryn Shevelow, *Women and Print Culture: The Construction of Femininity in the Early Periodical* (London: Routledge, 1989), 188–9.
17. Margaret Beetham, *A Magazine of Her Own?: Domesticity and Desire in the Woman's Magazine, 1800–1914* (London: Routledge, 1996), 171.
18. Jennie Batchelor, *The Lady's Magazine (1770–1832) and the Making of Literary History* (Edinburgh: Edinburgh University Press, 2022).
19. Beetham, *A Magazine of Her Own?*, 19.
20. 'Address to the Fair Sex', *Lady's Magazine* 1 (August 1770): [3].
21. Among the most successful periodicals for women across the first three-quarters of the eighteenth century (determined by longevity in the absence of verifiable circulation figures) were essay periodicals. Two previous *Lady's/Ladies' Magazines* achieved modestly successful runs. These include Jasper Goodwill's *Ladies Magazine* (1749–53) and *The Lady's Magazine; or Polite Companion for the Fair Sex* (1759–63).
22. Batchelor and Powell, 'Introduction', 16.
23. 'Address', *Lady's Magazine* (August 1770): [4].
24. Ibid., [3].
25. Ibid.

26. Ibid., [4].
27. Jenny DiPlacidi, '"Full of pretty stories": Fiction in the *Lady's Magazine* (1770–1832)', in *Women's Periodicals and Print Culture in Britain*, ed. Jennie Batchelor and Manushag N. Powell (Edinburgh: Edinburgh University Press, 2018), 263–77.
28. Gillian Hughes, 'Fiction in the Magazines', in *English and British Fiction, 1750–1820*, ed. Peter Garside and Karen O'Brien (Oxford: Oxford University Press, 2015), 463; Beetham, *A Magazine of Her Own?*, 21.
29. Alison Adburgham, *Women in Print: Writing Women and Women's Magazines from the Restoration to the Accession of Victoria* (London: George Allen and Unwin, 1972), 148.
30. 'Prospectus for the *Lady's Monthly Museum*', (1798), John Johnson Collection, Prospectuses of Journals, 32 (36), 1, Bodleian Library, University of Oxford.
31. Ibid., 2.
32. Ibid.
33. Ibid.
34. Ibid.
35. 'To the Public', *La Belle Assemblée* 1 (February 1806): n.p.
36. 'Address', *Lady's Magazine*, 1st n.s., 2 (January 1821): i.
37. Hilary Davidson, *Dress in the Age of Jane Austen: Regency Fashion* (New Haven: Yale University Press, 2019), 48.
38. 'Address', *Lady's Magazine* 1 (August 1770): [3].
39. Jennie Batchelor, 'Illustrated Magazines and Periodicals: Visual Genres and Gendered Aspirations', in *The Edinburgh Companion to Romanticism and the Arts*, ed. Maureen McCue and Sophie Thomas (Edinburgh: Edinburgh University Press, 2022), 408–26.
40. 'Address', 1st n.s., 2 (January 1821): i.
41. Ibid.
42. Ibid.
43. These section heads were: 'Original Communications', 'Miscellanies', 'Poetry', 'Fashions', 'Dramatic Intelligence', the 'Chronicle' (a news section), and births, marriages and deaths.
44. 'Address', *Lady's Magazine*, 2nd n.s., 2 (November–December 1830): 306.
45. 'Correspondence', *Lady's Magazine* 50 (February 1819): n.p.
46. James Grant, *The Great Metropolis* (London: Saunders and Otley, 1836), 2:331.
47. [Mary Russell Mitford], 'Our Village', *Lady's Magazine*, 1st n.s., 1 (December 1822): 645.

48. Ibid.
49. Hazlitt, 'The Periodical Press', 369.
50. Mitford to Haydon [May 1823], f. 472.
51. Ibid.
52. Ibid.
53. *Morning Advertiser*, 3 November 1831.
54. Ibid.
55. Marianne Van Remoortel, 'Women Editors' Transnational Networks in the *Englishwoman's Domestic Magazine* and *Myra's* Journal', in *Women's Periodicals and Print Culture in Britain, 1830s–1900s*, ed. Alexis Easley, Clare Gill and Beth Rogers (Edinburgh: Edinburgh University Press, 2019), 46.
56. Advertisement for the *Lady's Magazine*, *Old England* 94 (Sunday 5 May 1833): [1].
57. Advertisement for the *Lady's Magazine*, *Morning Herald* 15499 (Tuesday 1 January 1832): [1].
58. 'Address', *Lady's Magazine* 2nd n.s., 1 (July 1832): n.p.
59. 'Address', *Ladies' Magazine and Museum* 1 (July 1832): n.p.
60. The title page for the 1831 volume wrongly stated that the magazine was first published in 1756.
61. The arrangement with *Le Follet* continued.
62. 'Correspondence', *Court and Lady's Magazine and Monthly Critic* 19 (April 1844): 83.

8

Beyond the Literary Annuals: Felicia Hemans, Letitia Elizabeth Landon and Periodical Poetry

Caley Ehnes

In April 1830, *Blackwood's Edinburgh Magazine* published a collection of short poems under the title 'Poetical Portraits'. Over the course of two pages, the author – Robert Macnish, writing under the pseudonym 'A Modern Prometheus' – provides readers with brief poetic portraits of thirty-four British poets ranging from William Shakespeare, John Milton and William Wordsworth to Felicia Hemans and Letitia Elizabeth Landon.[1] The presence of Hemans and Landon in this portrait gallery of literary greats reminds us that while the work of the nineteenth-century popular poetess has often been dismissed as derivative and lightweight, nineteenth-century readers of the periodical press viewed these women and their sentimental, superficially iterative poetry very differently. Indeed, Macnish's gallery locates these female poets as part of an established literary canon, placing them in a seemingly random order alongside of and not separate from their male contemporaries and the canonical figures listed. The lack of hierarchy in Macnish's poem challenges critical divisions of popular and canonical literature by asserting the cultural and literary relevance of Hemans, Landon and the poetess tradition they represent. According to Macnish's poem, they are at the centre – and not the gendered margins – of British literary culture.

This chapter builds on the recent influx of scholarship studying the intersection of new media forms and the development of women's poetry and the public figure of the poetess.[2] While scholars of Hemans and Landon have previously considered the role of these poetesses in new media of the early nineteenth century, most have focused on their original contributions to the prominent literary periodicals and annuals of the 1820s.[3] Few have considered how their recirculation in new media of the 1830s simultaneously anticipates and contributes to the rise of the family literary periodical and its poetics at mid-century. My analysis of Hemans's and, to a lesser extent, Landon's reprinted poetry in *Chambers's Edinburgh Journal* between 1832 and 1841 begins to fill this gap. I argue that Hemans's and Landon's presence in this early Victorian journal encourages a reassessment of the function of the poetess and her poetry in the developing periodical culture of the early nineteenth century. Reading the poetess and her poetry as part of a 'culture of reprinting', to borrow a term from Meredith McGill, sheds new light on Yopie Prins's assertion that the poetess is 'an important figure within literary history as a shifting aesthetic category that is closely linked to historical transformations in modern reading practices'.[4] The reproduction and recirculation of the poetry and public-facing personas of Hemans and Landon in a publication like *Chambers's* emphasises how the poetry of the 1820s and 1830s set the stage both aesthetically and commercially for the rise of periodical poetry and the Victorian poetess. Thus, while the period between 1820 and 1840 has been described as 'a lacuna, a dash, or some other kind of punctuation mark',[5] this transitional moment is, in fact, integral to any history of nineteenth-century poetry, poetics and periodical culture. Hemans's and Landon's participation (both deliberate and unintended) in the new media of the 1820s and 1830s effectively positions periodical poetry as a key inheritor of the Romantic tradition.

This chapter begins with an overview of the poetess and her place in the ever-expanding periodical culture of the 1820s, tracing how Hemans's and Landon's engagement with the new media forms of the 1820s helped build the market for periodical poetry written by popular female poets. From there, I examine Hemans's and Landon's overlooked appearances in *Chambers's*, arguing that the reprinting of Hemans's and Landon's poetry in this early family literary periodical tells us a lot 'about what kinds of literature were demanded by [. . .] [the era's new reading public], what counted as literature in this culture, and how high art might be reconfigured for middle-class and working-class audiences'.[6] I conclude with a brief discussion of how the decisions made in the 1830s about whom to publish influenced the development of both periodical poetry and the mid-century family literary magazine as genres.

Periodicals, poetesses and the 1820s

The period in which Hemans and Landon were most active as poets represents a 'crucial transitional period', one largely defined by the poetry and literary production of women writers and the rise of new media in the form of literary periodicals and annuals.[7] The production of poetry in the 1820s and 1830s was an increasingly commercial venture dependent as never before on new media forms marketed towards the broadly defined middle-class reader. These new periodicals and annuals – filled with the poetry of women and non-canonical male poets – took the place of 'volumes of poetry by "canonical" male poets[,] [which consequently] suffered a decline in sales'.[8] Such 'drastic changes' within 'the institutions of literary production' required all authors to reconceptualise 'imaginative writing as a commercial activity' if they wanted to take advantage of the 'unprecedented print opportunities' offered by the era's new media.[9] Female poets, and, more specifically, poetesses like Hemans and Landon, succeeded in what Landon calls this 'new era' with 'a new set of aspirants [. . .] arisen, and a new set of opinions [. . .] to be won' because they capitalised on the demands and expectations of new media rather than fighting against them.[10] Hemans, for example, 'normally asked her publisher which subjects would appeal to the market before putting pen to paper', suggesting both her acute awareness of the market as well as her commitment to producing saleable poetry.[11] The nineteenth-century poetess, as represented by Hemans and Landon, is thus clearly a product of the democratisation of print and the concurrent commodification and professionalisation of authorship. For the most part, successful authors whose writing was their profession had to '[operate] within a commercial system in which they, and their advisors, and their publishers attempted to judge what the market wanted and how best to supply it'.[12] For poets writing in the 1820s and 1830s, this meant writing popular and accessible sentimental verse for the growing readerships of the era's new media forms. A huge part of these new readerships was women. Understanding this 'historical shift in reading practices' as being linked to the rise of new media forms and their diverse and female readerships confirms Easley's contention that 'the popular woman writer and reader arose in tandem as emblems of a distinctly "modern" print culture'.[13] I would, however, extend this even further to suggest that the same can be said of the popular

Victorian poetess, the literary periodical and its popular readership. They, too, developed almost simultaneously as emblems of a modern, middle-class print culture. Paying attention to the interplay between this triad of cultural forces suggests the existence of a literary tradition defined by the poetics of the poetess and nineteenth-century periodical culture.

The cultural force of Hemans, Landon and the poetess tradition they came to represent cannot be overstated. Within the evolving new media market of the 1820s and 1830s, their poetry was ubiquitous. Hemans and Landon dominated the pages of their era's periodicals in a way that few female poets could and would ever replicate.[14] Their work appeared in titles ranging from literary and critical juggernauts like *Blackwood's Edinburgh Magazine* and *The New Monthly Magazine*, to gilded annuals like *The Keepsake*, *The Bijou* and *The Literary Souvenir*, to cheap weeklies such as *Chambers's Edinburgh Journal* and *The Penny Magazine*. While data from the available indexes makes it clear that their work appeared most frequently in more expensive forms of new media such as the literary periodicals and annuals, their poetry, especially Hemans's, also went 'viral', as Easley states.[15] The editors of publications like *Chambers's* and *The Penny Magazine* reconfigured the poetry of Hemans and Landon, importing the cultural capital of their popular, but still literary, verse into their mass-market periodicals. In doing so, they transformed the poetesses' poetry into representative examples of the type of verse appropriate for both the readers and aspiring writers of the middle classes and, in the case of *The Penny Magazine*, those of the working classes. The positioning of Hemans's and Landon's poetry as exemplars of the genre also fulfilled the aims of the early family periodical to 'spark readers' desire for education, upward mobility, and moral self-improvement' by giving readers access to the ideas and literature of the day.[16] The presence of female poets and the content of their poetry functioned to further support claims of a publication's morality and propriety. It is here that Hemans's and Landon's reputations make a difference to their circulation and reproduction.

Throughout her career, Hemans's readers and publishers saw her poetry as offering 'a primer in the sphere of domestic affections, religious piety, and patriotic passion'.[17] She was seen as 'essentially feminine[,] [. . .] essentially domestic and self-sacrificing'.[18] This made her a perfect addition to a periodical intended to promote middle-class values to an audience that included women and girls. In contrast, Landon was unable to cultivate celebrity and still protect her reputation. The circulation and broad marketing of her poetry 'caused speculations about the promiscuous circulation of her literary character', making her a less valuable commodity in the world of the family magazine.[19] The data from *Chambers's* bears this out. Hemans's poetry appears fifteen times – the most of any female poet between the periodical's first issue in 1832 and the last appearance of either Hemans's or Landon's poetry in 1841. In contrast, Landon's poetry appears twice. The next section of this chapter reads Hemans's and Landon's appearances in *Chambers's* in light of McGill's contention that 'the culture of reprinting does not eliminate authors so much as suspend, reconfigure, and intensify their authority'.[20] I examine how the paratextual material surrounding the poems of both women suspends and intensifies the public narratives that grew around them. In addition, I consider how the content of the poems reprinted in *Chambers's* seems to define and anticipate the role of the periodical poetess for aspiring female poets, building on Easley's recent claim that Hemans's 'engagement with print culture anticipates and defines the market for women's poetry that emerged in the later years, 1832–60'.[21] Indeed, the fact that Landon appears only twice in *Chambers's* while Hemans appears the most out of any female poet published in the 1830s reinforces Hemans's centrality to the development of new media forms and periodical poetry in the early nineteenth century. Finally, this examination of Hemans's and Landon's appearances in *Chambers's* also serves to assert the importance of this early weekly to Victorian periodical culture and its poetics.

Hemans, Landon and *Chambers's Edinburgh Journal*

By the 1830s, Hemans's reputation had become a commodity exchanged in ways beyond her control. This is startingly evident in *Chambers's Edinburgh Journal*. Although Hemans was still actively writing for periodicals and publishing stand-alone poetry volumes at the time, all the poems attributed to Hemans in *Chambers's* were first published either in the literary periodicals of the 1820s, one of Hemans's poetry volumes or one of the many anthologies of her verse. For instance, *Chambers's* credits *The Works of Mrs. Hemans* for 'The Sunbeam' (16 April 1836), 'The Return' (19 September 1840) and 'The Voice of Home to the Prodigal' (24 October 1840). *Mrs. Hemans's Works* and *Mrs. Hemans's Poems* are named as the source for 'The Adopted Child' (12 August 1837) and 'The Song of Sight' (18 April 1840), respectively. *The New Monthly Magazine* is given as the source for 'The Treasures of the Deep' (28 September 1833), and the poems 'The Themes of Song' (31 May 1834), 'Ye Are Not Missed, Fair Flowers' (22 October 1836), 'The Home of Love' (24 December 1836) and 'Sonnet to the South Wind' (18 February 1837) are attributed to her collection *National Lyrics* (1834). The poem 'The Better Land' (8 December 1832) is accompanied by a note that identifies the poem as 'from Mrs. Hemans' Songs of the Affections', which was published in 1830. The periodical does not provide sources for 'The Voice of Spring' (14 April 1832), 'Farewell to the Dead' (11 January 1834), 'The Homes of England' (14 March 1835) and 'The Graves of a Household' (2 May 1835) although all four of these poems appeared in either *Blackwood's Edinburgh Magazine* or *The New Monthly Magazine* between 1823 and 1827.

The paratextual attributions offered (or omitted) by the editors of *Chambers's* provide insight into the role Hemans's poetry and persona played in the branding of the periodical. For example, the references to *The Works of Mrs. Hemans* and *Mrs. Hemans's Poems* evoke her cultural capital as an established poet, someone whose works deserve dedicated anthologies and thus possess literary value. While the references to anthologies draw on Hemans's established reputation, the presence of poems from her most recent collection, *National Lyrics*, draws attention to the fact that while the periodical is republishing poetry, it is nonetheless still publishing the literature of the moment. In the note attached to 'The Themes of Spring', for instance, the editor is careful to observe that *National Lyrics* was 'just published', highlighting the currency of the poem and thus reinforcing the value of the periodical's culture of reprinting.[22] The periodical's readers may not be able to afford the latest poetry volumes, but they can still keep up with the latest releases via *Chambers's*. Through such paratextual notes, the editors of *Chambers's* effectively brand the journal as a cheap and affordable alternative to the more expensive literary magazines, annuals and poetry volumes available on the market. Even the poems that lack attribution reinforce this point. 'The Graves of a Household' and 'The Homes of England' were two of Hemans's most popular poems, and *Chambers's* gives its readers the opportunity to own copies of these verses through their magazine. Ultimately, publishing the greatest and (sometimes) latest poems by the era's famous poets, including but not limited to Hemans, allowed the editors of *Chambers's* to locate their periodical – and thus its readers – at the centre of the era's literary culture, building the publication's brand as a purveyor of affordable, tasteful literature.

However, Hemans's presence in the periodical signals more than just William and Robert Chambers's interest in establishing the literary credentials of their magazine. In her work on the periodical, Easley observes that 'the firm insisted that entertaining readers must not be at the expense of maintaining propriety'; thus, the periodical's contents must always be 'tasteful and innocuous'.[23] The public persona and poetry of Hemans clearly aligns with this brief. As Mrs. Hemans, she is a safe female figure shrouded by the respectability of her signature, which allowed her publishers to market her 'as a poet who celebrated the "domestic affections," [. . .] a defender of hearth and home'.[24] This domestication of Hemans's life and work potentially explains why she is the most republished female poet in *Chambers's*: she offers an acceptable model of femininity for female poets and readers alike while her signature, to borrow from Linda Hughes's work on illustration and *Once a Week*, 'tacitly imports the symbolic capital' of her reputation as both a prominent poet and a defender and exemplar of middle-class domestic values.[25] Consequently, while Easley describes Hemans's career as 'an example of how [. . .] [a poet could] capitalize on new media forms, achieving celebrity while still maintaining a sense of middle-class respectability', [26] Hemans's ability to achieve respectable celebrity also transforms her into an example of how the new media of the nineteenth century used the cultural narratives associated with a particular version of the poetess – specifically, the middle-class and respectable model as defined Hemans – to build their branding and reputation.

The relative absence of Landon from *Chambers's* furthers this point. Unlike Hemans, whose poetry appears fifteen times in the family literary weekly, poems by Landon appear only twice: 'Verses on Thomas Clarkson' (14 December 1839) and 'A Long While Ago' (12 June 1841). Published posthumously in *Chambers's*, 'Verses on Thomas Clarkson' is preceded by a telling preface that describes the poem as having been composed by 'the lamented L. E. L.'[27] This description of Landon is juxtaposed with the editor's description of 'our excellent friend Mary Howitt', who is credited for taking over the *Literary Souvenir* after Landon's death.[28] It should be noted that by this time Howitt, a respectable wife and mother, was well known for the children's poem 'The Spider and the Fly' (1829) and her poetry collection *Hymns and Fireside Verses* (1839) – a biography and literary oeuvre very different from Landon's. The comparison suggested between Landon and Howitt (one lamentable, the other an excellent friend) hints at the public perception and reputation of Landon and perhaps explains why she is relatively absent from the pages of *Chambers's* despite her popularity. After her death, L. E. L. was increasingly defined as a tragic, pitiable figure – the doomed poetess who became a victim of her fame and suffered the consequences of her scandalous behaviour. As such, Howitt's seemingly unnecessary presence in the poem's introductory note adds a veneer of respectability to Landon's presence in the journal.[29] The content of the poem further elides Landon's reputation as a lovelorn poetess. 'Verses on Thomas Clarkson' is an abolitionist text, and its tone and argument are reminiscent of several of Hemans's contributions to the periodical, including her popular poem 'The Graves of a Household' (republished by *Chambers's* in May 1835). Landon's 'Verses' is simultaneously patriotic – 'England, how glorious thine estate!' – and subtly critical of empire – 'Oh England! For the guilty past / A deep atonement make'.[30] The poem thus aligns with the mass-market aesthetic categories privileged by *Chambers's* (and Hemans's poetry) rather than representing those 'treacherous currents of love' that garnered Landon her fame and popularity as a celebrity poetess.[31]

Landon's second appearance in *Chambers's* is prefaced by a note that identifies the source of the poem as her posthumous poetry volume, *The Poetical Remains of L. E. L.*, an evocative title that clearly conflates the poetess's physical body with her verse. This framing is deliberate as the editors could have credited the poem's original source: *The New Monthly Magazine*. Identifying the poem as part of a posthumous memorial collection of verse reconfigures the poem and the poet, fixing Landon and her poetry in a 'complex and heightened [form] of suspension' linked to the moment of her tragic, 'lamentable' death.[32] Like the unidentified 'she' spoken of in the poem, Landon 'hath a memory' in England: 'she was so much a part' of literary culture and society until her marriage and death took her away.[33] In his work on Landon,

Richard Cronin notes that her signature, L. E. L., functioned 'from the first' as 'a device that [. . .] invited the reader to decode and reveal the poet'.[34] In the case of 'A Long While Ago', the attribution of the poem's source combines with Landon's signature – and all it represents – to invite the reader to decode the poem and discover Landon's melancholy presence within, transforming a conventional periodical poem about loss and the passage of time into a seemingly poignant reflection on Landon's exile and death. Regardless of each poem's individual content, then, *Chambers's* reframes Landon's poems in ways that make them acceptable for consumption by middle-class readers, emphasising her pitiable state as England's doomed poetess and inserting her into the vetted and tasteful aesthetic of the journal.

While Landon's poetry had to be reconfigured to fit the aesthetic and moral categories privileged in *Chambers's*, Hemans's poetry seems tailor-made for a family periodical. Given her reputation as a poet of respectable British domesticity, it makes sense that *Chambers's* would define its poetry and model female poet through the nonthreatening and superficially conventional figure of Hemans.[35] The first of her poems republished in *Chambers's*, 'The Voice of Spring' (14 April 1832), epitomises the kind of popular, conventional verse that became identified with the poetess and mass-market periodical poetry, offering a master class of sorts on how to write a seasonal periodical poem. This superficially conventional poem demonstrates Hemans's deep understanding of the poet's craft. One example of the poem's careful construction is the kinetic energy that Hemans evokes in her description of the swelling streams of spring:

> They are sweeping on to the silvery main.
> They are flashing on down from the mountain-brows,
> They are flinging spray on the forest boughs –
> They are bursting fresh from their parry caves,
> And the earth resounds with the joy of waves.[36]

The anaphora in this passage suggests momentum, which is further reinforced through Hemans's diction as the verbs used to describe the water increase in intensity from the gentler sounds of 'sweeping' to the harsher consonant sounds of the 'st' in 'bursting'. The lines become onomatopoeic with the sounds of the words mimicking the sounds and movement of the water. Running alongside these 'streams and founts [. . .] loosed' by spring, however, is a hint of melancholy, a common feature in Hemans's poems.[37] As the poem draws to a close, spring leaves the human auditor of the poem, noting 'Ye are mark'd by care, ye are mine no more'.[38] The poem transforms from a description of the natural world to a meditation on the nature of human existence, drawing on the metaphorical meaning of spring as a stage of life. The poem thus gives the reader space within the busy pages of the periodical to reflect on mortality and the passage of time even as they (and *Chambers's*) mark the arrival of spring. Such space for reflection defines periodical poetry, especially verse published in newspapers.[39] The way Hemans's poetry simultaneously reflects the conditions of its publication and anticipates later patterns of periodical poetry supports Easley's reading of Hemans's poetry as portable and adaptable and introduces one of the central paradoxes of Hemans's poetics: it is at once bound to the periodicity of the periodical press and transcends it through its reproducibility and iterative content.[40]

While the appearance of 'The Voice of Spring' during *Chambers's* fourth month of publication provides readers with a relatively generic (re)introduction to Hemans's poetry, the periodical's republication of several poems from *National Lyrics* – in addition to some of Hemans's most popular patriotic poems – reinforces both the didactic nature of the periodical and its deliberate branding as a cheap family magazine appropriate for middle-class readers. In particular, the poems selected by the editors support Victorian ideals of domestic patriotism and sacrifice and include the kind of nondenominational devotional messaging that would become a defining feature of much periodical poetry. The second appearance of Hemans in *Chambers's* provides evidence of this. 'The Better Land' (8 December 1832) is a short lyric that contains both patriotic and religious messaging. The poem opens with a boy inquiring of his mother where the better land is located. In each stanza, the child describes landscapes tied to Britain's imperial project, asking if the better land is 'where the feathery palm-trees rise, / And the date grows ripe under sunny skies'.[41] The child's insistence on the better land's location in imperial spaces suggests the imaginative possibilities created through colonisation for those lacking opportunities on British soil. Significantly, however, a better life among the world of the living is not the focus of the poem. Rather than locating the better land in the imperial spaces alluded to by the child, the poem's maternal speaker describes the promise of a better land 'beyond the tomb'.[42] This correction and redirection of the child's hope to the promise of a better life in heaven after a life of suffering on earth both aligns with the devotional poetics of Hemans's contemporaries and anticipates the messaging present in the devotional poetry published in mid-century periodicals, reinforcing the connection between Hemans's poetics and Victorian periodical poetry as a genre.

Reprinted in *Chambers's* three years after 'The Better Land', Hemans's 'The Homes of England' (14 March 1835) explicitly brings together patriotism and faith; however, rather than looking beyond Britain's borders like the child speaker in 'The Better Land', the speaker of 'The Homes of England' focuses on identifiable British landscapes and scenes. As Lootens notes, Hemans's poem 'links [. . .] dwellings within a harmonious national hierarchy', moving from stately homes to cottages, from 'hut to hall'.[43] Each stanza depicts a domestic landscape that represents a part of Britain's national identity from its historical ancestral halls to its warm hearths and its quiet modern homes observing the Sabbath. All of these homes of England have their place and role in the definition of the nation. Significantly, the poem's final stanza depicts the domestic spaces of England (regardless of class) as places 'where first the child's glad spirit love / Its country and its God!'.[44] Domesticity and the home, the poem argues, are central to cultivating patriotism and faith in the nation's citizens, reinforcing middle-class ideologies about domesticity and ultimately serving the ideological and educational goals of the periodical. These themes also clearly identify *Chambers's* as an antecedent of the mid-century family literary magazine. Jennifer Phegley argues that 'women readers were crucial to the establishment of family literary magazines, which targeted women as consumers of literature and the dissemination of culture within the home'.[45] Hemans's republished poems in *Chambers's* fit the aims of the family literary magazine as defined by Phegley: her poems identify the home and mothers as the centre of British nationhood and culture – a fact reinforced by her signature, which emphasises her marital state. Moreover, the fact that only three male poets appear more times than Hemans in the periodical suggests that a female-orientated readership was central to the marketing plan of the periodical, speaking to the family periodical's investment in both promoting domesticity and supporting women's reading practices.[46]

Hemans's poems in *Chambers's* undoubtedly reify domestic spaces and celebrate patriotic sacrifice; however, they also contain contradictions seemingly glossed over in the mythologisation of Hemans's poetess persona, a myth-making process that seemingly influenced the reception and interpretation of her poetry in the nineteenth century and beyond. For instance, while Hemans was celebrated as a patriotic poet by her contemporaries, the mother's correction of her child in 'The Better Land' hints at Hemans's fraught and complicated relationship with imperialism. So, too, does her popular poem 'The Graves of a Household', republished in *Chambers's* in May 1835. Much has been written about the 'mournful patriotism' of the poem.[47] Like many of the other Hemans poems selected for republication in *Chambers's*, 'The Graves of a Household' participates in the broader project of cultivating a version of patriotism tied to domestic spaces and familial, especially maternal, love. However, it does so by tracing the lives and deaths of a pair of siblings, invoking the spectre of domestic and maternal grief through a brief reference to the 'fond mother'.[48] The poem's description of the scattered graves functions to highlight the private domestic tragedies caused by imperial progress, reminding us that the poems produced by popular poets (and poetesses) are not simple filler; they reflect complex reactions to and meditations on contemporary events and ideologies. The presence and republication of Hemans's mournfully patriotic poems in the popular media of their time suggests that readers were open to exploring poems that questioned contemporary ideologies as long as these questions were posed by a poet who otherwise embodied an ideal Victorian model of femininity. In his analysis of Hemans's poetry, Cronin asks, 'Is it really credible that Hemans could have contrived to win her place as the most successful poet in Britain by the production of poems that expose the destructive hollowness of the values her readers felt most dear?'[49] The republication of her poems in *Chambers's* suggests that the answer is yes – as long as this hollowness is softened by Hemans's reputation and the sentimental tone of her verse. This ability and the desire of her publishers and readers to smooth away her edges was central to the reception of periodical poetry in the years to come as female periodical poets both wrote within and often subtly challenged the demands of their editors through small, subversive acts. As Isobel Armstrong has noted, the simpler the surface of the sentimental poem, 'the more likely it is that a second and more difficult poem will exist beneath it'.[50] The readers of *Chambers's*, it seems, embraced both.

Equally important as the potential subversive messages in Hemans's verse is the way she and her poetry made space for female poets in the new media of the era, defining the poetics of periodical poetry for those following in her footsteps. Hemans does so directly in 'The Themes of Song' (31 May 1834) where she seemingly defines the subjects and themes appropriate for (popular) poetry. Originally published as part of Hemans's *National Lyrics*, the poem opens with a question: 'Where shall the minstrel find a theme?'[51] The answer is intensely patriotic in tone, matching the suggested focus of the collection's title: 'Where'er, for freedom shed / Brave blood hath dyed the ancient stream'.[52] The remainder of the poem, however, moves away from the martial imagery of the first stanza to poignant images of loss, including images of a 'forsaken grave' and 'a blessed home [. . .] / That now is home no more'.[53] The speaker concludes that

> *There* may the bard's high themes be found.
> We die, we pass away:
> But faith, love, pity – these are bound
> To earth without decay.[54]

The poem thus makes an argument for the value of affective verse, grounded (literally) in the subjects and emotions that define our earthly existence. These emotions, the speaker suggests, are the 'undying things' of existence that serve as the best theme for the poetry written by Britain's public poets.[55] The act of identifying the bard's themes as identical to those of Hemans's poems, including several of those published in *Chambers's Edinburgh Journal*, simultaneously makes a bold claim for the legitimacy and canonicity of such popular poetry as part of a broader British literary tradition and history and defines the 'recognized conventions' of both 'women's verse' and popular poetry as a genre.[56] Just as the American culture of reprinting created a '[mode] of authorship that middle-class women could comfortably apply',[57] the reprinting of Hemans's poems in *Chambers's* effectively established the form and formula for the kind of middlebrow periodical poetry that filled the pages of family literary magazines in the decades to come.

Conclusion

Studying the recirculation of Hemans's and Landon's verse in *Chambers's Edinburgh Journal* provides one window into how new media forms both shaped and responded to the market for women's poetry. It also highlights how the myths surrounding Hemans and Landon as opposite models of female authorship and celebrity determined and influenced their circulation among the new media forms designed to shape and entertain the era's growing middle class as debates about appropriate reading materials and the capacity of women to read critically evolved.[58] This preliminary examination of their republication in cheap weeklies like *Chambers's Edinburgh Journal* (facilitated by digitisation and the ongoing work of indexes like the Curran Index and the Digital Victorian Periodical Poetry Project) ultimately confirms and expands Stuart Curran's assertion that in the poetry and poetics of Hemans and Landon 'we can discern, what is almost strikingly absent in the male Romantic universe, an actual transition into the characteristic preoccupations of Victorian verse'.[59] Indeed, their careers illuminate far more than just a transition from Romantic to Victorian poetics. They also provide evidence for the existence of a concrete, traceable transition from the new media of the late Romantic era to that of the mid-nineteenth century.

The early years of *Chambers's* provide a valuable case study for how the new media forms of the 1820s and 1830s defined the market for cheap middlebrow periodical literature throughout the century. The culture of reprinting that defines the early years of *Chambers's* provides an important revision to Hughes's argument that the most important question in the study of periodical poetry is why 'original poetry mattered to Victorian editors and readers and what poetry can tell us about Victorian periodicals as a whole'.[60] As this chapter argues, we should also be asking why reprinted poetry mattered to the editors and readers of the new media forms that emerged in the lacuna of the 1830s. For periodicals like *Chambers's*, which entered the market in a moment of transition from old to new media forms, reprinting poems by popular canonical and noncanonical authors, from Hemans and Landon to Wordsworth and Scott, established the cultural value of the early nineteenth-century family magazine and created a market for (periodical) poetry among the broader reading public. It also provided the less affluent reader with the opportunity to own poetry written by prominent writers for a fraction of the cost required to purchase poetry volumes, literary annuals and the more expensive monthlies, making periodicals the main source of poetry for middle- and working-class readers. The poems selected for republication by the editors of these new media forms also established the expectations for original periodical poetry: affective, accessible verse appropriate for a middle-class readership that includes men, women and children. The result is a corpus of periodical literature dominated by an identifiable subset of poets who published across periodical titles from weeklies like *Chambers's* and *Household Words* to monthlies like *Macmillan's Magazine* and *Good Words*.[61]

Poets could easily publish across titles and publishing houses like Chambers's and Macmillan's because the proprietors of family literary magazines from the 1830s to the 1860s all aimed to provide middle-class readers with respectable contemporary literature that modelled middle-class values. For female poets, this meant producing poetry and maintaining a popular image that aligned with nineteenth-century notions of gender, propriety and the poetics of the popular poetess.[62] William Thackeray's rejection of Elizabeth Barrett Browning's 'Lord Walter's Wife' for publication in *The Cornhill Magazine* makes such expectations clear. He opens the letter by identifying Barrett Browning first as a wife and mother before writing that the *Cornhill*'s readers 'would make an outcry' if this poem depicting 'an unlawful passion felt by a man for a woman' appeared in their magazine.[63] In response, Barrett Browning submitted 'Little Mattie' (June 1861) a (seemingly) much more conventional periodical poem about maternal grief – a theme, uncoincidentally, often seen in Hemans's verse. As Thackeray's rejection of Barrett Browning's poetry at the height of her fame suggests, periodical poetry from Hemans and Landon onwards, especially verse by women, had to fit within certain aesthetic and thematic boundaries. In his work on Landon, Daniel Reiss argues that 'restoring her proper place' within the context of commercial literary venues such as the literary magazine 'allows us to understand and evaluate with greater clarity the work of the writers who precede and follow her'.[64] The same can, of course, be said of Hemans, as both poetesses arguably transformed the literary market, laying new paths for future poets. The decisions Hemans and Landon made about where to publish their work, considered alongside the uncontrollable afterlife of their poems, defined the expectations attached to periodical poetry and the popular poetess and contributed to the rise of the periodical as the main repository for poetry of the period.

Notes

1. Of the thirty-four poets, only five are women: Hemans, Landon, Mary Tighe, Joanna Baillie and Caroline Bowles.
2. For research on new media forms and women's poetry, see Alexis Easley, *New Media and the Rise of the Popular Woman Writer, 1832–1860* (Edinburgh: Edinburgh University Press, 2021); Terrence Hoagwood and Kathryn Ledbetter, *Colour'd Shadows: Contexts in Publishing, Printing, and Reading Nineteenth-Century British Women Writers* (New York: Palgrave Macmillan, 2005); Lindsy Lawrence, '"Afford[ing] me a Place": Recovering Women Poets in *Blackwood's Edinburgh Magazine*, 1827–1835', in *Women, Periodicals and Print Culture in Britain, 1830s–1900s: The Victorian Period*, ed. Alexis Easley, Clare Gill and Beth Rodgers, 400–12 (Edinburgh: Edinburgh University Press, 2019); Michele Martinez, 'Creating an Audience for a British School: L. E. L's Poetical Catalogue of Pictures in *The Literary Gazette*', *Victorian Poetry* 52, no. 1 (2014): 41–63; and Manuela Mourão, 'Remembrance of Things Past: Literary Annuals' Self-Historicization', *Victorian Poetry* 50, no. 1 (2012): 107–23. For a useful overview of the poetess and how to approach her verse, see Susan Brown, 'The Victorian Poetess', in *The Cambridge Companion to Victorian Poetry*, ed. Joseph Bristow, 180–202 (Cambridge: Cambridge University Press, 2000); Isobel Armstrong, *Victorian Poetry: Poetry, Poetics and Politics* (London: Routledge, 1993); and Jerome McGann, *The Poetics of Sensibility: A Revolution in Literary Style* (Oxford: Clarendon Press, 1996). For work on nineteenth-century periodical poetry more broadly, see Alison Chapman and Caley Ehnes, Introduction to a special issue of *Victorian Poetry* 52, no. 1 (2014): 1–20; Caley Ehnes, *Victorian Poetry and the Poetics of the Literary Periodical* (Edinburgh: Edinburgh University Press, 2019); and Linda K. Hughes, 'What the *Wellesley Index* Left Out: Why Poetry Matters to Periodical Studies', *Victorian Periodicals Review* 40, no. 2 (2007): 91–125.
3. See Lindsy Lawrence, 'Afford[ing] me a Place'; Martinez, 'Creating an Audience for a British School'; Daniel Reiss, 'Laetitia Landon and the Dawn of English Post-Romanticism', *Studies in English Literature, 1500–1900* 36, no. 4 (1996): 807–27; Sarah Anne Storti,

'Letitia Landon: Still a Problem', *Victorian Poetry* 57, no. 4 (2019): 533–56; and Mary Waters, 'Letitia Landon's Literary Criticism and Her Romantic Project: L. E. L.'s Poetics of Feeling and the Periodical Reviews', *Women's Writing* 28, no. 3 (2011): 305–30.

4. Meredith McGill, *American Literature and the Culture of Reprinting, 1834–1853* (Philadelphia: University of Pennsylvania Press, 2003), 17; Yopie Prins, 'Poetess', in *The Princeton Encyclopedia of Poetry and Poetics*, 4th ed., ed. Roland Greene, et al. (Princeton: Princeton University Press, 2012), 1052.
5. Richard Cronin, *Romantic Victorians: English Literature, 1824–1840* (New York: Palgrave, 2002), 2.
6. McGill, *American Literature*, 20.
7. Lawrence, 'Afford[ing] me a Place', 402.
8. Brandy Ryan, '"Echo and Reply": The Elegies of Felicia Hemans, Letitia Landon, and Elizabeth Barrett', *Victorian Poetry* 46, no. 3 (2008): 258.
9. McGann, *The Poetics of Sensibility*, 143, 145; Ryan, 'Echo and Reply', 258.
10. Letitia Elizabeth Landon, 'On the Ancient and Modern Influence of Poetry', *New Monthly Magazine* 35 (November 1832): 466.
11. William St Clair, *The Reading Nation in the Romantic Period* (Cambridge: Cambridge University Press, 2007), 160.
12. Ibid., 161.
13. Prins, 'Poetess', 1052; Easley, *New Media*, 242.
14. Based solely on the publications indexed in open-access resources such as the Digital Victorian Periodical Poetry Project and the Curran Index, Hemans published 129 poems in *Blackwood's Edinburgh Magazine* and 131 poems in *The New Monthly Magazine*. In addition, her poetry appeared in *The Keepsake* (two poems), *The Penny Magazine* (one poem), *The Bijou* (two poems), *Fraser's Magazine for Town and Country* (one poem) and *The Literary Souvenir* (twenty-five poems). Landon published over 300 poems in *The Literary Gazette* and over fifty in *The New Monthly Magazine*. She also published in *The Literary Souvenir* (twenty-eight poems), *The Bijou* (five poems), *Fraser's Magazine for Town and Country* (two poems) and *The Keepsake* (fifteen poems). These numbers are, of course, not representative of these writers' entire output, but they do begin to give us a sense of the scale of their participation in the periodical press.
15. Easley, *New Media*, 14.
16. Ibid., 135.

17. Susan Wolfson, 'Felicia Hemans and the Revolving Doors of Reception', in *Romanticism and Women Poets: Opening the Doors of Reception*, ed. Harriet Kramer Linkin and Stephen C. Behrendt (Lexington: University Press of Kentucky, 2015), 215.
18. Ibid., 215–16.
19. Prins, 'Poetess', 1052.
20. McGill, *American Literature*, 17.
21. Easley, *New Media*, 14.
22. Felicia Hemans, 'The Voice of Spring', *Chambers's Edinburgh Journal* 1 (14 April 1832): 87.
23. Easley, *New Media*, 152.
24. Paula R. Feldman, 'Introduction', in *Records of Woman, with Other Poems* by Felicia Hemans, ed. Paula R. Feldman (Lexington: University Press of Kentucky, 1999), xx. However, the reality was more complicated, as it often is. As Lootens notes, 'to sign "Poetess" is, then, to practice signature as a form of erasure'. Tricia Lootens, *The Political Poetess: Victorian Femininity, Race, and the Legacy of Separate Spheres* (Princeton: Princeton University Press, 2017), 3–4. Lootens's logic can be extended to include the chosen (and sometimes imposed) signatures of individual poetesses. In Hemans's case, her signature erased all aspects of her identity outside of her married respectability.
25. Linda Hughes, 'Inventing Poetry and Pictorialism in *Once a Week*: A Magazine of Visual Effects', *Victorian Poetry* 48, no. 1 (2010): 51.
26. Easley, *New Media*, 28–9.
27. Letitia Elizabeth Landon, 'Verses on Thomas Clarkson, by L. E. L.', *Chambers's Edinburgh Journal* 8 (14 December 1839): 376.
28. Ibid.
29. The editors of Hemans's anthologies were never mentioned.
30. Landon, 'Verses', 376.
31. Jerome McGann and Daniel Reiss, 'Introduction', in *Letitia Elizabeth Landon: Selected Writings*, ed. Jerome McGann and Daniel Reiss (Peterborough: Broadview Press, 1997), 20.
32. McGill, *American Literature*, 21; Letitia Elizabeth Landon, 'A Long While Ago', *Chambers's Edinburgh Journal* 10 (12 June 1841): 168.
33. Landon, 'A Long While Ago', 168. The quotations in this sentence are taken from the following lines of the poem: 'she who only hath a memory here, / She was so much a part of us, so cherish'd'.
34. Cronin, *Romantic Victorians*, 83.
35. See Wolfson, 'Felicia Hemans', 218–19.
36. Hemans, 'The Voice', 87.

37. Ibid. For more information about the melancholic tone of Hemans's poetry, see Cronin, *Romantic Victorians*.
38. Hemans, 'The Voice', 87.
39. For more information on newspaper verse, see Natalie Houston, 'Newspaper Poems: Material Texts in the Public Sphere', *Victorian Studies* 50, no. 2 (2008): 233–42.
40. 'The Voice of Spring' was particularly portable and adaptable. One year after its republication in *Chambers's*, it appeared in an early June issue of *The Penny Magazine*.
41. Felicia Hemans, 'The Better Land', *Chambers's Edinburgh Journal* 1 (8 December 1832): 359.
42. Ibid.
43. Tricia Lootens, 'Hemans and Home: Victorianism, Feminine "Internal Enemies", and the Domestication of National Identity', *PMLA* 109, no. 2 (1994): 248; Felicia Hemans, 'The Homes of England', *Chambers's Edinburgh Journal* 4 (14 March 1835): 56.
44. Hemans, 'Homes', 56.
45. Jennifer Phegley, *Educating the Proper Woman Reader: Victorian Family Literary Magazines and the Cultural Health of the Nation* (Columbus: Ohio State University Press, 2004), 6.
46. Those male poets are William Wordsworth, Robert Chambers and, in translation, Pierre-Jean de Beranger.
47. Lootens, 'Hemans and Home', 243.
48. Felicia Hemans, 'The Graves of a Household', *Chambers's Edinburgh Journal* 4 (2 May 1835): 112.
49. Cronin, *Romantic Victorians*, 68.
50. Armstrong, *Victorian Poetry*, 324.
51. Felicia Hemans, 'The Themes of Song', *Chambers's Edinburgh Journal* 3 (31 May 1834): 144.
52. Ibid.
53. Ibid.
54. Ibid.
55. Ibid.
56. Armstrong, *Victorian Poetry*, 321.
57. McGill, *American Literature*, 41.
58. See Phegley, *Educating the Proper Woman Reader*.
59. Stuart Curran, 'Romantic Poetry: The *I* Altered', in *Romantic Poetry: Recent Revisionary Criticism*, ed. Karl Kroeher and Gene W. Ruoff (New Brunswick: Rutgers University Press, 1993), 42.
60. Hughes, 'What the *Wellesley Index* Left Out', 91.

61. For instance, Dinah Mulock Craik published prolifically in *Chambers's* between 1839 and 1855, and she went on to contribute to *Good Words* and *Macmillan's Magazine* in the 1860s.
62. See Brown, 'Victorian Poetess', 189.
63. Gordon Ray, ed., *The Letters and Private Papers of William Makepeace Thackeray* (Oxford: Oxford University Press, 1946), 4:226–7.
64. Daniel Reiss, 'Laetitia Landon', 824.

9

A Familiar Transition: Dinah Mulock Craik's Early Career in Periodicals, 1841–45

Helena Goodwyn

The 'sense of a female literary invasion in the 1840s' was, writes Elaine Showalter in *A Literature of Their Own* in 1977, 'an illusion, an attempt to substitute a quantitative explanation for a qualitative phenomenon'.[1] This illusion, Showalter contends, can be attributed in part to the increased attention being given to the phenomenon of the woman writer in periodical criticism of the same period. Showalter cites another twentieth-century expert in the field, Richard Altick, whose early quantitative work established that between 1835 and 1870 'women were in fact a slightly *smaller* percentage of the literary professions than in other periods' and that 'the proportion of women writers to men remained steady at about 20 percent from 1800 to 1935' due to educational inequities and gender bias in the publishing world.[2]

More recent quantitative work that takes advantage of computational methodologies challenges these interpretations. Troy Bassett's digital humanities project At the Circulating Library – a biographical and bibliographical database of nineteenth-century British fiction – suggests that for published novelists in the period 1837–60, at least, equivalence was on the way to being reached, with novels by women making up 42 per cent of the total number of published novels in 1837, 50 per cent in 1850, 61 per cent in 1854 and 49 per cent in 1860.[3] Ted Underwood, David Bamman and Sabrina Lee have similarly demonstrated that by 1850, roughly 50 per cent of titles in their study, 'The Transformation of Gender in English-Language Fiction', were written by women.[4] Gaye Tuchman, in *Edging Women Out: Victorian Novelists, Publishers and Social Change*, found a gender imbalance in favour of women in published fiction even before 1840, though, as the title of her study suggests, this trend would be reversed after mid-century.[5] Whilst these studies focus their attention on the novelist, the wider research that informs them examines the conditions under which a woman might make a career in the nineteenth-century literary marketplace with its variety of publication formats.

Showalter, responding to Altick and Raymond Williams, argues that 'progress toward similar career patterns for male and female novelists was unsteady but distinct over a long period of time' and that 'there are three areas in which the career patterns of nineteenth century male and female writers show clear differences: education, means of support and age at first publication'.[6] In 'Making a Debut', Alexis Easley concurs that 'throughout the century, it was challenging for women to find success in a male-dominated literary marketplace' but that by the end of the century opportunities had improved.[7] The data provided by Bassett, Underwood, Tuchman and others suggests that, in fact, the mid-nineteenth century was a particularly fortuitous time for women to enter the literary marketplace. The early years of the novelist and poet Dinah Maria Mulock's (1826–87) career can be viewed in this context, but we must remember that she, like so many others of her generation, published her first works in the pages of the largely anonymous periodical press, which makes it more difficult to gauge the relative success of women and men as writers during this period.[8]

It is perhaps beyond the scope of any study to try to gauge the percentage increase of women working within the capacious boundaries of the periodical press over the course of the nineteenth century. As Margaret Beetham attests, 'we are constantly revising our estimates of how many Victorian periodicals there were', let alone the scale of the workforce behind those periodicals.[9] However, the 1891 census lists 660 women as 'author, editor or journalist', compared to 15 identifying as such in 1841. This is, of course, an unreliable estimate of the number of women who made a living by the press or contributed to it in a more irregular way; nevertheless, it does suggest that there was a significant increase in women who were comfortable with such a designation by the turn of the century.[10]

Whilst it is important to be able to situate individual case studies in larger trends and developments that inform our understanding of the nineteenth-century literary marketplace, Linda H. Peterson and others warn us against relying too heavily on macro 'historical' 'rise and fall' narratives.[11] Peterson, here, is following

Betty A. Schellenberg, who argues that, as the nineteenth century progressed, women could, increasingly, within a hugely expanded and expanding commercial press, construct 'their authorial identities self-consciously and diversely'.[12] Larger 'rise and fall' narratives can obstruct our view of these important stories of self-conscious authorial creation, as within these stories of individual and varied approaches to authorship, reasons Peterson, lay the future of the profession and 'the opening of new genres for women writers: the essay, the literary review, the periodical column, the biographical portrait and historical sketch, the travelogue, and the serialized tale'.[13] This is true of Dinah Mulock, whose oeuvre would later encompass poetry, essays, reviews, novels, translations, travelogues, short stories and children's literature.

In this chapter, I attempt to balance the kinds of quantitative studies mentioned above against the need for a nuanced understanding of the necessarily idiosyncratic ways many women writers found their place in the nineteenth-century literary marketplace. To do so, I look at the earliest publications of Dinah Mulock – latterly Craik, after her marriage to George Lillie Craik in 1865 – situating several of them in the hitherto unrecognised context of nineteenth-century popular music. As we have seen in the quantitative research conducted by Bassett, Underwood and others, the 1840s were a promising time, statistically, for a woman author to launch a career. Combining these findings with the qualitative context provided by Peterson, Schellenberg, Beetham and others, we can see that as mid-century approached, Dinah Mulock's route into the profession through periodicals was beginning to take on the air of an established model, one that young, ambitious writers could adopt and adapt to suit their needs, talents and interests.

At the same time, examining Mulock's entrance to the world of letters demonstrates just how 'self-conscious and diverse' finding a footing in the increasingly overcrowded periodicals marketplace needed to be. It could require a range of carefully calibrated acts, such as networking within an expatriate community or pitching content that displayed certain national leanings to a journal operating outside the dominant London domain. As I will go on to show, Mulock launched her career with numerous well-judged manoeuvres that led her to become a sensation in her own time. Her ability, from a young age, to respond to and manipulate the demands of the market demonstrates her awareness of the methods of her literary predecessors, who provided a range of inspirational models for Mulock to modify and experiment with in launching her career.[14]

Mulock's early success can also, in part, be attributed to the way in which she thought about her audience. She sought to represent and therefore engage a diverse readership by featuring voices from Scotland, Wales, Ireland, England and beyond in her earliest experimental submissions to periodicals and subsequent writings.[15] From the very beginning of her career, Mulock stands out as a writer concerned with representing a wide variety of voices. This is significant as these early writings were published in periodicals and magazines that were associated with the emergence of a 'mass media' – publications from many different regions and countries that achieved circulations in the tens and hundreds of thousands. Mulock also experimented with literary forms that were designed to appeal to middle-class and family audiences, often privileging the assumed interests and tastes of women and children. Her innovations are part of a larger story of radical change in literary culture, which led to the rise of sentimental poetry, social-problem fiction, children's literature and diverse other genres.

D. M. M.: Dinah Maria Mulock's initial publications (1841–44)

When Dinah Maria Mulock entered the literary marketplace as a teenager in the 1840s, she was by no means unusual in her precocity. As Laurie Langbauer and others note, many writers like Felicia Hemans, Lord Byron and Margaret Oliphant started writing at a young age.[16] The explosion of periodical culture that produced titles like *Blackwood's Edinburgh Magazine* (1817–1980), *The New Monthly Belle Assemblée* (1834–70), *Chambers's Edinburgh Journal* (1832–1956), *Bentley's Miscellany* (1837–68) and *The Westminster Review* (1824–1914) also created an abundance of opportunity for those seeking a career in letters. Moreover, as Karen Bourrier documents, another crucial influence on Dinah Mulock's early career was her move from Staffordshire to London in the summer of 1840 when she was fourteen years old. This introduced her to literary networks and soirées hosted by the likes of Mrs S. C. Hall and Jane Loudon, and provided her with access to the reading room at the British Library.[17] The move was engineered by Mulock's father, who had also facilitated her first appearance in print in the *Staffordshire Advertiser* on 16 January

1841: a 659-word poem entitled 'Stanzas on the Birth of the Princess Royal'.

Mulock confided to her childhood friend Rebecca Hallam, 'As you know I am guilty of scribbling sometimes. [. . .] Did you see in the "Advertiser" of last Saturday fortnight the 16th Jan, some verses on the Princess's birth, with "D. M. M., Brompton" at the bottom, they were mine.'[18] Mulock's performative self-deprecation of 'sometimes scribbling' is, of course, entirely undone by her palpable excitement and pride, conveyed clearly in the words 'they were mine'. Indeed, if this weren't enough evidence to suggest that Mulock was less than nonchalant about her first publication, she goes on to comment on the editorial note that accompanied her poem and which read, 'We insert the above Lines at the request of a Correspondent, who informs us that they are the production of a young Lady, in her 14th year only.'[19] Mulock reports to Hallam, 'I gave them to Papa [and] Mr. Crewe, [. . .] put [the verses] in, with that unlucky note at the bottom, which vexed me more than the insertion of my nonsensical lines pleased me.'[20] Mulock's return to self-deprecation – 'my nonsensical lines' – does not sufficiently disguise the fact that her displeasure at being outed as a fourteen-year-old girl outweighed the joy of seeing her work in print for the very first time. She is 'vexed' presumably because she hoped the poem would be seen as a professional work of poetry, rather than being contextualised as the accomplishment of a precocious child. Mulock's letter to Hallam helps us to establish that she viewed her work seriously from the outset of her career and saw this as a launch rather than a father's indulgence of a childish whim. Her youth was not a novelty in the literary culture of the period, yet the newspaper commented on it, suggesting to Mulock that her work had not yet achieved the quality to which she aspired.[21]

Nine months later, in October 1841, Mulock's second poem, 'Song of the Hours', was published in *Dublin University Magazine*, once again appearing under the signature D. M. M., Brompton. This was a quite a graduation from a local newspaper managed by a family friend to an expensive (2s 6d) 'thoroughly middle-class monthly magazine [. . .] with substantial general articles and reviews [. . .] intended for relatively well-educated readers'.[22] Once again, however, an editorial note was affixed:

> Our next is from the pen of another fair authoress. When we inform our readers, that she does not yet number sixteen years, we are sure

> they will agree with us that the following gives promise of future powers, which only require study of the art, careful examination of the best models, and a little more discipline and knowledge, to attain fame and distinction.[23]

'Song of the Hours' is an engaging, thoughtful piece that personifies time. 'The hours' address the reader arrestingly, asserting, 'We have come from the land of the viewless things.'[24] Made up of three twelve-line stanzas and composed of rhyming couplets throughout, the poem juxtaposes the 'pure of heart' who enjoy their time on earth with those who experience the passing of time painfully.[25] It was a rather more sophisticated poem than her celebration of the Princess Royal, so Mulock may have been disappointed to see yet another editorial intervention drawing the reader's attention to her age and literary abilities.

There is no record of any further publications by 'D. M. M.' for the next two years.[26] Then, in 1844, a steady succession of publications appeared in the annual *Friendship's Offering of Sentiment and Mirth* and in magazines such as *The New Monthly Belle Assemblée* and *Chambers's Edinburgh Journal*. In the intervening period, Bourrier explains, Mulock was developing the literary networks that would 'launch and sustain her career'.[27] In particular, she became immersed in musical culture, reporting to Hallam that in one week, she went to '*three* parties and a concert', where she heard Adelaide Kemble in the Bellini opera *Norma*.[28] Mulock describes how she regularly practised duets with Maria Knowles (daughter of the Irish dramatist Sheridan Knowles) who taught her 'to sing Italian music in the *orthodox* way', and, Aleyn Lyell Reade tells us, she was 'in great demand at parties as a vocalist' having amassed 'an immense stock of Irish, Scottish, Italian and English music'.[29] In addition, Mulock was studying French, Italian, Latin, Greek and Irish. As she playfully reported to Hallam, 'I shall be a Polyglot Lexicon, by-and-by.'[30] Her social circle was, in her own words, 'almost entirely Irish', including Mrs S. C. Hall, the scholar-tutor Thaddeus Connellan and a Mrs Cowley, who threw fabulous parties.[31]

It is beyond doubt that these are the influences we see in the next phase of Mulock's transition to a career in letters. Her doleful poem 'Verses', published in *Friendship's Offering of Sentiment and Mirth*, was accompanied this time by no patronising editorial note but one (presumably) from the author herself, which read:

'The sad story to which these lines relate, needs not be explained to those who know the history of one who perished on the scaffold in the dark year of the Irish Rebellion.'[32] This footnote is purposefully enigmatic, inviting some 'in the know' readers into dialogue and excluding others. However, the level of ambiguity present in the footnote also makes it difficult to firmly establish if Mulock is referring to the 1798 uprising or a later conflict such as the 1803 rebellion. Given the romantic subject matter of the poem, it may allude to Robert Emmet and Sarah Curran, who were memorialised in various different cultural forms, including popular song, after Emmet's death by hanging in 1803.[33]

Mulock's ancestry on her father's side was Irish, as was her social and cultural circle in London – both of which exerted a powerful influence on her young and intellectually hungry mind. It is likely that she would have heard at least some politically charged conversations at the various gatherings she attended and so would have gained a better understanding of the 'Irish Question' as experienced by the expatriates she found herself surrounded by.[34] Her collection of Irish music, too, which might have contained songs such as Thomas Moore's 'O Breathe Not His Name', a tribute to Robert Emmet's final speech from the dock, would have provided influence and inspiration for her own creations.[35]

Mulock's musical training in popular entertainments proved invaluable in her determination to become a regular contributor to fashionable periodicals. In April of 1844, she began her publishing relationship with *The New Monthly Belle Assemblée* by publishing two poems on the same page: 'A March Song' and the first of six poems/songs in a series entitled 'Songs for Stray Airs'. 'A March Song' consists of four stanzas and is a celebration of the coming of spring. The first stray air was titled 'The Mourner's Hope of Immortality. (A Funeral Hymn.)' and was accompanied by several directions to the reader. The first tells us that the song is a 'German air – the drinking chorus is *Robert le Diable*'.[36] The second gives further guidance: 'In adapting these words, the air should be played rather slowly, and with solemnity.'[37] Here we have evidence of Mulock capitalising on her 'immense stock' of music and burgeoning experience as an entertainer at parties. Imagining her female reader to be like her – well-versed in popular music of the day and in constant want of new entertainment – Mulock takes a chorus from a hugely popular opera, Giacomo Meyerbeer's *Robert le Diable* (1831), knowing that there would be a fair chance readers would be familiar with it and would be able to recall the music from memory. She then provides new lyrics and a slow, solemn air to put a fresh spin on an established song.[38] In an increasingly crowded literary marketplace, Mulock was thinking strategically about how to produce 'new' and entertaining content for the reader whilst using the resources she had available to her for inspiration. This mixture of the new and the familiar, innovation and reuse, was a shrewd tactic. It drew the reader into the dialogic relationship already established between Mulock and pre-existing music whilst inviting readers to add their own active participation and interpretation by playing and singing the song. In so doing, Mulock was borrowing from the tradition exploited by Thomas Moore, James Hogg, Robert Burns, Joanna Baillie and others in presenting readers with new lyrics to existing popular and familiar music.

Mulock's next 'stray air', 'The Shepherd's Wife', was published in the May edition of the *Assemblée*. It was a Scottish air, a strathspey (slow reel) meant to be played to the tune of 'Loch Erroch Side', a popular folk song.[39] In this experiment in folk music, Mulock attempted to emulate Scots, presumably for the reader and performer to copy:

The shepherd's wife cam' o'er the hill,
When night drew on sae drearie,
An' aye she sigh'd, an' aye she cried
'Come hame to me, my dearie!'
Her hair was wet wi' falling dew,
The saut tear fill'd her een sae blue,
She cried, as aye the darkness grew,
'Come hame to me, my dearie!'[40]

Mulock's use of Scots here would have been familiar to readers of publications such as the hugely popular, if somewhat condescending, *Whistle Binkie* song anthologies (1832–90), as well as novels by Walter Scott, James Hogg and others.[41] In fact, the use of Scots in literature and music had become so familiar that it was satirised as early as 1824 with the publication of Sarah Green's *Scotch Novel Reading; or Modern Quackery: A Novel Really Founded on Facts*.[42] Mulock's composition of new lyrics to a well-known folk song in the Scotch style shows her participating in the 'Caledonian Mania' identified by Green in her satirical novel. It is clear Mulock had a particular talent for such work: Bourrier cites the reminiscences of a Miss Winnard who witnessed Mulock's 'spirited singing of *Bonnie Dundee, Cam ye by Athol braes* and other Jacobite songs'.[43] Winnard further reported that the critic, editor and poet Leigh Hunt (1784–1859) also saw Mulock perform and that 'her songs took him by storm', so much so that he was 'charmed and excited [. . .] to an extent he never forgot'.[44] That Mulock chose to experiment linguistically as well as musically in these early works demonstrates her keen interest in 'finding the popular audience' by gauging the mood of the marketplace as well as her desire to hone her writerly skills by challenging herself to write in multiple formats and styles.[45]

Such experiences no doubt increased Mulock's confidence in her abilities, both as a performer and as a writer. This growing self-assurance may have influenced her decision to include her full name on her periodical publications. In the May 1844 edition of *The New Monthly Belle Assemblée*, her signature changes from 'D. M. M.' appended at the bottom of each publication to 'Dinah Maria Mulock' located at the top of each piece. This was more in keeping with the typical *Assemblée* style, which did publish authors known only by their initials but far more often printed contributors' full names. Mulock may have decided to change her signature because she was surrounded by literary women, including Mrs S. C. Hall, Camilla Toulmin and Jane Loudon, who published with their names – albeit in two of the three cases with married names; nevertheless, there was no obfuscation around who they were.[46]

The next month, in June of 1844, Mulock's third stray air, 'Carolan's War Cry', was published. This song was composed to a familiar Irish air, 'The Red Fox',[47] usually referred to as 'The Little Red Fox'. The earliest notation of this tune, according to Norman Cazden et al., is found in Robert A. Smith's *Irish Minstrel* of 1828, with a text by James Hogg entitled 'There's Gow[d] in the Breast'.[48] However, it is likely that Mulock's adaptation is inspired by Thomas Moore's lyrical variation to the tune, 'Let Erin Remember the Days of Old', from his *Irish Melodies*, published between 1808 and 1834, which Sarah McCleave tells us 'is arguably the most successful songster [songbook] of the nineteenth century'.[49] This same volume contained the previously mentioned 'O Breathe Not His Name', a tribute to Robert Emmet that may have inspired Mulock's poem 'Verses'. Mulock follows

Moore by setting English-language verse to an old Irish tune, and she does not attempt to alter her language to imitate an Irish accent, use vernacular phrasing or include many Gaelic words. She does, however, accurately use archaic formulations such as 'remaineth' and 'staineth' to indicate that her subject and speaker are historical:

> Oh, think of the days when our fathers bled,
> When the bands of the fierce assaulter
> Made Erin wail for her children dead!
> Then strike, for the Throne and Altar! –
> For the faith, which through long years opprest,
> Still shrin'd in our hearts remaineth –
> For the king, whose throne is the faithful breast,
> And the lip that no flattery staineth.[50]

Similarities of scansion and theme can be seen in Mulock's version above and Moore's lines:

> Let Erin remember the days of old,
> Ere her faithless sons betray'd her;
> When Malachi wore the collar of gold,
> Which he won from her proud invader;
> When her kings, with standard of green unfurl'd,
> Led the Red-Branch Knights to danger; –
> Ere the emerald gem of the western world
> Was set in the crown of a stranger.[51]

Moore writes of the tenth century whilst Mulock transports her reader to the seventeenth, but Mulock's air sits very lightly atop Moore's 'Let Erin Remember', functioning almost as a palimpsest. She follows the same rhyme scheme, the same irregular but iambic metre and the same wistful ahistorical tone, balanced by the use of apparently precise historical referents. In this way, Mulock creates a new song (lyrically) for the reader, performer and publisher, but one that is full of familiar resonances, anchoring it to Moore's well-known version and perhaps aiding recall of the tune.

Despite being surrounded by Irish expatriates, studying the language and culture of Ireland and regularly singing Irish songs, Mulock did not attempt to write in Hiberno-English when producing her 'Irish' airs. This may have been because there was not the same tradition of publications written in Hiberno-English as there was in Scots. As Norman Vance tells us,

> 'English' has been the dominant, but not the sole, language in which Irish people have written in modern times. [. . .] The period begins with the controversial passing of an Act of Union in 1800 which confirmed English as the language of government and administration (as it had been for centuries).[52]

As we have seen, Mulock was influenced by Moore's *Irish Melodies* in this regard, which became such a ubiquitous songster that it is credited with the popularisation of Gaelic musical culture in English and the idea that 'the "spirit" of Gaelic culture might be preserved and conveyed through the English language'.[53] Just like Moore, Mulock uses 'Erin', the Hiberno-English word for Ireland, to convey the sympathies of her imagined speaker, but like Moore, or James Hardiman, in his *Irish Minstrelsy* (1831), she uses very few other Hiberno-English words or phrases.[54]

Mulock published another piece that month entitled 'Forgive One Another', a seven-stanza poem made up of quatrains with alternate rhymes (ABAB) that preached the Christian message of forgiveness.[55] The fourth stray air, published in July, was 'A Barcarole', or Venetian boat song, to the tune of 'O Pescator, dell'onde', a well-known example of the style.[56] A version of this song had been popularised in Britain by Sir Henry Rowley Bishop (1786–1855) in his adaptation of Mozart's *Le nozze di Figaro* (1786) for the Theatre Royal, Covent Garden, 1819. Christina Fuhrmann makes the point that Bishop's version 'typified the world of nineteenth-century opera as a whole' in that 'cuts, substitutions, and translations accompanied every new production'.[57] These translations and adaptations often made their way into 'partial stage performances, concert excerpts and reams of sheet music variations', which 'splintered the work into individual numbers'.[58] Thus, 'O Pescator, dell'onde' may have made its way into Mulock's 'immense stock of Irish, Scottish, Italian and English music'.[59] Here again Mulock engaged in experimentation by reworking a well-known folk song, this time one that had been elevated by its association with Mozart's opera and which might have appealed to a slightly different reader as a result. By taking part in the practice of modifying songs in a variety of musical genres, Mulock developed her craft whilst also offering her reader a range of literary and musical experiences.

In August, Mulock published the fifth song in the series, 'Caoinhe Over an Irish Chieftain', another traditional Irish air sung to the tune of 'Brian Boroimhe's March'.[60] The only editorial intervention included is a note – 'Pronounced "keen"' – in keeping with the common practice of parsing Irish words for an English reader. Mulock also published a poem in the August edition of the *Assemblée*, 'The Country Sabbath', written in iambic heptameter, or 'fourteeners'. The poem is a pastoral tribute to the conditions of village and country life. With the publication of poems such as 'Forgive One Another' and 'The Country Sabbath' juxtaposed against 'Caoinhe over an Irish Chieftain' and 'A Barcarole', Mulock oscillated between experimenting with various national musical styles and themes and producing simple poems ideal for Sunday school recitations. By appealing to a variety of audiences and producing material appropriate for scrapbooks and the market for reprinting, Mulock ensured that her launch into the periodical marketplace would be a success.[61]

The final stray air, published in the September edition of the *Assemblée*, 'A Fire-Side Song', was designed to be played to the tune of Johann Strauss's 'Aurora Waltz', another popular piece that was guaranteed to be familiar to many readers.[62] These experiments in poetry and song allowed Mulock to play with different national themes that she had been learning about both in her studies and her social life. At the same time, she remained relatively protected from critical scrutiny as her compositions were linked to, and reliant on, pre-existing, well-known songs. Other poems she published at this time had conventional moral lessons or evoked episodes from history, thus also combining the new and the familiar, the innovative and the imitative.

Transition and translation: From poetry to prose (1845)

In 1845, Mulock began publishing translations, a natural next step from the stray airs that transformed old and familiar songs into fresh compositions. This is not to suggest that once Mulock began to publish stories she would leave poetry behind as a mere phase of her juvenile training in the literary trade; on the contrary, she would continue to publish poems prolifically throughout the rest of her career and even posthumously, as the Digital Victorian Periodical Poetry Project (DVPPP) demonstrates. Based on the content of the DVPPP, we know that between 1845 and 1892 Mulock published 191 poems in *Chambers's Edinburgh Journal*, *Macmillan's Magazine*, *All the Year Round*, *Good Words* and *Once a Week*.[63] In terms of the number of poems published, Mulock is second only in the database to 'Delta', the pseudonym of David Macbeth Moir (1798–1851), who published at least 370 poems during his lifetime, mainly in *Blackwood's Edinburgh Magazine*.

Like George Eliot, Mulock was able to transition from a primary focus on poetry writing to the field of translation.[64] Trading on a traditional view of translation as a 'derivative form of authorship', as 'mechanical' rather than 'creative', allowed Mulock to take further incremental steps into the competitive marketplace in these first years of her career.[65] Lesa Scholl explains that as the periodical press continued to expand over the course of the nineteenth century, translation became a valuable and reliable source of income for women such as Mary Howitt and Dinah Mulock, who could, if they wanted to, rely on a steady stream of texts for translation from their publishers. But the image conjured here of the translator as a passive recipient of texts belies the real relationship between translator, original text and translation which was, as Louis Kelly reminds us, both creative and generative, producing something new from a 'dialogic relationship'.[66] Just as Mulock's 'Carolan's War Cry' produces a dialogue between a traditional song, Moore's adaptation, Mulock's version and the reader/performer's interpretation, a text in translation is also a work of imagination and innovation. It allows readers to fancy themselves engaged with a different country from their own and to be a part of a more complex cultural exchange than they might otherwise be exposed to when reading British literature.

Mulock may have taken advantage of the common 'misplaced belief in translation's derivativity' in order to establish herself with one of the century's most successful periodical publishing houses: the Chambers brothers.[67] In a letter dating from March 1845, Mulock wrote to the firm, alternatively advocating for herself, performing self-effacing modesty and trading on the networks she had developed in London in order to publish her translations:

Gentlemen
The translation you have kindly accepted is taken from a little volume entitled 'Nouvelle [*sic*] morali di Francesco Soave' printed at Avignon 1816 – It is a collection of little stories, & true histories: by various authors. The one I chose is by L. Braumieri [*sic*] & seemed to me to bear the impress of truth. It may have been translated before – but never to my knowledge. I need not assure you that my translation is strictly from the original.

Allow me to thank you for your prompt & kind acceptance of my little translation, and to mention, what I was unwilling to do before, that I am happy to number among my friends Mrs. S. C. Hall & Miss Leslie, your contributors – & it was through them I heard of your encouragement to contributors previously unknown, and was therefore induced to send to you.

I leave to your judgment any alteration you may think necessary – and also the renumeration [*sic*] which you may deem it worthy – which will be acceptable to [*sic*].

Gentlemen
Yours obliged & obednt
Dinah M. Mulock[68]

The 'little' story Mulock is referring to here, by Luigi Bramieri, was published in the collection *Novelle Morali: Ad Uso Della Gioventù* (*Moral Short Stories: for the Use of Young People*) with the title 'Il Dovere e la Felicità' ('Duty and Happiness').[69] In her translation, Mulock renames the story 'Sophia of Wolfenbuttel'.[70] The story was published in the 3 May 1845 edition of *Chambers's Edinburgh Journal* without signature, as was in keeping with the journal's house style for this kind of work. But Mulock must have found it gratifying to see her work published in a popular journal with a circulation of at least forty thousand and for it to be one of her favourite magazines from childhood.[71] In her letter to the Chambers brothers, Mulock stresses that her translation is the first of its kind, and she also includes a carefully constructed reference to her London literary connections. As Bourrier notes, the 1840s were crucial years for Mulock in terms of her cultivation of a life of

> literary sociability that bridged her private life with her professional life and [which] capitalised on her ability to make friends among those in literary circles in London and Edinburgh. This model of

literary sociability, where writers and publishers met through literary parties and long visits, and formed plans to write and collaborate, was welcoming to young women, and differs significantly from a more conventional model of paternal influence and patronage.[72]

Mulock's ability to switch between genres – poetry, nonfiction, translation, short fiction and later the novel – meant that she was an impressive addition to any periodical's roster of writers. That Mulock was choosing the translations she offered for publication further demonstrates that she was attentive to popular tastes and had already developed a savvy social and business sense in dealing with periodical publishers.

The next translation the Chambers brothers accepted was of a short story entitled 'Eustace the Negro', which Mulock had chosen from a Parisian periodical, the weekly *Le Caméléon*.[73] In a letter dated 29 April 1845, Mulock writes:

> I beg to forward you a simple Tale, which may be suited for your Journal or Miscellany – I have translated it from an odd volume of a French Periodical 'Le Caméléon' – which contains other stories of the same kind which I think might meet your approval, as I trust this will.[74]

Mulock's use of the phrases 'odd volume' and 'may be suited for your Journal or Miscellany' shows us that she was keenly searching for suitable content and aiming her translations at multiple formats in the hopes of increasing her chances of publication. 'Eustace' is presented by Mulock as a 'simple and true history of an old negro slave, whose self-devotion, intelligence, and noble spirit are worthy of a higher commemoration'.[75] As Bourrier rightly highlights, it is a 'shockingly racist' story by modern standards.[76] However, British abolitionists picked up and utilised the story as part of their armoury of literature calling for the emancipation of enslaved people overseas after the abolition of slavery throughout the British Empire in 1834. Wilson Armistead's *A Tribute for the Negro: Being a Vindication of the Moral, Intellectual and Religious Capabilities of the Coloured Portion of Mankind* (1848) reproduced Mulock's translation of the story, crediting *Chambers's* as the source.[77] The culture of reprinting at this point in the century was considered normal and was even interpreted as a sign of a work's success.[78] That Mulock was choosing pieces for translation that would then go on to be included in such compendiums as Armistead's would have been an encouraging sign for both her publisher and her own sense of herself as writer, translator and cultural mediator. Just as Mulock's choice of stray airs had subtly political connotations, so too did her work as translator. As Scholl notes, translation is a 'political task of mediating between [. . .] two cultures [. . .] [creating] understanding across previously uncrossed boundaries'.[79] These early encounters with foreign-language texts, nations and cultures enabled Mulock to play with the physical and ideological boundaries imposed by English middle-class conventions and to carve a distinctive, respected position for herself in an already crowded competitive arena.[80]

Conclusion

In 1975, Elaine Showalter began her essay on 'Dinah Mulock Craik and the Tactics of Sentiment' with the following assertion:

> The second wave of Victorian women novelists – Margaret Oliphant, Charlotte Yonge, Mrs. Henry Wood, Dinah M. Craik, et al. – is seldom taken seriously by literary scholars. Born between 1820 and 1840 [. . .] these were the novelists with a purpose – self-disciplined and steadily productive over many years, active in journalism as well as literature.[81]

'Perhaps', Showalter continues, 'the disguises these women novelists assumed in order to conciliate as well as to conceal have worked too well'.[82] And so, 'misled by the public antifeminism of many female novelists, scholars have ignored the deeper content of the books, and the devices by which sentimental narratives articulated female conflict about achievement and affiliation'.[83] Bourrier points out that Dinah Mulock (now more commonly referred to by her married name, Mrs Craik) was to many a 'byword for Victorian respectability'.[84] She was fiercely protective of her privacy, disliked celebrity and maintained a respectable distance from her peers, so it would be easy to misconstrue her as an antifeminist writer.[85] However, as Showalter and others have shown, 'it was precisely this respectability that allowed her to flout convention'.[86] As Sally Mitchell highlights, 'in contrast to the images put forward by the society she lived in, Craik's [fictional] world is strikingly nonpatriarchal'.[87] Mitchell goes on to demonstrate the ways in which Craik's fiction rejected the idea that women 'face a world that says women should be protected [and] [. . .] fixed in childish dependency'.[88] We see this attitude even in Craik's commentary on her earliest publications: she was disappointed by editorial remarks about her age because she had made deliberate and autonomous decisions about the kinds of content that might appeal to publishers and readers. Soon thereafter she would remove any intermediary between herself and her publishers and begin to successfully navigate both the submission process and the face-to-face building of literary networks.

Since the late twentieth century, numerous scholars, such as Karen Bourrier, Martha Stoddard Holmes and Juliet Shields, have demonstrated the importance of Craik's contributions to nineteenth-century literary culture, and so her work need not be further defended here.[89] One negative association, however, has continued to follow Craik into the present day, despite increased scholarly attention, and that is the suggestion that she was in some way 'average' or mediocre in comparison to those of her peers who have been canonised. The famous dismissals of her work by Henry James and George Eliot are perhaps partly to blame for the critical underappreciation of her work.[90]

This disparaging view of Craik's work was evidently not shared by her readers and editors. In 1855, eleven years after her stray airs series was published in *The New Monthly Belle Assemblée*, the journal *Household Words* received a submission from her which Dickens described as 'the best Ghost story [. . .] that ever was written, and with an idea in it remarkably new'.[91] So remarkable was the story that Dickens could not believe a woman had written it. 'It is so very clever', he wrote to Miss Angela Burdett-Coutts 'that I think [. . .] it must have been written by some wild Frenchman'.[92]

In the decade since her stray air series, Craik had evidently studied her 'art' and obtained the 'discipline and knowledge' the *Dublin University Magazine* had requested of her as a sixteen-year-old.[93] Transitioning to the world of letters, Craik moved incrementally – establishing herself by skilfully combining innovation with familiarity in the earliest years of her career. She then moved to translation, a process that required great skill, impressive knowledge of the nuances of foreign languages and an eye for trends in the market for popular literature. She then proceeded to publish original short stories, novels and novellas.

As Dickens's comments on Craik's short story confirm, throughout the nineteenth century women continued to come up against obstacles to their progress in a 'male-dominated literary marketplace', where men typically held all the power over who and what was published.[94] Yet Craik, in her early years, was able to build the foundations of a successful literary career through a seemingly alchemical mix of volatile and uncertain circumstances, combined with some familial privilege and sheer determination. She managed to acquire an education by piggybacking on her brothers' studies and engaging in independent research. Her father's brief association with literary London keyed her into publishing networks at a crucial moment in her teen years, whilst her mother's death and her father's subsequent abandonment of the family provided a financial motivation for her to seek literary employment.[95] The 1840s were a fortuitous time for someone like Craik to launch a career in letters: the periodical press was expanding into new markets for the middle and working classes, as well as for women and children. Nevertheless, she was right to be cautious in transitioning into original writing slowly, developing relationships with multiple journals and publishers and honing her skills in a variety of styles and genres. In using all the resources at her disposal, Craik demonstrates the creative ways in which a young writer could begin to make a name for herself in periodicals of the early Victorian era. She networked, rewrote, reinterpreted, reimagined, translated, performed and socialised her way into some of the most successful periodical publications of her day, and she did so by skilfully combining innovation with familiarity.

Notes

1. Elaine Showalter, *A Literature of Their Own: British Women Novelists from Brontë to Lessing* (Princeton: Princeton University Press, 1977), 39.
2. Ibid. Showalter cites Richard Altick's 'The Sociology of Authorship: The Social Origins, Education, and Occupations of 1,100 British Writers, 1800–1935', *Bulletin of the New York Public Library* 66 (1962): 392.
3. Troy J. Bassett, 'Analysis: Data Visualizations', At the Circulating Library: A Database of Victorian Fiction, 1837–1901, 15 December 2022, http://www.victorianresearch.org.

4. Ted Underwood, David Bamman and Sabrina Lee, 'The Transformation of Gender in English-Language Fiction', *Journal of Cultural Analytics* 3, no. 2 (2018): 2.
5. Gaye Tuchman, *Edging Women Out: Victorian Novelists, Publishers and Social Change* (London: Taylor & Francis, 2012), 7.
6. Showalter, *Literature of Their Own*, 40.
7. Alexis Easley, 'Making a Debut', in *The Cambridge Companion to Victorian Women's Writing*, ed. Linda H. Peterson (Cambridge: Cambridge University Press, 2015), 15. Easley cites Sally Mitchell, 'Careers for Girls: Writing Trash', *Victorian Periodicals Review* 25, no. 3 (1992): 109.
8. I will refer to Dinah Maria Mulock (D. M. M.) as such in the main body of this chapter as this is how she was known in the early years of her career. In the final section, I will use Mulock Craik or Craik to reflect how she is now more commonly known.
9. Margaret Beetham, 'Periodical Writing', in *The Cambridge Companion to Victorian Women's Writing*, ed. Linda H. Peterson (Cambridge: Cambridge University Press, 2015), 222.
10. Beetham, 'Periodical Writing', 221–5.
11. Linda H. Peterson, *Becoming a Woman of Letters: Myths of Authorship and Facts of the Victorian Market* (Princeton: Princeton University Press, 2009), 3.
12. Ibid., 4.
13. Ibid.
14. See also Rory Moore's 'A Mediated Intimacy: Dinah Mulock Craik and Celebrity Culture', *Women's Writing* 20, no. 3 (2013): 387–403. Moore analyses Dinah Mulock Craik's early understanding of celebrity culture.
15. See, for example, Juliet Shields, 'The Races of Women: Gender, Hybridity, and National Identity in Dinah Craik's *Olive*', *Studies in the Novel* 39, no. 3 (2007): 284–300.
16. Laurie Langbauer, *The Juvenile Tradition: Young Writers and Prolepsis, 1750–1835* (Oxford: Oxford University Press, 2016); Alexis Easley, 'Making a Debut'; Christine Alexander and Juliet McMaster, ed., *The Child Writer from Austen to Woolf* (Cambridge: Cambridge University Press, 2005).
17. Karen Bourrier, *Victorian Bestseller: The Life of Dinah Craik* (Ann Arbor: University of Michigan Press, 2019), 24. Jane Loudon (1807–58) was predominantly a writer on botany and a magazine editor. Anna Maria Hall (1800–81) was also a writer and an editor of

periodicals including *Sharpe's London Magazine* (1852–3) and the *St James's Magazine* (1861–8).

18. Aleyn Lyell Reade, *The Mellards and their Descendants, Including the Bibbys of Liverpool, with Memoirs of Dinah Maria Mulock & Thomas Mellard Reade* (London: Arden Press, 1915), 60.
19. [Dinah Mulock], 'Stanzas on the Birth of the Princess Royal', *Staffordshire Advertiser*, 16 January 1841, 2.
20. Reade, *The Mellards*, 60. In her letter to Hallam, Mulock writes, 'I gave them to Papa [the verses on the Princess's birth] to do what he liked with, and he sent them to Mr. Crewe'. Reade notes that Frederick Crewe was a printer and secretary to Newcastle Mechanics' Institute, as well as being one of the trustees for Dinah's mother's legacy.
21. In *A Woman's Thoughts about Women* (1859) Mulock makes it clear to her reader that she considers herself a talented writer, perhaps even a 'genius'. Mulock argues that 'in any profession, there is nothing, short of being absolutely evil, which is so injurious, so fatal, as mediocrity'. And she condemns anyone who publishes a 'mediocre book' for lowering 'the standard of public taste, [filling] unworthily some better competitor's place' and doing a 'positive wrong to the community at large'. [Dinah Mulock], *A Woman's Thoughts about Women* (London: Hurst and Blackett, 1859), 51–2.
22. Elizabeth Tilley, 'Dublin University Magazine', in *The Dictionary of Nineteenth-Century Journalism* (online edition), ed. Laurel Brake and Marysa Demoor (London and Ghent: British Library and Academia Press, 2009). Sally Mitchell, *Dinah Mulock Craik* (Boston: Twayne, 1983), 21. Whilst we do not have background information on this publication from Reade, we might assume that the appearance of Mulock's poem in *Dublin University Magazine*, with a similar notice alluding to the author's age, was a result of her father using his literary connections to place her work. For more on Thomas Mulock, see Elihu Rich, 'Thomas Mulock: An Historical Sketch', *Transactions of the Royal Historical Society* 4 (1876): 424–38. See also Bourrier, *Victorian Bestseller*, and Reade, *The Mellards*.
23. Editorial note accompanying [Dinah Mulock], 'The Song of The Hours', *Dublin University Magazine* 18 (October 1841): 442.
24. [Mulock], 'Song of The Hours', 442.
25. Ibid.
26. This gap between publications may have been due to illness. We learn from Reade that in May 1841 Mulock wrote to Rebecca Hallam,

reporting that she had been ill: 'her chest is weak, and [. . .] she is not allowed to stoop over her writing'. Some months later, doctors allowed her to resume 'visits and enjoyment, but must not study'. Mulock's mother was also unwell in 1841 according to a letter sent by Thomas Mulock to Mrs Mayer, wife of Thomas Mayer, of Dale Hall, Burslem. Reade, *Mellards*, 61, 62. By 1842, Mulock's mother was very ill and died of breast cancer three years later. Bourrier, *Victorian Bestseller*, 38, 136.

27. Bourrier, *Victorian Bestseller*, 24.
28. Reade, *Mellards*, 63.
29. Ibid., 63, 65.
30. Ibid., 66.
31. Ibid., 64.
32. [Dinah Mulock], 'Verses', *Friendship's Offering of Sentiment and Mirth* (London: Smith, Elder, 1844), 217.
33. The 1798 rebellion is much more likely to be the 'dark year' referenced here, as it was on a more major scale than the 1803 attempt. This makes it more difficult to say for certain if Mulock's poem is about Emmet and Curran as this would mean that Mulock is slightly muddled in her dating of events. My thanks to colleagues James McConnel and Ultán Gillen for discussing the issue of Mulock's potentially inaccurate dating with me. In relation to Emmet, see, for example, Alison Morgan, '"Let no man write my epitaph": The Contributions of Percy Shelley, Thomas Moore and Robert Southey to the Memorialisation of Robert Emmet', *Irish Studies Review* 22, no. 3 (2014): 285–303; and Marianne Elliott, *Robert Emmet: The Making of a Legend* (London: Profile, 2003).
34. For more on the 'Irish Question', see George D. Boyce, *Nineteenth Century Ireland* (Dublin: Gill and Macmillan, 2005) and *The Revolution in Ireland, 1879–1923* (Dublin: Gill and Macmillan, 1988); Alan O'Day, *Irish Home Rule, 1867–1921* (Manchester: Manchester University Press, 1998). Despite these early sympathies, later in life Mulock expressed prejudice against the Irish, which may have stemmed, in part, from her difficult relationship with her father. See Bourrier, *Victorian Bestseller*, 101–2.
35. Thomas Moore, 'O Breathe Not His Name', in *A Selection of Irish Melodies with Symphonies and Accompaniments by Sir John Stevenson* (London: J. Power, 1808), 20–2. Casaliggi and Fermanis note that the publication of Thomas Moore's best-selling *Irish Melodies*, which contained 'O Breathe Not His Name', 'coincided with a period of intense debate about the 'Irish Question'.

Carmen Casaliggi and Porscha Fermanis, eds., *Romanticism: A Literary and Cultural History* (London: Routledge, 2016), 103.

36. [Dinah Mulock], 'The Mourner's Hope of Immortality. (A Funeral Hymn.)', *New Monthly Belle Assemblée* 20 (April 1844): 245.
37. Ibid.
38. Brown explains that the incredible success of *Robert le Diable* 'transformed Meyerbeer overnight into the most celebrated opera composer of the day'. Clive Brown, 'Giacomo Meyerbeer', in *The New Penguin Opera Guide*, ed. Amanda Holden (London: Penguin, 2001), 572.
39. It is difficult to establish the origins of this strathspey. George Eyre-Todd credits James Tytler (1745–1804), the editor of the second edition of *Encyclopædia Britannica*, as the original author, while others credit Niel Gow (1727–1807), a renowned Scottish violinist of the eighteenth century. James Tytler, 'Loch Erroch Side', in *Scottish Poetry of the Eighteenth Century*, vol. 2, ed. George Eyre-Todd (Glasgow: William Hodge, 1896): 88–9; Alfred Moffat, *The Minstrelsy of Scotland* (London: Augener, 1896), 244.
40. Dinah Maria Mulock, 'The Shepherd's Wife', *New Monthly Belle Assemblée* 20 (May 1844): 272.
41. Gerard Carruthers argues that standard critical narratives of nineteenth-century Scottish poetry chart the genre's descent into the 'sentimental, mawkish and comic' over the course of the century. The *Whistle Binkie* anthologies, which included such songs as 'Wee Willie Winkie' by William Miller, were indicative of this descent. Gerard Carruthers, *Scottish Literature* (Edinburgh: Edinburgh University Press, 2009), 58.
42. Sarah Green, *Scotch Novel Reading; or, Modern Quackery. A Novel Really Founded on Facts: by a Cockney* (London: A. K. Newman, 1824).
43. Bourrier, *Victorian Bestseller*, 34.
44. Ibid., 35.
45. Chapter two of Sally Mitchell's book on Craik is entitled 'finding the popular audience'. Mitchell, *Mulock Craik*, 19–38.
46. Mulock's books never carried her name on the title page, and elsewhere she would continue to publish anonymously or under the initials 'D. M. M.', as the house style of each publication required. Her work for *Chambers's*, for example, was mostly unsigned, and her short stories in *Dublin University Magazine* between 1847 and 1849 were variously unsigned or signed 'D. M. M.'

47. It is likely that the song referenced here is that which is more commonly referred to as 'An Maidrín Ruádh' or 'The Little Red Fox', in William Cole, ed., *Folk Songs of England, Ireland, Scotland & Wales* (New York: Doubleday, 1961), 68.
48. Norman Cazden, Herbert Haufrecht and Norman Studer, eds, *Folk Songs of the Catskills* (Albany: State University of New York Press, 1982), 535. In Cazden et al., the song is incorrectly referred to as 'There's Gows in the Breast'.
49. Sarah McCleave, 'The Genesis of Thomas Moore's Irish Melodies, 1808–1834', in *Cheap Print and Popular Song in the Nineteenth Century: A Cultural History of the Songster*, ed. Paul Watt, Derek B. Scott and Patrick Spedding (Cambridge: Cambridge University Press, 2017), 47.
50. Dinah Maria Mulock, 'Carolan's War Cry', *New Monthly Belle Assemblée* 20 (June 1844): 335. The accompanying footnote tells the reader, 'Terence Carolan, the blind Irish bard, was in his youth a warm adherent to the cause of James the Second, in the war that was terminated by the Battle of the Boyne. Carolan was a Catholic, and devoted to the prince whom he deemed his rightful sovereign.'
51. Thomas Moore, *Irish Melodies* (London: J. Power, 1821), 40–1.
52. Norman Vance, *Irish Literature Since 1800* (London: Taylor & Francis, 2002), 2.
53. Stephen Regan, 'Introduction', in *Irish Writing: An Anthology of Irish Literature in English, 1789–1939* (Oxford: Oxford University Press, 2004), xxvi.
54. James Hardiman, *Irish Minstrelsy, or Bardic Remains of Ireland* (London: Joseph Robins, 1831). Popular writers like Maria Edgeworth and popular collections by writers such as Thomas Crofton Croker (*Fairy Legends and Traditions of the South of Ireland*, 1825–8) peppered their Irish stories with Gaelic words and phrases, but almost always these were accompanied by a translation in a footnote or in the body of the text.
55. Dinah Maria Mulock, 'Forgive One Another', *New Monthly Belle Assemblée* 20 (June 1844): 346.
56. Dinah Maria Mulock, 'A Barcarole', *New Monthly Belle Assemblée* 21 (July 1844): 32; Charles Knight, *The English Cyclopaedia: A New Dictionary of Universal Knowledge* (London: Bradbury and Evans, 1859), 1:895.
57. Christina Fuhrmann, 'Introduction', in *Henry Rowley Bishop, Mozart's The Marriage of Figaro Adapted for Covent Garden, 1819* (Middleton, Wisconsin: A-R Editions, Inc. 2012), ix.

58. Ibid.
59. Reade, *Mellards*, 65.
60. Dinah Maria Mulock, 'Caoinhe over an Irish Chieftain', *New Monthly Belle Assemblée* 21 (August 1844): 76. Brian Boroimhe's 'March' is an ancient tune possibly dating from the eleventh century that memorialised the death of King Brian Boroimhe at the Battle of Clontarf. 'The Holy Places of Ireland', *Dublin Saturday Magazine* 1–2 (1865–6): 59.
61. Recitation was a key part of Sunday School pedagogy. See Rev. J. F. Serjeant, 'Our Sunday School Scholars', in *The Sunday School Teachers' Magazine and Journal of Education* 10 (1859): 342; Frederic Platt, 'Repetition', in *The Encyclopedia of Sunday Schools and Religious Education* (London: Thomas Nelson, 1915), 3:917–19. For more on scrapbooking, see Alexis Easley, 'Scrapbooks and Women's Leisure Reading Practices, 1825–60', *Nineteenth Century Gender Studies* 15, no. 2 (2019), https://www.ncgsjournal.com/issue152/easley.html.
62. Camille Crittenden, *Johann Strauss and Vienna: Operetta and the Politics of Popular Culture* (Cambridge: Cambridge University Press, 2006), 99.
63. Craik died in 1887, but the DVPPP credits the publication of 'In the Lane. A September Song' in *Good Words* to Craik for 1892. Alison Chapman et al., eds, Digital Victorian Periodical Poetry Project, University of Victoria, accessed 16 August 2022, https://dvpp.uvic.ca. The DVPPP database is another example of a large-scale digital project that gives us illuminating quantitative data about authors like Mulock which we can then use to make further qualitative discoveries.
64. Reade quotes Mulock's letters to her childhood friend Rebecca Hallam in which she reveals that she has been studying French, Italian and Latin. She also reports learning Greek with her brothers, 'who have a tutor at home to finish them'. This same tutor was teaching Dinah Irish. She proudly reports to Hallam, 'Did you ever know such a learned young lady as I shall be, in time? I shall be enough to frighten all the young gentlemen with my Latin, Greek and Irish!' Reade, *Mellards*, 65–6.
65. Lesa Scholl, *Translation, Authorship and the Victorian Professional Woman: Charlotte Brontë, Harriet Martineau and George Eliot* (London: Routledge, 2011), 2.
66. Ibid. Scholl cites Louis G. Kelly, *The True Interpreter: A History of Translation Theory and Practice in the West* (Oxford: Basil Blackwell, 1979), 44.

67. Scholl, *Translation*, 3.
68. Correspondence from Dinah Mulock Craik to William and Robert Chambers, 28 March 1845, W. & R. Chambers Papers, Dep. 341. National Library of Scotland, digitised by the Digital Dinah Craik Project, accessed 16 August 2022, https://tapasproject.org.
69. Luigi Bramieri, 'Il Dovere e la Felicità', in *Novelle Morali: Ad Uso Della Gioventù* (Brussels: Hauman, 1836), 64–73.
70. [Dinah Mulock] 'Sophia of Wolfenbuttel', *Chambers's Edinburgh Journal* 3 (1845): 277–8. The story is based on a 'legend' that emerged after the death of Princess Charlotte Christine Sophie von Braunschweig-Wolfenbüttel (1694–1715). Robert T. Clark, 'The Fusion of Legends in Zschokke's *Prinzessin von Wolfenbüttel*', *Journal of English and Germanic Philology* 42, no. 2 (1943): 185–96.
71. Mulock's poems in *Chambers's Edinburgh Journal* from this period (1845) were signed 'D. M. M.' In the 4 January 1845 edition of the *Journal*, an editorial entitled 'A Few Words to our Readers' indicates that 'the sale of the Journal in its magazine shape alone (the monthly part being strictly a magazine) is about forty thousand'. 'A Few Words to our Readers', *Chambers's Edinburgh Journal* 3 (4 January 1845): 1. In an article entitled 'Want Something to Read', published in the 8 May 1858 issue of *Chambers's*, Mulock tells of her childhood reading experiences and of a neighbour who bought a subscription to the magazine. She and her siblings used to 'rush in on Saturday afternoons to borrow it, and rush off again to some corner, where it could be read in quiet! How we hid it, and squabbled over it [. . .] till at last, as the only chance of peace, the Journal was forbidden ever to enter the house'. [Dinah Mulock], 'Want Something to Read', *Chambers's Edinburgh Journal* 227 (8 May 1858): 291.
72. Bourrier, *Victorian Bestseller*, 42–3.
73. James Poskett, *Materials of the Mind: Phrenology, Race, and the Global History of Science* (London: University of Chicago Press, 2009), 69.
74. Correspondence from Dinah Mulock Craik to William and Robert Chambers, 29 April 1845, W. & R. Chambers Papers, Dep. 341, National Library of Scotland, digitised by the Digital Dinah Craik Project, accessed 16 August 2022, https://tapasproject.org.
75. [Dinah Mulock], 'Eustace the Negro', *Chambers's Edinburgh Journal* 3 (1845): 332–4.
76. Bourrier, *Victorian Bestseller*, 49.

77. Wilson Armistead, *A Tribute for the Negro: Being a Vindication of the Moral, Intellectual and Religious Capabilities of the Coloured Portion of Mankind* (Manchester: William Urwin, 1848).
78. See M. H. Beals, 'Scissors and Paste: The Georgian Reprints, 1800–1837', *Journal of Open Humanities Data* 3, no. 1 (2017), https://doi.org/10.5334/johd.8; Catherine Feely, '"Scissors-and-Paste" Journalism', in *The Dictionary of Nineteenth Century Journalism* (online edition), ed. Laurel Brake and Marysa Demoor (Ghent and London: Academia Press and the British Library, 2009); Alison Hedley, *Making Pictorial Print: Media Literacy and Mass Culture in British Magazines, 1885–1918* (Toronto: University of Toronto Press, 2021), 119–28.
79. Scholl, *Translation*, 13.
80. Ibid., 1, 189.
81. Elaine Showalter, 'Dinah Mulock Craik and the Tactics of Sentiment: A Case Study in Victorian Female Authorship', *Feminist Studies* 2, no. 2/3 (1975): 5.
82. Ibid.
83. Ibid.
84. Bourrier, *Victorian Bestseller*, vii.
85. Once she began to publish novels, her books 'never carried her name on the title page'; instead, each new work was advertised as 'by the author of' the novels preceding it. Mitchell, *Mulock Craik*, 13.
86. Bourrier, *Victorian Bestseller*, viii.
87. Mitchell, *Mulock Craik*, 110.
88. Ibid., 111.
89. See, for example, Karen Bourrier, *Victorian Bestseller*; Helena Goodwyn, 'A Woman's Thoughts About Men: Malthus and Middle-Class Masculinity in Dinah Mulock Craik's *John Halifax, Gentleman*'. *Women's Writing* 28, no. 2 (2021): 231–49; Juliet Shields, 'The Races of Women'.
90. Henry James characterised Craik's works as suffering from 'excessive sentimentality', and Eliot dismissed Craik as 'a writer who is read only by novel readers, pure and simple, never by people of high culture'. Henry James, 'A Noble Life', in *Notes and Reviews* (Cambridge, MA: Dunster House, 1921), 169; George Eliot, *The George Eliot Letters*, ed. Gordon S. Haight (New Haven: Yale University Press, 1954), 3:302.
91. Anne Lohrli, 'Dinah Maria Mulock', Dickens Journals Online, accessed 29 March 2023, https://www.djo.org.uk/indexes/authors/dinah-maria-mulock.html.

92. Ibid.
93. [Mulock], 'Song of the Hours', 442.
94. Easley, 'Making a Debut', 15.
95. For more on Mulock's family history, see Bourrier, *Victorian Bestseller*.

10

Paratextual Navigation: Positions of Witnessing in *The Anti-Slavery Reporter*

Sofia Prado Huggins

In 1831, the momentum of nearly a decade of activism against colonial chattel slavery would soon bring about monumental legislative action. The tide of public opinion had turned. As the premiere outlet of the Anti-Slavery Society, *The Anti-Slavery Reporter* worked to sustain and increase the force of the antislavery movement in Britain. Although the end was in sight, the periodical continued to exert moral pressure to abolish chattel slavery throughout the British colonies. Inaugurated as a monthly journal in 1825, *The Anti-Slavery Monthly Reporter* transitioned to a bimonthly publication as *The Anti-Slavery Reporter* in 1831. While the textual tradition of the British antislavery movement was well established by the periodical's founding, *The Anti-Slavery Reporter* was one of the earlier and most successful examples of a reform periodical dedicated to the abolition of slavery. With its widespread global distribution, cross-class readership and direct political impact, the *Reporter* remains a striking example of the social force of nineteenth-century new media. Zachary Macaulay, the Scottish antislavery activist and Anti-Slavery Society member who founded *The Anti-Slavery Reporter* in 1825, continued to serve as editor, collecting and writing the lion's share of material each month.[1] Thomas Pringle, the secretary of the Anti-Slavery Society who edited Mary Prince's narrative, *The History of Mary Prince, a West Indian Slave* (1831), assisted Macaulay in his editorial duties.[2] From 1831 to 1833, Macaulay and Pringle worked steadily to produce new issues of *The Anti-Slavery Reporter* and provide information in support of parliamentary efforts to abolish colonial slavery in the British colonies.[3]

The Anti-Slavery Reporter played an integral role in the antislavery movement and the post-abolition development of the

British Empire. Concerned as it was with the connections between the metropole and the further reaches of British power in distant colonies, the periodical's engagement with geography is perhaps obvious. The ways in which readers interacted with and experienced the *Reporter*'s spatial dimensions were deeply local as well as global. The emotional relationship that the periodical encouraged readers to feel between themselves and locations both near and far depended on the intimate negotiations between textual elements that constructed the text as a space readers would navigate. To access an issue of *The Anti-Slavery Reporter* now, readers must travel to a research library, find a reprinted volume or open up a digital copy. In each instance, the reader inhabits space in the world and the periodical differently. In 1831, British readers would perhaps have walked to their regular bookseller or the *Reporter* office at 18 Aldermanbury, picked up a paperbound issue and carried it home to another part of London and read it there. These readers might have glanced at the periodical on their way home, although the dense copy did not invite peripatetic reading. Maybe one of the titles on the table of contents was particularly arresting and the buyer stopped for a closer look. However and wherever they read this issue, nineteenth-century readers experienced *The Anti-Slavery Reporter* both *in space* and *as space* that existed in their hands as ink and paper and in their minds as a forum for the exchange of ideas. It is easy to see how our experiences of space in the 'real world' can influence our understanding of a text; however, as geographers will attest, boundaries between spaces are imaginary and permeable.[4]

The world outside the pages of *The Anti-Slavery Reporter* was, in turn, shaped by how readers experienced the space of the periodical. Edward Soja's definition of 'thirdspace' provides a useful lens through which to analyse the *Reporter*. 'Thirdspace' is an alternative to the binary of real versus imagined space; it represents lived space that is real-and-imagined.[5] Thirdspaces such as *The Anti-Slavery Reporter* are complex and ever-evolving – a dynamic process of interplay between the world shaped by ideas and the ideas shaped by the world. Specific textual elements within *The Anti-Slavery Reporter* guided readers through the thirdspace of the periodical. In the 1830s, these elements worked together to position white British readers at the centre of the antislavery saga. By encouraging readers to function as witnesses, the periodical narrowed the emotional distance between British readers and the West Indian colonies. Understood geographically, these textual actants transported evidence from the colonies to Britain, where readers could appropriate it and transform themselves from passive recipients to witnesses whose testimony condemned slavery in the court of public opinion.[6] Although *The Anti-Slavery Reporter* was edited and printed in London, it depended on a global information and production network similar to how digital new media does today. However, the *Reporter* used paratextual elements to reinforce the importance of British moral force within the antislavery movement. Even though it was undeniably a successful social reform periodical, it exemplifies how new media can reproduce 'social, political, and economic inequalities'.[7] Although the repositioning of British supporters at the centre of the antislavery movement provided momentum to efforts to abolish colonial slavery, the *Reporter* emphasised Britain at the expense of colonial erasure.[8] At the same time, it negotiated a new definition of Britishness that brought the colonies more fully into the imperial fold to the exclusion of Black people, enslaved or free, across the globe.

Networks and network theory have proven valuable tools for considering how periodicals function in the world, particularly the communities of publishers, writers, printers and readers that interact with a periodical.[9] Textual elements in the publication itself are also actants, as described by Bruno Latour.[10] They interact with readers of *The Anti-Slavery Reporter*, serving as guides through the fraught spaces of the periodical and, beyond the boundaries of the page, to a new understanding of British identity in spaces across the globe. As in Latour's definition of the social, the relationships between actants in *The Anti-Slavery Reporter* and between the actants and readers are continually negotiated. There is no single straight path through the periodical. Instead, readers encounter a variety of actants that are often in competition for the reader's attention. This tension produces the *Reporter* as a space of influence within the antislavery movement.

In *For Space*, geographer Doreen Massey argues that space is constituted through social interactions; it is not a timeless arena for history but rather the contentious creation of relationships that are always in flux. By looking at *The Anti-Slavery Reporter* as a primary site of spatial and ideological 'relations of constructions', we can better understand how nineteenth-century readers of the periodical situated themselves within the antislavery movement in

Britain and the world beyond.[11] Thinking relationally about geography and space has profound political implications: in a movement dedicated to claiming social responsibility in the colonies, its primary textual outlet was instrumental in shaping the relations of the effort within Britain as well as the relationships of its readers to colonial populations, free and enslaved.

This approach to space requires an expansion of the purview of the social. In *Reassembling the Social*, Latour draws on literary criticism, using the term 'actants' to expand what sociology considers social beyond the human.[12] Like Massey on the notion of dynamic space, Latour insists that society is not static and a priori but rather that different webs of dynamic interactions between actors, only some of whom are human, compose the social. In the case of *The Anti-Slavery Reporter*, one can think of Zachary Macaulay, the longtime editor of the periodical, as an actant within a network. Additionally, any anonymous reader in Leeds was an actant. So was the mail coach that carried the issue of the *Reporter* to Leeds from London, the teams of horses that drew the coach, and the Royal Mail. This essay focuses on the actants on the page, specifically the self-referential footnotes in volumes 4 and 5 of *The Anti-Slavery Reporter*. It is perhaps unsettling to think of footnotes and verbal descriptions as having agency; however, as Latour notes, 'in addition to "determining" and serving as a "backdrop for human action", things might authorize, allow, afford, encourage, permit, suggest, influence, block, render possible, forbid, and so on'.[13]

Paratextual elements within *The Anti-Slavery Reporter* encouraged nineteenth-century British readers to serve as witnesses to colonial slavery, thereby positioning them at the centre of the anti-slavery movement even though they were geographically distant from the events detailed in the periodical. The role of the witness within the context of chattel slavery is emotionally and ethically complex because of the codification of witnessing as an exclusively white practice within colonial space. Such white witnessing enabled and legalised violence against enslaved persons in various forms throughout the British Empire. In most colonies, laws barred enslaved people from bearing witness against white colonists, making it virtually impossible to prosecute abuses against enslaved persons even when colonists broke colonial laws.[14] White colonists were immune to legal repercussions unless a white person bore witness against them. Black and enslaved persons were also unable to defend themselves against false accusations by white witnesses. Testifying against a white abuser often led to torturous punishment and even execution with little to no legal recourse. Substituting the white witnessing of its British readers for Black experience in *The Anti-Slavery Reporter* mirrored the violent erasure of Black testimony in the colonial legal systems that upheld chattel slavery.

The Anti-Slavery Reporter created space through relationships among predominantly white British readers of the periodical from 1831 to 1833 – a space of moral unity among island Britons that could be extended to white colonials if they removed the barrier of slavery. Simultaneously, *The Anti-Slavery Reporter*'s reliance on colonial sources countered the centring of white British voices within the movement and its own pages. Space is always contested; it is continually created through the push and pull of various forces. *The Anti-Slavery Reporter* exhibited 'a tension between the need to hearten the activist and the need to enlighten the unconverted', as Brian Harrison notes of pressure-group periodicals in general. Textual actants functioned slightly differently for regular versus new readers, with varying success. For example, regular readers familiar with the editorial tone of the *Reporter* might have lingered over a footnote detailing the editors' grievances against James Macqueen, a Scottish proslavery activist who was a fierce opponent of the Anti-Slavery Society in general and Macaulay and Pringle in particular.[15] New readers who were less interested in the interpersonal dramas of the antislavery movement might have skipped over such a footnote but pored over tables of population data from the colonies or a gory description of the punishment of an enslaved person. Regardless of their responses to various textual actants, it was rhetorically strategic to centre both those committed to and those newly interested in the antislavery movement within the thirdspace of *The Anti-Slavery Reporter*. In volumes 4 and 5 of the *Reporter*, format and layout, particularly self-referential footnotes, kept the focus on white witnessing in the periodical. These self-referential footnotes redirect readers to the *Reporter* by referencing previous or future issues or directing readers towards specific articles. These features employed visuality to engage readers. In the case of self-referential footnotes, the material separation of the note from the body text pulled the reader's gaze away from colonial source material to the role of the Anti-Slavery Society in the push for abolition.

Self-referential footnotes assisted the transformation of the reader from viewer to witness.

Just as recurring visual elements drew the reader's eyes towards self-referential footnotes, repetition in content marked them as distinct generic features of the antislavery periodical. In the pages that follow, I move between visual and content analysis – mirroring how readers might have intuited the relationship between layout and text in *The Anti-Slavery Reporter*. The slippage between the two forms of analysis corresponds to the interrelation of visuality and content on the periodical page, a space that is far more grey than black and white. I analyse the material elements of a single page in volume 4 of the *Reporter* – layout, typesetting and content – as a case study of how textual actants worked in concert to divert readers' attention from Black and colonial experiences to their roles as witnesses. Throughout this page and *The Anti-Slavery Reporter* as a whole, visuality and content collaborated to instill readers with a sense of their integral part in the antislavery movement. Building on this case study of a single page, I evaluate how self-referential footnotes throughout the periodical's 1831–3 volumes redirected readers' attention from its reliance on the colonial press and repositioned the Anti-Slavery Society and Britain at the centre of the global antislavery network. Self-referential footnotes, along with format and layout, functioned as textual actants in *The Anti-Slavery Reporter*; they closed the emotional distance between the British Isles and its colonies and promised unity throughout the empire after the abolition of colonial slavery. However, this unity would be bought at the expense of the exclusion of Black persons from the imaginary landscape of Britain.

On 25 June 1831, number 82 of *The Anti-Slavery Reporter* refuted the claims of the West Indian Manifesto, a document widely circulated by the proslavery faction in Britain. In my case study of the second page of this issue, I pay particular attention to the agency of punctuation marks, font size and page numbers, among other elements, to direct readers' movements not only visually through the page but also conceptually outwards, shaping readers' mental map of the British Empire. In *Paratexts: Thresholds of Interpretation*, Gérard Genette writes,

> More than a boundary or a sealed border, the pretext is a *threshold*, or [. . .] a 'vestibule' that offers the world at large the possibility of either stepping inside or turning back. It is an 'undefined zone'

> between the inside and the outside, a zone without any hard and fast boundary on either the inward side (turned toward the text) or the outward side (turned toward the world discourse about the text), an edge, or, as Philippe Lejeune puts it, 'a fringe which in reality controls one's whole reading of the text'.[16]

The porous zone of the paratext, Genette continues, is a zone of transaction between the text and its readers – a perfect example of a space created and defined by social relations. Throughout *Paratexts*, Genette describes reading as movement, a journey through the text. In that spirit, I explore a single page of *The Anti-Slavery Reporter* (Fig. 10.1).[17]

First, a reader's eyes find the top left-hand corner of the page, marked with the precise number 290. Subconsciously, this number situates this page within a broader socio-spatial context. The continuous pagination of the periodical across an entire volume gives readers a sense of the publication's longevity and the importance of its subject. The number 290, rather than 2, implies that this page is situated well within the conceptual space of *The Anti-Slavery Reporter* rather than at its beginning. When combined with the publication details on the previous page – volume 4, issue 10, number 82 – the page number 290 carries far greater weight than the light, paper-covered bimonthly issues that nineteenth-century readers would have held in their hands.

At the top of the page, dominating the visual landscape, are three columns of names. Distinct from the rest of the page, these columns immediately draw the reader's attention. Throughout this page, the textual elements redirect readers' focus back to these columns again and again. These are the names of the signees of the West Indian Manifesto, men who have willingly cosigned an argument for the continuation of slavery throughout the British dominions. As actants, various elements on this page work together to reinforce both their culpability and the importance of their names. A reader, drawn to the straight black line between the body text and the footnotes, might jump to the bottom of the page. This heavy line, or rule, counterbalances the visual weight of the columns. As in a landscape painting, the columns are the dominating figure, three mountains that immediately draw the eye and pull a viewer into a space that is both imaginary and real. The rule at the bottom is the foreground of the landscape – solid and essential for suggesting depth. The first footnote, marked with an

290 *West Indian Manifesto—Abstract of Laws.*

other classes of his Majesty's subjects'—and this 'at the earliest period compatible with the well-being of the Slaves themselves, with the safety of the Colonies, and with a fair and equitable consideration of the interests of private property.'

Simon H. Clarke, Bart.
Henry W. Martin, Bart.
W. Windham Dalling, Bart.
William H. Cooper, Bart.
William Fraser.
Wm. Max. Alexander.
J. L. Anderdon.
David Baillie.
John Baillie.
J. Foster Barham.
Æneas Barkly.
Andrew Colvile.
John Daniel.
Henry Davidson.
John H. Deffell.
James B. Delap.
John Fuller.
Alexander Grant.
Alexander Hall.
Robert Hibbert.
George Hibbert.
Thomson Hankey.
Isaac Higgin.
Hugh Hyndman.
John Innes.
William King.
Roger Kynaston.
David Lyon.
Neill Malcolm.
William Manning.
John P. Mayers.
Philip John Miles.
John Mitchell.
Rowland Mitchell.
G. H. Dawkins Pennant.
William Ross.
George Shedden.
A. Stewart.
George Watson Taylor.
Robert Taylor.
John Watson.*

London, April 29th, 1831.

"The Anti-Slavery Society declare—

"That the experience of the last eight years has demonstrated incontrovertibly, that it is *only* by the direct intervention of Parliament that any effectual remedy can be applied.'

"And one of the Resolutions proposed to the House of Commons at the close of the last Session, by Mr. T. F. Buxton, also declared—

"'That, during the eight years which have elapsed since the Resolutions of the House of Commons in 1823, the Colonial Assemblies have not taken adequate means for carrying those Resolutions into effect.'

"As it is, therefore, on the express ground of the alleged refusal of the Colonial Assemblies to take adequate measures for carrying into effect the Resolutions of 1823, that the Anti-Slavery party invoke the interference of Parliament, it has been thought fit to show what are the existing laws of the several Colonies, and which laws (with one exception, p. 12,)† are either entirely new, or have been re-enacted with great improvements, *within the last eight years*."

These *forty-one* gentlemen then proceed to give, what they call, an "Abstract of the existing laws of our West India Colonies" compiled, they say, from Parliamentary documents. The correctness of this abstract thus vouched, and the value of the enactments it boasts of, it shall now be our business to examine.

1. The "Abstract" commences with a view of the measures said to have been adopted in Jamaica for the benefit of the slaves, in pursuance of the suggestions of His Majesty's Government; and the first point which they select in proof of the compliance of the legislature of this island is that of "*Religious Instruction and the Observance of the Sabbath*." Now, we should be quite willing to rest the whole merits of this controversy on the truth or falsehood of the alleged compliance. The recommendation of the British Government was that Sunday markets and Sunday labour should be abolished, and a day in lieu of the Sunday given to the slaves for those purposes. But in what respect has the legislature of Jamaica complied with this suggestion? It has given the slaves no day in lieu of Sunday, nor do its present

* We have inserted the *forty-one* names subscribed to this paper by way of securing a lasting record of them. They are names which ought not to be forgotten.

† We shall hereafter show how unfounded is this statement.

Fig. 10.1 Page from *The Anti-Slavery Reporter* listing the forty-one signatories of the West Indian Manifesto, a proslavery document. *Anti-Slavery Reporter* 4, no. 10 (1831): 290.

asterisk, reads, 'We have inserted the *forty-one* names subscribed to this paper by way of securing a lasting record of them. They are names which ought not to be forgotten'.[18]

This footnote signals a 'local detour or a momentary fork in the text'.[19] The asterisk – John Watson* – invites readers to stop their traversal of the page. Unlike an endnote, which requires the effort of traveling a great distance to the end of the text, the footnote promises a short detour. Curious what the footnote has to say, readers find the second asterisk – '*forty-one* [. . .] names which ought not to be forgotten'. Readers travel back once again to the three columns of names. Now, perhaps, they read them more carefully. They commit the names to memory. Forty-one. Are there really so many? Perhaps the reader feels indignant that these British men would support so infamous a cause. The detour takes longer than they thought it would, but here they are again.

After the columns of names comes '*London*, April 29, 1831'. This date signals the spatial-temporal context of the manifesto and helps readers orient themselves within this context. Nineteenth-century readers might have recalled where they were and what they were doing on 29 April. The italics emphasise that the West Indian Manifesto was written in the heart of Britain rather than in far-off Jamaica or Antigua. For readers of the *Reporter* in 1831, the place and date bring the dangers of slavery closer to home. The section that follows quotes from the manifesto. It is less visually striking than the list of names and easier to pass over. Even if readers encounter them nearer to 'London, April 29, 1831', the legislative concerns might still seem remote from the concerns of everyday life. In the middle of this section, readers halt at another footnote marker. Down they travel once again to the other side of the black rule. This footnote reads, 'We shall hereafter show how unfounded is this statement'. Perhaps readers now go back and reread the excerpt from the Manifesto more carefully:

> As it is, therefore, on the express ground of the alleged refusal of the Colonial Assemblies to take adequate measures for carrying into effect the Resolutions of 1823, that the Anti-Slavery party invoke the interference of Parliament, it has been thought fit to show what are the existing laws of the several Colonies, and which laws [. . .] are either entirely new, or have been re-enacted with great improvements, *within the last eight years*.

The editorial footnote marking this passage from the proslavery document promises to disprove the manifesto's and its signees' claims. *The Anti-Slavery Reporter*, and by extension, the antislavery movement, repeatedly aligns itself with objectivity and empiricism. This footnote promises the reader another example of the underhanded dealings of the proslavery party. Readers might show renewed attention, as the issue now represents a moral contest between truth and lies.

The Anti-Slavery Reporter reinforces its alignment with veracity through the extensive use of direct quotations from other sources, in this case, the West Indian Manifesto.[20] Accordingly, the visual weight of the page emphasises the dominance of the *Reporter* over the manifesto. The quoted sections of the page use noticeably smaller font than the original content in the *Reporter*. Thus, although the excerpt from the proslavery manifesto takes up a more substantial portion of the page, the *Reporter*'s response dominates the conversation. The periodical dives right into its refutation of the West Indian Manifesto with the first point on its numbered list, the religious rights and practices of the enslaved population in the colonies. The number 1 implies both the reasoned, logical argumentation that is standard for *The Anti-Slavery Reporter* as well as the importance of religion to the antislavery movement as a whole. In its attacks against the proslavery argument, the Anti-Slavery Society consistently associates itself and its members with genuine religious feeling; meanwhile, it shows how proslavery activists twist religion to suit their self-interest. Placing the issue of religion at the top of the argument against the West Indian Manifesto reinforces the Anti-Slavery Society's position: that the debate about slavery involved a higher plane than mere political economy and consisted of virtuous Christians battling hypocritical proslavery activists.

Regular readers of *The Anti-Slavery Reporter* would be familiar with the debates about Sunday markets in the slave colonies. Despite the royal guidelines that the enslaved should have the Sabbath to devote to rest and religious observance, the periodical often detailed how enslavers forced them to labour on Sundays. The fact that the markets took place on Sundays so that enslaved persons could trade for the bare necessities of life produced significant moral outrage among antislavery activists. This exemplified the greed and depravity of white colonials; their pursuit of wealth obstructed the path to righteous Christian observance among the enslaved.[21] Antislavery activists argued that by forcing the enslaved to trade on Sundays, enslavers damned them and invalidated their claims that slavery was a means of converting heathens. Because proslavery activists argued that enslaving Africans was a Christian duty meant to lift them from heathenism to Christian brotherhood, antislavery activists regularly pointed to examples of colonial hypocrisy, which often made Christian observance and instruction for the enslaved a legal offense. Statutes and laws in the colonies prohibited the enslaved from gathering for services, reading the Bible or observing the Sabbath. By barring the enslaved from legal and religious marriage, antislavery activists argued that colonists forced them into concubinage and adultery. Despite casting blame on white colonists, these arguments did nothing to remove the moral burden of 'heathenish' practices from the enslaved.

Readers perhaps now find that they have made it to the black rule at the bottom of the page. The main text stops mid-sentence; they turn the page without thinking about it and continue reading. This page is only a small section of the path that threads throughout issue 82 of *The Anti-Slavery Reporter*; already, readers can see that the landscape is remarkably fertile. If they were to continue through the issue, they would see that some actants show up again and again – the italicised *forty-one* appears thirty-three times in this issue. It is impossible to ignore. This repetition ensures that readers recall the three columns of now-infamous names at the beginning of page 290. The footnote insists that these names 'ought not to be forgotten', and the thirty-three instances of the *forty-one* make it nearly impossible to do so.

Readers who were familiar with the recurring textual actants within *The Anti-Slavery Reporter* could traverse the space of the page as a matter of habit, much as they would take a familiar path through the city without significant conscious thought. Only by slowing down and looking around carefully does one notice all the little signposts and barriers that encourage movement down these familiar paths. The consistent use of actants such as self-referential footnotes encouraged readers to position themselves as witnesses to the horrors of colonial slavery. The witness created by the *Reporter*, published and read largely in Britain, looked at the evidence from the colonies as if from a great height. From this vantage point, the nineteenth-century British antislavery movement invested its moral capital in reshaping Britain's relationship with its colonies – one that promised greater unity across the empire but only for those who submitted to a rigid and racially exclusive social hierarchy.

The recursive nature of footnotes discussed above played a key role in how *The Anti-Slavery Reporter* managed readers' perceptions of its position at the centre of the antislavery movement. When the *Reporter* moved from monthly to biweekly publication in 1831 due to increasing support for the antislavery movement among the British public, the pressing need for more content increased significantly. Zachary Macaulay and Thomas Pringle used lengthy excerpts from other publications to fill issues. Information from the colonies had an important place within the *Reporter*, as it reinforced the periodical's assertions that it objectively reported facts about slavery, as opposed to the false claims of the proslavery movement. Newspapers such as *The Watchman, and Jamaica Free Press* and *The Christian Record* were useful sources of evidence against slavery and provided copy that Macaulay and Pringle did not have to write themselves.[22] Although some issues consisted almost entirely of material from colonial publications, the self-referential footnotes within *The Anti-Slavery Reporter* redirected readers' focus from the sources to the role of the periodical and, by extension, the Anti-Slavery Society as disseminators of reliable information.

Both pro- and antislavery activists recognised the importance of *The Watchman, and Jamaica Free Press* and *The Christian Record*. During the investigations of the Select Committee on the Extinction of Slavery Throughout the British Dominions in 1832, proslavery witness William Taylor referred to both of these Jamaican publications by name, claiming that they were 'unsafe reading for the slaves of Jamaica'.[23] Colonial antislavery activism posed a real threat to white safety in the West Indies, Taylor argued. *The Anti-Slavery Reporter*, on the other hand, was 'little known in Jamaica, and he did not believe it was read there'.[24] Although Macaulay, Pringle and the other members of the Anti-Slavery Society were probably more concerned with their British readers than with a colonial audience, Taylor's comment does call into question assumptions that Britain always claimed first place in the information network of the antislavery movement. The *Reporter* employed various rhetorical strategies that sought to balance the power of the colonial press's role as eyewitness and reclaim moral force as a distinctly British contribution to the antislavery movement. Self-referential footnotes in the *Reporter* negotiated the periodical's supremacy over colonial sources.

By drawing readers' attention back to the *Reporter* and other publications produced by the Anti-Slavery Society, the *Reporter* pulled focus from colonial publications back on itself, reinforcing the idea that Britain, rather than the colonies, was the primary battleground for the fight against slavery.

The footnotes in *The Anti-Slavery Reporter* have particular spatial gravity. Unlike an endnote, a footnote takes up space both on the page and in readers' minds. Although modern readers are perhaps more likely to skim or skip a footnote altogether, I propose that readers of *The Anti-Slavery Reporter*, whether regular or new, practiced alternative forms of reading encouraged by the spatial context of footnotes within the periodical. Of course, there is no way of knowing if these reading practices were standard. However, as the use of footnotes within the *Reporter* is noticeably different than how notes are used today, a little hypothesising about alternative reading practices opens up new paths through the periodical.

Footnotes in *The Anti-Slavery Reporter* often take up a significant amount of space on a page, sometimes more than the body of the text itself. These extended footnotes have a greater visual and conceptual pull than the rest of the page. The editorial voice, presumably Macaulay's, appears at full force in lengthy, discursive footnotes – with responses to personal attacks, barbs directed at specific proslavery activists or editorial asides seasoned with frustration and biting wit.[25] Since many of these footnotes take up more than half a page or even carry over several pages, they tend to upend the periodical's typical visual signals of importance. When extended over a wider space, the small, dense type visually intimates a verbal outpouring of feeling strong enough to interrupt more restrained arguments. Whereas the body text prioritises objectivity, the extended footnotes might signal for readers to

Table 10.1 Types of footnotes in volumes 4 and 5 of *The Anti-Slavery Reporter*

Type of Note	Occurrences
Additional information	6
Editorial asides	2
Self-referential footnotes	7
Original notes from *The Christian Record*	12

engage with more emotive, often aggressive, antislavery feelings. Longtime readers of *The Anti-Slavery Reporter* were perhaps more attuned to this emotional signaling, reading a long footnote as insiders privy to editorial sentiments. Thus, these extended editorial footnotes encouraged readers to traverse several pages, engaging with the parallel narrative contained within the *Reporter*'s paratextual material.

In contrast, newer readers might skip over footnotes and thus encounter a more sanitised, palatable antislavery discourse.[26] Thinking of footnotes in the *Reporter* as a parallel discourse to the body text also has implications for space outside the page. Many footnotes give specific locations, particularly Great Britain, greater prominence within the antislavery movement. This prominence translates to a conception of the British Empire where these exact locations also have more political and ideological weight. Throughout, the *Reporter* echoed the tension between the empirical body text and the sentiment in editorial footnotes, textually as well as visually.

Fifty-three direct references to *The Christian Record* appear in volumes 4 and 5 of *The Anti-Slavery Reporter*. Twenty-seven footnotes relating to the Jamaican periodical in the two volumes fall into four broad categories: additional information, editorial asides, self-referential footnotes and original footnotes from *The Christian Record*. Footnotes providing additional information offer minor clarifications of colonial details for British readers, whereas the *Reporter*'s barbs aimed at proslavery activists are usually presented as editorial asides. The majority of footnotes fall into the two latter categories. Twelve footnotes quote *The Christian Record*. Seven self-referential footnotes direct readers' attention away from the *Record*, either to previous (and, in one case, future) issues of the *Reporter*, other publications from the Anti-Slavery Society or its members, and parliamentary papers. Self-referential footnotes act in concert to position readers within a global antislavery discourse that minimises the role of the colonial press in favour of the Anti-Slavery Society's British publications. Readers are pulled in two directions by footnotes from *The Christian Record* – in one direction towards the Jamaican press as a source of empirical evidence against slavery and in the other direction back towards the Anti-Slavery Society as both gate and gatekeeper of the antislavery moment in Britain.

The footnotes quoted directly from *The Christian Record* indicate that it was a central source of information about slavery in the British colonies for the Anti-Slavery Society in Great Britain. The editors of *The Anti-Slavery Reporter* viewed *The Christian Record* as more than a well for sourcing fresh copy to fill its pages: by including footnotes from the *Record*, it was acknowledging the authority of the Jamaican paper.[27] Genette writes, 'The original authorial note, at least when connected to a text that is itself discursive and with which it has a relation of continuity and formal heterogeneity, belongs more to the text, which the note extends, ramifies, and modulates rather than comments on.'[28] Thus, the original notes from *The Christian Record* enrich its value as a source for *The Anti-Slavery Reporter*. By including so many of these notes, Macaulay and Pringle signal that they consider the *Record* a text that deserves nuanced reading.

Most of the notes quoted directly from *The Christian Record* in *The Anti-Slavery Reporter* provide further proof of claims made in the body text. These notes provide continuity between the original notes of the *Record* and original notes from the *Reporter*. Indeed, the *Reporter*'s signature editorial asides often accompany long quotations from the *Record*; this editorial interjection also 'extends, ramifies, and modulates' colonial evidence.[29] *The Anti-Slavery Reporter*'s heavy reliance on *The Christian Record*, including its editorial notes, diverges from the usual scissors-and-paste practices intended to fill pages. Macaulay and Pringle's interjections in *The Anti-Slavery Reporter* create a new hybrid text that blurs the lines between their roles as editors and authors.

Although *The Anti-Slavery Reporter*'s extended engagement with *The Christian Record* signalled a degree of respect for the colonial press as a source of objective evidence, the self-referential footnotes that peppered excerpts from the *Record* also served as a counterforce throughout the *Reporter*. These notes drew the reader's attention away from the *Record* and back to the *Reporter* and, by extension, to the Anti-Slavery Society's central role in abolition. Like the note on page 290 that urged readers to continually refer to the list of names at the top of the page, the self-referential notes accompanying excerpts from *The Christian Record* directed readers back to the Anti-Slavery Society's publications in Britain, *The Anti-Slavery Reporter* chief among them. This tension produced a dynamic, continuously negotiated relationship between the reader, the British periodical and the colonial press, which recalls Latour's definition of the social as constant process rather than a static medium. Through the self-referential footnotes that recursively brought the reader's attention back to the *Reporter*, the periodical co-opted the role of witness for itself and, by extension, its readers. In the moral battle waged between the antislavery and proslavery camps, this act of witnessing was a compelling claim on the part of the antislavery movement. The evidence against slavery carried more weight in the court of public opinion when it was vetted and presented by a British rather than a colonial source.[30]

The Anti-Slavery Reporter served as a map of the unfamiliar landscape of colonial slavery for readers in Britain. Paratextual cartographic devices helped readers position themselves within the space of the new British Empire imagined in the *Reporter* – a space that would be free of state-sanctioned slavery but that solidified the belief that white Britons were the rightful moral arbiters of the new world order. The goal of the *Reporter* was to move its British readers to action: beyond merely purchasing and reading the periodical, the members of the Anti-Slavery Society hoped that readers would materialise their support for the cause into donations and signatures on petitions, and would influence a more nebulous but equally crucial public opinion. The American Revolution was a recent example of the dangers of too great a distance between the colonies and Britain, a divide that somehow must be closed.[31] By conceiving of this space as a moral rather than a physical distance between proslavery advocates and Britons who 'never would be slaves', the antislavery movement successfully redefined the metrics of success for Britain's colonial relationships. If the colonists would only give up their slave system – the sin that separated them from full communion with the British nation – then Britain could be whole again.[32]

The Anti-Slavery Reporter remained an essential source of information and mobilisation for Britain's increasingly popular antislavery movement throughout its eleven years of uninterrupted publication. In addition to describing the horrors of slavery, asserting economic arguments in favour of abolition and making strident appeals to the moral necessity of ending slavery in the British colonies, *The Anti-Slavery Reporter* employed a sophisticated paratextual apparatus that encouraged its readers to engage with the text within a spatial dimension. A page of the *Reporter* is a space through which paratextual elements carve paths that readers are encouraged to follow across the periodical's broader terrain, be that a single issue, an annual volume or the entire run of the publication. Readers approach the periodical page as a sort of textual map in which paratextual devices function in much the same way as, say, a compass rose unfolds, with each device revealing another spatial component of the nineteenth-century periodical press. In the early nineteenth century's tumultuous political and cultural landscape, influential periodicals such as *The Anti-Slavery Reporter* were sources of both information and social cohesion. These periodicals assisted in the creation of new, at times revolutionary, terrain and then used their content and paratextual elements to suggest how readers should situate themselves therein. In the early 1830s, British readers engaged with the *Reporter* as a navigational tool, one that helped them position themselves in relation to the critical political issues of the day while simultaneously shaping their beliefs about Britain's place in the emerging world order.

Notes

1. Catherine Hall, *Macaulay and Son: Architects of Imperial Britain* (New Haven: Yale University Press, 2012), 84–5.
2. In addition to assisting Mary Prince in publishing her narrative, Pringle emigrated to South Africa and worked as a colonial official and journalist in the 1820s. He was also a major contributor in other publications produced for the Anti-Slavery Society. David Finkelstein, 'Thomas Pringle', in the *Oxford Dictionary of National Biography*, online edition (Oxford: Oxford University Press, 2004); Randolph Vigne, *Thomas Pringle: South African Pioneer, Poet and Abolitionist* (Rochester: Boydell and Brewer, 2012), 217–22.
3. The periodical includes evidence that information regarding colonial slavery was directly drawn from *The Anti-Slavery Reporter* and invoked during parliamentary discussions. During a debate on sugar duties, Lord Howick stated, 'We know the agents of the West Indian colonies circulated last year an abstract of the laws passed by the different local Legislatures, intended to shew that the Assemblies had, in many particulars, adopted the suggestions made to them, whilst on the other hand, the *Reporter*, if I may be permitted to allude to it, entered into a long argument to shew that the supposed compliances with those suggestions had been perfectly nugatory.' Zachary Macaulay, 'Debate on the Sugar Duties', *Anti-Slavery Reporter* 5, no. 4 (1832–3): 122.

4. Fernando J. Bosco, 'Emotions that Build Networks: Geographies of Human Rights Movements in Argentina and Beyond', *Tijdschrift Voor Economische En Sociale Geografie* 98, no. 5 (2007): 545–63; David Cooper and Ian N. Gregory, 'Mapping the English Lake District: A Literary GIS', *Transactions of the Institute of British Geographers* 36, no. 1 (2011): 89–108; Anne Kelly Knowles, et al., 'Inductive Visualization: A Humanistic Alternative to GIS', *GeoHumanities* 1, no. 2 (2015): 233–65; Doreen Massey, 'Politics and Space-Time', *New Left Review* 196 (1992): 65–84; Doreen Massey, *Space, Place, and Gender* (Minneapolis: University of Minnesota Press, 1994); Doreen Massey, *For Space* (London: SAGE, 2005).
5. Edward W. Soja, *Thirdspace: Journeys to Los Angeles and Other Real-and-Imagined Places* (Oxford: Blackwell, 1996), 188–93. Soja describes the Power of Place organisation's efforts to commemorate the life of Biddy Mason (1818–91), a formerly enslaved women who became 'the first African-American woman to own substantial property in [Los Angeles]' as an example of thirdspace (190). The Biddy Mason Park and the exhibition at UCLA reveal how the city is reshaped through the memorialising of Biddy Mason while the historical memory of her 'place' in the city of Los Angeles is shaped by the specific geographies created by the Power of Place organisation.
6. Bruno Latour, *Reassembling the Social: An Introduction to Actor-Network Theory* (Oxford: Oxford University Press, 2005).
7. Agnieszka Leszczynski and Sarah Elwood, 'Feminist Geographies of New Spatial Media', *Canadian Geographer* 59, no. 1 (2015): 12–28.
8. Jeremy W. Crampton, *Mapping: A Critical Introduction to Cartography and GIS* (New York: John Wiley, 2010), 92–4.
9. Laurel Brake, 'Time's Turbulence: Mapping Journalism Networks', *Victorian Periodicals Review* 44, no. 2 (2011): 115–27; Anne DeWitt, 'Advances in the Visualization of Data: The Network of Genre in the Victorian Periodical Press', *Victorian Periodicals Review* 48, no. 2 (2015): 161–82; John Fagg, Matthew Pethers and Robin Vandome, 'Introduction: Networks and the Nineteenth-Century Periodical', *American Periodicals: A Journal of History & Criticism* 23, no. 2 (2013): 93–104; Joanne Shattock, 'Professional Networking, Masculine and Feminine', *Victorian Periodicals Review* 44, no. 2 (2011): 128–40. Digitised editions of *The Anti-Slavery Reporter*, some of which I rely on in my analysis, should be considered as separate editions and not facsimiles. For more on the scholarly implications of digital editions of periodicals, see James Mussell,

The Nineteenth-Century Press in the Digital Age (Basingstoke: Palgrave Macmillan, 2012). Paul Fyfe also discusses digitised editions and in particular the erasure of BIPOC labour which is integral to the creation of these editions. Although reprints of *The Anti-Slavery Reporter* are available for purchase, digitised editions are behind paywalls that restrict access to this important source in ways that negatively impact BIPOC communities. Paul Fyfe, 'An Archaeology of Victorian Newspapers', *Victorian Periodicals Review* 49, no. 4 (2016): 546–77.

10. Latour, *Reassembling the Social*, 54.
11. Massey, *For Space*, 10.
12. Latour, *Reassembling the Social*, 54.
13. Ibid., 72.
14. The *Reporter* acknowledged the injustice of colonial laws that barred the enslaved from acting as legal witnesses against white defendants: 'He (Mr. Phillips) was in the Court-house when a person (whom he named) was brought up for trial under a charge of cruelly flogging a slave, in consequence of which he died; but there being no white or free witnesses against him, the murderer escaped with impunity: if 500 slaves had seen it they would not have been allowed to give evidence. Such is the law up to the present moment in Antigua'. Zachary Macaulay, 'Meeting at Bury St. Edmunds', *Anti-Slavery Reporter* 4, no. 2 (1831): 71.
15. James Macqueen was a Scottish proslavery activist, geographer and editor. Thomas Pringle, in particular, had a personal reason for singling out Macqueen for sharp criticism, as Macqueen and Pringle were embroiled in a libel case regarding *The History of Mary Prince* in 1832.
16. Gérard Genette, *Paratexts: Thresholds of interpretation* (Cambridge: Cambridge University Press, 1997), 1–2.
17. From 'The West Indian Manifesto Examined', *Anti-Slavery Reporter* 4, no. 10 (1831): 289–316. Subsequent references are to page 290 in this article.
18. Emphasis in the original.
19. Genette, *Paratexts*, 328.
20. Scissors-and-paste journalism, or the practice of using material originally printed in other sources, whether legally or pirated, was a common editorial practice during the eighteenth and nineteenth centuries. Considering that Macaulay, with Pringle's assistance, was responsible for putting out a new issue of *The Anti-Slavery Reporter* every two weeks, recycling copy from other publications might have

been the only way for him to meet the demands of his publication schedule. Catherine Feely, '"Scissors-and-Paste" Journalism', in *The Dictionary of Nineteenth-Century Journalism*, online edition, ed. Laurel Brake and Marysa Demoor (London: British Library, 2009).

21. The lack of observance of the Sabbath in the colonies provided the antislavery movement with substantial evidence of colonial irreligion. Enslavers often forced the enslaved to work on Sundays in order to maximise profits. Sundays were also the only days that enslaved persons were given time to farm meager plots of land from which they were expected to eke out their subsistence. The Sunday markets produced even more outrage among British antislavery activists, calling to mind the incident of Jesus' expulsion of the money lenders from the Temple of Jerusalem.
22. The editors of *The Jamaica Watchman*, Edward Jordan and Robert Osborn, were free Black men and advocates for the civil rights of Black Jamaicans and Jamaicans of colour, free and enslaved. Candace Ward, '"An Engine of Immense Power": *The Jamaica Watchman* and Crossings in Nineteenth-Century Colonial Print Culture', *Victorian Periodicals Review* 51, no. 3 (2018): 483–503.
23. Zachary Macaulay, 'Report of a Committee of the House of Commons', *Anti-Slavery Reporter* 5, no. 13 (1832): 339.
24. Ibid.
25. One such long editorial footnote, which spills across two pages, berates proslavery activists in Glasgow such as the infamous James Macqueen, editor of the *Glasgow Courier*, for their 'delusive and mendacious assertions' and 'matchless effrontery'. Zachary Macaulay, 'Meeting at Glasgow', *Anti-Slavery Reporter* 4, no. 2 (1831): 38.
26. Brian Harrison, 'Press and Pressure Group in Modern Britain', in *The Victorian Periodical Press: Samplings and Soundings*, ed. Joanne Shattock and Michael Wolff (Leicester University Press, Leicester, 1982), 284–5.
27. The original source footnotes are in quotation marks, distinguishing them from *The Anti-Slavery Reporter* notes.
28. Genette, *Paratexts*, 328.
29. Ibid.
30. This is troublingly similar to the act of witnessing in cases involving white abusers in the colonies who could only be convicted through the evidence of white witnesses, as the testimony of the enslaved was not legally admissible.

31. Christopher L. Brown, *Moral Capital: Foundations of British Abolitionism* (Chapel Hill: University of North Carolina Press, 2006).
32. British unity was clearly being redefined along other paths as well: Catholic Emancipation and the Reform Acts were debated at the same time as the future of colonial slavery.

11

The Media System of Charitable Visiting

Sara L. Maurer

The 1820s and 1830s mark a midway point between two landmark moments in the history of paperwork. The first is the French Revolution, which, as media historian Ben Kafka points out, unleashed a flood of documentation into everyday life. The levelling revolutionary spirit, with its commitment to 'political and administrative accountability', he notes, generated mountains of paperwork, 'in anticipation of an eventual public accounting'.[1] The second is the innovation of complex corporate communications systems designed to standardise geographically distant business operations. Joanne Yates documents the emergence of interlocking paperwork genres, storage systems and business meetings within post-Civil War American railway and chemical companies struggling to stay profitable as their operations expanded.[2] In both developments, media historians anticipate the rise of an impersonal, bureaucratic modern age. Lisa Gitelman, speaking of the blank printed forms that gradually transformed US corporate paperwork, asserts that 'because blank forms help routinize, they dehumanize'.[3] Kafka, too, concludes that 'our experience of paperwork's contradictions is an experience of carelessness', which becomes 'conflated with uncaring'.[4] Yates tacitly offers the same conclusion where paperwork is concerned, noting that the newly prescribed corporate genres of writing and recording had to be balanced out by meetings and in-house magazines designed to restore a human element to business transactions.[5]

In between these two historical moments in the evolution of paperwork lies the innovation of one high-profile media system in Great Britain – the system of charitable visiting. While the term 'visiting' might bring to mind informal calls made by the middle classes to the homes of the poor, as portrayed in novels by Charles Dickens or Elizabeth Gaskell, early century champions of the practice understood it as a methodical coordination of multiple genres of print and physical encounters designed for collecting information, efficiently distributing aid, and above all creating and sustaining channels of communication between the urban middle classes and their low-income neighbours. It has become a contemporary truism that the practice provided the prototype for modern casework associated with social work. However, this truism fails to account for how the steady proliferation of print circulation in the first third of the nineteenth century shaped the practice. In the 1820s and 1830s, when the practice enjoyed a sudden spike in popularity, charitable visiting depended on a media system that coordinated three different types of technical media: print material whose unidirectional communication conveyed messages to the poor; a host of printed blanks designed to collect information from the poor about their lives; and face-to-face encounters that were personalised yet were structured by the latter two types of print material.

I have two aims in describing early charitable visiting in these terms. For scholars of Victorian studies, I hope to suggest that the gradual rise of social work and the welfare state is a story as much about media as it is about new forms of modern governance. For media scholars interested in paperwork, I hope to complicate some conclusions about the seemingly inevitable inhumanity of the genre. Visiting was a system in which concern for poor people not immediately connected to one's own family or household called into being a complex system of paperwork that resembled care. I argue that early in the nineteenth century, the media system of visiting mitigated some of the most dehumanising effects of paperwork by associating this work with the practices of an intensive reader – a figure who carefully returned again and again to the same text, respectfully seeking what meaning might be pulled from it.

I make my argument in two parts. First, I explore Thomas Chalmers's early century vision of a visiting system undertaken on behalf of the church and state though executed entirely by volunteers. Chalmers's writing, largely responsible for the popularity of charitable visiting from the 1820s through the 1840s, offers few details about the circulation of printed forms or reading matter that would come to define the practice. Nonetheless, he writes of visitors deputised by the clergy to visit the poor, sent off to physical encounters whose dynamics resembled a broadcast. The visitor's face-to-face encounters are intended to bring the personality of the church and pastor to the poor. In turn, he (for Chalmers, visitors were always men) is expected to have a careful, readerly relationship to those he encounters in his visits, paying them the same respectful attention he would a devotional text. It is these media-like roots that spawn the multimedia interactions I explore in the second part of my paper. The literature generated by those promoting charitable visiting in Chalmers's wake not only offers a sharp picture of the proliferating genres of print literature and paperwork the practice occasioned but also shows that it fit uneasily into straightforward categories such as 'personal' or 'bureaucratic'. The printed forms and pre-established protocols of charitable visiting were designed, like standardised corporate forms later in the century, to eliminate individual idiosyncrasies from charitable visiting. At the same time, in literature associated with visiting, the analogy persists of the visitor as an intensive reader of the homes he or she visits. This vision of a charitable worker as someone making voluntary, attentive returns to limited spaces in order to seek understanding put the practice at odds with the impersonality of a modern bureaucracy. Visiting literature imagined the charity routine as a sign of devotion and care rather than underwriting a mechanical efficiency.

Chalmers and the visitor as media

To write about charitable visiting as a form of media, as I will do in this essay, might seem either misguided or naïvely obvious, depending on what definition of 'media' one is using. On the one hand, the entire practice of visiting was designed to create face-to-face encounters between the poor population of a city and those who might help them. Most advocates of the practice saw it as an opportunity for creating affective attachments between visitor and visited, much like the cross-rank ties they fantasised to have existed in pre-industrial villages. In this respect, it would seem the opposite of what we think of as technical media, which delivers content between humans physically distanced from one another.

Yet the practice unquestionably existed to create communication between classes of people understood to be distant from one another. The Scottish cleric Thomas Chalmers advised clergy to divide their parishes into districts whose households would be visited regularly by one responsible middle-class parishioner. The visitor could draw the unassimilated into a church network of schooling, worship and emergency assistance, thus allowing the pastor at the head of a rapidly expanding urban parish to develop 'a ready intermedium of communication between himself and the inhabitants'.[6] Even those who took up Chalmers's scheme for reasons other than church stewardship still saw the practice as acquainting the middle classes of a town with poor populations to which they might otherwise be oblivious. For instance, the explicitly nonsectarian Liverpool District Society began raising funds with the publication of a sermon which promised its audience that the society would return Liverpool to a condition that prevails 'in country parishes, where the population is thin' and where 'the tenant, the villager, the poor, all cling like the ivy to the oak to him [the richest man of the village] whose birth and fortune have placed him at their head'.[7]

District visiting, like many media systems, was not invented a single time in one location. Historians point out that the division of neighbourhoods into districts for routine visits by those concerned for their spiritual and temporal welfare can be identified as early as 1785, when the Quaker John Gardner started his Stranger's Friend Society.[8] But it wasn't until Chalmers published the first volume of *The Christian and Civic Economy of Large Towns* in 1819 that the model of visiting struck a wide group of people as a useful and reproducible practice.[9] For that reason, I examine Chalmers's own writing on the practice in order to establish two implicit aspects of his vision deeply enmeshed in media thinking. The first is that Chalmers assumes the charitable worker engaged in visiting to be an extension of the personality of the clergy, rather than appearing at the door of the poor as the bearer of his own personality. In broadcasting information to the poor, the visitor is expected to carry a message, not to create it. The second is Chalmers's repeated emphasis on the charitable workers' relationship to their district, which required a disciplining of their attention to focus on just one thing, much as a printed text might require a filtering out of the wider world for its consumption. In collecting information, a visitor would have to draw on dispositions first developed by most evangelicals to deal with a distracting environment of proliferating print.

In the first two volumes of *The Christian and Civic Economy of Large Towns*, published between 1819 and 1826, Chalmers recommended as a general practice the pastoral experiments he had undertaken in two urban parishes in Glasgow, appointing laymen to visit every household in the populous parishes to assess their needs for schooling, spiritual guidance and emergency aid – three functions that traditionally were the responsibility of the Scottish Established Church.[10] The popularity of Chalmers's system was due in no small part to his claim that this strategy for knowing the character and situation of every parish member significantly decreased the amount of church funds spent on the poor. Chalmers argued that a church that knew its members could more effectively assess when such help was truly called for, when friends or family might be called upon for such help instead and when such help would be useless.

But alongside this promise of less money spent on the poor, Chalmers imagined that the practice of visiting was the stuff of media, in the sense of widely shared material that binds consumers together into a common audience. Chalmers sees visiting as one way to gather communities into such 'common places of resort, as the parish church and the parish schools'.[11] But he also understands that visitors themselves act as a focal point that provides neighbours with a common subject for conversation, so that when 'contiguous families [. . .] come within the scope of the same household attentions [. . .] there is between them, through the week, a prolonged, and often a cherished sympathy'.[12] When Chalmers imagines this scenario, he is quite explicitly looking backwards, trying to recreate the hierarchical and deferential society that was the nineteenth century's recollection of small-town life in the preindustrial eighteenth century. But the scale at which he tries to accomplish this turns the project into a remediation, not a re-creation.[13] Chalmers never promises a community in which everyone becomes known to one another; instead, he imagines a community in which a few figures exist of whom everyone shares common knowledge. Chalmers advises clergy to maintain a personal relationship with 'the more remarkable cases' in the parish; however, 'as for [. . .] Christian acquaintanceship, he can spread it abroad by deputation' through the visitor.[14] In each district, the community shares knowledge of the visitor who attends them. But this knowledge is of the visitor who bears them 'Christian acquaintanceship' on behalf of the pastor and the church. Chalmers imagines the visitor to represent cultural and spiritual content whose source should be understood as the pastor. The visitors themselves are not identical to that content but instead become the means by which the content becomes more public, much in the same way a newspaper circulates content in its pages. This is a marked and deliberate change from the eighteenth-century visiting activities of the Stranger's Friend Society, a subscription-based visiting charity in which visitors pooled their own money and voted on the cases most meriting attention, with those donating the most money casting the weightiest votes.[15] Chalmers ensured that the church, rather than voluntary associations, sponsored the activity, transforming visitors from acting on their own initiative to simply mediating on behalf of someone else.

And much like a newspaper, the visitor, in his media-like character, is imagined as a vessel that might carry multiple types of content between the clergy and the people. On the one hand, the visitor fulfills the demands of evangelism, since, should the Holy Spirit descend, it would find 'its way, most readily, through the most free and frequented pathways of communication that have been opened up between the ministers of religion and the people'.[16] Chalmers asserts that 'by subdividing parishes we just multiply these pathways'.[17] But on the other hand, as heir to the Calvinist belief that salvation is reserved only for the elect few, Chalmers acknowledges that the salvific yield will be low. All the same, establishing channels of communication by means of district visiting remains worthwhile for Chalmers because 'the civic good [. . .] might be almost universal'.[18] A channel created to transmit spiritual messages serves just as well to communicate civic content, and in the end, the existence of the medium that connects counts for more than the message that might be passed through it.[19]

Chalmers's system is media at the most basic level in the sense that it extends the reach of the church both in terms of the number of people served and the physical distance spanned. Eager to sideline the social power of dissenting religion and secular organisations, his organisational plans borrow from many eighteenth-century innovations in sociability from corresponding clubs to Methodism.[20] And just like those new forms of organisation, an expansion in scale allows for new relationships made possible not just in spite of distance but because of it. This emerges sharply at moments when Chalmers imagines the rewards of visiting for the visitor and emphasises aspects of the experience that are possible because of distance and detachment.

Chalmers's emphasis on distance and detachment has been the subject of previous scholarly debate. For Mary Poovey, the distance indicates that Chalmers's project was always focused on training the middle classes to supervise and subordinate the poor.[21] Lauren Goodlad has countered this position by suggesting that Chalmers imagined his system would yield 'a deeply interpersonal relation' that would ultimately yield a whole society 'composed by inter-subjective relations'.[22] Yet neither critic quite captures the position the visitors occupy in relation to those they visit because they are, in the end, a part of the infrastructure and not its endpoint. Poovey's assumptions are overstated given Chalmers's repeated exhortations to the visitors not to set themselves up as patrons of the poor they visit. In urging visitors to stay focused on their role as ambassadors of the pastor, Chalmers's text works to undermine any middle-class assumption that they have regulatory control over the poor that is independent of the church. Goodlad is correct in that Chalmers does offer an account of reciprocity in which a social superior pays a call to a working-class home, and the poor, in turn, make an effort 'to afford him a decent reception, in the cleanliness of their houses, and the dress of their children'.[23] But this reciprocity is not his central interpretation of the dynamic between visitors and the poor. While Chalmers imagines a visitor who might bind neighbourhood inhabitants closer together by virtue of being a common topic of conversation, he tends not to emphasise that bonds between the visitors and the objects of their charity – or even among visitors working their separate districts – will strengthen in quite the same way.

Instead, Chalmers writes of a visitor who is strikingly solitary. He imagines each pastoral worker 'occupying his own little field'[24] and offers a surprisingly asocial vision of the work of urban ministers, who he says have 'each to concentrate the full influence of his character and office, on his own distinct and separate portion of the whole territory'.[25] Realising that they are responsible for broadcasting personalities not quite their own on to their districts, the visitors also begin to experience the district itself not as their immediate environment so much as a locale whose most salient feature seems to be its boundaries. Chalmers suggests that 'the very visibility of the limit [of the district], by constantly leading [the visitor] to perceive the length and the breadth of his task, holds out an inducement to his energies'.[26] Some of the pleasures he describes as arising from 'the very visibility of the limit' are decidedly nonreciprocal. A man gets a 'stronger pull' on his exertion when he is able to 'see the end of what he is embarked upon', Chalmers argues, suggesting one of the great pleasures of this sort of work is that those engaged in it are able to imagine its conclusion and thus hurry it along.[27] Likewise jarring is his suggestion that such a pastoral worker, assigned to work in only a small territory, 'will feel a kind of property in the families; and the very circumstance of a material limit around their habitations, serves to strengthen this impression'.[28] The same activities that are supposed to inspire communal ties among inhabitants seem to inspire in the pastoral worker a feeling of exclusive proprietorship.

Chalmers repeatedly defines visiting as work that calls for a sense of focus – a refusal to participate in endless charitable committees and clubs engaged in competing schemes to help the poor. Feelings of 'superior comfort' and 'superior productiveness, will soon make up to him for the loss of those more comprehensive surveys that are offered to his notice by Societies, which, however gigantic in their aim, are so inefficient in their performance'.[29] This, then, is the second consequence of Chalmers's vision: a requirement that visitors turn away from the wider social field and instead focus on 'a task so isolated' that it requires them to focus on 'particulars'.[30]

It would be easy to make the leap from Chalmers's account of the efficient district visitor to Adam Smith's worker under the division of labour, who becomes ever more efficient at his tiny, subdivided role within the pin factory. The charitable worker who feels proprietary pride in the neighbourhood he routinely visits also holds at least a superficial resemblance to Max Weber's bureaucratic worker, 'a single cog in an ever-moving mechanism', whose 'essentially fixed route of march' inspires in him 'an attitude set for habitual and virtuoso-like mastery of single yet methodically integrated functions'.[31] But in Chalmers's scheme, it is not the task of the charitable worker that is specialised: it is the place itself that must come to be known with a focused knowledge. Weber's dystopic understanding of bureaucracy leads to a starkly impersonal conclusion in which experts are each so minutely attuned to individual subdivided tasks that the organisation's leadership and ideology could change entirely without disrupting their work. But Chalmers's vision doesn't lead to the same entirely impersonal possibilities.

Specialised knowledge of a charitable district, after all, does not so much require the development of a specialised skill set than a capacity for repetitive alertness. For Romantic evangelicals, this is a capacity that also characterises an intensive approach to reading. 'Intensive reading' is the term book historians use to characterise reading carried out by those without access to a wide range of printed material. Performed 'repeatedly, deeply, with a reverence that corresponded to the often religious nature of the texts', intensive reading in an age of sparse print material generated a deep knowledge of the material, often deeply internalised if not also accurately memorised.[32] The intensive reader was the pious reader of sacred texts. Chalmers's own intensive evangelical reading also implied the calculated rejection of generalisation that emerged from extensive reading in a wide range of print material.[33] The truly Christian reader would derive a sharper, truer picture from repeated attention to orthodox texts.

William Wilberforce's *A Practical View of the Prevailing Religious System of Professed Christians*, a book that catalysed Chalmers's own evangelical conversion, might be seen as encouraging this sort of intensive reading.[34] He observes that while the idea of Christianity pervades Britain, most nominal Christians possess only the most 'barren generalities' concerning the topic, a state of affairs that might be corrected by 'the diligent perusal of Holy Scriptures'.[35] Thus, when Chalmers condemns 'a vague and vagrant philanthropy [. . .] which loses much of its energy in its diffusiveness, and which it were far better to fasten and to concentrate, and to confine, within the limits of a small locality', his dynamics echo an evangelical prescription for reading that privileges a contemplation of the specific over the general.[36] Wilberforce laments a nominally Christian population 'lost in generalities' with 'nothing precise and determinate, nothing which implies a mind used to the contemplation of its object'.[37] Chalmers adapts the complaint and its prescription of repeated returns to a specific text to his vision of visiting. Truly transformative work will be done, Chalmers opines, 'not by men, who eye, with imaginative transport, the broad and boundless expanse of humanity, but by men, who can work in drudgery and in detail, the separate portions of it'.[38]

Chalmers's emphasis on particularities over generalities – a single point of focus over an unlimited number of possible schemes – aligns well with evangelical reading advice during his lifetime, which frequently counselled the faithful to limit their reading material in spite of its sudden wide availability and to return always and faithfully to the Bible. Thus, even though Chalmers writes of efficiency as one payoff of his scheme, he also exhibits considerable interest in the charitable visitor retaining impressions of the district with the same sharpness with which intensive readers might retain the truth of the scriptural text to which they have returned again and again. The visitor having applied his efforts exclusively to one district, 'the objects of his liberality come so distinctly under his notice; that the good he has rendered, survives the exertion he has made in so separate and visible a form; that the families he has benefited can be so specifically pointed to'.[39] This is a relationship that is attentive and caring without being reciprocal; there is no expectation that the families might point back. In this sense, the concern lavished on those visited more closely resembles affective engagement with an important text rather than the full intersubjectivity of friendship or even the mutual recognition of class deference. Yet Chalmers's insistence that returning to the same district repeatedly matters and that careful attention also matters keeps the system from fully meeting Weber's criteria of a bureaucracy operated entirely 'without regard for persons'.[40]

In his elaboration of a church system of visiting, Chalmers imagines the 'intermedium of communication' that will integrate the urban poor into the established church, connecting them with the middle class.[41] His vision is not for a new technical material to do the work of transmission, storage and retrieval that the phonograph and the telegraph would provide a bit later in the century. Instead, Chalmers's intermedium is composed of the middle classes, who adhere to protocols that resemble on the one hand broadcasting to the poor and on the other, collecting information from a procedure that resembles intensive reading. But this protocol proved highly reproducible. Almost as soon as Chalmers published its description, local visiting societies sprang up in a wide variety of places, with a wide variety of aims. But it is striking that in this, one of the urtexts of Victorian visiting, Chalmers imagines the ties of sociability multiplying among the poor while the middle classes treat the poor as a revered text to be studied and imagine themselves operating as a sort of media whose consumption gives the poor a common bond. Against those who would interpret visiting only as a middle-class plan to subordinate the poor, it must be observed that the visitor who will act as mediator is the one whose focus comes in for so much disciplining in Chalmers's outline of the program. Visitors can act effectively only by collecting knowledge and concentrating their actions on clearly delimited areas. When Chalmers discusses visiting, he expresses far less concern over the behavior of the poor than he does over his hypothetical visitors' ability to confine their attention to one well-defined district and plan. This is surprising for a figure who contributed so richly to the Victorian notion of the 'deserving' poor.

Multimedia charitable visiting

The devotional readings aimed at pious Christians required the same close and confined attention expected of the charitable visitor. Both intensive reader and charitable visitor were expected to make disciplined returns to the same space or text for additional scrutiny. The resemblances of this new form of charity to old forms of reading may be one of the reasons it became, in historian Martin Hewitt's words, 'by far the most important Victorian technology of social knowledge'.[42] It might also explain to some extent the tendency Hewitt observes in literature that used observations from visiting to rely on 'conventional tropes and stock characters', offering 'little in the way of direct social description'.[43] After all, pious readers of a sacred text don't return to it for an original reading. They return to a text to derive a fresh impression of the force of a message whose broad contours are already familiar. When Victorians 'championed' what Hewitt calls 'the visiting mode' as 'the only means by which many social facts could be observed, recorded, and publicised', there are reasons to believe that the lingering associations between visiting and the virtues evangelicals saw in intensive reading could have bolstered its authority considerably.[44] The resemblance is also the reason I so strongly concur with Hewitt's account of visiting as an investigative mode that did not render the poor district as abstracted, empty space populated by so many fungible statistics.[45] Under the eyes of the district visitor, the poor district was an intensively read text, a space clearly separate from the observer, distant in the sense that its contents required repeated scrutiny. But the concentration it required for understanding meant that Chalmers, at least, did not see it as easily controllable or subordinated to the person under whose gaze it fell.

This dynamic of intensive reading persisted even as Chalmers's practice was widely adopted in the next twenty years by organisations that also incorporated the circulation of printed tracts or the use of printed forms into their charitable visiting. Visiting became a practice that proliferated print, drawing on an interlocking structure of text, printed forms and face-to-face meetings to help keep alive the sense of keen and focused attention Chalmers first associated with the activity. The project of visiting gradually became a media system in which three communication technologies – broadcast print, dialogic printed forms and face-to-face communication – all combine to create a system that does not quite behave according to one medium's set of affordances.

The media complexity the system acquired in the next two decades is summarised by the Reverend Robert A. Simpson, who in his 1842 *Clergyman's Manual* advises clergy to divide up their parish into visiting districts of a size that will allow them to visit each household once a week to read scripture, leave a tract, check on the sick and injured, encourage Sunday school and church attendance, and promote routine donations to missionary societies and deposits to savings schemes while also administering plans that will allow households to purchase on installment 'BIBLES, PRAYER BOOKS, HYMN BOOKS, AND FAMILY PRAYERS'.[46] The distribution of religious tracts, usually loaned out singly and exchanged for new ones at the next visit, became more sharply associated with the practice of charitable visiting. Quite often these tracts were composed of brief excerpts from devotional texts that a century earlier had been the mainstays of intensive reading, as if the fact of their having once been intensively read could improve the quality of lower-class encounters with them.[47]

In an environment of increased print, visitors were pressured to model intensive reading practices, not only in terms of their close attention to the districts they visited but also in terms of their religious reading. This is illustrated by the 1836 pocket volume *Jowett's Christian Visitor or, Scripture Readings with Expositions and Prayers; Designed to Assist the Friends of the Poor and Afflicted*, enthusiastically endorsed by Simpson.[48] The book collects brief passages from the Bible, each accompanied by concise reflections and a concluding prayer. In a preface that was also reproduced in a short-lived 1830s periodical, *The District Visitor's Record*, the author, William Jowett, explains the volume as the product of his own habitual marking out of 'Select Passages' in the course of his Bible reading that might be used 'in visiting the Poor and the Sick'.[49] He suggests that inexperienced clergymen and charitable visitors alike might benefit from his brief accounts of what he might say to the suffering, comments that are the fruits of his own intensive reading. He anticipates that those who benefit most from his books will be charitable visitors who have been devoted to their visits but perhaps not to their Bibles. In a passage that clearly treats visiting the poor as its own sort of intensive reading, the writer observes that the most devout visitors understand that 'their best lessons' are learned not in church or private prayer but 'when the circle around us is a room full of poor sufferers. [. . .] There [. . .] the mind of Christ is more copiously imbibed by the Visitor while he is doing the work of his Master.'[50]

Such readers might need Jowett's guide to select passages and interpretations, but Jowett cautions that visitors still cannot expect the book to do all of the reading for them. While Jowett provides the material, he recommends that 'the pious Visitor should previously meditate on the portion of Scripture to be explained; and then, with his heart full of it, read slowly and if he pleases, comment a little on the exposition that follows'.[51] In this way, even though Jowett has put into print his own thoughts for the poor, he imagines that the most effective form of communication with them still depends on the presence of a reflective, physically present body to read the material out loud. Jowett insists that his book will only be properly used if 'the Portions be *read* to the Poor, rather than left to be *looked at by* them'.[52] Print alone can't deliver what needs to be communicated from his lessons, at least not to the poor, and Jowett professes to trust only 'the Human Voice' to start 'the sacred thought flowing on more warmly to the heart of every hearer'.[53] The intensive reading that produced the books in the first place requires intensive pre-reading from the middle classes before it is delivered and demands physical presence if the message is to be communicated across class lines.

Jowett clearly enjoys contemplating the added reach that his foray into print gives his thoughts, but he resists celebrating a charitable project whose extensions are limited only by how far a book can travel or how many books a press can print.[54] He modestly entreats the reader 'who may possess this Manual, to read to the Poor a little of what [Jowett's] heart has indited for them', but the results he imagines still require physically present bodies.[55] This is an ethic that a later philanthropist frames as creating a fair playing field in which the media capital of the middle classes cannot by themselves vanquish the working classes without their own bodily labour. In a sermon excerpted in the

1840 *District Visitor's Manual*, a compendium of sermons, advice and stories about visiting, the Reverend C. Benson positions the bodily presence of the middle-class visitors as key to its success: 'When we [. . .] minister to our dependents with our own hands', we commit acts that 'most of all tend to effect the great purpose of all charity' because the poor who earn their keep with physical labour 'know well the value of personal services'.[56]

At first the claim that visiting can be understood as personal service stands in bold contradiction to the fact that charitable visiting's popularity also came with a surge in mass-produced print. Perhaps the best exemplar of the connection between visiting and a sharp increase in paperwork is the appearance of the General Society for Promoting District Visiting in the 1830s. This evangelical Anglican association, housed in Exeter Hall, sought to coordinate district visiting schemes across London and set itself up as provider of 'registers, journals containing instructions to visitors, and monthly reports carefully arranged for the use of visitors' for everyone involved in local schemes.[57] But even organisations in no way associated with the London society seemed infected with a rage to multiply print. The Liverpool Visiting Provident Society, whose operations focused on encouraging the poor to join provident savings schemes, deposits that district visitors collected on a regular basis, published an account of itself that the title page announced to be 'Intended as a Manual for the Formation of Similar Institutions'. The manual includes multiple samples of 'blanks' – forms printed so that they could be filled out by hand – ostensibly so that other societies could copy them.[58]

These print traces at first seem to suggest an ambition for endless scaling up of visiting efforts, an ethic which embraces the technology of mass production for the ends of charity. But the ubiquity of printed blanks, rather than indicating the imminent domination of impersonal paperwork over all charitable projects, acts as yet another restraint on the scale of the work. Printed forms, after all, pin print consumption to physical presence. As Gitelman reminds us of printed forms designed to be filled in with handwritten information, 'blanks help to demonstrate as well as to ensure the continued interdependence of the oral, the written, and the printed'.[59] As 'print that incites manuscript', forms depend on 'oral promptings' and call our attention to the media limits that restrained the scale of visiting.[60] Infinitely reproducible pieces of paper still relied on limited numbers of bodies to hold the pens and ask the questions. In the case of visiting, there was an assumed direct link between the hand that wrote the answers into the blanks, the eyes that witnessed the living conditions of those about whom they wrote and the body that shared a presence with those whose conditions were being written down.

Understanding visiting as a practice that aspired to peg the distribution of print to present bodies might also expand the ways we can understand the religious tract, the brief genre aimed at a general audience whose circulation became one of the main tasks of charitable visiting. The religious tract was not a printed blank eliciting information from those visited. However, its co-presence among the registers and forms carried by visitors must have imbued it with some of the same associations. Gitelman makes the distinction that blanks 'are printed and used, not [. . .] authored or read', and from the brief descriptions of the use to which visitors put them, we might conclude the same thing about religious tracts, in spite of their design as printed instruments intended to broadcast evangelical content.[61] A writer using the pseudonym 'Amicus' reminds his readers that they shouldn't worry too much about which tracts they are distributing since 'the tracts, however, though tending to edification, are not the only, perhaps not the principal, benefit of the system. They are a card of introduction to the Visitors, between whom and the poor a friendly intercourse is thus kept up'.[62] *The Clergyman's Manual* likewise explains its recommendation that each district visiting society settle on a list of tracts for visitors to distribute because 'a tract will, in many cases, become the medium of an introduction to the poor, and afford a subject of conversation at future visits'.[63]

In all of these accounts, the tract emerges less as a vessel carrying a message to be communicated to the poor and more as an object enabling free passage for the visitor. As Peter Stallybrass observes, what is written on a ticket or a passport is not as important as the condition it permits – the admission of a person somewhere they otherwise would not be allowed.[64] While the tract carried information in print, distributors imagined it as a relationship, not a set of declarations about religion. And we know from the wide variety of ephemera printed for charitable visitors that tickets themselves – for relief or medical care – were routinely part of the currency for visiting. The printed tract was charged with multiplying the conditions under which individual human connection, forged in the physical presence of one another, could thrive.

In the media system of visiting, print aimed primarily at the visitors, such as *Jowett's Christian Visitor*, was imagined as standardising the face-to-face procedures they were being asked to undertake, allowing a uniformity of messaging for both religious organisations and those simply looking to encourage thrifty or self-reliant behaviour among the poor. But print aimed primarily at those visited, such as the tract, was tasked with generating the human particularity of each encounter. Even the tract's lack of a periodical rhythm that might be found in newspapers or cheap magazines reinforced the rhythm of human particularity: each new tract came only when a human being arrived at the front door. And it was the human particularity that made visiting such an authoritative source of knowledge about the poor, one that offered an 'intensely personalised and situated' glimpse into their lives.[65]

This left in place an uneven dynamic between visitor and visited. Visitors were responsible for producing a 'personalised and situated' reading of the homes they visited, but that reading shouldn't be confused with the creation of an intersubjective peer-to-peer relationship. Instead, it featured the same unevenness produced by a reader's relationship with a complex text in which the responsibility for interpreting lies entirely with the reader. In this, the poor were not understood to share the same quality of agency that the visitors had as intensive readers. At the same time, if poor people were complex texts to be read, they were not without richness or importance, and it was the visitors who were expected to cultivate their own ability to focus repeatedly in a disciplined way in order to unearth what might be known. The General Society for Promoting District Visiting might print thousands of identical visitors' registers to be used across the country, but it also placed on the visitor an imperative to turn away from other schemes in order to focus on a limited neighbourhood. This clearly discouraged an assumption that all poor homes would yield precisely the same data to be written down on their preprinted lines.

The poor themselves were not imagined as readers of any sort in the encounter, either as figurative readers of their surroundings or even as literal readers of the printed material they were offered by charitable visitors. We see this in the case of William Jowett, who warns visitors that 'a Tract left [at a poor household], is not always read; and even if it be, yet, in reading with the eye, the thoughts travel too fast'.[66] But the failure to credit the poor with powers of reflective perception was also a tacit acknowledgement of all the ways that visitors did not yet know how to reach the very people they were visiting in encounters that seemed to assign visitors unlimited responsibility for doing the reaching. When modern readers encounter Charles Dickens's depiction of Mrs Pardiggle's overbearing charitable visiting in *Bleak House*, they tend to read it as a condemnation of the existing practice. But the scene Dickens writes might provide us with more truth about the affordances of the media system of charitable visiting than condemnation. Even faced with Pardiggle, an unbearably inhumane charitable visitor – 'much too businesslike and systematic' as our narrator, Esther, explicitly tells us – the brickmaker understands her proffering of the tract as an attempt to create a channel for communication, which he immediately uses quite freely and without discernible repercussions: 'Have I read the little book wot you left? No, I an't read the little book wot you left. There an't nobody here as knows how to read it; and if there wos, it wouldn't be suitable to me. It's a book fit for a babby, and I'm not a babby.'[67] Even Dickens understood that the media system of charitable visiting left the poor free not to read what was offered while offering feedback all the same.

Notes

1. Ben Kafka, *The Demons of Writing: Powers and Failures of Paper* (Brooklyn: Zone Books, 2012), 21.
2. Joanne Yates, *Control Through Communication: The Rise of System in American Management* (Baltimore: Johns Hopkins University Press, 1989).
3. Lisa Gitelman, *Paper Knowledge: Towards a Media History of Documents* (Durham: Duke University Press, 2014), 31.
4. Kafka, *Demons of Writing*, 14. One striking exception to this consensus is Matthew P. Brown's recent 'Blanks: Data, Method, and the British American Print Shop', *American Literary History* 29, no. 2 (2017): 228–47. Brown reads the materiality of eighteenth-century American contracts as bearing marks of human subjectivities that negotiate between freedom and voluntary constraint.
5. Yates, *Control Through Communication*, 17–18.
6. Thomas Chalmers, *The Christian and Civic Economy of Large Towns*, 3 vols. (1821–6, reprint, Cambridge: Cambridge University Press, 2013), 1:26.
7. Rev. James Aspinall, *A Sermon Preached at St. Michael's Church, Liverpool, on Sunday, April 4, 1830, upon the Subject of the*

Provident District Society, Now Forming in That Town (Liverpool: Cruikshank, 1830), 7–8.

8. See George K. Behlmer, *Friends of the Family: The English Home and Its Guardians, 1850–1940* (Stanford: Stanford University Press, 1998), 32; Donald M. Lewis, *Lighten Their Darkness: The Evangelical Mission to Working-Class London, 1828–1860* (New York: Greenwood Press, 1986), 36; F. K. Prochaska, *Women and Philanthropy in Nineteenth-Century England* (Oxford: Oxford University Press, 1980), 99.
9. See Stewart J. Brown, *Thomas Chalmers and the Godly Commonwealth in Scotland* (Oxford: Oxford University Press, 1982), 376; and Stewart J. Brown, 'Thomas Chalmers, 1780–1847', in the *Oxford Dictionary of National Biography*, online edition (Oxford: Oxford University Press, 2004).
10. A. C. Cheyne, 'Introduction: Thomas Chalmers Then and Now', in *The Practical and The Pious: Essays on Thomas Chalmers*, ed. A. C. Cheyne (Edinburgh: Saint Andrew Press, 1985), 9–30. See especially pages 14–15.
11. Chalmers, *Christian and Civic Economy*, 2:74.
12. Ibid., 1:100.
13. It might not make sense, at first, to refer to Jay David Bolter and Richard Grusin's idea of remediation, the refashioning of old media into new, when talking about the reimagination of the relations of a preindustrial village in the form of parish visiting. After all, the village was an environment and not a medium. But charitable visiting's double impulses – imagining that a physical visit to the homes of the poor would provide real knowledge, on the one hand, and its hypermediacy in the proliferation of print forms that came to be associated with it, on the other – give it much in common with the media Bolter and Grusin analyse in *Remediation: Understanding New Media* (Cambridge: MIT Press, 1998).
14. Chalmers, *Christian and Civic Economy*, 1:26.
15. Daniel Weibren, 'Supporting Self-Help: Charity, Mutuality, and Reciprocity in Nineteenth-Century Britain', in *Charity and Mutual Aid in Europe and North America Since 1800*, ed. Bernard Harris and Paul Briden (New York: Routledge, 2007). See especially page 69.
16. Chalmers, *Christian and Civic Economy*, 2:30.
17. Ibid.
18. Ibid., 2:38.
19. This might, in fact, be seen as Chalmers's distinctive contribution to the idea of charitable visiting. While church auxiliaries existed in

district-like structures for providing linens for women about to give birth or to look after those who did not qualify for local poor relief, Chalmers envisioned a district-visiting system that might distribute all types of aid and communicate many types of knowledge along its channels. For background on the types of charities preceding Chalmers's, see Prochaska's *Women and Philanthropy*.

20. See Clifford Siskin and William Warner, 'This Is Enlightenment: An Invitation in the Form of an Argument', in *This is Enlightenment*, ed. Clifford Siskin and William Warner, 1–36 (Chicago: University of Chicago Press, 2010), 13.
21. Mary Poovey, *Making a Social Body: British Cultural Formations, 1830–1864* (Chicago: University of Chicago Press, 1995), 99–105.
22. Lauren M. E. Goodlad, *Victorian Literature and the Victorian State: Character and Governance in a Liberal Society* (Baltimore: Johns Hopkins University Press, 2004), 41, 43.
23. Chalmers, *Christian and Civic Economy*, 2:36.
24. Ibid., 1:87.
25. Ibid., 1:87, 1:96.
26. Ibid., 1:57.
27. Ibid., 1:157.
28. Ibid., 1:56.
29. Ibid., 1:73.
30. Ibid., 1:171–2.
31. Max Weber, *Max Weber: Essays in Sociology*, ed. and trans., Hans Heinrich Gert and C. Wright Mills (New York: Oxford University Press, 1958), 228–9.
32. Matthew P. Brown, *The Pilgrim and the Bee: Reading Rituals and Book Culture in Early New England* (Philadelphia: University of Pennsylvania Press, 2007), 220n3. David Hall, 'Introduction: The Uses of Literacy in New England, 1600–1850', in *Printing and Society in Early America*, ed. William L. Joyce, David D. Hall, Richard D. Brown and John B. Hench (Worcester: American Antiquarian Society, 1983), 1–45.
33. For more on intensive evangelical reading, see Sara L. Maurer, 'Reading Others Who Read: The Early-Century Print Environment of the Religious Tract Society', *Victorian Studies* 61, no. 2 (2019): 222–31.
34. William Wilberforce, *A Practical View of the Prevailing Religious System of Professed Christians* (London: T. Caddell, Jr., and W. Davies, 1797).
35. Ibid., 7, 16.
36. Chalmers, *Christian and Civic Economy*, 1:139.

37. Wilberforce, *A Practical View*, 66.
38. Chalmers, *Christian and Civic Economy*, 1:86.
39. Ibid., 1:156.
40. Weber, *Max Weber*, 215.
41. Chalmers, *Christian and Civic Economy*, 1:26.
42. Martin Hewitt, *Making Social Knowledge in the Victorian City: The Visiting Mode in Manchester, 1832–1914* (New York: Routledge, 2020), 17.
43. Ibid., 19.
44. Ibid., 43. This would echo trends noticed by Stephen Collini in *Public Moralists: Political Thought and Intellectual Life in Britain, 1850–1930* (Oxford: Clarendon Press, 1991), and Boyd Hilton in *The Age of Atonement: The Influence of Evangelicalism on Social and Economic Thought, 1795–1865* (Oxford: Clarendon Press, 1988), both of whom argue that evangelical logic ultimately seeped into the structure of Victorian secular thought.
45. Hewitt, *Making Social Knowledge*, 93.
46. Robert Simpson, *The Clergyman's Manual* (London: R. Groombridge, Panyer Alley, 1842), 194.
47. David Hall notes that '19th c[entury] Evangelicalism and tract societies keep parts of [intensively read seventeenth-century religious authors] alive' ('Introduction', 45).
48. Simpson, *The Clergyman's Manual*, 188. Jowett's work was also endorsed in *The District Visitors' Record* 1 (April 1836): 40–3.
49. William Jowett, *The Christian Visitor* (London: R. B. Seeley, 1836), v.
50. Ibid., vii.
51. Ibid., x.
52. Ibid., xi.
53. Ibid.
54. In this way, charitable visiting might be understood as a system that restrained the otherwise vast ambition of the evangelical enterprise, detailed compellingly in Joseph Stubenrauch's *The Evangelical Age of Ingenuity in Industrial Britain* (Oxford: Oxford University Press, 2016).
55. Jowett, *Christian Visitor*, xii.
56. Christopher Benson, *The District Visitor's Manual: A Compendium of Practical Information and of FACTS for the Use of District Visitors*, 2nd ed. (London: John W. Parker, 1840), 19–20.
57. Simpson, *Clergyman's Manual*, 189.
58. James Shaw, *An Account of the Liverpool District Provident Society* (Liverpool: Mitchell, 1838).

59. Gitelman, *Paper Knowledge*, 26.
60. Ibid.
61. Ibid., 25.
62. Benson, *District Visitor's Manual*, 70.
63. Simpson, *Clergyman's Manual*, 190. See also Peter Stallybrass, who observes, 'Many printed sheets fulfill their function without being read. [. . .] Unable to understand a word of what a tax form says, I fill it in and affix my signature under the guidance of a tax lawyer.' Peter Stallybrass, '"Little Jobs": Broadsides and the Printing Revolution', in *Agent of Change: Print Culture Studies after Elizabeth L Eisenstein*, ed. Sabrina Alcorn Baron, Eric N. Lindquist and Eleanor F. Shevlin (Boston: University of Massachusetts Press, 2007), 340.
64. Stallybrass, 'Little Jobs', 340. Leah Price observes this ticket-like function in her account of religious tracts but emphasises the tract as scrap paper, a category that had monetary value, especially in the first three decades of the nineteenth century. Leah Price, *How To Do Things with Books in Victorian Britain* (Princeton: Princeton University Press, 2012), 156–60.
65. Hewitt, *Making Social Knowledge*, 23.
66. Jowett, *Christian Visitor*, xi.
67. Charles Dickens, *Bleak House* (New York: Vintage, 2012), 107.

12

Invincible Brothers: The Pen and the Press in *The Compositors' Chronicle*, 1840–43

Françoise Baillet

After the first Reform Act and well into the 1840s, working-class education was one of the main issues of concern among radical theorists and utilitarian philanthropists. While the former group saw in it a formidable political tool for excluded workers to shape a sense of class consciousness and power, the latter thought that a knowledgeable labouring class would be more inclined to support the existing social order.[1] As popular education developed through schools, churches, temperance societies, libraries and poetry readings, radical publications such as Cobbett's *Political Register* and the SDUK-supported penny periodicals filled their columns with informative and enlightening stories.[2] As Greg Vargo explains in *An Underground History of Early Victorian Fiction*, both radical writers and middle-class authors encouraged and employed popular literary forms, with each reading and writing community benefiting from the other. The reduction of the stamp duty in 1836 also resulted in a considerable growth of specialised periodicals and thus a segmentation of reading audiences. This included trade journals that encouraged creative contributions from their readers.

Printed and published by R. Thompson, the office keeper for the London Union of Compositors (LUC), *The Compositors' Chronicle* first appeared in September 1840 as a monthly priced at twopence.[3] Between that date and August 1843, when the magazine ceased publication, thirty-six regular issues and a single supplementary number were put in circulation and were later reprinted as a single volume. A typical issue of the *Chronicle* carried a leading article consisting either of national union news or reports from regional typographical societies affiliated with the LUC. The aim of this column, which formed the bulk of the magazine, was to inform readers on questions concerning the general interests of the trade and to establish the journal as the organ of a healthy, efficient and representative debate between compositors and pressmen across the country.[4] Open to 'all correspondents whose aim is to promote the interests of the profession', the *Chronicle* harnessed the creative aspirations of its readers, providing a venue for the 'literary effusions of the members of the trade upon all subjects'.[5] While Chartist and other radical publications addressed a working-class audience, the *Chronicle*'s intended readership was more skilled and narrowly defined.[6] Nineteenth-century compositors, Patrick Duffy writes, were the aristocrats of the printing world; better paid than any other group of workers, they enjoyed a privileged position within the printing business, particularly in London, where their wages could be twice or even three times as high as those of their fellow workers in the rest of the United Kingdom.[7] In *Movable Types*, David Finkelstein accounts for such a status by explaining that printers and compositors had been 'at the forefront of early nineteenth-century social and trade union movements, in terms of union organisation, social support, establishing libraries and educational centres, and in organising and actively engaging in literary and cultural events'.[8] The pages of the *Chronicle* certainly reflect this sense of entitlement. Averse to Chartism, which it once referred to as 'the mummery of 1838', the journal heavily relied on the spirit of evangelicalism and utilitarianism that permeated the early Victorian social landscape.[9] Writing for what many then called the enlightened working class, the journal strove to elaborate its own ideological pathway and construct its own creative community.

Concentrating on a selection of thirty items of prose and verse, original or reprinted from various sources, this essay will complement and extend the work of previous analyses, interrogating the connection between 'those invincible brothers, the Pen and the Press', as it was played out in the pages of *The Compositors' Chronicle* between 1840 and 1843.[10] More specifically, it will investigate the 'complete articulation between aesthetics, utilitarianism and economics' that Mike Sanders questions in his volume on *The Poetry of Chartism*.[11] As considered through the lens of the *Chronicle*, the creative activity of printers in the early 1840s was overwhelming. Ranging from work-related anecdotes to historical essays, short stories, inspirational fables and poetry, the magazine's columns are remarkable for their variety, scope and political agency. After characterising the general nature of the *Chronicle*'s contents and concerns, this essay will examine a selection of the journal's prose narratives, focusing on the contradiction between the journal's progressive political stance in defence of printing trade interests and its participation in the discourse on useful knowledge, which was steeped in traditional and religious values. A second section of the essay will investigate the *Chronicle*'s poetry as an ideological genre situated within the rich and complex textual environment of the printed page and within an array of other discourses outside the trade press.

Leafing through the pages of *The Compositors' Chronicle*, one is struck by the sense of connection that existed between editors and readers. Columns devoted to entertainment, science, poetry, satire or readers' correspondence resonated with the leading articles, echoing, interrogating or reappropriating the same subject matter in creative and humorous ways. As scholars of the Victorian press have shown, the printed page is a composite text offering what Lorraine Janzen Kooistra calls 'a dynamic set of possibilities, within set constraints, for readers to activate and engage'.[12] The sophisticated layout of the *Chronicle* certainly favoured this engagement, suggesting a set of relationships between the different sections available and transforming the surface of the page into 'a virtual program, interactive, dialogic, dynamic in the fullest sense'.[13] A regular section entitled 'To Correspondents, &c.' answered each query personally, using individual readers' initials. In the October 1840 issue, for instance, a correspondent from Hull is given confirmation that his suggestion of notifying all regional secretaries of the *Chronicle*'s recent launch will be attended to, while the anonymous author of 'A Leaf from a Scrap-Book' is informed that Hogarth is 'not buried in Westminster-Abbey, but at Chiswick'.[14] Information contained in this section ranges from practical messages to printers (lost and found cards, notes to local or regional offices, reprints of the *Chronicle*), to historical, scientific, philosophical or literary knowledge.

Humour and satire were never absent from this column, which in July 1842 informed 'T. S. H.' that the journal had 'laid it down as a rule not to insert advertisements in [its] columns, not only because it would occasionally engross [its] space, but [because it] would give rise probably to an opinion that the love of money had more influence with [the editors] than the advocacy of those rights [they] profess to uphold'.[15] The *Chronicle* also published a 'Facts and Scraps' column largely devoted to matter-of-fact notices and specific messages to union members across the country. This included where to find local secretaries and new appointments, as well as enrolment figures and reports of celebrations. The column was not only designed to inform readers but also to provide them with instruction and amusement. Besides entries on various subjects of interest to printers, it contained puns and jokes, often at the expense of eccentric, idle or improper characters. The September 1841 issue, for example, mocks the Welsh maid who, because a candle 'was fell in the water' has 'put hur in the oven to dry' [*sic*].[16] The same column asks, 'Why is a dandy pickpocket like a heavy sea?' and answers, 'Because he is a dangerous swell'.[17] Another tells the story of the lady who fed her sixteen lap dogs a strict diet of veal shoulder and 'Savoy biscuits steeped in Burgundy'.[18] Largely based on the widely circulated social stereotypes which in these years also filled the pages of *Punch* and its competitors – the rustic character, the foolish aristocrat or the conceited idler – these quips fulfilled several functions. Beyond the cheerful tone they conveyed in a journal devoted to the protection of trade interests that were perceived as being endangered, they constructed the *Chronicle*'s readers as the spectators, and not the objects, of derision and mockery. By drawing such a line, they assumed a reassuring stance that relied on a shared set of assumptions between writers, editors and readers about the indispensable difference between decency and impropriety, respectability and immorality, self and other. As David Finkelstein has convincingly argued, print-trade periodicals of the 1840s and 1850s supported and sustained the development of a shared professional identity, helping compositors and pressmen project a creative identity meant to distinguish them from other, less literate, workers.[19]

'On the pleasures of intellectual exertion'

Aimed both at printers and at those among the ruling classes who might take an interest in their communications, trade journals also fulfilled a political function. In a context in which the parliamentary reform of the 1830s had left most British workers disenfranchised, the London Union of Compositors felt that the 'instability and ignorance of the masses', as described in its annual reports of 1834 and 1836, could result in widespread popular protest and disorder.[20] Many typographical societies believed that improving and enlightening the working classes could be one way to avert such a danger. In line with the spirit of evangelicalism and utilitarianism that was a ubiquitous part of the Victorian social landscape, *The Compositors' Chronicle* carried a series of moral and philosophical essays designed to foster a culture of respectability and to reimagine printers as virtuous, literate and sociable men.[21] These stories were authored by in-house compositors, submitted by correspondents from across the United Kingdom or reprinted from other magazines in the cut-and-paste journalistic tradition of the day. They broached key utilitarian concepts, echoing Charles Knight's *Penny Magazine*, *Chambers's Edinburgh Journal*, or other magazines already in circulation such as *The Literary Gazette*, *The National Omnibus* or *The Athenaeum*.

Specifically addressing a carefully controlled, conservative trade, the *Chronicle* relied heavily on an ideology of self-help, regularly putting forward its strong connections with such figures as George Birkbeck (1776–1841) and Henry Brougham (1778–1868).[22] A long-time proponent of education for the working classes, Birkbeck delivered free lectures on science in Glasgow before founding the London Mechanics' Institution, whose purpose was to impart scientific knowledge to working men through classes, lectures and libraries. In its substantial obituary for Birkbeck published in March 1842, the *Chronicle* acknowledges its indebtedness to him 'for much useful instruction'.[23] A close supporter of Birkbeck's initiative was Lord Brougham, a lawyer and journalist who had helped found the *Edinburgh Review* in 1802. Sharing with Jeremy Bentham a strong interest in education, Brougham had also spearheaded the creation of the Society for the Diffusion of Useful Knowledge, whose principal object was 'to elevate the minds of people, and draw them from sordid and sensual pursuits and pleasures, to the cultivation of the pure gratifications of the mind'.[24] Throughout the early months of 1841, the *Chronicle* published a series of articles expressing concern about the new Copyright Bill, which Brougham and the radicals saw as a hindrance to the expansion of the British press, which was already hampered by the so-called 'taxes on knowledge'.

In the 'Advertisement' for its 1843 bound volume, the *Chronicle* warmly acknowledges a writer named 'Cephas' who, 'by the contribution of [his] papers, has aided [the journal's] object'.[25] Although no clarification is provided as to this object, the contents of the numerous pieces written by Cephas between 1841 and 1843 shed interesting light on the *Chronicle*'s ideological framework. In the March issue of the journal, Cephas approaches the topic of education through a fable based on the lives of three figures: Daniel Defoe, James Ferguson and William Tell. Highlighting the necessity of providing every youth with 'a suitable guide to direct him', the story promotes the virtues of proper, well-structured instruction, insisting on the key role played by 'guardians and instructors of the rising race' who should 'endeavour to ascertain the dispositions of those with whom they are entrusted, and [. . .] direct them in a course which shall not only be creditable to themselves, but promote the well-being of the society they shall have to associate with in riper years'.[26]

This advocacy of a durable and stratified social order is reiterated in the second instalment of the series in which the specific role of women in young men's education is given ample scope. The 'grand turning point on which the welfare of a nation turns', Cephas insists, 'is the training up of its youth in *right* principles and pursuits'.[27] To that end, women should be kept away from universities since a 'stern atmosphere might not merely stunt these fair perennials, but blight their opening blossoms'.[28] Instead, women should be exclusively tutored within an 'endearing society, which the parental retreat supplies – "sweet home", where "hearts in unison meet"'.[29]

Considered from the perspective of a printers' union, this insistence on a regulated society in which men and women would play distinct roles within separate spheres can easily be accounted for. At a time when the introduction of new typesetting machinery gave employers the opportunity to hire underpaid labour, the gradual admittance of women into the composing room was perceived by many journeyman printers as a major threat to their status. The incursion of women into the printing trade was perhaps best exemplified by *The Family Herald* (1842–1940), a journal owned and edited by James Elishama Smith (known as 'Shepherd Smith'), which was the first publication created entirely by female labour on the pianotype printing machine (featured in the masthead of the journal). This was also the case for the weekly *London Phalanx*, a small-circulation magazine that promoted the theories of Charles Fourier, a utopian socialist advocating a style of community in which women could be employed as well as men. Between September 1841 and May 1843, the *Chronicle* published no less than a dozen letters and essays on the subject of pianotype compositing, expressing a widely shared concern in the profession about this 'infernal machine'.[30]

Throughout the three years of the *Chronicle*'s existence, Cephas published fifteen prose narratives and at least one poem, probably more. In line with the pious spirit which his biblical pseudonym announced, Cephas praised the bliss of domestic life, defined friendship as 'the very offspring of virtue', celebrated artisans and mechanics as 'the foundation which supports the whole body politic', and warned his readers against the lure of wealth which, 'in too many instances may be the cause of irresistible temptation'.[31] Printers, he implied, should not aspire to rise above their positions but instead give themselves the means to be recognised as respectable and reliable men. From this perspective, 'fickleness of mind' should be avoided as 'an insuperable bar to improvement, enjoyment, and usefulness'.[32] In subsequent instalments, Cephas criticised the deliberate excitation of feeling, insisting on the dangers of dilettantism and advocating instead for a regular diet of sound and useful reading matter. 'Knowledge', 'Genius' and 'Authors and Readers', all published in the early months of 1843, warn the 'wise man' against the pitfalls of 'slothfulness of mind' and entice him to turn away from 'the large masses [. . .] sunk in all the deformities and degradations consequent upon ignorance!'[33]

Another leading voice of the *Chronicle*, 'Philo', specialised in reflective and sometimes metaphysical fiction. Based in Birmingham, this correspondent contributed a six-part series celebrating 'The Beauties of Nature', published between December 1840 and July 1841.[34] 'The Beauties of Nature' is a parable enjoining the reader to take inspiration from 'nature's glad creation' and discard 'strife, envy, jealousy, revenge, and a thousand evil passions' to embrace a peaceful and harmonious existence.[35] While Philo's professed object 'is merely to point out a few of the prominent beauties which nature everywhere and in all seasons displays to the admiring lover of the beautiful', his text strongly echoes Benthamite utilitarianism. He advocates for a society in which human labour would be 'regulated so as to be in accordance with the great principle of man's happiness', allowing the working man to have 'his physical comforts attended to, his faculties developed, by good and kind training, to their fullest extent'.[36]

Within the pages of the *Chronicle*, the inspirational essays of Philo and Cephas were printed alongside extracts from biographies and historical fables meant to elevate readers, to reinforce their faith in the social order and to provide direct evidence that they could safely be entrusted with the vote. The figure of Benjamin Franklin, whose career had begun in the printing trade, attracted much attention from the journal's editors. In December 1841, the *Chronicle* devoted six columns to a lecture on 'The Life and Character of Dr [Benjamin] Franklin' delivered in Liverpool by the influential Reverend M'Neile as part of an event organised by the Printers' Pension Society.[37] The long speech reconstructed the American scientist's early career as a printer, insisting on his moral qualities. Franklin is described as having 'habits of temperance' that 'greatly improved' his intellectual capacities.[38] His activity as a printer is used to demonstrate his 'unwearied industry', 'morality of living' and 'magnificent benevolence'.[39] Less than a year later, the *Chronicle* also reprinted extracts from Lord Brougham's *Historical Sketches of Statesmen Who Flourished in the Time of George III*, in which Franklin was described as 'the most remarkable man in our time'.[40] The same celebratory rhetoric suffused the two-column biography devoted to William Blake, which described the artist as being 'always at work' or 'maintaining himself respectably'.[41] His wife Catherine Blake was reimagined as a prefiguration of Patmore's angel in the house, '[setting] his house in good order, [preparing] his frugal meal, [learning] to think as he thought [. . .] and [becoming], as it were, bone of his bone, and flesh of his flesh'.[42] These representations of printers and artists as exemplars of domestic bliss, self-respect, discipline and success were meant to provide the *Chronicle*'s readers – and possibly their families – with models of Victorian respectability within their own trade. In those years when printers – apprentices as well as journeymen – were still commonly described as improvident and disreputable, this celebratory rhetoric allowed them to project a respectable public image. To borrow Patricia Hollis's words, it is quite clear that, for the journal, 'politics, property and education dovetailed in various ways to structure the political community'.[43]

'The arts of printing and making poetry are nearly akin'

Another key genre within the printing trade journals was poetry, as shown in the pages of *The Compositors' Chronicle*. In September 1841, it carried the following notice:

> Poetry – From the numerous poetical favours we receive we begin to think that the arts of printing and making poetry are nearly akin. Elegies, sonnets, songs and odes (among the last-named, we have 'An Ode on a Shooting-Stick,' consisting of about 200 lines) innumerable have been forwarded to us, which we cannot insert, but recommend the writers to 'try again'.[44]

And 'try again' they did. The volume of correspondence addressed to Bouverie Street was so robust that from August 1842, a separate 'Poet's Gallery' was introduced in the magazine, presenting a monthly selection of up to six poems. This rhythm, however, decreased in the following months, progressively returning to an average of three to four poems per issue. A major proportion of the *Chronicle*'s poems, around forty compositions, may be classified as sentimental – evoking death, grief, motherhood, beloved pets, family bonds, married love and the sublimity of nature. The rest of the poetry column is devoted to what Kirstie Blair calls 'associational verse', that is, 'poems written for a specific audience at a meeting, event, dinner, or other special occasion'.[45] This latter section featured ballads such as the unpublished 'Ode on a Shooting-Stick' mentioned above, in which compositors and pressmen depicted the tools, sounds and experience of the printing office.[46] Other compositions dealt with the harsh working conditions of typographers, questions of working-class poverty or wider political questions of interest to printers. I will now successively examine a selection of poems in each of these categories.

As recent scholarship of the periodical press has shown, poetry was ubiquitous in Victorian newspapers and magazines. Andrew Hobbs, for example, estimates that five million poems were published in English provincial newspapers during the nineteenth century.[47] This underscores the significance of the local press as a publishing platform for literary content. Many 'labour laureates' were also active within the typographical trade press during the Victorian era. In *Movable Types*, David Finkelstein lists over 200 poems published in six key British and overseas printers' journals between 1840 and 1870, evoking in particular the names of William Dorrington, Alfred Knott, John Lash Latey and David Walkinshaw, all of whom were active contributors to *The Compositors' Chronicle*.[48] With an average of two poems per week, the *Chronicle*'s output certainly corresponds to this estimation: over the thirty-six months of its existence, the journal published no less than sixty-four compositions. Following the nineteenth-century journalistic tradition of anonymity, most of these poems were unsigned or were signed with their author's initials and location. Regular prose writers like 'Cephas' and 'Philo' also contributed original verse while other poems were reprinted or adapted from canonical works.

Considered as a whole, the sentimental poems published by the *Chronicle* bespeak a middle-class attachment to the family as the primary form of social organisation. In line with the values associated with evangelical Christianity, they depict the relations between men and women as characterised by moral earnestness and express sensitivity to the plight of the weak and the helpless. The subject of seventeen compositions, love is defined not as 'a cringing, fawning spirit' but as a 'Virtue's offspring', a long-lasting 'steady affection' between husband and wife.[49] As represented by the *Chronicle*, men and women occupy separate spheres: while self-sacrificial and devoted mothers watch over their offspring, invested with the divine power 'to form the young immortal's mind', their husbands, brothers and sons are active in the outer world.[50] At a time when infant and child mortality rates were very high, lyrics evoking loss and grief also pervade the poetry columns, often borrowed from other periodicals, as was the case with Letitia Elizabeth Landon's 'The Little Shroud', reprinted from *The Literary Gazette*, or 'The Angel and the Child', adapted from a poem by Jean Reboul, a working-class poet from southern France.[51] Attachment to the home and, by extension, to the motherland also featured in the *Chronicle*. In August 1842, the newly created 'Poets' Gallery' included a reprint of Aubrey George Spencer's 'The Exile's Adieu', which had originally appeared in *The Keepsake* in 1834. Although this poem deals with emigration – Spencer worked as a missionary in Newfoundland and Bermuda before being appointed Bishop of Jamaica in 1843 – the themes it touches upon certainly appealed to many printers then obliged to resort to the 'tramping' system, by which journeymen in search of employment could find relief and shelter nationwide. During the year 1842, as a major recession hit the printing sector, the *Chronicle* ran a series of articles on the subject.[52] As scholarship of periodical poetry has shown, newspaper poems 'never exist as single units, but in relation to other publications within the same issue or paper, and as part of a constantly evolving body of literature associated with a particular paper'.[53] Dramatic representations of uprootedness and nostalgia may therefore have resonated strongly with the experience of many readers at the time.

Despite the distress experienced by many in the profession, or possibly because of it, a significant proportion of the poetry carried in the journal struck a lighter note, celebrating nature and its beauties. Seven poems, several of them original compositions, suggest a form of escape from the grind of the printing office. Signed 'T. J. O.', 'Song of the Earth to the Moon' is a ten-stanza lyrical evocation of the natural world. Composed of five lines rhyming a/b/a/b/a, with a repetition of the first and last line of each stanza, the poem was intended to be set to music and sung during one of the numerous social occasions for printers.[54] The night scene is described in dreamy and mysterious terms, conveying a sublime quality reminiscent of early nineteenth-century Romantic poetry. While the 'magic eye' of the moon peeps through the 'clouds of snow', the earth emerges from its slumber, brought back to life by the 'pearly rays' of the night star.[55] The song also possesses an erotic quality, repeatedly evoking the 'blissful' encounter in terms of 'sprinkling silver' and 'amorous lays', the earth's 'flower-cups open[ing] their lips, as though in prayer'.[56] Like many other poems in the *Chronicle*, 'The Song of the Earth and Moon' relies on the conventions of traditional poetry, demonstrating a familiarity with the canon. By doing so, it associates the journal's literary community with middle- and upper-class knowledge and practices, implicitly defining this community as literate and thus worthy of full British citizenship. 'The association of poetry, more than any other genre, with cultural capital and intellectual ability', Kirstie Blair explains, 'meant that the ability to write a poem that fell within the "horizon of expectation" for Victorian popular poetry, and the ability to vote, were intimately linked'.[57] This horizon of expectation also included the humorous pieces that peppered the pages of the magazine throughout its three-year existence, such as the moving 'Ode to a Dead Poodle' by 'Belinda', published in December 1841, or 'Jolly Nose', printed in May 1843, a playful obituary in memory of Joseph Knight, 'a once cheerful and facetious companion' well-known to all the readers.[58]

'An interplay between the aesthetic and the democratic'

In *The Compositors' Chronicle*, a significant proportion of the poetry tackled more pressing subjects, thus allowing authors, readers and editors to initiate and sustain what Mike Sanders calls an 'interplay between the aesthetic and the democratic'.[59] The *Chronicle*'s 'associational verse' fulfils a major function within the journal. Considered as a whole, the poems belonging to this category express shared views, experiences and aspirations on professional, social and political subjects. Original or republished from eclectic sources, they articulate the connectedness of printers across the country, echoing the union reports and associative columns printed within the same or adjacent pages of the magazine. Natalie Houston has underlined the visual impact of periodical poetry, showing how 'the indenting of poetic lines makes even shorter poems like sonnets visually stand out among the paper's six tightly packed columns'.[60] The white space around the poems, Houston explains, 'possibly caused some readers to look more closely at the text'.[61] Thoughtfully elaborated, the *Chronicle*'s layout certainly suggested a dynamic reading process, providing the reader with various and complementary entries into high-profile topics. Among these were leading columns on the nature and cost of the many trade disputes that erupted in British printing offices.[62] Numerous reports were also devoted to the excessive hiring of apprentices, opposition to the new Young & Delcambre typesetting machine, or the Copyright Bill of 1842.[63] Throughout the journal's existence, two dozen poems broached these questions, shedding emotional and sometimes humorous light on the printers' living and working conditions and reasserting the role of the press within a free society. 'Lines to a Worn-Out Font of Type', reprinted by Charles Henry Timperley in the 1845 edition of *Songs of the Press and Other Poems*, appeared for the first time in the May 1842 issue of the *Chronicle*. Subtitled 'In a note to a friend' and addressed to 'George', the anonymous poem unfolds as an epic recounting the central role of printing in the expansion of the written word. Composed of eight lines arranged in an a/b/c/b a/b/c/b rhyme scheme, the nine stanzas evoke the range of journalistic and literary information available to nineteenth-century readers. From 'tales of horror' in the penny dreadfuls to the broadsheets' reports on 'earthquakes and suicides' or the argumentative columns of the parliamentary press, all writing, the poem says, originates in printing rooms.

Other items celebrating the printing office are 'The Typographical Song' and John Critchley Prince's 'The Pen and the Press'. 'The Typographical Song' is a ballad written in 1823 by John Scott Walker (1791–1850), editor of the *Liverpool Mercury*. Intended for special occasions, when printers meet 'to feast and to drink', the song weaves technical printing terms into a romantic story. The poem uses italics to highlight words and phrases extracted from their ordinary printing context, their meaning twisted into an amusing tale in which 'a fair slender female of *paragon* face' and '*nonpareil* figure' makes an 'impression' on a '*tramp*' who seduces and '*hotpresses*' her.[64] Cupid's '*shooting-stick*' eventually leads the couple to the '*chapel*' where a '*father* [binds] them in one'.[65] As Mike Sanders remarks about Chartist poetry, such texts constitute 'both a distinctive form of agency and a unique form of historical knowledge'.[66] Restricting their intended audience to those familiar with printing tools and publishing idioms, they suggest a cognisant complicity across the real and imaginary community of compositors and pressmen in the United Kingdom. John Critchley Prince's 'The Pen and the Press' considers such questions from a wider perspective.[67] Presented with an anonymous piece entitled 'The Printer's Song', the poem comes from *Hours with the Muses* (1841), which Prince had published while working as a yard warehouseman in Manchester. A strong critic of socialism, Prince also disapproved of Chartism, writing mostly about nature and religious faith.[68] 'The Pen and the Press' mythicises the written word as a 'glorious thing' whose 'magical use' was brought to the world by the Promethean figure of a 'Young Genius'.[69] It also reminds the reader of the role of newspapers as defenders of citizens' rights. 'Those invincible brothers, the Pen and the Press' are here constructed as protectors of an enlightened and powerful people now able to 'snap the rod of the tyrant like a reed'.[70]

Such lyrics fulfilled other, wider functions than the sole development of a cooperative spirit. As David Finkelstein observes, 'compositor-poets were ubiquitous voices in fundraising events for indigent printer families and trade-based social causes.'[71] In periods of widespread unemployment, efforts were made by typographical unions to provide relief to vulnerable members like tramping journeymen or aged printers. While a Printers' Pension Society had already been established in London in 1827, the 1841–2 recession was such that the London Union of Compositors decided on the setting up of a 'Printers' Asylum' that recurrently features in the pages of the *Chronicle*.[72] The sixty-two-line text written by 'W. R.' for the benefit of the Printers' Pension Society addresses the 'assembled patrons of the glorious Press', imploring them to hear 'the worn and aged Printer's humble claim' and support him while 'his hand falters and his eye grows dim'.[73] The rest of the ballad insists on the benefits brought by the press to the world, considering each sector of activity and referring to the great names of English literature such as Milton and Shakespeare. The impact of this 'Address' may have been strengthened by its publication in the same December 1840 issue of another ballad, 'Victoria, a Political Poem'.[74] Strategically placed on the first page of the journal, this poem is a short extract from the eponymous text Richard Wemyss had then just published with Effingham Wilson. Wilson was a familiar figure in radical circles: he had assisted William Hone in preparing his defence in a libel trial of 1817 and had published Jeremy Bentham's *Church-of-Englandism* (1818) and the 'unpublishable' *Elements of the Art of Packing* (1821). The *Chronicle* presents Wemyss as 'an aspiring poet' who will 'by patient perseverance, attain no mean station in the walks of poesy', echoing the author's own preface to the volume, where he evokes his 'unskilful tongue or pen'.[75] The passage selected comes from the very beginning of the political epic and, in line with the topic of the December 1840 issue, specifically addresses the persistence of inequalities in a post-Reform British society: 'Then lordling fell – their ill-used power destroy'd – / Their places lost, which were too long enjoy'd. / But still their power – the hateful power of gold – / Is felt 'mongst voters, as it was of old'.[76]

Within a trade publication whose main object was to protect print workers from the 'misconduct and tyranny' of some employers, the choice of advertising Wemyss's work is significant. *Victoria, a Political Poem*, the full-length version of the ballad excerpted in *The Compositors' Chronicle*, was written in the late 1830s.[77] Celebrating the ascent of a 'virtuous Queen' to the British throne, the forty-page epic denounces 'a disease in the government of the country', explaining that 'the only way to effect a cure is to go to the root of the evil'.[78] Successively addressing several high-profile parliamentary figures of the day – not only John Russell,

Lord Melbourne (William Lamb) and Sir Robert Peel but also Daniel O'Connell, leader of Ireland's Repeal Association – the poem evokes the 'evils' hampering Britain: the disenfranchisement of voters, the persistence of the Corn Laws and the questionable logic of Lord Palmerston's foreign policy on the Eastern Question.[79] One of the solutions, Wemyss suggests, would be for Victoria's ministers to 'Bend [their] ear unto a nation's prayer; / And let th' enlightened poor the franchise share'.[80] The Chartists, the poem further notes, should also mend their ways: 'The narrow path of virtue they must tread / And lead the people, not be knaves be led'.[81] By recommending a poem denouncing both 'furious Chartists and bigot Tories', the *Chronicle* sheds light on its own ideological stance, later confirmed by a reference to Chartism as 'the mummery of 1838'.[82] But the topic of the New Poor Law (1834) reveals something of a disagreement between Wemyss and *The Compositors' Chronicle*. While Wemyss attacks 'a poor-law by high Heaven abhorr'd', Thompson's magazine largely supports the text, publishing in July 1841 a series of extracts from *Letters to the Working People on the New Poor Laws*, in which John Lash Latey listed the 'evils' of the old system while clarifying the purpose of the new.[83]

Conclusion

The January 1843 issue of *The Compositors' Chronicle* included a song entitled 'Wanted, an Editor',[84] a witty parody of John Orlando Parry's 'Wanted, a Governess' (c. 1840). The four-stanza ballad capitalises on the popularity of its source text to advertise an editorial position at the *Chronicle*'s office.[85] The song portrays the ideal trade press editor as 'Learned, yet practical', with a capacity to 'unite / Natural talent with science'.[86] 'Neither a Radical, Tory, nor Whig', the perfect candidate must above all 'please every party' without ever offending a subscriber.[87] The song also lists a number of references and personalities familiar to the London journalistic and literary scene, such as 'the Camden', one of the many 'printing clubs' that had sprung up in the late 1830s, or the name of Sir Peter Laurie, a former lord mayor of London then occupying the position of chairman of the Union Bank of London. Later reprinted in Timperley's *Songs of the Press*, 'Wanted, an Editor' humorously evokes the exigencies of a function that the London Union of Compositors' registrar, R. Thompson, had then held for more than two years.[88] As the January 1843 number went to press, *The Compositors' Chronicle* was going through major financial difficulties, mostly on account of a lack of subscribers and outstanding debts contracted to keep the magazine afloat.[89] The *Chronicle* eventually ceased publication in August 1843, later replaced by *The Printer, or Compositors' and Pressmen's Chronicle* (1843–5), whose more comprehensive title was also intended as a symbolic gesture towards new categories of print workers.[90]

Behind the pages of the *Chronicle*, the London Union of Compositors was collapsing. Rumours of the dissolution of the union had begun to circulate in 1842, as many unemployed members became crippled by dispute payments and began to fall into arrears. The Bouverie Street office was closed, and the LUC dissolved and reorganised as the London Society of Compositors, affiliated with the South Eastern District of the National Typographical Association, which had been formed the previous year. The collapse of the National Typographical Association in 1848 led to the breakaway and re-establishment of the London Society of Compositors, joined in 1853 by the London Daily Newspaper Compositors. The society was registered in 1879 and by the end of the century moved to St Bride Street, where it remained until the 1950s.[91] It was during the mid- and late Victorian period that London compositors, facing tremendous changes in all aspects of the trade, negotiated significant agreements with master printers, agreements that would prove significant to the printing industry. Meanwhile, the British political landscape had changed considerably, gradually becoming more representative, especially after the Third Reform Act (1884–5). In printing offices and elsewhere, compositors and pressmen continued to write poetry and prose, some of them rising to fame. As David Finkelstein notes, 'Laureates of the print trade featured in practically every issue of relevant journals from the 1840s through to the early 1870s, either through their poetry, through reviews of their work, or in reports of their creative activities.'[92] Within the trade press, the celebration of facts and useful knowledge turned out to encourage artistic self-expression.

Notes

1. Patricia Hollis, *The Pauper Press. A Study in Working-Class Radicalism of the 1830s* (Oxford: Oxford University Press, 1970), 8.

2. Hollis, however, specifies that, according to Cobbett, the tracts of the Society for the Diffusion of Useful Knowledge (SDUK) were 'gingerbread dolls to stop the poor from asking awkward questions' (20).
3. In London, typesetters were mostly supported by the London Union of Compositors, an organisation founded in March 1834 with the amalgamation of the London Trade Society of Compositors (1816) and the London General Trade Society of Compositors (1826).
4. Compositors, also called typesetters, were in charge of assembling individual type letters on a composing stick, while pressmen were in charge of operating the press to produce the printed page. All adult workers were referred to as journeymen.
5. 'Address', *Compositors' Chronicle* 1 (September 1840): 1.
6. Mike Sanders, *The Poetry of Chartism. Aesthetics, Politics, History* (Cambridge: Cambridge University Press, 2009), 17; Kirstie Blair, *Working Verse in Victorian Scotland: Poetry, Press, Community* (Oxford: Oxford University Press, 2019), 21.
7. Patrick Duffy, *The Skilled Compositor, 1850–1914: An Aristocrat among Working Men* (Aldershot: Ashgate, 2000), 82–4. See also Ellic Howe, ed., *The London Compositor: Documents Relating to Wages, Working Conditions and Customs of the London Printing Trade, 1785–1900* (Oxford: Oxford University Press, 1947), 58.
8. David Finkelstein, *Movable Types: Roving Creative Printers of the Victorian World* (Oxford: Oxford University Press, 2018), 152.
9. 'To Correspondents, &c.', *Compositors' Chronicle* 17 (January 1842): 132.
10. 'The Pen and the Press', *Chronicle* 17 (January 1842): 131.
11. Sanders, *Poetry of Chartism*, 19.
12. Lorraine Janzen Kooistra, 'Charting Rocks in the Golden Stream: Or, Why Textual Ornaments Matter to Victorian Periodicals Studies', *Victorian Periodicals Review* 49, no. 3 (2016): 376. See also James Mussell, *The Nineteenth-Century Press in the Digital Age* (Basingstoke: Palgrave Macmillan, 2012), 29–30.
13. Joanna Drucker, 'The Virtual Codex from Page Space to E-space', The Book Arts Web, 25 April 2003. http://www.philobiblon.com/drucker/.
14. 'To Correspondents, &.c', *Chronicle* 2 (October 1840): 12.
15. 'To Correspondents, &.c', *Chronicle* 24 (July 1842): 189.
16. 'Facts and Scraps', *Chronicle* 13 (September 1841): 104.
17. Ibid.
18. 'Facts and Scraps', *Chronicle* 20 (April 1842): 157.
19. Finkelstein, *Movable Types*, 111.

20. Albert Edward Musson, *Trade Union and Social History* (London: Routledge, 2006), 128.
21. Richard D. Altick, *The English Common Reader: A Social History of the Mass Reading Public, 1800–1900* (Chicago: University of Chicago Press, 1957), 103, 129.
22. Duffy, *Skilled Compositor*, 82. On London compositors' scale of prices, see also Howe, *London Compositor*, 58.
23. 'The Late G. Birkbeck', *Chronicle* 19 (March 1842): 150.
24. 'Society for the Diffusion of Useful Knowledge', *The Times*, 19 May 1828, 3.
25. 'Advertisement', *Chronicle*, general preface, 1843.
26. 'On Education', *Chronicle* 7 (March 1841): 55.
27. 'On Education – Essay II', *Chronicle* 8 (April 1841): 63–4.
28. Ibid.
29. Ibid.
30. 'New Composing Machine', *Chronicle* 13 (September 1841): 99; 'The Infernal Machine', *Chronicle* 27 (October 1842): 212.
31. 'Friendship – Essay IV', *Chronicle* 14 (October 1841): 107; 'Home – Essay VI', *Chronicle* 18 (February 1842): 143–4; 'Reverses of Fortune', *Chronicle* 20 (April 1842): 155.
32. 'On the Varieties of Change – Essay VII', *Chronicle* 20 (April 1842): 154.
33. 'Knowledge', *Chronicle* 33 (April 1843): 258.
34. In the August 1841 issue of the *Chronicle*, Philo also contributed a song entitled 'I Wish I Could Forget Her!' (89).
35. 'The Beauties of Nature', *Chronicle* 5 (January 1841): 34; 6 (February 1841): 42.
36. 'The Beauties of Nature', *Chronicle* 4 (December 1840): 26; 6 (February 1841): 42.
37. The Printers' Pension Society, which had been set up in 1827 to provide relief for elderly and unemployed printers and their widows, complemented the action of the journeymen's unions and associations.
38. 'Lecture on the Life of Dr Franklin', *Chronicle* 16 (December 1841): 121.
39. Ibid.
40. 'The Character of Franklin – By Lord Brougham', *Chronicle* 27 (October 1842): 210.
41. 'Biography – Blake the Artist', *Chronicle* 21 (May 1842): 166.
42. Ibid.
43. Hollis, *Pauper Press*, 3.
44. 'To Correspondents, &c.', *Chronicle* 13 (September 1841): 100.

45. Blair, *Working Verse*, 35.
46. Shooting sticks were pieces of hardwood used to lock type inside the chase (or forme).
47. Andrew Hobbs, 'Five Million Poems, or the Local Press as Poetry Publisher, 1800–1900', *Victorian Periodicals Review* 45, no. 4 (2012): 488–92.
48. Finkelstein, *Movable Types*, 111–24.
49. J. P. S. B., 'Tripartite Effusions', *Chronicle* 12 (August 1841): 96.
50. E. de la Mont, 'To a Mother', *Chronicle* 16 (December 1841): 128.
51. Between September 1840 and August 1843, at least seven poems evoke the loss of a child or a sibling: 'A Voice from the Grave' (96), 'She Lived in Beauty' (103), 'The Last of Seven' (152), 'The Corpse-Candle' (200), 'The Serenade' (200), 'The Little Shroud' (237) and 'The Angel and the Child' (261).
52. 'The Tramp System' (109–10), 'Tramping – Its Evil Results and its Remedy' (114–15), 'Tramping' (127), 'The Tramp System' (132), 'Tramping' (215), 'Improvement in the Present Tramp System' (234–5) and 'Tramping' (248).
53. Kirstie Blair, '"A Very Poetical Town": Newspaper Poetry and the Working-Class Poet in Victorian Dundee', *Victorian Poetry* 52, no. 1 (2014): 105.
54. Finkelstein, *Movable Types*, 137.
55. T. J. O., 'Song of the Earth to the Moon', *Chronicle* 11 (July 1841): 88.
56. Ibid.
57. Blair, *Working Verse*, 11.
58. 'Ode to a Dead Poodle', *Chronicle* 4 (December 1840): 31; 'Jolly Nose', *Chronicle* 34 (May 1843): 269.
59. Sanders, *Poetry of Chartism*, 8.
60. Natalie Houston, 'Newspaper Poems: Material Texts in the Public Sphere', *Victorian Studies* 50, no. 2 (2008): 236.
61. Ibid.
62. During this period, major industrial conflicts occurred in Dublin (September–December 1840, then February–March 1841). Many reports sent by the Irish Typographical Union were regularly featured in *The Compositors' Chronicle* throughout 1841 and 1842.
63. On apprentices, see 'The Apprentice System' (4–5, 10, 19) and 'Origin of Apprentices' (56, 59, 70). On the Young & Delcambre typesetting machine, see 'New Composing Machine' (99, 145–6, 192, 197), 'The Infernal Machine' (212–3, 251), 'Machinery – The

New Composing Machine (220, 225–6, 233) and 'The Triumph of Machinery' (268–9). On the Copyright Bill, see 'The Copyright Question' (36–7, 45, 54–5) and 'New Copyright Bill' (156–7, 173). *The Compositors' Chronicle: An Epitome of Events Interesting to Printers, from September 1840 to August 1843* (London: R. Thompson, 1843).

64. 'The Typographical Song', *Chronicle* 7 (March 1841): 55.
65. Ibid., 55–6.
66. Sanders, *Poetry of Chartism*, 3.
67. 'The Pen and the Press', 131.
68. James Sambrook, 'Prince, John Critchley (1808–66)', in the *Oxford Dictionary of National Biography*, online edition (Oxford: Oxford University Press, 2004).
69. 'The Pen and the Press', 131.
70. Ibid.
71. Finkelstein, *Movable Types*, 139.
72. On unemployment relief, see 'Gifts to Printers' (28, 48, 56, 72), 'General Distress in the Printing Business' (124), 'Relieving the Distress of Unemployed Printers' (155, 165) and 'Financial Statement of the London Relief Committee' (171, 256). On printers' pensions see 'Printers' Asylum' (12, 21, 29, 37, 40, 45, 53, 64, 69, 77, 81, 93, 109, 117, 125, 133, 141, 153, 161, 170, 173, 189, 197, 205, 228, 245, 253, 269) and 'Printers' Pension Society' (8, 53, 69, 80, 85, 109, 149, 153, 173, 189). *The Compositors' Chronicle: An Epitome of Events Interesting to Printers, from September 1840 to August 1843* (London: R. Thompson, 1843).
73. Sanders, *Poetry of Chartism*, 3; 'An Address', *Chronicle* 4 (December 1840): 31.
74. 'Victoria, a Political Poem', *Chronicle* 4 (December 1840): 25.
75. Richard Wemyss, *Victoria, a Political Poem* (London: Effingham Wilson, 1840), iv.
76. 'Victoria, a Political Poem', 25.
77. In a footnote, Wemyss specifies that the text was written 'while the war in Spain [1838–9] was hotly raging'. Wemyss, *Victoria*, 18.
78. Ibid., iv.
79. In July 1840, Lord Palmerston, then Foreign Secretary in the Whig government of Lord Melbourne, engineered an agreement between Britain, Russia, Austria and Prussia to preserve Turkey as a sufficiently strong state capable of standing up to Russian ambitions. This alliance compromised Britain's relations with France, which then deteriorated.

80. Wemyss, *Victoria*, 14.
81. Ibid., 32–3.
82. 'To Correspondents, &c.', 132.
83. 'Poor Laws', *Chronicle* 11 (July 1841): 87.
84. 'Wanted, an Editor', *Chronicle* 30 (January 1843): 233.
85. John Parry, 'Wanted, a Governess', The Lester S. Levy Sheet Music Collection, Johns Hopkins Sheridan Libraries & University Museums, https://levysheetmusic.mse.jhu.edu/collection/049/080.
86. 'Wanted, an Editor', 233.
87. Ibid.
88. The ledger book of the LUC Trade Council for 1840–5 reveals that Thompson had initiated the launch of *The Compositors' Chronicle*, declaring during the 1 September 1840 meeting of the Council that he proposed 'publishing monthly a digest of trade matters, on his own responsibility, but would not do so if there were any objections to it on the part of the Trade Council'. London Union of Compositors, Trade Council, LSC/D/1/8, MSS.28/CO/1/1/8, item 1840–45, Modern Records Centre, University of Warwick.
89. 'To proceed as we have hitherto is impossible, and the plan we have sketched for our future conduct a few words will explain. We purpose to suspend our labours for one month. Should the sale of our stock and the payment of our outstanding accounts during that period be equal to our wishes, we shall resume our labours on the first of October'. 'Advertisement', *Chronicle*, 1843.
90. *The Printer* was also published and edited by R. Thompson.
91. Arthur Marsh and John B. Smethurst, *Historical Directory of Trade Unions* (London: Routledge, 2006), 43–6.
92. Finkelstein, *Movable Types*, 124.

Bibliography

Adburgham, Alison. *Women in Print: Writing Women and Women's Magazines from the Restoration to the Accession of Victoria*. London: George Allen and Unwin, 1972.

'Address'. *Compiler; or, Literary Banquet* 1 (1807): iii.

'Address'. *Compositors' Chronicle* 1 (September 1840): 1.

'An Address'. *Compositors' Chronicle* 4 (December 1840): 31.

'Address'. *Lady's Magazine* (August 1770): [3–4].

'Address'. *Lady's Magazine*, 1st n.s., 2 (January 1821): i.

'Address'. *Lady's Magazine*, 2nd n.s., 2 (November–December 1830): 306.

'Address'. *Lady's Magazine* 2nd n.s., 1 (July 1832): n.p.

'Address'. *Ladies' Magazine and Museum* 1 (July 1832): n.p.

'Address of the Editors'. *Chambers's Edinburgh Journal* 9 (25 January 1840): 8.

'Address to the Fair Sex'. *Lady's Magazine* 1 (August 1770): [3].

'Advertisement'. *Compositors' Chronicle*, general preface (1843).

'Advertisement'. *Figaro in London* 1 (17 March 1832): 60.

'Advertising Considered as an Art'. *Chambers's Edinburgh Journal* 52, n.s. (28 December 1844): 401–3.

Alexander, Christine, and Juliet McMaster, eds. *The Child Writer from Austen to Woolf*. Cambridge: Cambridge University Press, 2005.

Algee-Hewitt, Mark, et al. (The Multigraph Collective). *Interacting with Print: Elements of Reading in the Era of Print Saturation*. Chicago: University of Chicago Press, 2018.

'Allegory on Impudence and Modesty'. *Australian Magazine* 1, no. 1 (1 May 1821): 21–2.

Altick, Richard D. *The English Common Reader: A Social History of the Mass Reading Public, 1800–1900*. 1957. Chicago: University of Chicago Press, 1998.

———. *The Shows of London: A Panoramic History of Exhibitions, 1600–1862*. Cambridge: Belknap Press, 1978.

———. 'The Sociology of Authorship: The Social Origins, Education, and Occupations of 1,100 British Writers, 1800–1935'. *Bulletin of the New York Public Library* 66 (1962): 389–404.

Anderson, Christopher G. *London Vagabond: The Life of Henry Mayhew*. London: Anderson, 2018.

Armistead, Wilson. *A Tribute for the Negro: Being a Vindication of the Moral, Intellectual and Religious Capabilities of the Coloured Portion of Mankind*. Manchester: William Urwin, 1848.

Armstrong, Isobel. *Victorian Poetry: Poetry, Poetics and Politics*. London: Routledge, 1993.

Aspinall, Rev. James. *A Sermon Preached at St. Michael's Church, Liverpool, on Sunday, April 4, 1830, upon the Subject of the Provident District Society, Now Forming in That Town*. Liverpool: Cruikshank, 1830.

Atkin, Lara, and Emily Bell, eds. The Curran Index, 2017–present. https://curranindex.org.

Barnes, James J., and Patience P. Barnes. 'Resassessing the Reputation of Thomas Tegg, London Publisher, 1776–1846'. *Book History* 3 (2000): 45–60.

Barrett Browning, Elizabeth. 'Stanzas Addressed to Miss Landon, and Suggested by Her "Stanzas on the Death of Mrs. Hemans"'. *New Monthly Magazine* 45 (September 1835): 82.

Bassett, Troy J. 'Analysis: Data Visualizations'. At the Circulating Library: A Database of Victorian Fiction, 1837–1901. 15 December 2022. http://www.victorianresearch.org.

Batchelor, Jennie. 'Illustrated Magazines and Periodicals: Visual Genres and Gendered Aspirations'. In *The Edinburgh Companion to Romanticism and the Arts*, edited by Maureen McCue and Sophie Thomas, 408–26. Edinburgh: Edinburgh University Press, 2022.

———. *The Lady's Magazine (1770–1832) and the Making of Literary History*. Edinburgh: Edinburgh University Press, 2022.

Batchelor, Jennie, and Manushag N. Powell, eds. *Women's Periodicals and Print Culture in Britain, 1690s–1820s*. Edinburgh: Edinburgh University Press, 2018.

Beals, M. H. 'Scissors and Paste: The Georgian Reprints, 1800–1837'. *Journal of Open Humanities Data* 3, no. 1 (2017): https://doi.org/10.5334/johd.8.

'The Beauties of Nature'. *Compositors' Chronicle* 4 (December 1840): 26; 5 (January 1841): 34; 6 (February 1841): 42.

Beetham, Margaret. *A Magazine of her Own?: Domesticity and Desire in the Woman's Magazine, 1800–1914*. London: Routledge, 1996.

———. 'Open and Closed: The Periodical as a Publishing Genre'. *Victorian Periodicals Review* 22, no. 3 (1989): 96–100.

———. 'Periodical Writing'. In *The Cambridge Companion to Victorian Women's Writing*, edited by Linda H. Peterson, 221–35. Cambridge: Cambridge University Press, 2015.

Behlmer, George K. *Friends of the Family: The English Home and Its Guardians, 1850–1940* Stanford: Stanford University Press, 1998.

Benjamin, Walter. *Illuminations*. Edited by Hannah Arendt. Translated by Harry Zorn. London: Pimlico, 1999.

Bennett, Andrew. *Romantic Poets and the Culture of Posterity*. Cambridge: Cambridge University Press, 1999.

Benson, Christopher. *The District Visitor's Manual: A Compendium of Practical Information and of FACTS for the Use of District Visitors*. 2nd ed. London: John W. Parker, 1840.

'Biographical Particulars of Celebrated Persons, Lately Deceased: Mr. Douglas, the Botanist'. *New Monthly Magazine* 44 (June 1835): 269–70.

'Biographical Particulars of Celebrated Persons, Lately Deceased: Mrs. Hemans'. *New Monthly Magazine* 44 (June 1835): 265–8.

'Biographical Particulars of Celebrated Persons, Lately Deceased: Richard Sharp, ESQ'. *New Monthly Magazine* 44, no. 174 (June 1835): 268–9.

'Biographical Particulars of Celebrated Persons, Lately Deceased: Sir George Tuthill'. *New Monthly Magazine* 44, no. 174 (June 1835): 268.

'Biography – Blake the Artist'. *Compositors' Chronicle* 21 (May 1842): 166.

Blackmantle, Bernard. *The Punster's Pocket-Book, or The Art of Punning*. London: Sherwood, Gilbert, and Piper, 1826.

Blair, Kirstie. '"A Very Poetical Town": Newspaper Poetry and the Working-Class Poet in Victorian Dundee'. *Victorian Poetry* 52, no. 1 (2014): 89–109.

———. *Working Verse in Victorian Scotland: Poetry, Press, Community*. Oxford: Oxford University Press, 2019.

Bolter, Jay D., and Richard Grusin. *Remediation: Understanding New Media*. Cambridge: MIT Press, 1998.

Borsuk, Amaranth. *The Book*. Cambridge: MIT Press, 2018.

Bosco, Fernando J. 'Emotions That Build Networks: Geographies of Human Rights Movements in Argentina and Beyond'. *Tijdschrift Voor Economische En Sociale Geografie* 98, no. 5 (2007): 545–63.

Bourrier, Karen. *Victorian Bestseller: The Life of Dinah Craik*. Ann Arbor: University of Michigan Press, 2019.

Boyce, Charlotte. 'At Home with Tennyson: Virtual Literary Tourism and the Commodification of Celebrity in the Periodical Press'. In *Victorian Celebrity Culture and Tennyson's Circle*, edited by Charlotte Boyce, Páraic Finnerty and Anne-Marie Millim, 18–52. Basingstoke: Palgrave Macmillan, 2013.

Boyce, George D. *Nineteenth-Century Ireland*. Dublin: Gill and Macmillan, 2005.

———. *The Revolution in Ireland, 1879–1923*. Dublin: Gill and Macmillan, 1988.

Brake, Laurel. 'Nineteenth-Century Newspaper Press Directories: The National Gallery of the British Press'. *Victorian Periodicals Review* 48, no. 4 (2015): 569–90.

———. 'The Serial and the Book in Nineteenth-Century Britain: Intersections, Extensions, Transformations'. *Memoirs du Livre Studies in Book Culture* 8, no. 2 (2017): 1–16.

———. 'Time's Turbulence: Mapping Journalism Networks'. *Victorian Periodicals Review* 44, no. 2 (2011): 115–27.

Bramieri, Luigi. 'Il Dovere e la Felicità'. In *Novelle Morali: Ad Uso Della Gioventù*, 64–73. Brussels: Hauman, 1836.

Braudy, Leo. *The Frenzy of Renown: Fame and Its History*. New York: Oxford University Press, 1986.

Brock, Claire. *The Feminization of Fame, 1750–1830*. Basingstoke: Palgrave Macmillan, 2006.

Brown, Christopher L. *Moral Capital: Foundations of British Abolitionism*. Chapel Hill: University of North Carolina Press, 2006.

Brown, Clive. 'Giacomo Meyerbeer'. In *The New Penguin Opera Guide*, edited by Amanda Holden, 570–7. London: Penguin, 2001.

Brown, Matthew P. 'Blanks: Data, Method, and the British American Print Shop'. *American Literary History* 29, no. 2 (2017): 228–47.

———. *The Pilgrim and the Bee: Reading Rituals and Book Culture in Early New England*. Philadelphia: University of Pennsylvania Press, 2007.

Brown, Stewart J. 'Thomas Chalmers, 1780–1847'. In the *Oxford Dictionary of National Biography*, online edition. Oxford: Oxford University Press, 2004.

———. *Thomas Chalmers and the Godly Commonwealth in Scotland*. Oxford: Oxford University Press, 1982.

Brown, Susan. 'The Victorian Poetess'. In *The Cambridge Companion to Victorian Poetry*, edited by Joseph Bristow, 180–202. Cambridge: Cambridge University Press, 2000.

'Buckland – on Antediluvian Fossil Bones'. *Quarterly Review* 27 (July 1822): 459–76.

Burton, Antoinette. *Empire in Question: Reading, Writing, and Teaching British Imperialism*. Durham: Duke University Press, 2011.

Cale, Luisa. *Fuseli's Milton Gallery: Turning Readers into Spectators*. Oxford: Clarendon Press, 2006.

'Captain Raine's Narrative of a Visit to Pitcairn's Island, in the Ship Surry, 1821'. *Australian Magazine* 1, no. 3 (1 July 1821): 80–4.

Carlyle, Thomas. *Past and Present*. London: Chapman and Hall, 1843.

Carruthers, Gerard. *Scottish Literature*. Edinburgh: Edinburgh University Press, 2009.

Casaliggi, Carmen, and Porscha Fermanis, eds. *Romanticism: A Literary and Cultural History*. London: Routledge, 2016.

Cassel, Monika Irene. 'Poetesses at the Grave: Transnational Circulation of Women's Memorial Verse in Nineteenth-Century England, Germany and America'. PhD diss., University of Michigan, 2002. ProQuest Dissertations Publishing (3042050).

A Catalog of Books and Newspapers Printed by John Bell and by John Browne Bell. London: First Edition Club, 1931.

Cazden, Norman, Herbert Haufrecht and Norman Studer, eds. *Folk Songs of the Catskills*. Albany: State University of New York Press, 1982.

Chalmers, Thomas. *The Christian and Civic Economy of Large Towns*. 3 vols. 1821–6. Reprint, Cambridge: Cambridge University Press, 2013.

Chandler, James K. *England in 1819: The Politics of Literary Culture and the Case of Romantic Historicism*. Chicago: University of Chicago Press, 1998.

Chapman, Alison et al., eds. *Digital Victorian Periodical Poetry Project* (beta). 10 April 2022. https://dvpp.uvic.ca/.

Chapman, Alison, and Caley Ehnes. Introduction to a special issue of *Victorian Poetry* 52, no. 1 (2014): 1–20.

'The Character of Franklin – By Lord Brougham'. *Compositors' Chronicle* 27 (October 1842): 210.

Cheyne, A. C. 'Introduction: Thomas Chalmers Then and Now'. In *The Practical and The Pious: Essays on Thomas Chalmers*, edited by A. C. Cheyne, 9–30. Edinburgh: Saint Andrew Press, 1985.

Chorley, Henry. 'Personal Recollections of the Late Mrs. Hemans, No. I'. *Athenaeum* 398 (13 June 1835): 452–545.

'Civilization of the Aborigines'. *Arden's Sydney Magazine* 1, no. 2 (October 1843): 65–82.

Clark, Robert T. 'The Fusion of Legends in Zschokke's *Prinzessin von Wolfenbüttel*'. *Journal of English and Germanic Philology* 42, no. 2 (1943): 185–96.

Cole, William, ed. *Folk Songs of England, Ireland, Scotland & Wales*. New York: Doubleday, 1961.

Collini, Stephen. *Public Moralists: Political Thought and Intellectual Life in Britain, 1850–1930*. Oxford: Clarendon Press, 1991.

Colman, George. *The Circle of Anecdote and Wit*. 7th ed. London: John Bumpus, 1825.

The Compositors' Chronicle: An Epitome of Events Interesting to Printers, from September 1840 to August 1843. London: R. Thompson, 1843.

Cooper, David, and Ian N. Gregory. 'Mapping the English Lake District: A Literary GIS'. *Transactions of the Institute of British Geographers* 36, no. 1 (2011): 89–108.

Copeland, Edward. *The Silver Fork Novel: Fashionable Fiction in the Age of Reform*. Cambridge: Cambridge University Press, 2012.

'Correspondence'. *Court and Lady's Magazine and Monthly Critic* 19 (April 1844): 83.

'Correspondence'. *Lady's Magazine* 50 (February 1819): n.p.

Crampton, Jeremy W. *Mapping: A Critical Introduction to Cartography and GIS*. New York: John Wiley, 2010.

The Cream of the Jest: A Fund of Chaste Wit and Humour. Derby: Henry Mozley, 1826.

Crittenden, Camille. *Johann Strauss and Vienna: Operetta and the Politics of Popular Culture*. Cambridge: Cambridge University Press, 2006.

Cronin, Richard. *Paper Pellets: British Literary Culture after Waterloo*. Oxford: Oxford University Press, 2010.

———. *Romantic Victorians: English Literature, 1824–1840*. New York: Palgrave, 2002.

Cruikshank, George. *My Sketch Book*. London: George Cruikshank, 1834.

Curran, Stuart. 'Romantic Elegiac Hybridity'. In *The Oxford Handbook of the Elegy*, edited by Karen Weisman, 238–50. Oxford: Oxford University Press, 2010.

———. 'Romantic Poetry: The *I* Altered'. In *Romantic Poetry: Recent Revisionary Criticism*, edited by Karl Kroeher and Gene W. Ruoff, 38–43. New Brunswick: Rutgers University Press, 1993.

D'Arcy Wood, Gillen. *The Shock of the Real: Romanticism and Visual Culture*. Basingstoke: Palgrave, 2001.

Davidson, Hilary. *Dress in the Age of Jane Austen: Regency Fashion*. New Haven: Yale University Press, 2019.

DeWitt, Anne. 'Advances in the Visualization of Data: The Network of Genre in the Victorian Periodical Press'. *Victorian Periodicals Review* 48, no. 2 (2015): 161–82.

[Dickens, Charles]. 'Bill-Sticking'. *Household Words* 2 (22 March 1851): 601–6.

———. *Bleak House*. 1853. New York: Vintage, 2012.

DiPlacidi, Jenny. '"Full of pretty stories": Fiction in the *Lady's Magazine* (1770–1832)'. In *Women's Periodicals and Print Culture in Britain, 1690s–1820s*, edited by Jennie Batchelor and Manushag N. Powell, 263–77. Edinburgh: Edinburgh University Press, 2018.

D'Israeli, Isaac. 'Review of "Memoirs of Percival Stockdale"'. *Quarterly Review* 1 (May 1809): 326–39.

Doran, Amanda-Jane. 'Landells, Ebenezer (1808–1860)'. In the *Oxford Dictionary of National Biography*, online edition. Oxford: Oxford University Press, 2004.

Drucker, Joanna. 'The Virtual Codex from Page Space to E-space'. Book Arts Web. 25 April 2003. http://www.philobiblon.com/drucker/.

Duffy, Patrick. *The Skilled Compositor, 1850–1914: An Aristocrat among Working Men*. Aldershot: Ashgate, 2000.

Duncan, John [John Brighte]. *The Book to Keep the Spirits Up*. Wakefield: William Nicholson, n.d.

E. de la Mont. 'To a Mother'. *Compositors' Chronicle* 16 (December 1841): 128.

Easley, Alexis. *First-Person Anonymous: Women Writers and Victorian Print Media, 1830–70*. Aldershot: Ashgate, 2004.

———. 'Imagining the Mass-Market Woman Reader: *The News of the World*, 1843–77'. In *The News of the World and the British Press, 1843–2011*, edited by Laurel Brake, Chandrika Kaul and Mark W. Turner, 81–99. Houndmills: Palgrave Macmillan, 2016.

———. 'Making a Debut'. In *The Cambridge Companion to Victorian Women's Writing*, edited by Linda H. Peterson, 15–28. Cambridge: Cambridge University Press, 2015.

———. *New Media and the Rise of the Popular Woman Writer, 1832–1860*. Edinburgh: Edinburgh University Press, 2021.

———. 'Scrapbooks and Women's Leisure Reading Practices, 1825–60'. *Nineteenth-Century Gender Studies* 15, no. 2 (2019): https://www.ncgsjournal.com/issue152/easley.html.

Eckhardt, Joshua, and Daniel Starza Smith. *Manuscript Miscellanies in Early Modern England*. London: Routledge, 2019.

Ehnes, Caley. *Victorian Poetry and the Poetics of the Literary Periodical*. Edinburgh: Edinburgh University Press, 2019.

Eisner, Eric. *Nineteenth-Century Poetry and Literary Celebrity*. Basingstoke: Palgrave Macmillan, 2009.

Eliot, George. *The George Eliot Letters*. 9 vols. Edited by Gordon S. Haight. New Haven: Yale University Press, 1954–78.

Elliott, Marianne. *Robert Emmet: The Making of a Legend*. London: Profile, 2003.

Erickson, Lee. *The Economy of Literary Form: English Literature and the Industrialization of Printing, 1800–1850*. Baltimore: Johns Hopkins University Press, 1996.

'Facts and Scraps'. *Compositors' Chronicle* 13 (September 1841): 104.

'Facts and Scraps'. *Compositors' Chronicle* 20 (April 1842): 157.

Fagg, John, Matthew Pethers and Robin Vandome. 'Introduction: Networks and the Nineteenth-Century Periodical'. *American Periodicals: A Journal of History & Criticism* 23, no. 2 (2013): 93–104.

Faxon, Frederick W. *Literary Annuals and Gift Books: A Bibliography 1823–1903*. London: Private Libraries Association, 1973.

Fay, Elizabeth A. *Fashioning Faces: The Portraitive Mode in British Romanticism*. Durham: University of New Hampshire Press, 2010.

Feely, Catherine Clare. '"Scissors-and-Paste" Journalism'. In *The Dictionary of Nineteenth-Century Journalism*, online edition. Edited by Laurel Brake and Marysa Demoor. Ghent and London: Academia Press and the British Library, 2009.

Feldman, Paula R. 'Introduction'. In *Records of Woman, with Other Poems* by Felicia Hemans, edited by Paula Feldman, xi–xxix. Lexington: University Press of Kentucky, 1999.

———. 'The Poet and the Profits: Felicia Hemans and the Literary Marketplace'. *Keats-Shelley Journal* 46 (1997): 148–76.

Ferris, Ina. 'A Bookish Intervention: Thomas Bewick's *British Birds* and the Reconfiguration of Illustrated Natural History'. *Romanticism* 28, no. 1 (2022): 72–86.

'A Few Words to Our Readers'. *Chambers's Edinburgh Journal* 3 (4 January 1845): 1–3.

Finkelstein, David. *Movable Types: Roving Creative Printers of the Victorian World*. Oxford: Oxford University Press, 2018.

———. 'Thomas Pringle'. In the *Oxford Dictionary of National Biography*, online edition. Oxford: Oxford University Press, 2004.

Fisher, Judith L. '"In the Present Famine of Anything Substantial": *Fraser's* "Portraits" and the Construction of Literary Celebrity; Or, "Personality, Personality Is the Appetite of the Age"'. *Victorian Periodicals Review* 39, no. 2 (2006): 97–135.

Forrester, Alfred, and Charles Forrester. *The Battle of the "Annuals": A Fragment*. London: A. H. Baily, 1835.

[Francis, George Henry]. 'The Age of Veneer'. *Fraser's Magazine* 42 (September 1850): 437–45; 45 (January 1852): 87–93.

'Friendship – Essay IV'. *Compositors' Chronicle* 14 (October 1841): 107.

Fuhrmann, Christina. 'Introduction'. In *Henry Rowley Bishop, Mozart's The Marriage of Figaro: Adapted for Covent Garden, 1819*, ix–xvi. Middleton: A-R Editions, 2012.

Fun for the Million. London: Sherwood, Gilbert and Piper, n.d.

Furr, Derek. 'Sentimental Confrontations: Hemans, Landon, and Elizabeth Barrett'. *English Language Notes* 40, no. 2 (2002): 29–47.

Fyfe, Paul. 'An Archaeology of Victorian Newspapers'. *Victorian Periodicals Review* 49, no. 4 (2016): 546–77.

Garvey, Ellen Gruber. 'Scissorizing and Scrapbooks: Nineteenth-Century Reading, Remaking, and Recirculating'. In *New Media, 1740–1915*, edited by Lisa Gittelman and Geoffrey B. Pingree, 207–27. Cambridge: MIT Press, 2003.

———. *Writing with Scissors: American Scrapbooks from the Civil War to the Harlem Renaissance*. Oxford: Oxford University Press, 2013.

Genette, Gérard. *Paratexts: Thresholds of Interpretation*. Cambridge: Cambridge University Press, 1997.

Gitelman, Lisa. *Paper Knowledge: Towards a Media History of Documents*. Durham: Duke University Press, 2014.

'Godfrey Gimcrackiana'. In *The Comical Budget of Fun and Frolic*. Derby: Thomas Richardson, c. 1830.

Goodlad, Lauren M. E. *Victorian Literature and the Victorian State: Character and Governance in a Liberal Society*. Baltimore: Johns Hopkins University Press, 2004.

Goodwyn, Helena. 'A Woman's Thoughts About Men: Malthus and Middle-Class Masculinity in Dinah Mulock Craik's *John Halifax, Gentleman*'. *Women's Writing* 28, no. 2 (2021): 231–49.

Grant, James. *The Great Metropolis*. 2 vols. London: Saunders and Otley, 1836.

Gray, Erik. 'Victoria Dressed in Black'. In *The Oxford Handbook of the Elegy*, edited by Karen Weisman, 272–87. Oxford: Oxford University Press, 2010.

Gray, Valerie. *Charles Knight: Educator, Publisher, Writer*. Aldershot: Ashgate, 2006.

Green, Sarah. *Scotch Novel Reading; or, Modern Quackery. A Novel Really Founded on Facts: by a Cockney*. London: A. K. Newman, 1824.

Gretz, Daniela, Marcus Krause and Nicolas Pethes, eds. *Miszellanes Lesen Reading Miscellanies/Miscellaneous Reading*. Hannover: Wehrhahn Verlag, 2022.

Hall, Catherine. *Macaulay and Son: Architects of Imperial Britain*. New Haven: Yale University Press, 2012.

Hall, David. 'Introduction: The Uses of Literacy in New England, 1600–1850'. In *Printing and Society in Early America*, edited by William L. Joyce, David D. Hall, Richard D. Brown and John B. Hench, 1–45. Worcester: American Antiquarian Society, 1983.

Hall, Samuel Carter. 'Literature in 1834'. *New Monthly Magazine* 40 (April 1834): 497–505.

———. 'Notes on Periodicals'. *New Monthly Magazine* 39, no. 156 (December 1833): 424–31.

Hamilton, Samuel. 'Prospectus for a New Series of the *Lady's Magazine*' (1820). John Johnson Collection, Prospectuses of Journals 32 (36), 1. Bodleian Library, University of Oxford.

Hardiman, James. *Irish Minstrelsy, or Bardic Remains of Ireland*. London: Joseph Robins, 1831.

Harris, Katherine D. 'Borrowing, Altering and Perfecting the Literary Annual Form – Or What It Is Not: Emblems, Almanacs, Pocket-Books, Albums, Scrapbooks and Gift Books'. Poetess Archive 1 (2007): http://idhmc/tamu.edu/poetess/index.html.

———. *Forget Me Not: The Rise of the British Literary Annual, 1823–1835*. Athens: Ohio University Press, 2015.

Harrison, Brian. 'Press and Pressure Group in Modern Britain'. In *The Victorian Periodical Press: Samplings and Soundings*, edited by Joanne Shattock and Michael Wolff, 261–96. Leicester: Leicester University Press, 1982.

Haydon, B. R. *Life of Benjamin Robert Haydon, from His Autobiography and Journals*. 3 vols. Edited by Tom Taylor. New York: Harper & Brothers, 1853.

[Hayward, Abraham]. 'The Advertising System'. *Edinburgh Review* 77 (February 1843): 1–43.

Hazlitt, William. *The Complete Works of William Hazlitt*. 21 vols. Edited by P. Howe. London: J. J. Dent, 1930–4.

———. 'The Periodical Press'. *Edinburgh Review* 38 (May 1823): 349–78.

Hedley, Alison. *Making Pictorial Print: Media Literacy and Mass Culture in British Magazines, 1885–1918*. Toronto: University of Toronto Press, 2021.

Heffernan, Megan. *Making the Miscellany: Poetry, Print, and the History of the Book in Early Modern England*. Philadelphia: University of Pennsylvania Press, 2021.

Hemans, Felicia. 'The Better Land'. *Chambers's Edinburgh Journal* 1 (8 December 1832): 359.

———. 'The Graves of a Household'. *Chambers's Edinburgh Journal* 4 (2 May 1835): 112.

———. 'The Homes of England'. *Chambers's Edinburgh Journal* 4 (14 March 1835): 56.

———. *The Poetical Works of Mrs. Felicia Hemans*. London: Evert Duyckinck, 1828.

———. 'The Themes of Song'. *Chambers's Edinburgh Journal* 3 (31 May 1834): 144.

———. 'Thoughts During Sickness'. *New Monthly Magazine* 43 (March 1835): 328–30.

———. 'The Voice of Spring'. *Chambers's Edinburgh Journal* 1 (14 April 1832): 87.

Hewitt, Martin. *Making Social Knowledge in the Victorian City: The Visiting Mode in Manchester, 1832–1914*. New York: Routledge, 2020.

Higgins, David. *Romantic Genius and the Literary Magazine: Biography, Celebrity, Politics*. London: Routledge, 2005.

Hill, Isabel. 'A Stage Driver', 87–90. *Comic Offering*. London: Hurst, Chance, 1832.

Hilton, Boyd. *The Age of Atonement: The Influence of Evangelicalism on Social and Economic Thought, 1795–1865*. Oxford: Clarendon Press, 1988.

Hindley, Diana, and Geoffrey Hindley. *Advertising in Victorian England, 1837–1901*. London: Wayland, 1972.

Hoagwood, Terence, and Kathryn Ledbetter. *Colour'd Shadows: Contexts in Publishing, Printing, and Reading Nineteenth-Century British Women Writers*. New York: Palgrave Macmillan, 2005.

Hobbs, Andrew. 'Five Million Poems, or the Local Press as Poetry Publisher, 1800–1900'. *Victorian Periodicals Review* 45, no. 4 (2012): 488–92.

Hollis, Patricia. *The Pauper Press: A Study in Working-Class Radicalism of the 1830s*. Oxford: Oxford University Press, 1970.

'The Holy Places of Ireland'. *Dublin Saturday Magazine* 1–2 (1865–6): 58–9.

'Home – Essay VI'. *Compositors' Chronicle* 18 (February 1842): 143–4.

[Hood, Thomas]. 'The Art of Advertizing Made Easy'. *London Magazine and Review* 1 (February 1825): 246–53.

Hope, Eva. 'Felicia Hemans: The Poet of Womanhood'. In *Queens of Literature of the Victorian Era*, 261–301. London: Walter Scott, 1886.

Houston, Natalie. 'Newspaper Poems: Material Texts in the Public Sphere'. *Victorian Studies* 50, no. 2 (2008): 233–42.

Howe, Ellic, ed. *The London Compositor: Documents Relating to Wages, Working Conditions and Customs of the London Printing Trade, 1785–1900*. Oxford: Oxford University Press, 1947.

Howitt, Mary. *An Autobiography*. Edited by Margaret Howitt. 2 vols. London: William Isbister, 1889.

———. *Birds and Flowers and Other Country Things*. London: Darton and Clark, 1838.

———. 'Mountain Children'. In *The Winter's Wreath*, 397–8. London: George C. Whittaker and George Smith, 1829.

———. *My Own Story; or, the Autobiography of a Child*. London: Thomas Tegg, 1844.

———. *Sketches of Natural History*. London: Effingham Wilson, 1834.

Howitt, William, and Mary Howitt. *The Desolation of Eyam*. London: Wightman and Cramp, 1827.

Hughes, Gillian. 'Fiction in the Magazines'. In *English and British Fiction, 1750–1820*, edited by Peter Garside and Karen O'Brien, 461–77. Oxford: Oxford University Press, 2015.

Hughes, Linda K. 'Inventing Poetry and Pictorialism in *Once a Week*: A Magazine of Visual Effects'. *Victorian Poetry* 48, no. 1 (2010): 41–72.

———. *Victorian Women Writers and the Other Germany: Cross-Cultural Freedoms and Female Opportunity*. Cambridge: Cambridge University Press, 2022.

———. 'What the *Wellesley Index* Left Out: Why Poetry Matters to Periodical Studies'. *Victorian Periodicals Review* 40, no. 2 (2007): 91–125.

———. 'Women Poets and the Poetess Tradition'. In *Victorian Literature: Criticism and Debates*, edited by Lee Behlman and Anne Longmuir, 75–83. London: Routledge, 2015.

Hughes, Linda K., and Michael Lund. *The Victorian Serial*. Charlottesville: University of Virginia Press, 1991.

Hunnisett, Basil. *Engraved on Steel: The History of Picture Production Using Steel Plates*. Aldershot: Ashgate, 1998.

Hunt, Tamara L. 'Louisa Sheridan's *Comic Offering* and the Critics: Gender and Humour in the Early Victorian Period'. *Victorian Periodicals Review* 29, no. 2 (1996): 95–115.

'The Infernal Machine'. *Compositors' Chronicle* 27 (October 1842): 212.

J. P. S. B. 'Tripartite Effusions'. *Compositors' Chronicle* 12 (August 1841): 96.

Jackson, H. J. *Romantic Readers: The Evidence of Marginalia*. New Haven: Yale University Press, 2008.

James, Henry. 'A Noble Life'. In *Notes and Reviews*, 167–72. Cambridge: Dunster House, 1921.

James, Louis. *Fiction for the Working Man, 1830–50*. 1963. Reprint, Brighton: Everett Root, 2017.

[Johnstone, Christian.] 'Mary Howitt's Sketches of Natural History. Dr. Bowring's Minor Morals for Young People'. *Tait's Edinburgh Magazine* 1 (August 1834): 443–6.

'Jolly Nose'. *Compositors' Chronicle* 34 (May 1843): 269.

Jones, Linda. 'The *New Monthly Magazine*, 1821 to 1830'. PhD diss., University of Colorado at Boulder, 1970. ProQuest Dissertations Publishing (7121596).

Jowett, William. *The Christian Visitor*. London: R. B. Seeley, 1836.

Kafka, Ben. *The Demons of Writing: Powers and Failures of Paper*. Brooklyn: Zone Books 2012.

Karbiener, Karen. 'Scribbling Woman into History: Reconsidering a Forgotten British Poetess from an American Perspective'. *Wordsworth Circle* 32, no. 1 (2001): 48–52.

Kelly, Louis G. *The True Interpreter: A History of Translation Theory and Practice in the West*. Oxford: Basil Blackwell, 1979.

Kirkpatrick, Robert J. *Pennies, Profits and Poverty: A Biographical Dictionary of Wealth and Want in Bohemian Fleet Street*. London: Kirkpatrick, 2016.

Klancher, Jon P. *The Making of English Reading Audiences, 1790–1832*. Madison: University of Wisconsin Press, 1987.

Knight, Charles. 'Advertisement'. In *A Volume of Varieties*, v. London: Charles Knight, 1844.

———. *The English Cyclopaedia: A New Dictionary of Universal Knowledge*. 3 vols. London: Bradbury and Evans, 1859.

———. *Passages of a Working Life During Half a Century; with A Prelude of Early Reminiscences*. 3 vols. London: Bradbury and Evans, 1864.

Knight, Mark. 'Periodicals and Religion'. In *The Routledge Handbook to Nineteenth-Century British Periodicals and Newspapers*, edited by Andrew King, Alexis Easley and John Morton, 355–64. London: Routledge, 2016.

'Knowledge'. *Compositors' Chronicle* 33 (April 1843): 258.

Knowles, Anne Kelly, Levi Westerveld and Laura Strom. 'Inductive Visualization: A Humanistic Alternative to GIS'. *GeoHumanities* 1, no. 2 (2015): 233–65.

Kooistra, Lorraine Janzen. 'Charting Rocks in the Golden Stream: Or, Why Textual Ornaments Matter to Victorian Periodicals Studies'. *Victorian Periodicals Review* 49, no. 3 (2016): 375–95.

———. *Poetry, Pictures and Popular Publishing: The Illustrated Gift Book and Victorian Visual Culture, 1855–1875*. Athens: Ohio University Press, 2011.

Kunzle, David. 'Between Broadsheet Caricature and "Punch": Cheap Newspaper Cuts for the Lower Classes in the 1830s'. *Art Journal* 43, no. 4 (1983): 339–46.

[Landon, Letitia Elizabeth]. 'A Long While Ago'. *Chambers's Edinburgh Journal* 10 (12 June 1841): 168.

[———]. 'On the Ancient and Modern Influence of Poetry'. *New Monthly Magazine* 35 (November 1832): 466–71.

———. 'On the Character of Mrs. Hemans's Writings'. *New Monthly Magazine* 44 (August 1835): 425–33.

———. 'The Parting Word'. *New Monthly Magazine* 45 (October 1835): 155.

———. 'Stanzas on the Death of Mrs. Hemans'. *New Monthly Magazine* 44 (July 1835): 286–8.

[———]. 'Verses on Thomas Clarkson, by L. E. L.' *Chambers's Edinburgh Journal* 8 (14 December 1839): 376.

Langbauer, Laurie. *The Juvenile Tradition: Young Writers and Prolepsis, 1750–1835*. Oxford: Oxford University Press, 2016.

'The Late G. Birkbeck'. *Compositors' Chronicle* 19 (March 1842): 150.

Latour, Bruno. *Reassembling the Social: An Introduction to Actor-Network Theory*. Oxford: Oxford University Press, 2005.

Law, Graham. *Serializing Fiction in the Victorian Press*. Basingstoke: Palgrave, 2000.

Lawrence, Lindsy. '"Afford[ing] me a Place": Recovering Women Poets in *Blackwood's Edinburgh Magazine*, 1827–1835'. In *Women, Periodicals and Print Culture in Britain, 1830s–1900s: The Victorian Period*, edited by Alexis Easley, Clare Gill and Beth Rodgers, 400–12. Edinburgh: Edinburgh University Press, 2019.

Lears, Jackson. *Fables of Abundance: A Cultural History of Advertising in America*. New York: Basic Books, 1994.

Leary, Patrick. 'Googling the Victorians'. *Victorian Literature and Culture* 10, no. 1 (2005): 72–86.

———. *The Punch Brotherhood: Table-Talk and Print Culture in Mid-Victorian London*. London: British Library, 2010.

'Lecture on the Life of Dr Franklin'. *Compositors' Chronicle* 16 (December 1841): 121.

Ledbetter, Kathryn. *British Victorian Women's Periodicals: Beauty, Civilization, and Poetry*. New York: Palgrave Macmillan, 2009.

Lee, Amice. *Laurels and Rosemary: The Life of William and Mary Howitt*. London: Oxford University Press, 1955.

Leszczynski, Agnieszka, and Sarah Elwood. 'Feminist Geographies of New Spatial Media'. *Canadian Geographer* 59, no. 1 (2015): 12–28.

Lewis, Donald M. *Lighten Their Darkness: The Evangelical Mission to Working-Class London, 1828–1860*. New York: Greenwood Press, 1986.

Lilti, Antoine. *The Invention of Celebrity: 1750–1850*. Translated by Lynn Jeffress. Cambridge: Polity Press, 2017.

'Lines to a Worn-Out Font of Type'. *Compositors' Chronicle* 21 (May 1842): 168.

Lohrli, Anne. 'Dinah Maria Mulock'. Dickens Journals Online. Accessed 29 March 2023. https://www.djo.org.uk/indexes/authors/dinah-maria-mulock.html.

London Union of Compositors. Ledger book of the LUC Trade Council. 1840–5. MSS.28/CO/1/1/8, LSC/D/1/8. Modern Records Centre, University of Warwick.

Lootens, Tricia. 'Hemans and Home: Victorianism, Feminine "Internal Enemies," and the Domestication of National Identity'. *PMLA* 109, no. 2 (1994): 238–53.

———. *The Political Poetess: Victorian Femininity, Race, and the Legacy of Separate Spheres*. Princeton: Princeton University Press, 2017.

Lytton, Edward Bulwer. *The Siamese Twins: A Tale of the Times*. 2nd ed. London: H. Colburn and R. Bentley, 1831.

Macaulay, Zachary. 'Debate on the Sugar Duties'. *Anti-Slavery Reporter* 5, no. 4 (1832–3): 113–34.

———. 'Meeting at Bury St. Edmunds'. *Anti-Slavery Reporter* 4, no. 2 (1831): 69–75.

———. 'Meeting at Glasgow'. *Anti-Slavery Reporter* 4, no. 2 (1831): 34–9.

———. 'Report of a Committee of the House of Commons'. *Anti-Slavery Reporter* 5, no. 13 (1832): 314–72.

Macleod, Jock. 'Noticing the Dead: The Biographical Sketch in Victorian Periodicals'. *Victorian Periodicals Review* 50, no. 3 (2017): 534–59.

Macnish, Robert. 'Poetical Portraits'. *Blackwood's Edinburgh Magazine* 27 (April 1830): 632–3.

[Maginn, William]. 'Address to Contributors and Readers'. *Fraser's Magazine* 7 (January 1833): 1–15.

———. 'Female Fraserians'. *New Monthly Magazine* 13 (January 1836): 78–9.

Maidment, Brian. 'Beyond Usefulness and Ephemerality: The Discursive Almanac, 1828–60'. In *British Literature and Print Culture*, edited by Sandro Jung, 158–94. Woodbridge: Boydell and Brewer, 2013.

———. *Comedy, Caricature and the Social Order, 1820–1850*. Manchester: Manchester University Press, 2013.

———. *Reading Popular Prints, 1790–1870*. Manchester: Manchester University Press, 1996.

———. *Robert Seymour and Nineteenth Century Print Culture*. Abingdon: Routledge, 2021.

———. 'Scraps and Sketches: Miscellaneity, Commodity Culture and Comic Prints, 1820–40'. *19: Interdisciplinary Studies in the Long Nineteenth Century* 5 (2007): http://www.19.bbk.ac.uk.

———. '"Thief of the name of Kidd": Unscrupulous Opportunism and Cheap Print in Late Regency London'. *Victorian Popular Fictions* 3, no. 2 (2021): 21–44.

Marsh, Arthur, and Smethurst John B. *Historical Directory of Trade Unions*. London: Routledge, 2006.

Martinez, Michele. 'Creating an Audience for a British School: L. E. L.'s *Poetical Catalogue of Pictures* in *The Literary Gazette*'. *Victorian Poetry* 52, no. 1 (2014): 41–63.

Mason, Nicholas. *Literary Advertising and the Shaping of British Romanticism*. Baltimore: Johns Hopkins University Press, 2013.

Massey, Doreen. *For Space*. London: SAGE, 2005.

———. 'Politics and Space-Time'. *New Left Review* 196 (1992): 65–84.

———. *Space, Place, and Gender*. Minneapolis: University of Minnesota Press, 1994.

Maurer, Sara L. 'Reading Others Who Read: The Early-Century Print Environment of the Religious Tract Society'. *Victorian Studies* 61, no. 2 (2019): 222–31.

McCleave, Sarah. 'The Genesis of Thomas Moore's Irish Melodies, 1808–1834'. In *Cheap Print and Popular Song in the Nineteenth Century: A Cultural History of the Songster*, edited by Paul Watt, Derek B. Scott and Patrick Spedding, 47–70. Cambridge: Cambridge University Press, 2017.

McGann, Jerome. *The Poetics of Sensibility: A Revolution in Literary Style*. Oxford: Clarendon Press, 1996.

McGann, Jerome, and Daniel Reiss. 'Introduction'. In *Letitia Elizabeth Landon: Selected Writings*, edited by Jerome McGann and Daniel Reiss, 11–31. Peterborough: Broadview, 1997.

McGill, Meredith. *American Literature and the Culture of Reprinting, 1834–1853*. Philadelphia: University of Pennsylvania Press, 2003.

McPherson, Heather. *Art & Celebrity in the Age of Reynolds and Siddons*. University Park: Pennsylvania State University Press, 2017.

Miller, Elizabeth Carolyn. *Extraction Ecologies and the Literature of the Long Exhaustion*. Princeton: Princeton University Press, 2021.

Miller, John. 'The Evolving Forms of Animal Studies'. *Victorian Studies* 62, no. 2 (2020): 306–19.

Mirth in Miniature, or Bursts of Merriment. Derby: Henry Mozley 1825.

Mitchell, Sally. 'Careers for Girls: Writing Trash'. *Victorian Periodicals Review* 25, no. 3 (1992): 109–13.

———. *Dinah Mulock Craik*. Boston: Twayne, 1983.

Mitford, Mary Russell. Letter to Benjamin Robert Haydon [May 1823], qB/TU/MIT, vol. 4, f. 472. Reading Central Library.

[———]. 'Our Village'. *Lady's Magazine*, 1st n.s., 1 (December 1822): 645.

Moffat, Alfred. *The Minstrelsy of Scotland*. London: Augener, 1896.

Moir, D. M. '[Critical Comment on] Sabbath Sonnet'. *Blackwood's Magazine* 38 (July 1835): 96–7.

Mole, Tom. *Byron's Romantic Celebrity: Industrial Culture and the Hermeneutic of Intimacy*. Basingstoke: Palgrave Macmillan, 2007.

———. *What the Victorians Made of Romanticism: Material Artifacts, Cultural Practices, and Reception History*. Princeton: Princeton University Press, 2017.

Moore, Rory. 'A Mediated Intimacy: Dinah Mulock Craik and Celebrity Culture'. *Women's Writing* 20, no. 3 (2013): 387–403.

Moore, Thomas. *Irish Melodies*. London: J. Power, 1821.

———. *A Selection of Irish Melodies with Symphonies and Accompaniments by Sir John Stevenson*. London: J. Power, 1808.

Morgan, Alison. '"Let no man write my epitaph": The Contributions of Percy Shelley, Thomas Moore and Robert Southey to the Memorialisation of Robert Emmet'. *Irish Studies Review* 22, no. 3 (2014): 285–303.

Mourão, Manuela. 'Remembrance of Things Past: Literary Annuals' Self-Historicization'. *Victorian Poetry* 50, no. 1 (2012): 107–23.

Mulock, Dinah Maria (Craik). 'A Barcarole'. *New Monthly Belle Assemblée* 21 (July 1844): 32.

———. 'Caoinhe over an Irish Chieftain'. *New Monthly Belle Assemblée* 21 (August 1844): 76.

———. 'Carolan's War Cry'. *New Monthly Belle Assemblée* 20 (June 1844): 335.

———. 'The Country Sabbath'. *New Monthly Belle Assemblée* 21 (July–December 1844): 101.

[———]. 'Eustace the Negro'. *Chambers's Edinburgh Journal* 3 (22 November 1845): 332–4.

———. 'Forgive One Another'. *New Monthly Belle Assemblée* 20 (1844): 346.

[———]. 'A March Song'. *New Monthly Belle Assemblée* 20 (April 1844): 245.

[———]. 'The Mourner's Hope of Immortality. (A Funeral Hymn.)'. *New Monthly Belle Assemblée* 20 (April 1844): 245.

———. 'The Shepherd's Wife'. *New Monthly Belle Assemblée* 20 (May 1844): 272.

[———]. 'The Song of the Hours'. Dublin University Magazine 18 (October 1841): 442–3.

[———]. 'Sophia of Wolfenbuttel'. *Chambers's Edinburgh Journal* 3 (3 May 1845): 277–8.

[———]. 'Stanzas on the Birth of the Princess Royal'. *Staffordshire Advertiser*, 16 January 1841, 2.

———. 'Verses'. *Friendship's Offering of Sentiment and Mirth*, 216–17. London: Smith, Elder, 1844.

[———]. 'Want Something to Read'. *Chambers's Edinburgh Journal* 227 (8 May 1858): 289–92.

[———]. *A Woman's Thoughts about Women*. London: Hurst and Blackett, 1859.

Mussell, James. 'Digitization'. In *The Routledge Handbook to Nineteenth-Century British Periodicals and Newspapers*, edited by Andrew King, Alexis Easley and John Morton, 17–28. London: Routledge, 2016.

———. 'Elemental Forms: The Newspaper as Popular Genre in the Nineteenth Century'. *Media History* 20 (2014): 4–20.

———. *The Nineteenth-Century Press in the Digital Age*. Basingstoke: Palgrave Macmillan, 2012.

———. '"Of the making of magazines there is no end": W. T. Stead, Newness, and the Archival Imagination'. *English Studies in Canada* 41, no. 1 (2015): 69–91.

———. 'Repetition: Or, "In Our Last"'. *Victorian Periodicals Review* 48, no. 3 (2015): 345–6.

Musson, Albert E. *Trade Union and Social History*. 1974. Reprint, London: Routledge, 2006.

Nevett, T. R. *Advertising in Britain: A History*. London: Heinemann, 1982.

'New Composing Machine'. *Compositors' Chronicle* 13 (September 1841): 99.

The New Fun-Box Broke Open. London: Dean and Munday, 1822.

Newlyn, Lucy. *Reading, Writing, and Romanticism: The Anxiety of Reception*. Oxford: Oxford University Press, 2000.

'The Newspaper Press in London', *London Journal* 1 (19 July 1845): 328.

North, Julian. *The Domestication of Genius: Biography and the Romantic Poet*. Oxford: Oxford University Press, 2009.

———. 'Portraying Presence: Thomas Carlyle, Portraiture, and Biography'. *Victorian Literature and Culture* 43, no. 3 (2015): 465–88.

Nye, Eric W. 'Effingham Wilson, Radical Publisher of the Royal Exchange'. *Publishing History* 36 (1994): 87–102.

O'Day, Alan. *Irish Home Rule, 1867–1921*. Manchester: Manchester University Press, 1998.

Odds and Ends, Being a Collection of the Best Jokes, Comic Stories, Anecdotes, Bon mots, Etc. Glasgow: n.p., c. 1830.

'Ode to a Dead Poodle'. *Compositors' Chronicle* 4 (December 1840): 31.

'On Advertisements; and Advertising, Considered as One of the Fine Arts; in Which the Theory and the Practice Are Combined'. *Tait's Edinburgh Magazine* 2 (September 1835): 575–82.

'On Education'. *Compositors' Chronicle* 7 (March 1841): 55.

'On Education – Essay II'. *Compositors' Chronicle* 8 (April 1841): 63–4.

'On the Varieties of Change – Essay VII'. *Compositors' Chronicle* 20 (April 1842): 154.

Onslow, Barbara. 'Gendered Production: Annuals and Gift Books'. In *Journalism and the Periodical Press in Nineteenth Century Britain*, edited by Joanne Shattock, 66–83. Cambridge: Cambridge University Press, 2017.

———. *Women of the Press in Nineteenth Century Britain*. Basingstoke: Macmillan, 2000.

'Original Papers: Mrs. Hemans'. *Athenaeum* 395 (23 May 1835): 391–2.

'Our Leader'. *Thief* 1 (21 April 1832): 1.

Parry, John. 'Wanted, a Governess'. The Lester S. Levy Sheet Music Collection. Johns Hopkins Sheridan Libraries & University Museums. https://levysheetmusic.mse.jhu.edu/collection/049/080.

Patten, Robert. *George Cruikshank's Life, Times, and Art*. 2 vols. Cambridge: Lutterworth Press, 1992.

Peltz, Lucy. *Facing the Text: Extra-Illustration, Print Culture, and Society in Britain, 1769–1840*. San Marino: Huntington Library, 2017.

'The Pen and the Press'. *Compositors' Chronicle* 17 (January 1842): 131.

Peterson, Linda H. *Becoming a Woman of Letters: Myths of Authorship and Facts of the Victorian Market*. Princeton: Princeton University Press, 2009.

Pettitt, Clare. *Serial Forms: The Unfinished Project of Modernity, 1815–1848*. Oxford: Oxford University Press, 2020.

Phegley, Jennifer. *Educating the Proper Woman Reader: Victorian Family Literary Magazines and the Cultural Health of the Nation*. Columbus: Ohio State University Press, 2004.

———. 'Family Magazines'. In *The Routledge Handbook to Nineteenth-Century British Periodicals and Newspapers*, edited by Andrew King, Alexis Easley and John Morton, 276–92. London: Routledge, 2016.

Platt, Frederic. 'Repetition'. *The Encyclopedia of Sunday Schools and Religious Education*. 3 vols. London: Thomas Nelson, 1915.

Pointon, Marcia. *Hanging the Head: Portraiture and Social Formation in Eighteenth-Century England*. New Haven: Yale University Press, 1993.

'Poor Laws'. *Compositors' Chronicle* 11 (July 1841): 87.

Poovey, Mary. *Making a Social Body: British Cultural Formations, 1830–1864*. Chicago: University of Chicago Press, 1995.

Porter, Roy. *Health for Sale: Quackery in England, 1660–1850*. Manchester: Manchester University Press, 1989.

Poskett, James. *Materials of the Mind: Phrenology, Race, and the Global History of Science*. London: University of Chicago Press, 2009.

Postman, Neil. *Technopoly: The Surrender of Culture to Technology*. New York: Knopf, 1992.

'Preface'. *Australian Magazine* 1 (1821): iii–v.

'Preface'. *Mirror of Literature, Amusement and Instruction* 1 (21 May 1823): n.p.

Preface to *The Comic Annual*, v–x. London: Hurst, Chance, 1830.

Preface to *The Comic Offering*, v–viii. London: Smith, Elder, 1831.

Price, Leah. *How To Do Things with Books in Victorian Britain*. Princeton: Princeton University Press, 2012.

Prince, Mary. *The History of Mary Prince, a West Indian Slave*. London: Penguin, 2001.

Prins, Yopie. 'Poetess'. In *The Princeton Encyclopedia of Poetry and Poetics*, 4th ed., edited by Roland Greene, Stephen Cushman, Clare Cavanagh, Jahan Ramazani, Paul Ouzer, Harris Feinsod, David Marno and Alexandra Slessarev, 1051–4. Princeton: Princeton University Press, 2012.

'The Printer's Song'. *Compositors' Chronicle* 17 (January 1842): 131.

Prochaska, F. K. *Women and Philanthropy in Nineteenth-Century England*. Oxford: Oxford University Press, 1980.

'Prospectus'. *Australian Magazine* 1, no. 1 (1 May 1821): 3.

'Prospectus'. *Companion to the Newspaper* 1 (1 March 1833): 1.

'Prospectus for the *Lady's Monthly Museum*' (1798). John Johnson Collection, Prospectuses of Journals 32 (36). Bodleian Library, University of Oxford.

'Prospectus for a *New Series of the Lady's Magazine*'. 1820. John Johnson Collection, Prospectuses of Journals 32 (36). Bodleian Library, University of Oxford.

'Puns on Punning; Or, Hints to a Punster'. *New Comic Annual*, 69–70. London: Hurst, Chance, 1831.

'Railway Press'. *Newspaper Press Directory* 1 (London: C. Mitchell, 1846): 25–32.

Ray, Gordon, ed. *The Letters and Private Papers of William Makepeace Thackeray*. 4 vols. Oxford: Oxford University Press, 1946.

Reade, Aleyn Lyell. *The Mellards and their Descendants, Including the Bibbys of Liverpool, with Memoirs of Dinah Maria Mulock & Thomas Mellard Reade*. London: Arden Press, 1915.

'Reading for All'. *Penny Magazine* 1 (31 March 1832): 1.

Regan, Stephen. 'Introduction'. In *Irish Writing: An Anthology of Irish Literature in English, 1789–1939*, xiii–xxxix. Oxford: Oxford University Press, 2004.

Reiss, Daniel. 'Laetitia Landon and the Dawn of English Post-Romanticism'. *Studies in English Literature, 1500–1900* 36, no. 4 (1996): 807–27.

'Reverses of Fortune'. *Compositors' Chronicle* 20 (April 1842): 155.

Rich, Elihu. 'Thomas Mulock: An Historical Sketch'. *Transactions of the Royal Historical Society* 4 (1876): 424–38.

Richards, Thomas. *The Commodity Culture of Victorian England: Advertising and Spectacle, 1851–1914*. Stanford: Stanford University Press, 1990.

Roach, Joseph. 'Public Intimacy: The Prior History of "It"'. In *Theatre and Celebrity in Britain, 1660–2000*, edited by Mary Luckhurst and Jane Moody, 15–30. Basingstoke: Palgrave Macmillan, 2005.

Rovee, Christopher. *Imagining the Gallery: The Social Body of British Romanticism*. Stanford: Stanford University Press, 2006.

Ryan, Brandy. '"Echo and Reply": The Elegies of Felicia Hemans, Letitia Landon, and Elizabeth Barrett'. *Victorian Poetry* 46, no. 3 (2008): 249–77.

Salmon, Richard. *The Formation of the Victorian Literary Profession*. Cambridge: Cambridge University Press, 2013.

Sambrook, James. 'Prince, John Critchley (1808–66)'. In the *Oxford Dictionary of National Biography*, online edition. Oxford: Oxford University Press, 2004.

Sampson, Henry. *A History of Advertising from the Earliest Times*. London: Chatto and Windus, 1874.

Sanders, Mike. *The Poetry of Chartism: Aesthetics, Politics, History*. Cambridge: Cambridge University Press, 2009.

Schaffer, Talia. *Communities of Care: The Social Ethics of Victorian Fiction*. Princeton: Princeton University Press, 2021.

Scholl, Lesa. *Translation, Authorship and the Victorian Professional Woman: Charlotte Brontë, Harriet Martineau and George Eliot*. London: Routledge, 2011.

Serjeant, J. F. 'Our Sunday School Scholars'. In *The Sunday School Teachers' Magazine and Journal of Education* 10 (1859): 337–43.

Shattock, Joanne. 'Professional Networking, Masculine and Feminine'. *Victorian Periodicals Review* 44, no. 2 (2011): 128–40.

Shaw, James. *An Account of the Liverpool District Provident Society*. Liverpool: Mitchell, 1838.

Shevelow, Kathryn. *Women and Print Culture: The Construction of Femininity in the Early Periodical*. London: Routledge, 1989.

Shields, Juliet. 'The Races of Women: Gender, Hybridity, and National Identity In Dinah Craik's *Olive*'. *Studies in the Novel* 39, no. 3 (2007): 284–300.

Showalter, Elaine. 'Dinah Mulock Craik and the Tactics of Sentiment: A Case Study in Victorian Female Authorship'. *Feminist Studies* 2, no. 2/3 (1975): 5–23.

———. *A Literature of Their Own: British Women Novelists from Brontë to Lessing*. Princeton: Princeton University Press, 1977.

Simpson, Robert. *The Clergyman's Manual*. London: R. Groombridge, Panyer Alley, 1842.

Siskin, Clifford, and William Warner. 'This Is Enlightenment: An Invitation in the Form of an Argument'. In *This Is Enlightenment*, edited by Clifford Siskin and William Warner, 1–36. Chicago: University of Chicago Press, 2010.

'Society for the Diffusion of Useful Knowledge'. *The Times*, 19 May 1828, 3.

Soja, Edward W. *Thirdspace: Journeys to Los Angeles and Other Real-and-Imagined Places*. Oxford: Blackwell, 1996.

St Clair, William. *The Reading Nation in the Romantic Period*. Cambridge: Cambridge University Press, 2007.

Stallybrass, Peter. '"Little Jobs": Broadsides and the Printing Revolution'. In *Agent of Change: Print Culture Studies after Elizabeth L Eisenstein*, edited by Sabrina Alcorn Baron, Eric N. Lindquist and Eleanor F. Shevlin, 315–41. Boston: University of Massachusetts Press, 2007.

Steinlight, Emily. '"Anti-Bleak House": Advertising and the Victorian Novel'. *Narrative* 14, no. 2 (2006): 132–62.

Stewart, David. *The Form of Poetry in the 1820s and 1830s: A Period of Doubt*. London: Palgrave Macmillan, 2018.

Storti, Sarah Anne. 'Letitia Landon: Still a Problem'. *Victorian Poetry* 57, no. 4 (2019): 533–56.

Strachan, John. *Advertising and Satirical Culture in the Romantic Period*. Cambridge: Cambridge University Press, 2007.

Stubenrauch, Joseph. *The Evangelical Age of Ingenuity in Industrial Britain*. Oxford: Oxford University Press, 2016.

Styler, Rebecca. 'Revelations of Romantic Childhood: Anna Jameson, Mary Howitt, and Victorian Women's Spiritual Autobiography'. *Life Writing* 11, no. 3 (2014): 313–30.

Sweet, Nanora. '*The New Monthly Magazine* and the Liberalism of the 1820s'. *Prose Studies* 25, no. 1 (2002): 147–62.

T. J. O. 'Song of the Earth to the Moon'. *Compositors' Chronicle* 11 (July 1841): 88.

Teukolsky, Rachel. *Picture World: Image, Aesthetics, and Victorian New Media*. Oxford: Oxford University Press, 2020.

[Thackeray, William M]. 'Half-a-Crown's Worth of Cheap Knowledge'. *Fraser's Magazine* 17 (March 1838): 279–90.

Thomas, Sophie. *Romanticism and Visuality: Fragments, History, Spectacle*. New York: Routledge, 2007.

Thompson, Hilary. 'Enclosure and Childhood in the Wood Engravings of Thomas and John Bewick'. *Children's Literature* 24 (1996): 1–22.

Thornton, Sara. *Advertising, Subjectivity and the Nineteenth-Century Novel: The Language of the Walls*. Houndmills: Palgrave Macmillan, 2009.

Tilley, Elizabeth. 'Dublin University Magazine'. In *The Dictionary of Nineteenth-Century Journalism* (online edition), edited by Laurel Brake and Marysa Demoor. London and Ghent: British Library and Academia Press, 2009.

Timperley, Charles Henry. *Songs of the Press and Other Poems Relative to the Art of Printers and Printing*. London: Fisher, Son & Co., 1845.

'To Correspondents, &c'. *Compositors' Chronicle* 2 (October 1840): 12.

'To Correspondents, &c'. *Compositors' Chronicle* 13 (September 1841): 100.

'To Correspondents, &c'. *Compositors' Chronicle* 17 (January 1842): 132.

'To Correspondents, &c'. *Compositors' Chronicle* 24 (July 1842): 189.

'To the Editor of the Australian Magazine'. *Australian Magazine* 1, no. 1 (1 May 1821): 27.

'To the Editor of the Australian Magazine'. *Australian Magazine* 2, no. 2 (1 June 1821): 48–52.

'To the Public'. *La Belle Assemblée* 1 (February 1806): n.p.

'To the Public'. *News of the World*, 1 October 1843, 4.

Tom and Jerry, or Life in London: A Burletta of Fun, Frolic and Flash. London: J. Robinson, 1825.

Tuchman, Gaye. *Edging Women Out: Victorian Novelists, Publishers and Social Change*. London: Taylor & Francis, 2012.

Tuite, Clara. *Lord Byron and Scandalous Celebrity*. Cambridge: Cambridge University Press, 2015.

Turner, Mark W. 'Companions, Supplements, and the Proliferation of Print in the 1830s'. *Victorian Periodicals Review* 43, no. 2 (2010): 119–32.

———. 'Serial Culture in the Nineteenth Century: G. W. M. Reynolds, the Many *Mysteries of London*, and the Spread of Print'. In *Nineteenth-Century Serial Narrative in Transnational Perspective, 1830s–1860s, Popular Culture – Serial Culture*, edited by Daniel Stein and Lisanna Wiele, 193–211. Basingstoke: Palgrave, 2019.

———. 'Seriality, Miscellaneity and Compression in Nineteenth-Century Print'. *Victorian Studies* 62, no. 2 (2020): 283–94.

'The Typographical Song'. *Compositors' Chronicle* 7 (March 1841): 55–6.

Tytler, James. 'Loch Erroch Side'. In *Scottish Poetry of the Eighteenth Century*, 2 vols., edited by George Eyre-Todd, 88–9. Glasgow: William Hodge, 1896.

Underwood, Ted, David Bamman and Sabrina Lee. 'The Transformation of Gender in English-Language Fiction'. *Journal of Cultural Analytics* 3, no. 2 (2018): 1–25.

The Universal Songster or Museum of Mirth. 3 vols. London: John Fairburn, 1825–8.

Van Remoortel, Marianne. 'Women Editors' Transnational Networks in the *Englishwoman's Domestic Magazine* and *Myra's Journal*'. In *Women's Periodicals and Print Culture in Britain, 1830s–1900s*, edited by Alexis Easley, Clare Gill and Beth Rogers, 46–56. Edinburgh: Edinburgh University Press, 2019.

Vance, Norman. *Irish Literature Since 1800*. London: Taylor & Francis, 2002.

Vargo, Gregory. *An Underground History of Early Victorian Fiction*. Cambridge: Cambridge University Press, 2018.

'Victoria, a Political Poem'. *Compositors' Chronicle* 4 (December 1840): 25.

Vigne, Randolph. *Thomas Pringle: South African Pioneer, Poet and Abolitionist*. Rochester: Boydell and Brewer, 2012.

'Wanted, an Editor'. *Compositors' Chronicle* 30 (January 1843): 233.

Ward, Candace. '"An Engine of Immense Power": *The Jamaica Watchman* and Crossings in Nineteenth-Century Print Culture'. *Victorian Periodicals Review* 51, no. 3 (2018): 483–503.

Waters, Mary. 'Letitia Landon's Literary Criticism and Her Romantic Project: L. E. L.'s Poetics of Feeling and the Periodical Reviews'. *Women's Writing* 28, no. 3 (2011): 305–30.

Webby, Elizabeth. 'Australia'. In *Periodicals of Queen Victoria's Empire: An Exploration*, edited by J. Don Vann and Rosemary T. VanArsdel, 19–58. Toronto: University of Toronto Press, 1996.

Weber, Max. *Max Weber: Essays in Sociology*. Edited and translated by Hans Heinrich Gert and C. Wright Mills. New York: Oxford University Press, 1958.

'Weekly Newspapers'. *Westminster Review* 10 (April 1829): 466–80.

Weibren, Daniel. 'Supporting Self-Help: Charity, Mutuality, and Reciprocity in Nineteenth-Century Britain'. In *Charity and Mutual Aid in Europe and North America Since 1800*, edited by Bernard Harris and Paul Briden, 67–88. New York: Routledge, 2007.

Wemyss, Richard. *Victoria, a Political Poem*. London: Effingham Wilson, 1840.

'The West Indian Manifesto Examined'. *Anti-Slavery Reporter* 4, no. 10 (1831): 289–316.

Westover, Paul. *Necromanticism: Traveling to Meet the Dead, 1750–1860*. Basingstoke: Palgrave Macmillan, 2012.

Wicke, Jennifer. *Advertising Fictions: Literature, Advertisement, and Social Reading*. New York: Columbia University Press, 1988.

Wilberforce, William. *A Practical View of the Prevailing Religious System of Professed Christians*. London: T. Caddell, Jr., and W. Davies, 1797.

Williams, Andy. 'Advertising and Fiction in *The Pickwick Papers*'. *Victorian Literature and Culture* 38, no. 2 (2010): 319–35.

Williams, Raymond. 'Advertising: The Magic System'. In *Problems in Materialism and Culture*, 170–95. London: Verso, 1980.

Wolfson, Susan J. *Borderlines: The Shiftings of Gender in British Romanticism*. Stanford: Stanford University Press, 2006.

———. 'Felicia Hemans and the Revolving Doors of Reception'. In *Romanticism and Women Poets: Opening the Doors of Reception*, edited by Harriet Kramer Linkin and Stephen C. Behrendt, 214–41. Lexington: University Press of Kentucky, 2015.

———. *Romantic Interactions: Social Being and the Turns of Literary Action*. Baltimore: Johns Hopkins University Press, 2010.

Woodring, Carl. *Victorian Samplers: William and Mary Howitt*. Lawrence: University of Kansas Press, 1952.

Woolf, Virginia. 'Aurora Leigh' (1932). Reprinted in *Aurora Leigh*, by Elizabeth Barrett Browning, edited by Margaret Reynolds, 439–46. New York: Norton, 1996.

Wordsworth, William. *The Prelude; Or, Growth of a Poet's Mind. An Autobiographical Poem*. New York: D. Appleton, 1850.

Yates, Joanne. *Control Through Communication: The Rise of System in American Management*. Baltimore: Johns Hopkins University Press, 1989.

Index

Printed and bound by CPI Group (UK) Ltd, Croydon, CR0 4YY
20/03/2025
01835113-0004